MASS COMMUNICATION LAW

IN A NUTSHELL

Sixth Edition

By

T. BARTON CARTER
Professor of Communication and Law
Chairman, Department of Mass Communication,
Advertising and Public Relations
College of Communication
Boston University

JULIET LUSHBOUGH DEE
Associate Professor of Communication
College of Arts and Science
University of Delaware

HARVEY L. ZUCKMAN
Emeritus Professor of Law
The Catholic University of America
Founding Director
Institute for Communications Law Studies,
Washington, D.C.

THOMSON

WEST

Mat #40357966

Nutshell Series, In a Nutshell, the Nutshell Logo and West Group are trademarks registered in the U.S. Patent and Trademark Office.

COPYRIGHT © 1983, 1988, 1994 WEST PUBLISHING CO.
© West, a Thomson business, 2000
© 2007 Thomson/West
      610 Opperman Drive
      P.O. Box 64526
      St. Paul, MN 55164–0526
      1–800–328–9352

Printed in the United States of America

ISBN–13: 978–0–314–16020–1
ISBN–10: 0–314–16020–5

 TEXT IS PRINTED ON 10% POST CONSUMER RECYCLED PAPER

For Kendra, Gregory, and Charlotte

*

PREFACE

To appreciate the interrelationship of law and mass communication, look at a daily newspaper. Each day one is likely to find news of important court decisions, news of new legislation and news about the judiciary. Even the sports page may contain as much news about law suits between team owners, unions and players as about team performance. There has been a veritable explosion in media coverage of legal issues since the early 1960s. The media's increasing influence has resulted in more problems for them, especially in the areas of First Amendment protection and Federal Communication Commission regulation, deregulation and reregulation of broadcasting and cable, as well as the emergence of the Internet.

In this book we attempt to meet a continuing need for a basic text in communication law, not only for law students but journalism and communication students as well.

Readers will note that the authors have made every effort to achieve gender neutral exposition in this edition. We believe the time has long since passed when we might ignore the need for equality of opportunity and the achievements of both men and women in the fields of law and communication. In this regard, Professor Zuckman is proud to report that his daughter Jill has been the Congressional correspondent for a large midwestern newspaper for several years. Professor Zuckman's son Michael is a practicing attorney with a Washington, D.C. law firm which does telecommunications work.

We wish to acknowledge our heavy debt to the following individuals and organizations in the preparation of this text: Professor Thomas I. Emerson, whose many writings greatly influenced our thinking on First Amendment issues, and the editorial board of Law and Contemporary Problems for permitting us to reprint material from Professor Emerson's article "The Doctrine of Prior Restraint," appearing in a symposium on Obscenity and the Arts in Law and Contemporary Problems (Vol. 20, No. 4, Autumn, 1955), published by Duke University School of Law, Durham, North Carolina, copyright 1955, by Duke University; the late Dean William L. Prosser, founding author of the Handbook of the Law of Torts, whose works greatly shaped our thinking in Chapters II and III on the law of defamation and privacy; Professor Dan B. Dobbs, author of the Handbook of the Law of Remedies (now in its second edition), for his guidance on the law of damages in defamation actions; the late Professor Melville B. Nimmer, without whose brilliant thinking on the law of copyright infringement actions no rational discussion of those subjects could be presented; the editorial board of the Texas Law Review for permission to paraphrase portions of the article by Donna Murasky, Esquire, "The Journalist's Privilege: Branzburg and Its Aftermath," 52

Texas Law Review 829 (1974); the editorial board of the Washington Law Review for permission to paraphrase portions of the article by Professors Don R. Pember and Dwight L. Teeter, Jr., "Privacy and the Press Since Time, Inc. v. Hill," 50 Washington Law Review 57 (1974); Charles B. Blackmar, distinguished jurist and former teaching colleague and cherished friend of Professor Zuckman, for his insights into First Amendment problems engendered by lawyer advertising (he argued and won In re R.M.J. in the United States Supreme Court); and West Publishing Company for its computerized storage and retrieval system that made the progression from galley to page proof to publication so much easier for the authors and helped keep typographical errors to a minimum.

We would also like to thank Erica Hepp and Adrian Li, students at Boston University Law School, reference librarian Patrick Petit of the Columbus School of Law of the Catholic University of America, and reference librarian Rebecca Knight of the University of Delaware. Finally, we express our utmost gratitude to Hubert Alpert, M.D., Herman B. Segal, M.D. and Ronald Rodriguez, M.D., without whose skill and dedication, Professor Zuckman might not be making these acknowledgements.

T. BARTON CARTER
JULIET L. DEE
HARVEY ZUCKMAN

September 2006

*

OUTLINE

OUTLINE

Page

PART TWO. REGULATION OF THE ELECTRONIC MASS MEDIA

OUTLINE

TABLE OF CASES

References are to Pages

TABLE OF CASES

TABLE OF CASES

TABLE OF CASES

TABLE OF CASES

TABLE OF CASES

TABLE OF CASES

TABLE OF CASES

TABLE OF CASES

TABLE OF CASES

TABLE OF CASES

TABLE OF CASES

L

TABLE OF CASES

*

MASS COMMUNICATION LAW

IN A NUTSHELL

Sixth Edition

*

PART ONE

THE FIRST AMENDMENT AND MASS COMMU- NICATIONS

CHAPTER I

THE FIRST AMENDMENT IN PERSPECTIVE

A. INTRODUCTION

The development of mass communication throughout the western world and particularly in the United States in the twentieth century is a product of both science and law. Science has given us the technology by which individuals may communicate information, ideas and images across time and space to other individuals. For this we owe a debt of gratitude to scientists and inventors such as Edison, Bell, Marconi, DeForest, and Zworykin.

However, technology does not exist in a vacuum. It operates in organized societies governed by laws. These societies may be open ones in which the members are relatively free to express themselves and to communicate with others by whatever means available, or they may be relatively closed, with the modes of communication tightly controlled by a

1

very few persons. Gutenberg's invention of moveable type gave promise of spreading both literacy and ideas to the masses, but in Elizabethan England and beyond, licensing acts severely limited access to the printing press to a few printers considered "safe" by the ruling authorities. It was this legal restriction on the utilization of the first technology of mass communication that led the great poet John Milton to make his stirring call for a free press in "Areopagitica." In our own time the vast promise of cable television was retarded for years because of the complex of statutes and Federal Communications Commission regulations designed to reign in this new technology in order to protect existing economic interests.

Thus, while technology is the necessary antecedent to mass communication, a society's laws ultimately determine how the technology will be developed and how "mass" will be its reach.

In our country the fountainhead of the law governing mass communication is the First Amendment to the Constitution which says in spare but sweeping language "Congress shall make no law ... abridging the freedom of speech or of the press; ..." The way this mandate is carried out tells us much about the kind of society we have. For as that giant of electronic journalism Edward R. Murrow once noted, what distinguishes a truly free society from all others is an independent judiciary and a free press.

B. BACKGROUND, THEORIES AND DIRECTION OF THE FIRST AMENDMENT

1. Background

At the time Madison was directed by Congress to draft the amendment to the Constitution expressly protecting free speech and press from governmental encroachment, he and the other founders of the Republic were acutely aware of the long history of suppression in England and the Colonies of free expression, particularly that concerning the affairs of government. Even after Parliament refused to renew the last of the licensing acts in 1695, the Crown was largely able to retain its control over the press by the imposition of heavy taxes on periodicals in England, by the refusal to permit the introduction of printing presses in many of the American colonies and, most importantly, by vigorous enforcement of the criminal law of seditious libel everywhere.

Under that law printers and publishers who offended the government and its ministers could be severely punished even when their statements were true. The maxim at common law was "the greater the truth the greater the libel." The journalistic exposure of a Watergate or Teapot Dome style scandal would have been virtually impossible under that law. Worse yet for the defendant, it was the Crown's judges who determined whether the utterance or writing was defamatory to the government. Needless to say, the prosecutors won nearly all of their cases, including one against Daniel Defoe for a satirical essay "Shortest Way with Dissenters." For his efforts Defoe was fined, pilloried and imprisoned.

Much the same fate befell a number of colonial printers and publishers until the royal governor of New York, William Cosby, instituted a prosecution for seditious libel against a New York printer, John Peter Zenger. Zenger had had the temerity to criticize Cosby's administration of the colony in the pages of his Weekly Journal. In the face of the uncontested fact of publication by Zenger and the common law of libel previously described, the jury refused to convict and the seed of a free press was planted in America.

Doubtless, then, with this history in mind, the press guarantee of the First Amendment was aimed at the very least at the abuses of licensing, censorship and punishment of political expression. Indeed, when Alexander Hamilton asked what was meant by freedom of the press, Madison responded that it meant freedom from despotic control by the federal government. Beyond this, the drafters failed to hand down to us any clear theory of the Amendment.

Only after the outbreak of World War I and the consequent increase in radical agitation in the country, did the Supreme Court and constitutional scholars begin to search for coherent theories to explain the allowance or suppression of expression in specific cases. This search for theory was further encouraged by the ruling in Gitlow v. New York (1925) that the constraints of the First Amendment applied to the states through the operation of the due process clause of the Fourteenth Amendment.

2. Theories and Tests of the First Amendment

Over the years a number of general theories have been espoused to justify the existence of the First Amendment guarantees of free speech and free press. The most famous of these is the "free trade of ideas" espoused by Justices Holmes and Brandeis in their dissenting opinion in Abrams v. United States (1919) and their concurring opinion in Whitney v. California (1927). By this theory the First Amendment stands as a protector of truth emerging from the public discussion of competing ideas.

Another major theory is the so-called Meiklejohn interpretation of the First Amendment. Named after its leading proponent, Professor Alexander Meiklejohn, this interpretation, broadly stated, holds that ours is a self-governing society and the First Amendment protects the freedom of thought and expression directed to the process by which we govern ourselves. Thus, it is concerned with the need for the citizenry to acquire such qualities of mind and spirit and such information as will make possible responsible self-governance. Implicit in this form of government is the idea that while the people delegate certain responsibility to their elected representatives, they reserve for themselves the means to oversee their government and that the elected representatives may not abridge the freedom of the people in maintaining this oversight. Thus, in the Meiklejohn view, the central meaning of the First Amendment is the protection it affords to the public power of the people collectively to govern themselves. See Meiklejohn, "The First Amendment is an Absolute," 1961 Sup.Ct.Rev. 245, 253–263.

Practically, what this thesis translates into is absolute protection for all thought, expression and communication which bears on the citizen's role of self-government. Major emphasis is placed on political expression: punishment for seditious libel becomes an impossibility. However, Meiklejohn would also include within the coverage of the First Amendment all aspects of educational, philosophical, scientific, literary and artistic endeavors because sensitivity to humanistic values and rationality in judgment are dependent upon these pursuits. Other expression not directly or indirectly related to the process of self-government would be beyond the pale of the First Amendment, as perhaps horror comic books.

Although no Supreme Court decision has completely accepted the Meiklejohn thesis, it has been embodied to some extent in the law of defamation. See e.g., New York Times Co. v. Sullivan (1964). There, the Court found the state's defamation law constitutionally deficient in failing to provide safeguards for freedom of speech and press in libel actions brought by public officials against critics of their official conduct. Justice Brennan, speaking for the Court, quoted James Madison. "If we advert to the nature of Republican Government, we shall find that the censorial power is in the people over the Government, and not in the Government over the people." This idea is, of course, at the heart of the Meiklejohn interpretation. See also Near v. Minnesota (1931) for an earlier Supreme Court expression of the same idea.

Other general theories of the First Amendment include the somewhat cynical "safety valve" idea of permitting individual members and groups in society to "let off steam" without seriously affecting the status quo, and the more idealistic belief that free expression is a necessary aspect of individual development and growth.

Traditionally, a common underpinning of these theories was the belief that protecting the individual's right to free speech against government attempts to restrict inevitably served societal interests as well. As a result, First Amendment jurisprudence concerned limitations on the power of government or its agencies to act in certain ways, e.g., the power of courts to enter judgments in defamation actions. However, there are now those who argue that the free speech rights of individuals are not always in concert with those of society as a whole. For example, broadcast regulation has been heavily influenced by a theory largely developed by Professor Jerome A. Barron that the First Amendment actually compels the government to act affirmatively to insure freedom of expression by requiring citizen access to the mass media. Although this theory has been rejected by the Supreme Court with regard to the print media, it has been instrumental in forcing a wide ranging re-examination of the nature of the First Amendment in the late twentieth century and early twenty-first century. The communitarian, as opposed to libertarian, approach to the First Amendment is also the basis for proposals to limit various forms of hate speech.

a. Absolutism

However, these general theories and principles do not resolve hard cases. Thus, the quest has been for operative or functional tests permitting reasonably consistent decisions in the field of free expression.

The most extreme approach is the idea that the First Amendment provides a central core of protection for expression in all circumstances—the so-called absolutist approach. Although this approach has been characterized as holding that the "no law" injunction of the First Amendment *means* no law, the absolutist schools of thought are more complex than that.

The absolutists agree that the First Amendment does provide a central core of protection, but to determine whether particular expression is protected in the face of governmental efforts at regulation, the broad language of the First Amendment must be defined. What does "no law" mean? What constitutes abridgment? What is the expression that is to be protected? "No law" is defined generally to include not only statutes but administrative regulations promulgated pursuant to statutes, municipal ordinances, executive orders and court orders. Insofar as abridgment is concerned, the absolutists would permit limitations on free expression incidental to reasonable regulation promulgated pursuant to a "law" directed solely to controlling the time, place and manner of expression. In determining whether a challenged regulation is reasonable, the absolutists would reject any regulation based on a law that does not contain appropriate safeguards to limit administrative discretion. If such safeguards are present the absolutists would then look to see whether the regulation has created a sufficient inroad on expression by its nature, degree and impact so as to constitute an "abridgment" of free expression.

The key to understanding the absolutist's view of abridgment is recognition that regulation must relate only to time, place and manner of the presentation of expression and that such regulation must not be so restrictive as to interfere with the *substance* of expression. See, e.g., Saia v. New York (1948), in which Justice Douglas, an adherent of absolutism, while conceding that some narrow regulation of sound trucks to prevent abuses would be constitutionally permissible, held unconstitutional a local ordinance which forbade the use of sound amplification devices except with the permission of the chief of police. The grant of such permission was placed in the chief's sole discretion and thus under the ordinance he was in a position to determine not only the time, location and volume of operation but the kind of speech that might be amplified and the particular groups that might use amplification equipment.

Of the various absolutist views of the scope of the First Amendment, perhaps the most celebrated is that held by the late Justice Hugo Black. Justice Black was an adherent of the Holmes–Brandeis view of the First Amendment as primarily a protector of the free market in ideas. However, he was wary of their "clear and present danger test" discussed below, because judges could hold that certain expression in certain circumstances failed the test for First Amendment protection. Rather, Justice Black came to believe that all ideas and their expressions, including the libelous and the obscene, are to be given absolute protection. This view of the scope of the First Amendment is, of course, more expansive than that taken by Meiklejohn and has never commanded majority adherence on the Court.

While Justice Black was an implacable foe of any infringement of free expression except the most incidental occasioned by reasonable "time, place and manner" regulation, "speech" and "press" were to him technical terms and only expression encompassed within those terms was to be protected. Justice Black normally defined "speech" and "press" more broadly than anyone else on the Court, but in the context of public demonstrations he defined "speech" very narrowly so as to exclude expression bound up with essentially physical conduct. For instance, in Adderley v. Florida (1966), he spoke for the Court in upholding the convictions of

32 students who demonstrated in a nonviolent manner on a nonpublic jail driveway to protest the arrests of fellow students and local segregation policies. The 32 were among 200 students who had apparently blocked the driveway and had engaged in singing, clapping and dancing to protest what they believed to be an unjust situation. Among the dissenters in the Adderley case were Justice Black's usual allies in First Amendment cases, Justices Douglas and Brennan and Chief Justice Warren.

At bottom, whatever their differences as to the reach of the First Amendment, the late Justice Black and the other absolutists were attempting to remove from the judiciary the power to balance the interest in free expression against the exigencies of the times. For them, the balance was struck once and for all in favor of freedom of speech and press by the drafters of the Bill of Rights and that balance may not be disturbed.

b. The "Clear and Present Danger" Test

Another approach reflective of the free trade of ideas approach, was the "clear and present danger" test. Proposed by Justice Holmes in Schenck v. United States (1919), the test permitted the punishment of expression when "the words used are used in such circumstances and are of such a nature as to create a clear and present danger that they will bring about the substantive evils that Congress has a right to prevent. It is a question of proximity and degree."

In Schenck, the expression was in the form of a leaflet authorized by the American Socialist Party attacking the Conscription Act of World War I and urging recent conscripts to resist serving in the armed forces by asserting their alleged rights under the Thirteenth Amendment. The defendant, an officer of the party, was indicted, inter alia, for conspiracy to violate the Espionage Act of 1917 by causing and attempting to cause insubordination in the military forces and obstruction of the recruiting and enlistment service during a period of war. In the circumstance of war time, Holmes, who had himself been an officer in the Union Army during the Civil War, found that the leaflet created a danger of disruption of the war effort of sufficient proximity and magnitude to permit punishment in the face of the sweeping guarantees of the First Amendment.

Aside from the problem that it frankly permits the Congress in certain circumstances to legislate punishment of expression, the test is vague and difficult to apply. As Brandeis and Holmes admitted in their concurring opinion in Whitney v. California (1927), the Supreme Court had not yet "fixed the standard by which to determine when a danger shall be deemed clear; how remote the danger may be and yet be deemed present; and what degree of evil shall be deemed sufficiently substantial to justify resort to abridgement of free speech and assembly as the means of protection."

Moreover, even if there were a common understanding of the meaning of the test, the results of its application to challenged legislation directly or indirectly prohibitive of expression would vary according to extrinsic circumstances such as war or peace, cold war or detente, and prosperity or depression. Expression that might be afforded First Amendment protection from legislative repression in one social context might be denied it in another, and the speaker or publisher would not know whether his particular expression was safeguarded until the courts passed upon it. Thus, the test might have the effect of discouraging borderline writings or utterances.

In recent years, doubts about the test by civil liberties oriented justices and constitutional scholars and the hostility of those more state security oriented, have sapped "clear and present danger" of its vitality as constitutional doctrine. For instance, Brandenburg v. Ohio (1969) involved a prosecution for violation by certain members of the Ku Klux Klan of the Ohio criminal syndicalism statute. Although this prosecution was much like earlier prosecutions in which the "clear and present danger" test had been employed (compare Whitney v. California (1927) involving a similar state criminal syndicalism statute), the per curiam opinion of the Supreme Court striking down the state law as an infringement of the First Amendment did not mention the test. Rather, the Court simply drew a distinction between advocacy of forcible or illegal political action in the future and advocacy directed to inciting *imminent* lawless action and likely to produce just such action. Only the latter is unprotected speech.

It was long thought that the requirement of imminence provided almost absolute protection for the mass media against suits for inciting members of the audience to inflict physical harm on themselves or others. A recent U.S. Court of Appeals case has challenged this assumption. In Rice v. Paladin (1997), the family of a murder victim sued the publisher of a how-to book for hitmen. The murderer had used techniques described in the book to commit the murder. The appellate court overturned the dismissal–on First Amendment grounds–of the suit, concluding that the book was not protected by the First Amendment.

c. *Ad Hoc Balancing of Interests*

In Justice Frankfurter's dissent in Bridges is the seed of another general approach to First Amendment cases. In his opinion Justice Frankfurter emphasized that other interests protected by the Bill of Rights were also at stake—the interests of due process of law and fair trial. He would not give any special deference to the interests protected by the First Amendment. "Free speech is not so absolute or irrational a conception as to imply paralysis of the means for effective protection of all the freedoms secured by the Bill of Rights.... In the cases before us, the claims on behalf of freedom of speech and of the press encounter claims on behalf of liberties no less precious." Bridges v. California (1941).

Frankfurter would resolve competing claims by weighing their relative importance in each case. In

Bridges, he came to the conclusion that the interest in the impartial administration of justice outweighed the competing interest in allowing the Los Angeles Times through its editorial pages to attempt to prevent a judge from granting a request for probation from several labor organizers convicted of strong arm tactics, or in allowing Harry Bridges, a Pacific Coast longshoremen's union leader, to proclaim in the newspapers his threat to tie up the entire Pacific Coast shipping business if a court order of which he disapproved was enforced.

Frankfurter's approach formed the basis for the ad hoc balancing of interests. This balancing of First Amendment interests was embraced by a majority of the Court in American Communications Association v. Douds (1950), in which certain labor unions attacked a provision of the Labor Management Relations Act barring unions from access to procedures important to the collective bargaining process unless their officers executed affidavits declaring, among other things, that they were not members of or affiliated with the Communist Party. The unions contended that the provision violated union leaders' fundamental rights guaranteed by the First Amendment such as the right to hold and express whatever political views they choose and to associate with whatever political groups they wish. In concluding that the section of the act was compatible with the First Amendment, Chief Justice Vinson weighed First Amendment interests against the interest to be fostered by the statute in question, i.e., interstate commerce free from the disruption of political strikes.

Perhaps the most explicit statement of this approach was made by Justice Harlan in Konigsberg v. State Bar of Cal. (1961). There Konigsberg, a candidate for admission to the California Bar, was denied a license to practice law because he had refused to answer questions put to him by a bar committee (acting as a state agency) concerning his alleged membership in the Communist Party. Konigsberg challenged the state's action on several grounds including violation of protected rights of free speech and association. In rejecting this challenge Justice Harlan said, "Whenever ... these constitutional protections are asserted against the exercise of valid governmental powers a reconciliation must be effected, and that perforce requires an appropriate weighing of the respective interests involved [citations omitted].... With more particular reference to the present context of a state decision as to character qualifications, it is difficult, indeed, to imagine a view of the constitutional protections of speech and association which would automatically and without consideration of the extent of the deterrence of speech and association and of the importance of the state function, exclude all reference to prior speech or association on such issues [concerning bar membership] as character, purpose, credibility or intent." Following this standard, a majority of the Court found that the state's interest in safeguarding the bar from possible subversive influence outweighed interests protected by the First and Fourteenth Amendments.

A major question raised by the balancing approach is the relative weight to be given to each interest. How strong does the government's interest have to be to outweigh the free-speech interest? This depends on the type of restriction that is at issue in the case. Where the restriction is based on the content of the speech, the Court applies strict scrutiny. Under strict scrutiny, in order to prevail, the government must demonstrate a compelling government interest and show that the restriction on speech is the least restrictive means of achieving that interest. If the restriction is content neutral, intermediate scrutiny applies. The government need only show that the restriction serves an important government interest and that the restriction is narrowly tailored to serve that interest.

The ad hoc balancing approach has the virtue of pragmatism. It recognizes the importance of First Amendment interests but permits the making of pragmatic judgments as to when those interests should prevail over other and conflicting interests, often of a state security nature. But this virtue may also be a vice, for the protections afforded by the First Amendment are stated in absolute terms and the Amendment makes no provision for restricting freedom of speech and press when other interests are in conflict. This approach also suffers from vagueness. Because it is ad hoc, no consistent weight can be given to conflicting interests and the lower court judges are left on their own to determine when First Amendment interests are outweighed. Under such an approach a judge's predilections either for state security or individual liberties may be easily rationalized and, as with the "clear and present danger" test, the individual can never have any advance notice whether his interest in freedom of expression will outweigh some competing interest of the state expressed in its legislation. See Frantz, "The First Amendment in the Balance," 71 Yale L.J. 1424, 1440–1443 (1962).

d. Definitional Balancing

Another approach to the balancing of government and speech interests was first enunciated in Chaplinsky v. New Hampshire (1942), which addressed the constitutionality of a New Hampshire statute construed to ban "words likely to cause an average addressee to fight."

In upholding the statute, the Court stated that certain classes of speech had never been thought to raise a constitutional problem. They included the lewd and obscene, the profane, the libelous and insulting or "fighting words."

At first glance this approach, placing entire classes of speech outside the protective ambit of the First Amendment, gives much more guidance for future decisions than the ad hoc approach. Often however, it creates a different uncertainty due to the difficulty of defining these classes of speech. Thus, the court has struggled for more than thirty years to define obscenity, a struggle that reduced Justice Stewart to declaring in Jacobellis v. Ohio

(1964), that he couldn't define hard core pornography but he knew when he saw it. Similar problems exist with the definition of commercial speech. See, e.g., Central Hudson Gas & Electric Corp. v. Public Service Commission of New York (1980) (Justice Steven's concurring opinion).

The other problem with definitional balancing is that there is a danger of overreaching. Essentially, definitional balancing is a finding that the societal interest in restricting a certain type of speech always outweighs the value of that speech, regardless of context or circumstances. Thus, prior to 1964, there was no constitutional protection for libel, even for discussions of the performance of public officials. This, of course, was changed by New York Times Co. v. Sullivan.

The preceding approaches or tests have not been consistently applied by their proponents to all First Amendment problem areas and when they are applied the competing approaches do not always yield results in conflict with each other. But, again with the caveat that tests or theories cannot always be relied upon to predict the outcome of specific cases, an understanding of them is useful in predicting the direction of the Supreme Court in relation to the First Amendment.

3. Present Direction of the Supreme Court

The transition from the Burger Court to the Rehnquist Court did not present anywhere near the radical change in direction that occurred between the Warren and Burger courts. Even though many of the Justices have not clearly articulated their approach to the First Amendment and two new Justices joined the Court in 2005, it is possible to make some judgments about the direction of the current Supreme Court regarding First Amendment philosophy.

It appears that the entire Court has embraced an ad hoc balancing approach, some justices perhaps more completely than others. This ad hoc balancing approach has produced a more limited view of the First Amendment than existed in the Warren era.

Often, as part of its attempt to balance the particular interests at stake, the Court will apply a "test" or set of guidelines to the specific facts of the case. For example, in Central Hudson Gas & Electric Corp. v. Public Service Commission of New York (1980), Justice Powell enunciated a four-part test to determine the constitutionality of restrictions on commercial speech. First, is the commercial speech protected by the First Amendment? (At a minimum, it should not involve illegal activity, nor should it be false or misleading.) Second, is there a substantial government interest in restricting the speech? Third, does the regulation directly advance the asserted government interest? Fourth, is the regulation no broader than necessary to serve the asserted government interest?

This "test," essentially a form of intermediate scrutiny, is typical of the Court's approach in that it forces the government to articulate a competing public interest that justifies restricting First

Amendment rights, recognizes that such competing interests can outweigh First Amendment rights, and requires the government to narrowly tailor its restrictions. See also Press–Enterprise Company v. Superior Court (II) (1986).

One developing trend is a blurring of the traditional distinction between strict scrutiny and intermediate scrutiny. One example of this is the use of "narrowly tailored" in applying strict scrutiny. See, e.g., McIntyre v. Ohio Elections Commission (1995). Justice Breyer took this one step further by using a new formulation in analyzing a series of regulations aimed at indecent cable programming. He asserted that the analysis should be whether a regulation "properly addresses an extremely important problem, without imposing, in light of the relevant interests, an unnecessarily great restriction on speech." Denver Area Educational Telecommunications Consortium, Inc. v. Federal Communications Commission (1996).

In addition, some Justices seem to be limiting content regulation, and thus, the application of strict scrutiny, to those laws that discriminate not merely on content, but rather on viewpoint. For example, in Turner Broadcasting System, Inc. v. Federal Communications Commission (1997), the majority applied intermediate scrutiny even though the Congressional findings of fact which formed the justification for the cable must-carry rules referred to the importance of broadcast stations' providing educational and informational programming, as well as local news and public affairs programming.

Obviously, whenever ad hoc balancing is used, one of the keys is the weight given to the First Amendment interest involved. In the Court's eyes all First Amendment rights are not created equal. Rather, the Court has established at least three distinct hierarchies of speech that are used to determine the degree of First Amendment protection involved.

One hierarchy is based on the actual content of speech. In what is essentially a refined version of definitional balancing the Court has taken the position that protected expression is not monolithic but divisible into categories with the extent of First Amendment protection dependent upon the intrinsic worth of the expression in each category. See Young v. American Mini Theatres (1976); Federal Communications Commission v. Pacifica Foundation (1978) (opinion of Justice Stevens joined by Chief Justice Burger and Justice Rehnquist); 44 Liquormart, Inc. v. Rhode Island (1996). This position raises some very thorny questions for the courts: what criteria should they use in categorizing protected speech; how will individual judges be able to cast aside their own personal value systems in determining objectively the comparative worth of particular expression; and finally, what degree of First Amendment protection will be afforded each of the categories of expression? These questions led some Justices to question this approach in 44 Liquormart. (Opinions of Justices Stevens, Thomas, and Scalia).

The mode of transmission of speech is also used to determine the degree of First Amendment protection available. The Court has long held that differences in the characteristics of new media justify the application of different First Amendment standards. Thus, in Miami Herald Publishing Company v. Tornillo (1974) the Court declared unconstitutional a statute granting an individual attacked by a newspaper the right to have a response printed in that newspaper; yet the Court upheld a similar regulation applying to broadcasters in Red Lion Broadcasting Company v. FCC (1969). The proliferation of new communication technologies is forcing the Court to address the issue more frequently. See Turner Broadcasting System v. Federal Communications Commission (1997) (Upholding the must-carry rules for cable); Reno v. A.C.L.U. (1997) (Holding restrictions on indecent material transmitted over the Internet unconstitutional). As the number of new communication technologies continues to grow and the technologies continue to converge (e.g., what is the difference between a movie transmitted over the Internet accessed by a cable modem, and regular cable programming?), the Court may find it more and more difficult to differentiate them in terms of appropriate First Amendment standards.

Finally, recognizing that the right to publish news can be seriously restricted by limitations on the right to gather news, the Court has extended some First Amendment protection to newsgathering, often under the rhetoric of a right of access. See Branzburg v. Hayes (1972); Richmond Newspapers, Inc. v. Virginia (1980). However, the degree of protection afforded newsgathering is nowhere near as extensive as that given dissemination of news.

The good news for advocates of strong First Amendment protection is that the decisions produced by the ad hoc balancing approach tend to make small adjustments in the law as opposed to sweeping changes. The bad news is that because the ad hoc approach depends so heavily on the value that each Justice attaches to the government interest asserted, as well as to the speech involved, there is much less guidance for the lower courts.

Other trends in the Court's approach to the First Amendment include a continued departure from the idea that time, place and manner restrictions on protected expression may not be influenced by the content of the expression except where captive or juvenile audiences are involved, i.e., the restrictions must be "content neutral." In Young v. American Mini Theatres, Inc. (1976), a five-justice majority upheld a Detroit zoning ordinance that required dispersal of "adult" bookstores and motion picture theaters but not other bookstores and theaters in order to protect established commercial and residential neighborhoods. This "place" restriction was justified on the basis of the type of books sold and the motion pictures exhibited. In other words, the majority "peeked" at the content of the expression here and, having peeked, upheld the place restriction embodied in the ordinance because of the content. See also City of Renton v. Playtime Theaters, Inc. (1986); Reno v. A.C.L.U. (1997) (Opinion of

Justice O'Connor joined by Chief Justice Rehnquist).

Also, in the past, the Court, perhaps to conserve judicial energy, occasionally avoided the philosophical struggle over the proper approach to the First Amendment by nullifying statutes, ordinances and governmental regulations infringing free expression simply on the basis of their "vagueness" or "overbreadth." See, e.g., Erznoznik v. Jacksonville (1975) (ordinance making it a public nuisance and a criminal offense for a drive-in movie theater to exhibit any film containing nudity if the screen is visible from the street held overbroad and struck down as violative of the First Amendment). However, the Court now seems to be narrowing the application of the "vagueness" and "overbreadth" devices. See, e.g. Young v. American Mini Theatres, Inc. (1976) (all opinions); New York v. Ferber (1982) (statute prohibiting the promotion of a sexual performance by a child by distributing material which depicts such performances held not substantially overbroad).

For the first time in more than a decade, there will be new justices on the Court. It is far too early to determine what effect Chief Justice John Roberts and Justice Samuel Alito will have, either in terms of approach or results. However, there are a number of areas ranging from reporters' privilege to limitations on indecency to the application of the First Amendment to new technologies which seem likely to come before the Court, leading to the possibility that the new justices may have a major impact.

C. THE DICHOTOMY BETWEEN PRIOR RESTRAINT AND SUBSEQUENT PUNISHMENT OF EXPRESSION

On one point adherents of all schools of thought appear to agree. At a minimum the First Amendment was adopted to prevent the federal government—and later the state governments through the Fourteenth Amendment—from instituting a general system of prior restraint on speech or press similar to that employed in England and the Colonies in the seventeenth and eighteenth centuries, i.e., licensing of the press and censorship of expression.

There were those, including Blackstone in his Commentaries on the Laws of England, who believed that freedom of the press consisted only in proscribing prior restraints upon publication and that once publication was made the publisher had to accept the consequences which might be imposed upon him by an offended government or individual. That First Amendment protection extended also to attempts by government to punish completed utterances and publications through imposition of criminal sanctions was not fully settled until the formulation of the "clear and present danger" test in Schenck v. United States (1919). That the Amendment further provided the publisher or speaker some protection against subsequent civil defamation actions was not recognized until New York Times Co. v. Sullivan, supra.

Despite the fact that the threat of subsequent criminal punishment and civil judgments for damages may have a substantial deterrent effect upon free expression, the Supreme Court has not, as indicated in the preceding sections, achieved anywhere near the consistency of doctrine that it has regarding the condemnation of administrative and judicial prior restraints.

There are many reasons besides the historical for the Court's hostility toward governmental action smacking of prior restraint. Professor Emerson in his classic article "The Doctrine of Prior Restraint," 20 Law and Contemporary Problems 648 (1955), provides us with a modern catalogue of these reasons. A system of prior restraint is broader in its coverage, more uniform in its effect and more easily and effectively enforced than subsequent punishment. Everything which is published or publicly uttered would be subject to scrutiny. Then, too, expression which is banned never sees the light of day and that which is not banned may be so delayed in the administrative mill that it becomes superfluous or obsolete when it is "cleared." The procedural safeguards of the criminal judicial process, including public scrutiny, are not present to the same degree in the administrative censorial process. Finally, the entire process is geared toward suppression and the censor will be impelled to find things to suppress.

The landmark case recognizing the dangers of prior restraint is Near v. Minnesota (1931). There, a state statute provided for the abatement as a public nuisance of "malicious, scandalous, and defamatory" publications. The statute further provided that all persons guilty of such a nuisance could be permanently enjoined from further publication of malicious, scandalous and defamatory matter. A county attorney brought an action under the statute to enjoin The Saturday Press on the ground that it accused law enforcement agencies and officials of the city of Minneapolis with failing to stop vice and racketeering activities allegedly controlled by a "Jewish Gangster." In the face of the publisher's claim that his activities were protected by the First and Fourteenth Amendments, the trial court perpetually enjoined him from conducting a public nuisance under the name of The Saturday Press or any other name. The state supreme court affirmed the injunctive order. The United States Supreme Court reversed. Cutting through the peculiar procedures of the statute, the Court indicated that its object and effect was to suppress further publication. This they equated to prior restraint of the press. Moreover, if the person enjoined were so bold as to resume his or her publishing activities, he or she would have to submit the material to the appropriate judicial officer for clearance prior to publication in order to avoid being held in contempt of court for violation of the injunctive order. To the Court this constituted effective censorship prohibited by the due process clauses of the First and Fourteenth Amendments.

This decision stands out for many reasons. It was the Court's first definitive statement concerning the constitutionality of prior restraint on expression. More than this, it made clear that what was important was not the form governmental action took but its effect on speech and press. Furthermore, because it indicated that the constitutional ban on prior restraints was not absolute and did permit certain narrow exceptions, it opened up the question of the precise limits of the First Amendment in this area. Finally, it made the point very clearly that while expression was generally protected from prior restraint, it might subsequently be punished if it were determined that the expression was unlawful. This dichotomy drawn by the Court in Near persists today. It was relied upon expressly by four of the Justices in their separate opinions in New York Times Co. v. United States (1971) (the "Pentagon Papers" case). See also Vance v. Universal Amusement Co., Inc. (1980).

D.　INFORMATION AS PROPERTY

As the United States moves further towards an information-based economy, there is an increasing conflict between the property rights in information and the free flow of ideas protected by the First Amendment.

1. Conflict Between Economic Interests and Information Flow

The primary motivation for information owners restricting others' First Amendment rights is an economic one. Often it is simply a question of seeking compensation for what is seen as the use of someone else's property. In other words, anyone who is willing to pay can disseminate the information. Other times the purpose is to obtain a competitive edge through exclusive coverage of a news or entertainment event. For example, ABC originally claimed exclusive rights to some of the July 4, 1986 Statue of Liberty festivities.

Sometimes, however, the primary motivation is not an economic one. For example, a Boston cable news channel attempted unsuccessfully to prevent Congressional candidate James Roosevelt from using an unauthorized tape of its interview with his opponent, Joseph Kennedy, in his campaign advertisements. The cable channel claimed that this particular use of its programming would damage its credibility as a news organization.

In another case author J.D. Salinger sought to enjoin a biography of him containing excerpts from personal letters that he had donated to various school libraries. Here, the issue was not who would get to distribute the information or profit from it, but whether it would be distributed at all.

The conflict between information rights and First Amendment values can take place within the framework of many different areas of the law including right of publicity, trademark law, trade secret law, and contract law. However, copyright law is probably the best illustration of the problems raised by the conflict and attempts to strike an accommodation between these competing interests.

2. Copyright and the First Amendment

The legal concepts of American copyright law and the provisions of the Copyright Act of 1976, 17 U.S.C.A. § 101 et seq., 90 Stat. 2541 (1976) are summarized in another volume of the "Nutshell" series and will not be generally repeated here. It is enough to say that the Congress, pursuant to constitutional authority, can and does protect the owners of intellectual property in fixed form such as writings, photographs, and sight and sound recordings from having their creations copied and appropriated by others. Such copying and appropriation of copyrighted works constitutes infringement for which the copyright holder may seek civil remedies and the federal government may in certain cases seek criminal sanctions.

Although the aim of copyright law to encourage the production of intellectual property is laudable, it can have the effect of limiting distribution of copyrighted material even in the face of First Amendment claims by the news media.

Thus in Roy Export Co. v. Columbia Broadcasting System, Inc. (1982), CBS's claim of First Amendment protection in the use, on the occasion of Charlie Chaplin's death, of a special compilation of excerpts from Chaplin's motion pictures in which

Roy Export Co. held the copyright was rejected by
the United States Court of Appeals. In affirming
that CBS had been guilty of copyright infringement
in using "the compilation" originally prepared for
the 1972 Academy Award Presentations during
which Chaplin received a special "Oscar," the Second Circuit made clear that it would be a very rare
case in which copyrighted material was so imbued
with news value as to subordinate the copyright
holder's protection to First Amendment claims.

It should be noted, however, that raw news and
information are not subject to copyright and are in
the public domain for anyone to disseminate. See
International News Service v. Associated Press
(1918) in which the Supreme Court recognized that
the substance of the news of the day was not
copyrightable because of the obvious public policy
that such history should be made freely available to
all. However, the way news or information is organized, including the words used and the manner
chosen by the reporter or publisher to express the
news or information gathered, is copyrightable.

Sometimes the line between the news and someone's expression of the news is a difficult one to
draw. The determination of when two descriptions
of an event are similar enough to constitute copyright infringement is not governed by any clear
guidelines.

It should be obvious that copyright protection
provides a serious limitation on the use of existing
material by the news media. However, the noncon-

stitutional "fair use" defense to copyright infringement suits provides at least limited protection for
First Amendment values by affording journalists
some right to publish copyrighted material.

This defense is not statutory in origin but was
created by the courts, apparently in the belief that
public policy requires persons other than the copyright owner to be able to use the owner's work
under strictly limited conditions in certain contexts
in which it will be of value to the public. This
defense has often been misunderstood by the courts
and has not been defined with any great precision.
Nevertheless, certain features of the defense can be
discerned. One may be protected in copying another's copyrighted work where the copying is not
likely to hurt the present and potential markets for
the copyrighted work and where the copying is
likely to be of substantial benefit to the public. In
determining whether the use of another's creation
is a "fair use," the purpose of the defendant's work,
the amount of copying involved, the public interest
in the copyrighted material, the nature of the media
involved and the effect of the copying on the market
value of the plaintiff's work are all factors to be
considered. An example of the balancing of these
factors is Time, Inc. v. Bernard Geis Associates
(1968), in which a book publisher reproduced several frames of the Zapruder home movie of the Kennedy assassination in a book about the assassination. In holding the reproduction of the frames a
fair use, the court balanced the great public interest
in information concerning the assassination against

the doubtful effect of the reproduction on the market value of Time, Inc.'s copyright in the entire film.

These principles have now been given explicit statutory recognition in § 107 of the 1976 Copyright Act which states that in determining whether the use made of a work in any particular case is a fair use, the following four factors shall be considered:

1. the purpose and character of the use, including whether such use is of a commercial nature or is for nonprofit educational purposes;

2. the nature of the copyrighted work;

3. the amount and substantiality of the portion used in relation to the copyrighted work as a whole; and

4. the effect of the use upon the potential market for or value of the copyrighted work. 17 U.S.C.A. § 107.

The public interest is central to a successful invocation of the fair use defense. Statutory protection of expression encourages authors and artists to continue to produce original works; continued production and dissemination of these works aids the flow of ideas throughout society. However, statutory protection can also retard the flow of ideas, offering a work so much protection that the ideas contained therein are no longer free to enter the marketplace. The fair use defense moderates this overprotection, thus stimulating the circulation in society of the ideas and information that the copyrighted work contains. This rationale for the defense explains some of the more common examples of fair use, such as the quotation or paraphrase of passages from books in book reviews and the limited quotation of copyrighted materials in news stories.

At bottom, then, two elements predominate in determining the availability of the fair use defense: (1) the intensity of the public interest in the free dissemination of portions of particular copyrighted works (e.g., the desire of the public for as much opinion and information about the Kennedy assassination as possible); and (2) the effect such free dissemination will have on the property value of or income from the particular copyrighted work (e.g., parody of a literary work or motion picture in such detail that an audience exposed to the parody will have little desire to pay for the privilege of reading or viewing the original).

Harper & Row Publishers, Inc. v. Nation Enterprises (1985) is a good example of the difficulty of applying the fair use defense in a "news" context. Harper & Row had contracted for various exclusive rights to President Gerald Ford's memoirs, "A Time to Heal," including the right to license prepublication excerpts. Harper & Row had then granted Time Magazine the right to excerpt 7,500 words from President Ford's account of his decision to pardon President Nixon in return for $25,000 (half in advance), such publication to take place one week before the publication of the book. Prior to Time's scheduled publication, Victor Nevasky, editor of The Nation Magazine, obtained an unauthorized copy of "A Time to Heal." Working directly from this manuscript, he produced a 2,250 word article consisting exclusively of quotes, paraphrases and facts drawn from the Ford manuscript. This article appeared before the scheduled publication of the Time article. As a result Time did not publish its article and refused to pay Harper & Row the remaining $12,500.

In the ensuing copyright action, The Nation relied on fair use and the First Amendment to defend its actions. In a 6–3 decision the Court held that The Nation's excerpt was not a fair use. In applying the four factors of fair use, the Court first held that the general purpose was indeed news reporting, but that the more specific purpose was to supplant "the copyright holder's commercially valuable right of first publication."

In examining the nature of the copyrighted work, the Court acknowledged that it was a factual work and that the need to disseminate factual works is greater than that for fictional works. Having done so, however, the Court then focused on the unpublished nature of the work and decided that fair use has a more limited application to *unpublished* works.

A key issue was the amount and substantiality of the portion used. Here, although there was some dispute as to exactly how much of The Nation's article consisted of infringing material, it was clear that overall it was a very small amount when compared to the entire text of "A Time to Heal." The Court, however, viewed this as a qualitative as well as a quantitative issue, and found that the material on the Nixon pardon was the heart of the book and that the quotes used in The Nation's article were the essence of that article. In that sense the portion used was substantial.

For the Court, the easiest part of the test was the effect on the market for the copyrighted work. Harper & Row had lost $12,500 when Time cancelled its projected article as a result of The Nation's article. When considered in conjunction with the analysis of the other three factors, the finding against fair use was clear.

Justice Brennan wrote a sharp dissent accusing the majority of extending copyright protection to information and ideas. In his view the purpose of the work—news reporting—and the nature of the copyrighted work—historical and factual—supported a fair use defense. He found the amount taken not to be excessive even though it dealt with the most important part of the book. Because he believed that the cancellation by Time was as much a result of information contained in The Nation article as expression appropriated from Ford's book, he did not find that the infringement had any serious effect on the market for the copyrighted material.

The significance of this case is in some ways difficult to determine. Some would argue it is limited to the rather unusual facts of the case. Although there was no proof the manuscript was stolen, the Court appeared to assume that it was. Also, the infringing work was published prior to the copyrighted work, a fact emphasized by the Court. Given that most fair use cases involve someone copying an already published work, it may be relatively easy to distinguish Harper & Row.

On the other hand, if it operates, as Justice Brennan suggested, to restrict the fair use defense to a point where information itself acquires some copyright protection, then it presents a serious threat to the free flow of information protected by the First Amendment.

The limitations of fair use as a vehicle for First Amendment protection became even more apparent in Salinger v. Random House, Inc. (1987). Author J.D. Salinger sought to restrain the publication of a biography of him on the grounds that it contained excerpts from copyrighted letters that he had written. The biographer, Ian Hamilton, had obtained copies of the letters from various college libraries to which they had been donated by their recipients. As in Harper & Row the case was treated strictly as a copyright case with no real First Amendment issues. For the court of appeals, the key question was whether or not the use of the excerpts from the letters constituted fair use.

The court of appeals relied heavily on Harper & Row for its fair use analysis because it was "the court's first delineation of the scope of fair use as applied to unpublished works."

In considering the application of the four fair use factors to Hamilton's use of the Salinger letters, the court started by categorizing the purpose of the use alternatively as "criticism," "scholarship," or "research." All of these categories are viewed as appropriate to a fair use. The court went on, however, to specifically reject the idea that a biographer is entitled to an especially generous application of the defense.

The court noted that as long as the biographer took only the factual content of the letter, there was no copyright problem. But the court did not recognize any need to take the expression contained in the letter.

Turning to the second factor, the court focused on the unpublished nature of the work as being of critical importance. In essence, the court viewed it as creating a heavy presumption against a finding of fair use.

With regard to the amount and substantiality of the use, the court of appeals found that copyrighted expression was used on at least 40% of the book's 192 pages.

Finally, the court found that due to the substantial amount taken by Hamilton and his extensive use of the phrases "he wrote" and "he said" that at least some members of the public might be misled into believing that they had read the essence of Salinger's letters, thus reducing the potential market for a book of his letters. This led the court of appeals to conclude that the fourth fair use factor—

effect on the potential market for the work—weighed slightly in Salinger's favor. Based on this analysis the court ordered an injunction prohibiting the sale of the biography.

Similarly, the court of appeals reversed a district court's finding that the First Amendment precluded an injunction against an infringing work in New Era Publications International v. Henry Holt & Co. (1989). The case involved a biography of L. Ron Hubbard, the founder of the Church of Scientology. Russell Miller, the author of "Bare–Faced Messiah," had used quotations from Hubbard's own unpublished letters and diaries to support his contention that Hubbard was a bigot and a hypocrite. The district court, despite finding that the quotations exceeded the bounds of fair use, had denied a request for an injunction. Noting the "abhorrence of the First Amendment to prior restraint," the district court concluded that the damage remedy would adequately protect the copyright holder's interests.

The court of appeals upheld the denial of the injunction, but only on the ground of laches. With regard to the First Amendment question the court concluded that all First Amendment claims were encompassed by the fair use doctrine and thus, no separate First Amendment analysis was warranted.

In Wright v. Warner Books, Inc. (1991), the court of appeals seemingly retreated somewhat from its position on the application of fair use analysis to unpublished works, when it upheld a district court finding that the use of excerpts of unpublished letters in a biography of Richard Wright was a fair use. However, the court once again failed to apply a separate First Amendment analysis.

Just to be certain that the judges of the Second Circuit did not regress to their earlier approach, the Congress in 1992 enacted, and President Bush signed, legislation adding the following language to the Fair Use Section of the Copyright Act. 17 U.S.C.A. § 107: "The fact that a work is unpublished shall not by itself bar a finding of fair use if such finding is made upon consideration of all the above factors."

Perhaps the most important conclusion that can be drawn from Salinger, New Era and Wright is that courts are unwilling to examine any copyright case for First Amendment problems. The assumption is that the idea-expression dichotomy and the defense of fair use provide a proper accommodation between the sometimes competing interests. The distinction between prior restraint and subsequent punishment recognized by the Supreme Court in Near and the "Pentagon Papers" case does not apply to copyright cases.

Thus in Salinger and New Era the court of appeals was not concerned that the expression in Salinger's letters or the evidence for Miller's assertions about Hubbard might be withheld from the public for many years. Nor did the court address the fact that the real interests of the copyright holders (privacy in Salinger and limiting criticism in

New Era) would have been insufficient to justify an injunction had the cases been subjected to First Amendment as opposed to copyright analysis.

Parodies present another troubling conflict between the property rights protected by copyright and the free flow of ideas protected by the First Amendment. In Campbell v. Acuff–Rose (1993), the Sixth Circuit, rejecting a claim of fair use, found 2 Live Crew's song "Pretty Woman" had infringed the copyright for Roy Orbison's "Oh, Pretty Woman." The Supreme Court reversed, holding that the court of appeals' fair use analysis was flawed.

The first error was holding that the parody was presumptively unfair because of its commercial nature. The Court held that § 107 does not set out bright line rules, but rather calls for case-by-case analysis. Thus, in terms of the purpose of the use, the fact that the song was a parody weighed in favor of fair use, while the fact that it was commercial weighed against it.

A second error was holding that because the parody took the heart of the song, the amount and substantiality taken from the original was too great. As the Court noted, in order for a parody to be effective, it must take enough so as to make it clear what work is being parodied. Sometimes this makes it necessary to take the heart of the work, in this case the opening bass line. Thus, in applying the third fair use factor, it is necessary to examine the context. Taking only the amount necessary to conjure up the original favors a finding of fair use.

The final error was presuming from the commercial nature of the parody that it had harmed the market for the original. The Court explained that there are two ways a parody can harm the market for the parodied work. The first, offering a substitute for the original work or for any potential derivative work (such as a rap version of the original), weighs heavily against a finding of fair use. Damage to the original resulting from the criticism expressed in the parody, however, does not weigh against fair use. The case was remanded for further proceedings consistent with the Court's opinion.

As illustrated by these cases, there is an increasing conflict between property rights in information and the free flow of ideas protected by the First Amendment. Courts attempting to balance these sometimes competing interests have so far produced inconsistent results. As will be discussed more extensively in Chapter 12, the advent of the Internet and related digital technologies which allow easy, rapid and inexpensive transmission and copying of everything from print to video has exacerbated this conflict.

———

In the chapters that follow, the First Amendment will be considered in several specific contexts. These include the permissible scope of defamation and invasion of privacy actions in tort, the efforts of government to suppress pornography, government efforts to safeguard national security, the possible conflict between protection of a free press and the Fifth and Sixth Amendment guarantees of a fair and impartial trial, the existence or non-existence of a newsperson's privilege not to reveal his or her sources of information when compelled to do so, and the permissible limits of governmental regulation of advertising.

CHAPTER II

DEFAMATION AND MASS COMMUNICATION

A.   INTERESTS IN CONFLICT

One of the interests that has competed with the interest in freedom of expression down through the centuries is that of reputation, both personal and proprietary. The importance of this interest should not be minimized. As Justice Stewart said in his concurring opinion in Rosenblatt v. Baer (1966), "The right of a man to the protection of his own reputation from unjustified invasion and wrongful hurt reflects no more than our basic concept of the essential dignity and worth of every human being— a concept at the root of any decent system of ordered liberty."

The early common law courts considered reputation to be an interest deserving of protection by recognizing an action for money damages to compensate for injury resulting from defamatory communications. This action has evolved into the complex (some would say "confused and confusing") twin tort actions of libel and slander. There is no doubt that the ever present fear that one may have to respond in damages for what one publishes has a limiting effect on the work of the modern journalist

45

or public speaker. One reason for the demise of Pulitzer's New York World was the drain on its resources from numerous libel actions.

The thrust of the recent significant cases in the field of defamation has been the recognition of the unavoidable conflict between these two interests and the attempt to provide a measure of legal protection for both.

B. COMMON LAW DEFAMATION

1. Definition and Elements

Defamation has been defined as the injury to reputation by words that tend to expose one to public hatred, shame, contempt or disgrace, or to induce an evil opinion of one in the minds of right-thinking persons and to deprive one of their confidence. Kimmerle v. New York Evening Journal (1933). Although this definition provides a good starting place for understanding the nature of defamation, it fails to place any emphasis on loss of reputation in one's business or profession. Moreover, the loss of reputation need only be with regard to a small but significant segment of the community, whether "right-thinking" or not. Finally, as the late Dean William L. Prosser pointed out, one may be defamed by imputations of insanity or poverty, which would instead arouse pity or sympathy—feelings that diminish esteem and respect. W. P. Keeton, editor, Prosser and Keeton on the Law of Torts 773 (5th Ed. 1984). An example of this would be a false statement that an individual is a hopeless alcoholic.

In the past, defamation actions have been either criminal or civil in nature. Although criminal libel laws have an odious historical association with prosecutions for political sedition, a few prosecutors have stooped to using them during the past half-century, as in Louisiana's prosecution of New Orleans district attorney James Garrison for his verbal attacks on certain sitting criminal court judges. Garrison v. Louisiana (1964). The criminal action had nearly fallen into disuse until it was revived in a flurry of cases during the last five years. In the first conviction for criminal libel since 1974, publishers David Carson and Edward Powers were convicted of criminal libel for falsely claiming that a mayor and a judge lived outside the county in which they worked. Kansas v. Carson (2004). A Utah prosecutor brought criminal libel charges against a high school student who falsely accused the principal of having an affair with the high school secretary; the charges were later dropped. In re I.M.L. v. State of Utah (2002). An Alabama prosecutor charged a lawyer with criminal libel in a case that ended only after the Alabama Supreme Court found the criminal defamation law unconstitutional. Ivey v. Alabama (2001). Only 17 states had criminal libel statutes in 2005. In any event, the focus of this chapter will be the modern civil actions of libel and slander.

The essential elements common to both libel and slander actions are (1) the making by the defendant of a defamatory statement; (2) the publication to at least one other than the plaintiff of that statement;

and (3) the identification in some way of the plaintiff as the person defamed.

a. The Defamatory Statement

The words complained of must be such as will injure the reputation of a living person or existing organization because only the injured party may sue for defamation. Some words such as "thief," "cheat," "murderer" or "whore" are almost universally understood to hurt someone's reputation. Other words may have that effect in relation to the times and the victim's position. Falsely labeling one a Communist during the World War II period of United States–Soviet cooperation was not actionable. However, the same false label was considered defamatory after the "Cold War" began.

In general, defamation suits tend to involve false charges that fall into the following categories:

    1.   accusation of a crime;

    2.   sexual impropriety or other immoral behavior;

    3.   having a loathsome disease or being mentally ill;

    4.   professional incompetence or misconduct in one's business;

    5.   bankruptcy, financial irresponsibility or dishonesty;

    6.   disgraceful behavior such as child abuse or substance abuse;

7. product disparagement or trade libel (discussed in Chapter IX)

The plaintiff's situation in life may also give a damaging effect to otherwise innocent words. The selling of pork is normally a respectable occupation, but suggesting that a kosher butcher sells bacon has been considered defamatory, for clearly it would cause religiously oriented customers to think less of the butcher and to take their business elsewhere. See Braun v. Armour & Co. (1930).

Defamatory words can be presented in numerous ways. One need not attack with a verbal axe. The stiletto of ridicule may suffice. Provided that even one person other than the plaintiff understands the communication to be defamatory and such understanding is reasonable, given its content and context, a court may accept the plaintiff's argument that it is defamatory. Of course, the defendant may attempt to show that the communication had at least one nondefamatory meaning and others understand it in that sense, or that the communication was made in jest and could not reasonably be taken seriously. Courts in Illinois, for example, have fashioned the "innocent construction rule" which gives defendants the benefit of the doubt; in other words, if there are two reasonable ways to interpret a statement, one defamatory and the other nondefamatory, the court will choose the "innocent" meaning. However, the great majority of states do not follow this rule.

Sexual slurs instigate numerous libel suits. Saying that a woman is "unchaste" or is having sex with a man to whom she is not married is defamatory. Even falsely stating that a woman is a rape victim is defamatory. To falsely report that someone is gay or bisexual is defamatory in 47 states, although courts in North Carolina, Colorado and Massachusetts have ruled that saying a person is gay or bisexual is not defamatory because it merely indicates sexual preference. See Donovan v. Fiumara (1994); Miles v. National Enquirer (1999); Amrak Productions v. Morton (2005). Of course, if some members of the community think less of a plaintiff who is said to be a rape victim or who is gay, one could characterize this as "wrong-thinking." Judges, however, must "take the world as they find it," and must be attuned to "right-thinking," "average-thinking," and "wrong-thinking" people in deciding what is defamatory and what is not.

Libel has normally been a tort of commission. Can it also be a tort of omission? In a Spokane, Washington case, television reporter Tom Grant reported that store owners Eliot and Louise Mohr had filed charges of trespassing and harassment against a man with Down's syndrome with the mental capacity of a five year-old after he offered to clean their windows in exchange for candy. The news story appeared unsympathetic toward the Mohrs, but Grant omitted the fact that the Down's syndrome man had threatened Mohr and his wife, making slashing motions across his throat and shouting that he would shoot them. Mohr and his wife sued Grant for defamation by omission. Although the Washington Court of Appeals ruled in Mohr's favor, the Supreme Court of Washington reversed, granting summary judgment for KXLY–TV and Grant because Mohr had not shown that the news report was false, despite its omissions. Mohr v. Grant (2005). The U.S. Supreme Court has never directly ruled on a libel-by-omission claim. See also Janklow v. Newsweek (1985)(U.S. Court of Appeals for Eighth Circuit held that former South Dakota Governor Bill Janklow could not proceed in liable-by-omission case when Newsweek reported that he had been accused of raping his 15 year-old babysitter).

If a person's reputation in the community is so irredeemable that a few added insults do not hurt (if the person is a convicted felon, for example), that person may be termed "libel-proof." Numerous federal and state courts have embraced the doctrine of the "libel-proof" plaintiff, as in the case of a convicted kidnapper who sued for libel, objecting to the news report saying that he had been dressed as a woman when he abducted his victim. Lamb v. Rizzo (2004).

Like the idea of a plaintiff being libel-proof, the idea that a company can sue for trade libel or product disparagement is relatively new. Many states have passed laws designed to protect the reputations of certain businesses such as banks and insurance companies, and more recently, fruits and vegetables. Because it is closely related to commercial speech, trade libel is discussed further in Chapter IX.

b. Publication

Publication is a legal term of art, meaning that someone has communicated the defamatory message, whatever its form, to someone other than the person defamed. Publication in the sense of printing and distribution of printed matter is not required. For example, publication occurs if a patient makes a serious statement in a loud voice in a crowded waiting room directly to a licensed physician that he or she is a "quack" and one or more of the other patients overhears it.

In this situation, it is clear that the communicator either intends that others overhear his or her accusation or is so uncaring whether it is overheard as to be deemed reckless in his or her conduct. Where one does not intend the communication to be conveyed to anyone other than the target of his or her attack, however, and the means chosen to convey the communication will in the normal course prevent reception by third persons, there is no publication. For instance, Able writes his former business partner Baker a letter in which he accuses Baker of causing the downfall of their business by "stealing the company blind." Able places the letter in a sealed envelope, marks it "personal," addresses it to Baker and mails it to his house. Baker's son, curious about the letter from his father's former associate, opens and reads the letter prior to Baker and without authority. There is no publication here and hence, no actionable defamation.

Moreover, since it is the *defamer* who must intentionally or recklessly promote publication, the requirement is not met if the victim publicizes the communication to others. If in the above hypothetical, Baker opened the letter and then showed the letter to his son, the result would be the same—no publication. Where there is publication, however, repetition of the original defamation by persons other than the victim constitutes republication, for which the original communicator will also be held liable provided the republication is foreseeable. Of course, the person who does the republishing may also be held liable.

A question of special significance to the print media is whether the distribution of each copy of a press run is a separate publication providing the basis for multiple defamation actions or whether the press run is to be viewed as constituting one publication. The early English cases suggested the first alternative but they were decided before the advent of high speed presses, large press runs and mass distribution. Shortly before World War II American courts began to move toward what has become known as the "single publication rule." The rule provides that only one cause of action for defamation arises when the product of a press run or printing is released by the publisher for distribution, no matter how many separate transactions may result. A corollary is that the statute of limitations for defamation begins to run from the moment of first release. See Gregoire v. G.P. Putnam's Sons (1948), the leading case for the single publication rule. This case held that a libel action based on the sale of a single copy of a book whose last printing was more than two years prior to the sale was barred by New York's one-year statute of limitation. Reinforcing this judicial trend is the Uniform Single Publication Act (see Restatement Second of Torts § 577A) promulgated by the National Conference on Uniform State Laws in 1952. This model legislation extends the single publication concept to radio, television and motion pictures. The act has been adopted by statute in nine states, including California, Illinois and Pennsylvania, and has been adopted by judicial decision in at least 17 states. See Keeton v. Hustler Magazine (1988).

c. *Identification*

Published defamation is not actionable unless the complaining party can establish that it was he or she who was defamed. Very often the target of a defamatory communication is not clearly named therein and thus the identification of the complaining party with the communication becomes a problem of analyzing extrinsic circumstances.

Furthermore, a disclaimer does not necessarily preclude a finding of liability in a defamation suit. For example, when Boston Magazine published the May 2003 article "The Mating Habits of the Suburban High School Teenager," it included a picture of five students at a high school dance, one of whom was Stacey Stanton. The article described an increase in casual sex and promiscuity among teenagers, although it added the following disclaimer: "The photos on these pages are from an award-winning five-year project on teen sexuality taken by photojournalist Dan Habib. The individuals pictured are unrelated to the people or events described in this story." Stanton sued for defamation and invasion of privacy, but the federal district court in Massachusetts, relying on the disclaimer, dismissed her suit. She appealed, and the U.S. Court of Appeals for the First Circuit reversed and remanded her case, ruling that a "reasonable reader" could easily miss "the crucial second sentence" of the disclaimer and assume that Stanton herself was one of the teenagers who engaged in promiscuous behavior, thus identifying her in a defamatory context. Stanton v. Metro Corp. (2006).

Identification may also be difficult when a group is defamed. In the past it was possible to criminally libel a large group or race of people, as in Beauharnais v. Illinois (1952). In this case white racist Joseph Beauharnais was fined $200 for distributing pamphlets insulting to blacks who were integrating the white Chicago suburb of Cicero. The Supreme Court upheld Beauharnais' conviction on the grounds that such libelous speech was not protected by the First Amendment. Most legal scholars would probably agree that the Beauharnais ruling is no longer viable, however, in light of New York Times Co. v. Sullivan, discussed below. The case of R.A.V. v. City of St. Paul, Minnesota (1992), in which the Supreme Court struck down a St. Paul ordinance against hate speech, further suggests that Beauharnais may no longer be viable.

In the five decades since Beauharnais, the general rule has changed so that the courts will not enter-

tain an action for group libel when the complainant
is a member of a large group that has been defamed. In the case of defamation of small homoge-
neous groups, the courts will permit actions by the
individual members of the group. But how many
people constitute a small group? There is no magic
number, but any group under 100 may be small
enough for a court to find that one or more members have been identified. The inclusiveness of the
language affects identification; generally, a court
will ask a jury to determine the degree to which
other people would find a defamatory statement
attaching to an individual or to everyone in the
group. For example, in Fawcett Publications v. Mor-
ris (1962), a member of the 1956 University of
Oklahoma football team sued *True* magazine when
it published an article implying that the Sooners
had used stimulant drugs. Although no players were
named in the article and more than 60 were on the
squad, the Oklahoma Supreme Court held that the
suit could be maintained, concluding that the article
defamed every member of the team, including the
plaintiff. Some courts will allow individual actions
by certain members of small groups when the defamatory communication is directed to a segment of
the group. Of course, in this last case the plaintiff
must convince the finder of fact (normally the jury)
that he or she was a member of the segment attacked. See Neiman–Marcus Co. v. Lait (1952) for
an application of these rules regarding civil actions
for group defamation, and Hudson v. Guy Gannett
Broadcasting Co. (1987).

d. Economic Loss

In addition to establishing the defamatory nature of the communication, its publication and the necessary identification, plaintiffs in certain cases must also plead and prove that they suffered actual pecuniary or economic loss (special damages). In determining when this additional requirement must be met, we are confronted with the herculean task of sorting out libel from slander, libel per se from libel per quod and slander per se from all other slander.

2. The Contrast Between Libel and Slander

Broadly differentiated, the tort of libel includes defamatory communications of a more or less permanent sort such as printed material, photographs, paintings, motion pictures, signboards, effigies and even statuary, while slander includes more ephemeral communications such as the spoken word, gestures and sign language. The distinction arises out of the historical development of common law court jurisdiction. In wresting jurisdiction from the ecclesiastical courts of England, which heard cases of slander, and in succeeding to the jurisdiction of the notorious Star Chamber over printed defamation, the common law courts kept the two types of defamation separate. See Donnelly, "History of Defamation," 1949 Wis.L.Rev. 99.

Although classification of communications as slander or libel might not have been too difficult in the late seventeenth century with the limited communications then available, it becomes troublesome in an electronic age with its dependence on telephones, radio, television and even computers for communication. Indeed, the courts have never agreed on the taxonomy of radio and television defamation. For example, in eight states including California, a defamatory broadcast is considered to be slander. Connecticut and Tennessee, seeking greater discrimination, classify it as libel if read from a script and slander if the remark is ad libbed. Courts in 13 states have held that broadcasting is libel. However, the majority of states do not distinguish between libel and slander with regard to broadcasting; instead, they simply refer to "broadcast defamation" and courts deal with it under the general laws of defamation in those states.

What too many courts appear to do when they are confronted with defamation via a new medium is to fix their gaze on the medium rather than on the interest the law is trying to protect and the reasons supporting the libel-slander dichotomy. The interest is, of course, reputation and the sting of defamation is its injury to reputation. Initially, the main justification for labeling writings as libelous, with concomitantly more serious consequences, including fine or imprisonment, was the greater permanence of the defamation and the correspondingly greater potential for wider distribution and greater injury to the victim. As new media have emerged, the distinctions among radio and television, print media or streaming video on the Internet have blurred with regard to the question of which medium can do the most damage to one's reputation. The potential injury to reputation from electronic defamation via broadcasting, cable or the Internet can be devastating. On principle it justifies the libel classification, whether the defamation is read from a script, made extemporaneously, or posted to an Internet web site.

There is no real way to avoid the troublesome task of classifying defamation since the requirement of special damages rests upon that classification. Generally, if the defamatory communication is held to constitute libel, the complaining party is not required to plead and prove as part of his or her case actual pecuniary loss resulting from the libel. On the other hand, if the communication is categorized as a slander, the complaining party generally has to establish such loss. As a practical matter many slander suits are quashed in the law office when the angry prospective plaintiff is informed by his or her own attorney to forget a lawsuit because he or she has no out-of-pocket loss. There is, however, a qualification to the requirement of financial sting in slander actions.

a. *The Special Cases of Slander*

The common law courts established three special categories of slander which were to be actionable without regard to the existence of special damages, meaning pecuniary loss: (1) imputation of crimes recognized by the common law courts such as larceny or larceny by trickery; (2) imputation of certain loathsome diseases (limited to sexually transmitted diseases, leprosy and the black plague); and (3) imputations affecting the victim in his or her business, trade, profession or office. Later, by statute or common law decision a fourth category, the imputation of unchastity to a woman, was created. Most courts recognize these four categories of slander as permitting a plaintiff to sue his or her slanderer without establishing special damages.

While from a plaintiff's perspective the existence of these special categories provides a liberalizing force in the law of slander, a somewhat parallel development in the law of libel has had the opposite effect.

b. Libel Per Se and Per Quod

As the tort of libel developed, the rule became fixed that in contrast to slander actions, the plaintiffs did not have to plead and prove special damages in order for them to recover. An explanation often given for this distinction is that the written communication once had greater potential for mischief because of its more permanent form. Therefore, some injury to the victim could be conclusively presumed.

Courts made no distinction between those libelous communications plain upon their face (libel *per se*) such as "John Doe committed arson" and those which require reference to extrinsic circumstances to give them the necessary defamatory meaning (libel *per quod*). The classic example of libel per quod is the erroneous newspaper story stating that Mary Doe of 1234 Shady Lane has just given birth to twins at a local hospital. The story is libelous because of the extrinsic fact that Mrs. Doe has been married only one month before and several persons reading the story know this fact.

Originally, then, if the defamatory communication was broadly classified as libel, special damages were not essential to a successful action. This is still stated to be the majority rule by the American Law Institute's Restatement of the Law of Torts Second, Section 569. But the late Dean William L. Prosser noted that at least 35 American jurisdictions draw a distinction between libel per se and per quod and hold that libel per quod is to be treated like slander, meaning that it is actionable only with the pleading and proving of special damages unless the libel falls within one or more of the four special categories associated with slander. W. Prosser, Handbook of the Law of Torts (4th ed. 1971) 763. Moreover, the presumption of damage required by libel per se is now constitutionally suspect with regard to libelous communication of public concern not made with actual malice. See Gertz v. Robert Welch, Inc. (1974); W. Prosser and W. Keeton, Handbook of the Law of Torts (5th ed. 1984) 796, 843. A major reason for this apparent change in the common law appears to be the reluctance of courts to hold newspapers and other media broadly liable for communications which they may not even be aware are defamatory.

To summarize:

1. Slander is actionable only with a showing of special damages . . .

2.   ... unless the slander imputes to the complaining party (1) criminal conduct recognized as involving moral turpitude; (2) infection with a sexually transmitted disease, leprosy or the plague; (3) misconduct or mismanagement in business, trade, profession or office; or (4) unchastity (if the victim is a female).

3.   Libels per se in all jurisdictions and libels per quod in a large number of jurisdictions (including New York) are actionable without the need for special damages.

4.   Libels per quod in other jurisdictions are now actionable only with a showing of special damages unless they fall into one of the four special categories established originally for slander.

The above rules and the proper classification of defamation cases under them are extremely important since the establishment of special damages, meaning pecuniary loss as a result of the defamatory communication, is often difficult for the plaintiff to prove.

3.   Theories of Liability

At common law, so long as the defendant intended to publish to a third person that which is ultimately adjudged to be defamatory toward the plaintiff, the defendant was strictly liable in tort, absent a valid defense. The plaintiff needed only to establish the intention of the defendant to publish and did not have to establish that the defendant intended the publication to be defamatory. Peck v. Tribune Co. (1909). Thus, a publisher under this rule "published at his own peril" and would be held liable for coincidences and honest errors as well as for intended defamatory attacks. The Supreme Court decisions in New York Times Co. v. Sullivan (1964) and Gertz v. Robert Welch, Inc. (1974) (discussed infra at pp. 95–112) ended strict liability for the media.

4. Remedies

Once the plaintiff has established his or her cause of action and assuming the defendant has not interposed any valid defense, the focus of the defamation suit shifts from the question of liability to the question of remedies available to the defamed person. The major remedy for injury to reputation is the award of monetary damages.

a. Damages

We have already seen that in cases of libel per quod in at least some jurisdictions and in cases of slander, excluding the four special categories, proof of special damages is necessary for liability. Of course, such damages may be established in any defamation action. Such damages require rather specific pleading and proof by the plaintiff of pecuniary or economic loss actually resulting from the defamatory communication and reasonable foreseeability of the plaintiff's loss by the defendant. Obvious cases are the loss of one's employment, the loss of opportunity for business profits and impaired credit rating because others are influenced by the defamation.

The existence of special damages may influence the jury's award of general damages. These are damages awarded for actual losses to the plaintiff from the defamation and cover both proven and unproven pecuniary and nonpecuniary loss for such injuries as hurt feelings, embarrassment, mental and emotional distress and physical consequences. Unless the action is one that specifically requires the showing of special damages, such damages are not a prerequisite for the award of general damages.

The jury will consider many factors in attempting to determine reasonable and appropriate general damages. These are catalogued by a leading authority as including (1) the nature of the defamation (irrational name calling or insinuation of serious wrongdoing); (2) the form and permanency of the publication (oral conversations between individuals or communication by the mass print or electronic media); (3) the degree of dissemination; (4) the degree to which the defamatory communication is believed; (5) the nature of the plaintiff's reputation; (6) in certain cases, the good faith of the defendant in publishing the defamatory matter and (7) the defendant's subsequent conduct in retracting the complained of communication or in making apology. Dan Dobbs, Law of Remedies: Damages–Equity–Restitution 259–276 (1993).

If spite, evil motive or reckless disregard for the truth is present, the jury will be instructed that it may award the plaintiff punitive damages subject to state law. Courts in Louisiana, Massachusetts, Michigan, Nebraska, New Hampshire, Oregon and Washington have declared that *no* punitive damages may be awarded to any libel plaintiff, regardless of proof at trial. Eight more states, Colorado, Florida, Georgia, Kansas, Montana, Mississippi, North Dakota and Virginia, have limited punitive damage awards. As the term implies, such damages are designed to punish the defamer and are not compensatory in nature. If such damages are to make the defendant "smart" for his or her indiscretion and deter him or her in the future, the jury must be entitled to know the defendant's net worth and to reduce it to where it hurts.

Punitive damages may have too great a deterrent effect. One lower court has suggested that when First Amendment interests are balanced against the interests of the state in punishing defamers, the "chilling effect" of punitive damages on freedom of expression is too great a price for a free society to pay in attempting to rid itself of defamation. Maheu v. Hughes Tool Co. (1974).

In the 1990s, former district attorney Vic Feazell won a $58 million libel judgement (later set aside and settled for an undisclosed sum) against WFAA–TV in Dallas, and attorney Richard Sprague won a $34 million judgment against Philadelphia Newspapers (later settled for an undisclosed amount of money). A Texas jury awarded $222.7 million (later set aside) to a bond brokerage firm against the Wall Street Journal for reporting that the Securities and

Exchange Commission was investigating it. MMAR Group, Inc. v. Dow Jones & Co., Inc. (1999).

Until recently there were no guidelines controlling the award of punitive damages in tort actions. In 1996, however, the Supreme Court struck down a $2 million punitive damage award to an Alabama physician who had bought a "new" BMW sedan with repaired body damage and retouched paint. The Supreme Court called the damage award "grossly excessive," and set out three guidelines for juries in imposing punitive damages. Triers of fact must consider 1) the reprehensibility of the defendant's conduct, 2) the ratio between the compensatory damages awarded and the punitive damages contemplated, and 3) the difference between the contemplated punitive damages and the civil or criminal sanctions which could be imposed for comparable misconduct. BMW of North America, Inc. v. Gore (1996).

In 2003 the U.S. Supreme Court overturned an award of $1 million in compensatory damages and $144 million in punitive damages that a Utah jury had given a couple who had sued State Farm insurance company. Justice Anthony Kennedy wrote that the ratio of 144 to 1 resulted in a damage award that was "neither reasonable nor proportionate to the wrong committed" and was based more on the fact that State Farm had deep pockets. State Farm v. Campbell (2003).

The huge punitive damage awards for Vic Feazell, Richard Sprague and the MMAR Group mentioned above were all set aside on appeal. Even if over-turned after numerous appeals, however, such large damage awards will inevitably cause journalists and their publishers to be more timid.

b. Use of a Permanent Injunction to Restrain Defamatory Speech

On occasion plaintiffs in defamation cases do not seek monetary damages; rather, they seek a permanent injunction to silence the person who is defaming them. The U.S. Supreme Court had invalidated a prior restraint that a court issued against a newspaper publisher for libeling various public officials in Near v. Minnesota (1931). The U.S. Supreme Court was poised to consider the issue in Tory v. Cochran (2005). This case began in 1999 when Ulysses Tory, his wife Ruth Craft and others started picketing the late Johnnie Cochran's law office and a Los Angeles courthouse carrying signs with messages such as "Unless you have O.J. [Simpson's] millions—you'll be screwed if you use J. L. Cochran." Cochran sued Tory in 2000 for defamation, seeking no money damages but instead a court order to stop Tory. When the trial court granted the permanent injunction against Tory and he received no relief from California's appellate courts, he appealed to the U.S. Supreme Court. Tory presented just one question: "whether a permanent injunction as a remedy in a defamation action, preventing all future speech about an admitted public figure, violates the First Amendment." At that point Johnnie Cochran died of a brain

tumor. The U.S. Supreme Court substituted Johnnie Cochran's widow Sylvia Cochran as a respon-
dent. The Court declared the case not moot because
of the uncertainty of California law on this question
and the Court's belief that the injunction continued
to restrain Tory's speech, thus presenting an ongoing federal controversy. The question for which
certiorari was issued was not resolved, however.
Instead the Court remanded the case on the
grounds that Cochran's law firm or his widow Sylvia Cochran might still seek injunctive relief, but
that the previous injunction was overbroad and as
written, had lost its underlying rationale due to
Cochran's death. The Court expressed no view on
whether a more narrowly tailored injunction might
be constitutional. Tory v. Cochran (2005).

See also Willing v. Mazzocone (1978)(Pennsylvania Supreme Court struck down injunction against
a woman who wore a "sandwich-board" accusing
two lawyers of stealing money from her); Nolan v.
Campbell (2004)(Nebraska Court of Appeals upheld
permanent injunction forbidding re-publication of
false charges against a city administrator); Humin-
ski v. Corsones (2005)(U.S. Court of Appeals for
Second Circuit struck down no-trespassing order
restraining speech of self-styled "citizen-reporter"
who criticized Vermont Judge Nancy Corsones).

C.   THE COMMON LAW DEFENSES

Once the plaintiff has provided sufficient evidence
of the elements necessary to establish a prima facie

case of defamation, the defendant is put to his or her defense. He or she may, of course, deny one or more elements of the plaintiff's case such as the defamatory nature of the communication or the publication of the offending communication. In addition or alternatively, he or she may attempt to establish one or more of the complete common law affirmative defenses of truth, privilege and fair comment in order to defeat liability, or to attempt to establish certain incomplete defenses to reduce the award of damages. In resorting to these defenses, the defendant accepts the burden of pleading them in his or her answer and then proving them by a preponderance of the evidence at trial.

1. Truth or "Justification"

Although British common law in the American colonies held that "the greater the truth, the greater the libel," in criminal libel cases involving criticism of a public official, even British common law respected truth as a defense in civil actions for defamation.

The defense of truth can be risky, however. Most states recognize truth as a complete defense regardless of the speaker's motives. A few states, however, require that the truth be spoken with "good motives" or "justifiable ends" or both. In Rhode Island the defense of truth fails if spoken with bad motive. For example, when 50 to 75 people at a restaurant heard a man loudly accuse his ex-wife of being a "whore," she sued him for defamation. The court reviewed her past liaisons with a few men, some of whom she had married and some of whom she had not, and after consulting Black's Law Dictionary for the definition of a "whore," the court concluded she was indeed a whore. Because her ex-husband had made a truthful accusation with ill will, however, the court required that he pay compensatory (but not punitive) damages. Johnson v. Johnson (1995).

Knowing something to be true and proving it in a court of law are, of course, two different things. In many situations only the plaintiff will have access to the necessary proof and, understandably, he or she will not make it easy for the defendant to establish the defense.

Moreover, the defense must be as broad in its reach as the communication complained of. The defense will fail if only a portion of the allegation is verified. For example, a newspaper charge that X is an habitual vice law offender is not justified by the paper establishing one conviction of X for a gambling violation. A statement that a reliable source has informed the communicator that X is guilty of tax evasion is not justified by establishing only that someone informed the defendant about X and that someone is indeed a reliable source. The truth of the charge itself must be established even though the defendant was not the originator of the story. This does not mean that defendants have to verify every detail of their communication, however. The defense is available if the substance of the communication can be established. An individual who publicly accuses his or her neighbor of embezzling

$1500 from the neighborhood association treasury will escape liability by proving embezzlement of $150, for example.

2. Privilege

As with most intentional torts, the common law recognizes the defense of privilege in certain cases of defamation. Even if plaintiffs suffer harm to their reputations from the defamation, the defamers may be shielded from liability. This can happen because the law accords supremacy to conflicting interests of the defendant in communicating the defamation or of the public generally in encouraging free expression of matters of general concern. The defense, which is relatively narrow in scope, is divided into two aspects: the absolute privilege to defame and the qualified privilege.

a. *Absolute Privilege*

One who possesses an absolute privilege to defame or, perhaps more accurately, an absolute immunity from suit is not required to establish his or her good faith in making the defamatory communication. Motivation is immaterial. The public proceedings in which the absolute privilege is available are divided into the legislative, judicial, executive and administrative.

All who speak in a legislative forum—U.S. Congresspersons, state representatives, city council members—enjoy an absolute privilege to speak without fear of being sued for libel. But the comments must be made in a legislative forum. The

Supreme Court has ruled that although a senator's speech on the floor of the Senate is completely immune from a libel suit, newsletters and press releases about the speech issued from the senator's office are not immune. Only speech that is "essential to the deliberations of the Senate" is protected by this privilege, and neither newsletters nor press releases are part of the deliberative process. Hutchinson v. Proxmire (1979).

The absolute privilege is also conferred on all communications in judicial forums such as courtrooms or grand jury rooms. Judges, lawyers, witnesses, defendants and plaintiffs are immune from a libel action provided the remark occurs during the official portions of the hearing or trial.

Finally, people who work in the executive and administrative branches of government—presidents, governors, mayors, heads of government agencies—may also enjoy absolute privilege for official communications or statements. For example, in Barr v. Mateo (1959), a department head distributed a press release explaining why two federal employees had been fired. In its decision, the Supreme Court accorded to government officials an absolute privilege to make defamatory statements within the bounds of their offices.

The reasons for the absolute privilege are clear: if participants are forced to analyze their remarks for strict legal relevance and risk civil liability should they be in error, their fearlessness and independence may be impaired and their actions on the public's behalf inhibited. Unfortunately, like any privilege, the absolute privilege can be abused. One of the worst abusers of the privilege was Senator Joseph McCarthy, who destroyed the careers of hundreds of people during the McCarthy Era when he accused them of being Communists. As long as McCarthy made his accusations on the floor of the Senate, he was immune from all libel suits.

Aside from speech by government representatives in their official capacity and communications between husband and wife, the absolute privilege does not obtain. The report of a credit rating enjoys an absolute privilege in some states but not in others.

b. *Qualified Privilege*

In contrast to the absolute privilege discussed above, the qualified privilege to communicate defamatory matter is defeated if the plaintiff establishes malice on the part of the defendant. This entails proving a publication was motivated chiefly by some consideration other than furthering the interest for which the law accords the privilege in the first place. The law's recognition of this lesser privilege reflects the idea that some of the interests competing with that of reputation, while not as compelling as those which justify an absolute privilege or immunity for the publisher, are still sufficiently important to justify a lesser degree of protection.

Depending on the jurisdiction, there is a qualified common law privilege for an employer to comment on an employee's performance to a manager or to someone requesting a reference for the employee, for communication to an employer regarding an employee's conduct toward a customer, and for a plant manager to tell employees that plaintiffs were terminated for theft of plant property. See Gonzalez v. Avon Products, Inc. (1985). A qualified privilege exists for a plant supervisor to tell employees that a plaintiff was demoted because he could not perform his job, and for a union member to make charges against the union's business manager. See Battista v. Chrysler Corp. (1982) and Pierce v. Burns (1962). There is also a qualified common law privilege for a physician to criticize a pharmacist's competence in talking with a patient, and for a bank officer to make a charge of forgery to a police officer. See Newark Trust Co. v. Bruwer (1958).

The media are granted a qualified privilege with the expectation that they will engage in public oversight of government activity. Even when the oversight function is not involved, the public has a legitimate need to be informed of public proceedings of both governmental and private organizations in order to guard against potential abuses of power which could occur if all proceedings were kept secret. The qualified privilege that has developed is sometimes called the privilege of "record libel," meaning that a journalist may report what occurs in government proceedings even if some of the speakers are not truthful—provided that the journalist gives a fair and accurate summary of what transpired.

(1) Limitations on the Scope of the Privilege

The courts have placed certain limitations on the scope or availability of the privilege to the media in reporting public proceedings. Most courts, for instance, led by Massachusetts, take the position that the privilege does not extend to reporting allegations or statements contained in complaints, affidavits or other pretrial papers unless and until such papers are brought before a judge or magistrate for official action. See Sanford v. Boston Herald–Traveler Corp. (1945). Thus the reporter must be alert to the law of his or her state and, if it follows the majority view, must be wary of the content of court papers filed with the clerk of court but not yet acted upon by a judicial officer vested with discretionary authority. The minority view is that the report of the contents of papers properly filed and served on the required parties may be privileged because the filing and serving of pleadings or other papers authorized by the rules of court are public and are official acts done in the course of judicial proceedings. Campbell v. New York Evening Post, Inc. (1927).

Then, too, reports of the activities of executive officers or administrative agencies are generally not privileged until the officer or agency has taken some definite final action, as a district attorney filing a criminal information or obtaining an indictment. The report of a district attorney's preliminary investigation would not in most jurisdictions be privileged. Police proceedings are especially dangerous for the newsperson to report because of the significant variations from state to state regarding the point at which the privilege attaches. The status of the police blotter, the record of arrests and charges and the oral reports of police officers concerning their preliminary investigations varies according to the jurisdiction involved.

With regard to the legislative process, so long as the particular proceeding reported upon is authorized, the report itself will be privileged, assuming conformity with the general requirements discussed below.

The proceedings subject to the privilege must normally be public in nature unless a statute provides otherwise. Thus, a report of secret grand jury deliberations would not be considered privileged though such deliberations are official proceedings. Exceptions to the "public proceeding" requirement are occasionally recognized. Coleman v. Newark Morning Ledger Co. (1959). In Coleman, the court held that a journalist's fair and accurate report of Senator Joseph McCarthy's press conference summarizing the secret proceedings of his subcommittee's investigation into alleged communist activity at Fort Monmouth, New Jersey, was privileged. The dissenting judge pointed out that there was no verification of whether Senator McCarthy's report of the secret legislative proceeding was itself fair and accurate; thus, the privilege should not have applied. Such exceptions are rare and reporters should not assume from them that there is legal justification for publishing reports of secret governmental proceedings. Also, the qualified privilege would not extend to a confidential police report that is unavailable to the public because such a confidential report would not qualify as an official government act or proceeding. Wynn v. Smith (2001).

(2) General Requirements of the Privilege

As indicated by the Coleman case, if the qualified privilege is to attach, the report must be fair and accurate and motivated by a sense of duty to make disclosure to those receiving the report. The privilege will be unavailable if it is held to be either an unfair or inaccurate account of that portion of the proceeding covered. The report need not, of course, be verbatim, but its condensation, abridgment or paraphrasing must accurately and fairly reflect what transpired. An erroneous detail will not destroy the privilege so long as it does not affect the essential accuracy or fairness of the report. A report may, of course, be literally accurate so far as it goes and yet unfairly portray the proceedings and the complaining person's involvement in them because the report ends at a critical point or omits important facts favorable to that person.

Moreover, if the defamatory report is made chiefly for a purpose other than to inform those who have a "need to know," the publication will be considered malicious and the privilege will be destroyed. Malice is found when the main reason for the publication is not the proper one of informing the public. A fair and accurate account of a proceeding containing defamatory matter given to a friend at a party to make idle cocktail conversation could be considered malicious because the proper motivation for making the account is missing. The privilege will not obtain if the communication is motivated mainly by some selfish objective of the reporter or publisher such as enhancing their business interests at the expense of a competitor who is unfavorably referred to in the public proceeding reported.

Another type of qualified privilege is that of fair comment, which was the most popular of the common law defenses. It is now made less important by the holding in New York Times Co. v. Sullivan (1964), supra. The constitutional privilege found in that case regarding public figures is broader than the traditional fair comment privilege.

As traditionally viewed, fair comment involved the honest expression of the communicator's opinion on a matter of public interest based upon facts correctly stated or inferred in the communication. Such expression had to be free of speculation as to the motivation of the person whose public conduct is criticized unless such discussion was warranted by the facts. See Foley v. Press Publishing Co. (1929). Chief among the unique characteristics of this defense are (1) its emphasis upon opinion based upon fact rather than the reporting of the facts themselves and (2) its broader scope, permitting comment on all matters of public interest rather than simply proceedings of a public nature. It is these characteristics which made possible political and artistic criticism by the media prior to New York Times v. Sullivan. The courts gave broad meaning to fair comment. Commentaries containing exaggeration, illogic, sarcasm, ridicule and even viciousness were protected if at all justified by the underlying facts. Opinion is not *per se* protected by the First Amendment. Thus, the rules of fair comment apply to determining whether a particular opinion is protected by the common law privilege.

Malice would negate the defense of fair comment but it could not be inferred merely from the words chosen by the publisher or speaker. Malice could only be found from an examination of the communicator's motives in publishing. The defense is also negated in a majority of jurisdictions if the comment or opinion is based on a major error of fact. Furthermore, the defense of fair comment will not succeed unless the factual basis for the opinion is disclosed with it or is generally known to the audience. For example, if a newspaper columnist writes, "Dr. Jones is a murderer," this would be defamatory if it is false. If readers know that Dr. Jones performed euthanasia in one case, however, they are free to agree or disagree with the opinion that he is a murderer.

The defense of fair comment encompasses a form of exaggeration known as "rhetorical hyperbole," provided that the writer gives enough context for readers to know that a defamatory term should not be taken literally. Greenbelt Cooperative Publishing

Association v. Bresler (1970). For example, Geraldo Rivera interviewed Neal Horsley, who maintained a web site that listed the names and addresses of doctors who performed abortions. If a doctor was murdered, as was Dr. Bernard Slepian, his name was crossed off the list. Rivera described Horsley as "an accomplice to murder," on a live CNBC broadcast. When Horsley sued for libel, the U.S. Court of Appeals for the Eleventh Circuit held that the First Amendment protected Rivera's opinion because it constituted rhetorical hyperbole. Horsley v. Rivera (2002). See also Finebaum v. Coulter (2003)(radio shock jock's accusation that sportscaster was having oral sex with football coach protected as rhetorical hyperbole).

3.   Incomplete Defenses

Certain defenses in defamation actions are labeled incomplete because they do not bar liability even if successful but only reduce the amount of damages that the plaintiff can recover. Chief among them is that of retraction. If the defamer publishes a retraction of the defamatory communication punctually and with essentially the same prominence as he or she gave to the defamation, the danger of a punitive damages award will be negated and compensatory damages may be reduced.

It should be emphasized that the retraction must be complete and unequivocal. Less than full retraction or a veiled continuance of the defamation will not mitigate damages but, in fact, may increase them. It will not do to state that "John Doe hasn't the morals of a tom cat" and then be willing to "retract" by stating that "John Doe does have the morals of a tom cat." It should also be noted that the availability of the partial retraction defense, the effects of retraction and the consequences of a refusal to retract are governed in a number of states such as California by statute. The California retraction statute figured prominently in comedienne Carol Burnett's celebrated libel suit against the National Enquirer. The statute by its terms applies to and provides partial protection for newspapers. In the Burnett case the trial court ruled that the National Enquirer was a magazine and thus, although it had published a retraction of the libelous material about Burnett, it was not protected against the imposition of punitive damages. Burnett v. National Enquirer, Inc. (1984).

Somewhat akin to retraction is the idea of allowing the defamed party to reply to a personal attack. The voluntary agreement by media defamers to allow use of their facilities by victims to reply to attacks does not necessarily establish the defamer's good faith and the award of punitive damages remains a possibility. The actual injury to the defamed party may be reduced, however, because of the opportunity afforded to reach and favorably influence those whose good opinion of him or her has been affected. However, any effort by government to mandate the right of reply insofar as the print media are concerned would appear to violate the First Amendment. See Miami Herald Publishing Co. v. Tornillo (1974). The U.S. Supreme Court makes a distinction regarding broadcasters, however, who may be compelled to extend the right to reply, in certain narrow circumstances, to those personally attacked over their facilities. Red Lion Broadcasting Co. v. Federal Communications Commission (1969).

————

This completes the discussion of common law defamation, a law in many respects quite favorable to the defamed party's interest in reputation. Witness, for instance, its theory of strict liability. Conversely, this law imposes many restrictions upon and dangers for those who seek to exercise their right of free expression under the First Amendment. Damage awards by juries began to increase dramatically in the 1980s. The Brown & Williamson Tobacco Corporation won a $3 million damage award from CBS in 1987 that was upheld on appeal. Brown & Williamson Tobacco Corp. v. Jacobson (1987). Even when the media win, the costs of defending themselves are so high that self-censorship and a chilling effect will be the inevitable result. ABC allegedly spent $7 million defending itself against a series of lawsuits by Synanon, and Consumers Union spent $5 million defending itself in a product disparagement case before the case even went to trial. Suzuki Motor Corp. v. Consumers Union of United States, Inc. (2003).

With such daunting legal fees, libel suits can be an intimidating form of harassment. In recent years, wealthy corporations have begun suing citizen activists for defamation if they speak against a corporate development project or circulate petitions to oppose it. Such lawsuits comprise an entirely new genre of libel suits called Strategic Lawsuits Against Public Participation (SLAPP) suits. SLAPP suits are not filed in order to restore a corporation's reputation; indeed, they are filed simply to punish or harass anyone critical of the corporation. The Church of Scientology has filed numerous SLAPP suits against its critics. Church of Scientology v. Wollersheim (1996); Church of Scientology International v. Behar (2001).

In order to protect citizen activists from SLAPP suits, 18 state legislatures (California, Delaware, Georgia, Hawaii, Indiana, Louisiana, Massachusetts, Minnesota, Missouri, Nevada, New Mexico, New York, Oregon, Pennsylvania, Rhode Island Tennessee, Utah and Washington) have passed laws that either immunize citizens against SLAPP suits or provide for early dismissal of such complaints. Thus, when a real estate developer in Rhode Island filed a SLAPP suit against a neighborhood group that criticized the developer after the developer tried to open a gravel pit in a residential neighborhood, the neighborhood group won dismissal of the developer's suit under Rhode Island's anti-SLAPP statute. South County Sand & Gravel v. South Kingston Neighborhood Congress (1999). Likewise, when an environmental assessment company filed a SLAPP suit against a retired college professor for questioning the company's competence during an environmental review of a proposed development project, the court dismissed the suit under California's anti-SLAPP statute. Dixon v. Superior Court of Orange County (1994).

Anti–SLAPP laws protect newspapers as well as individual citizens. For example, the owners of a non-accredited "university" sued the San Francisco Chronicle when it reported that this "university" offered a Ph.D. in "sensuality" and offered courses in "teasing" and "mutually pleasurable stimulation." The Chronicle also correctly reported that the proprietors of the "university" had faced drug-related criminal charges. Under California's anti-SLAPP law, the court dismissed the libel suit. Lafayette Morehouse Inc. v. Chronicle Publishing Co. (1995).

Against the backdrop of skyrocketing legal fees and SLAPP suits intended merely to harass defendants, the common law principles set out above are still applied in whole to communications that do not involve public figures or matters of public concern, and in part to communications which do. They are thus worthy of continued discussion. The very serious question posed to the Supreme Court by New York Times Co. v. Sullivan, however, was whether the application of all aspects of the common law of defamation to newspapers and other media is consistent with the guarantees of the First Amendment. The answer to that important question and its qualifications is the subject of the next section of this chapter.

D. THE CONSTITUTIONAL LAW OF DEFAMATION

1. New York Times Co. v. Sullivan

In New York Times Co. v. Sullivan (1964), a civil rights group bought a full page advertisement in the New York Times, entitled "Heed Their Rising Voices." The ad charged that the police of Montgomery, Alabama had improperly "ringed" a black college campus to put down a peaceful demonstration for civil rights. It added that certain unnamed "southern violators" had bombed Martin Luther King's home, had physically assaulted him, arrested him seven times for "speeding," "loitering" and similar "offenses;" and finally charged him with "perjury." Some of these statements were erroneous in whole or part.

Although no "southern violator" was named in the ad, L. B. Sullivan, the Commissioner of Public Affairs for Montgomery, Alabama, filed suit for libel. Sullivan persuaded the jury that the ad identified him because he was the city commissioner in charge of the police at all times in question and thus would have been responsible for the "ringing" of the campus and the multiple arrests of Dr. King for minor infractions as part of the alleged lawless campaign of harassment and intimidation. Sullivan also contended that being identified as a "southern violator" in conjunction with the arrests had resulted in his further identification in the public mind with the other lawless acts listed. Several Montgomery residents so testified. L. B. Sullivan sought and won a jury award of $500,000 against the New York Times. The Alabama Supreme Court affirmed the judgment under ordinary common law rules of defamation, rejecting the argument that the ad was protected by the First Amendment.

No more graphic illustration of the dangers posed to a free press by the common law can be suggested than the decision of the Alabama Supreme Court in this case. That decision was, in almost all respects, in accord with accepted common law principles concerning the elements of libel, malice, compensatory and punitive damages and the recognized defenses.

The effect of that litigation in the state courts was to cause the New York Times Company to halt distribution of its newspaper in Alabama for a time. The litigation also saddled the New York Times with a massive judgment for $500,000 damages (along with a potential $2,500,000 more in damages claimed in other pending related suits). If not reversed, this judgment would have weakened the Times' financial position, with all the implications that that might have had for the Company's continued ability to adhere to its motto "all the news that's fit to print."

The U.S. Supreme Court reversed a judgment for Sullivan. The Court acknowledged that the paid advertisement in question did contain erroneous information that, if satisfactorily identified with Sullivan, would be considered defamatory toward him at common law. However, the Court held that there was not adequate proof of identification of

Sullivan to support liability of the defendants for defamation and thus reversed the state court judgment for him. Because the Court held that the general reference to "southern violators" did not constitute "identification" of L. B. Sullivan, this finding by itself would have been sufficient to dispose of the case.

This raises the question of why journalists would need a Constitutional privilege to protect them when they make honest mistakes; furthermore, why did the High Court use the Sullivan case as a vehicle to establish a Constitutional privilege when none had existed before? The ruling included a second completely separate holding.

It seemed clear to the Court that, at most, the New York Times Company was guilty of negligence in publishing the advertisement without checking the facts alleged therein against its own news files to verify the accuracy of the advertisement. If the media made honest mistakes amounting to negligence when they published defamatory material about public officials—and then had to pay large sums of money in damages—this would interfere with debate on public issues. The Court explained that the encouragement of such debate was part of the central meaning of the First Amendment. The Court therefore laid down the rule that public officials may not recover damages for defamatory falsehoods relating to their official conduct unless they prove with "convincing clarity" that the statements are made with actual malice. The Court defined "actual malice" as publication with knowledge that the statement in question is false, or is made with "reckless disregard" for whether or not it is false.

Thus, for the first time in the long history of this country, the Supreme Court accorded constitutional protection to certain false and defamatory communications, provided they were not maliciously made. This historic ruling represents a corollary to Barr v. Matteo (1959), discussed above, in which the Court held that government officers have an absolute privilege to make defamatory communications if specifically related to the discharge of their official duties. Critics of official conduct are given an equivalent privilege in order to encourage public oversight of these same officers.

2.   Effects of the New York Times Case

The effects of the New York Times case on common law defamation have been profound. Briefly summarized, they include the following:

1.   The idea of "fair comment" is broadened to include facts and to permit the communication of erroneous facts, and is raised to a constitutional privilege when the comment concerns conduct of public officials relating to their offices.

2.   Strict liability for defamatory comments about public officials is eliminated and a new fault standard of intentional or reckless conduct is substituted.

3.   The definition of actual malice to mean evil motive, spite or ill will is rejected and a new

definition of knowing falsehood or reckless disregard for the truth is substituted when public officials and public figures are complaining parties. Even hard-hitting investigative reporting begun with a preconceived point of view and an "adversarial stance" does not indicate actual malice where the reporter conducts a detailed investigation and writes a story therefrom that is substantially true. Tavoulareas v. Piro Co. (1987); Church of Scientology v. Behar (2001).

4. Under common law the defense of privilege, including lack of actual malice, was for the defendant to establish. After New York Times the plaintiff public official has the burden of negating the defendant's constitutional privilege by proving that the defendant acted with actual malice (intentionally or recklessly) in publishing the false and defamatory material. Implicit in this is the shifting of the burden of proof on the issue of truth to the plaintiff. He or she must now establish falsity as part of his or her prima facie case. See Philadelphia Newspapers, Inc. v. Hepps (1986).

5. The plaintiff's proof of malice and his or her identification as the party defamed must now be made with convincing clarity; at common law the normal standard of proof for defamation is mere preponderance of the evidence. See Cobb v. Time, Inc. (2002).

Another important effect of New York Times v. Sullivan is somewhat more indirect. As a practical matter, plaintiff public officials have had a very hard time in making out their defamation cases against media defendants because of the difficulty of establishing actual malice under the convincing clarity standard. An exception to this rule occurred in Harte–Hanks Communications, Inc. v. Connaughton (1989), discussed below, in which a public official did establish actual malice. In general, however, responsible media organizations rarely traffic in known falsehoods or act recklessly in disseminating news or information. Very often then when there is no real dispute as to the material facts, defendants are able to obtain summary judgments on the basis of preliminary papers, documents and affidavits showing insufficient proof of actual malice and thus do not have to defend themselves at trial. See Anderson v. Liberty Lobby, Inc. (1986).

3. The New York Times Progeny

As great a charter as the New York Times case is for the mass media, it raised more questions than it answered, and only the existence of four decades of subsequent court decisions permits an assessment of the true boundaries and impact of that case. One of the questions raised was the meaning of "reckless disregard." In New York Times itself, the facts pointed so strongly to honest mistake in publication that no real clue was given as to the boundaries of the concept.

A faint ray of light is cast on this issue in St. Amant v. Thompson (1968). During a televised speech, St. Amant, a candidate for local office, re-

peated a union leader's charges that a deputy sheriff had taken bribes. The union leader had made his
charges in an affidavit under oath, and St. Amant
made no attempt to verify the charges, which
turned out to be false. The state court held that St.
Amant had been reckless, but the U.S. Supreme
Court reversed. Justice Byron White said that
"[t]here must be sufficient evidence to permit the
conclusion that the defendant in fact entertained
serious doubts as to the truth of his publication."
See also Herbert v. Lando (1979). This came very
close to requiring the public official to prove knowing publication of falsehood and appeared by implication to protect those publishers who deliberately
avoid discovering the truth.

But this implication was put to rest in Harte–
Hanks Communications, Inc. v. Connaughton
(1989). There, a jury found the Hamilton (Ohio)
Journal–Beacon guilty of actual malice. One of its
editors not only failed to check his own news
sources but also refused to listen to a tape recording
which would have cast doubts on the veracity of a
story the paper published about Daniel Connaughton, a candidate for judge in a local election. The
Supreme Court held that the editor's refusal to
listen to the tape recording created evidence of
actual malice. This was the first time the Court had
upheld a libel judgment involving actual malice
since the 1960s. See also Bentley v. Bunton (2002)
(Texas Supreme Court affirmed $8 million damage
award for actual malice after talk-show host Joe

Bunton carried out "personal vendetta" against Judge Bascom Bentley III).

In another case, the U. S. Supreme Court held that knowingly misquoting a source may constitute actual malice. In Masson v. New Yorker Magazine, Inc. (1991), the Court ruled that a serious misquotation that hurts a person's reputation may be libelous if the quotation is rephrased to result in a "material change in the meaning." In this case, psychoanalyst Jeffery Masson sued The New Yorker magazine for libel. Its free-lance writer Janet Malcolm quoted Masson as calling himself an "intellectual gigolo" who would turn the Sigmund Freud Archives into a "place of sex, women and fun" and would become "the greatest analyst who ever lived." Those exact phrases were not in the 40 hours of tape-recorded interviews Malcolm had conducted with Masson. The Supreme Court remanded the case, and a jury found free-lance writer Janet Malcolm guilty of actual malice, but could not agree on the damages, and the case ended in a mistrial. Masson v. Malcolm (1993).

In 1995, Malcolm said she had found her long-lost notes from the non-tape-recorded interviews; these notes included a few key statements that Masson had denied, including the "intellectual gigolo" quotation. In a second trial, a different jury found that Malcolm had not acted with actual malice. Masson appealed, but the U.S. Court of Appeals affirmed the jury verdict and barred Masson from any further libel suits against Malcolm or The New Yorker based on Malcolm's interview. Masson v. New Yorker Magazine, Inc. (1996).

In addition to the definition of malice, another question expressly left open in New York Times Co. is the meaning of "official conduct." This concept now appears to parallel closely the boundaries of an executive or administrative officer's duties and responsibilities in office set forth in Barr v. Matteo, supra. As long as the defamatory material is published within the constitutional and statutory bounds of his or her office, the public official would be bound by the New York Times Co. rule. Cf. Butz v. Economou (1978). In addition, erroneous charges of criminal conduct on the part of public officials and candidates for public office, no matter how remote in time or place, are protected by the constitutional privilege because such charges are always relevant to the question of fitness to hold or seek office. Monitor Patriot Co. v. Roy (1971); Ocala Star–Banner Co. v. Damron (1971). On the other hand, even public officials are entitled to private lives. Thus, false and defamatory communications relating thereto would not be protected by the privilege established in the New York Times case. For instance, if a newspaper negligently publishes the false accusation that a (male) county assessor likes to wear ballet tutus while he vacuums his carpets, the story would not be protected because wearing a tutu is not a crime and is not relevant to the conduct of his office.

The Court in New York Times v. Sullivan also declined to provide a general definition of "public official." The cases that followed New York Times have established that "public official" includes at least those in governmental hierarchies who have or appear to have substantial responsibility for the conduct of government business, from judges to public park supervisors. The term also includes former office holders who exercised substantial responsibility while in office and who are attacked for their past official conduct. See Rosenblatt v. Baer (1966), (no finding of malice and hence no defamation on part of publisher of newspaper column critical of supervisor of public recreation facility, who qualified as public official).

Although the term "public official" is thus an expansive one, it covers only a small percentage of public personages. Recognizing this, the Court subsequently extended the reach of the New York Times Co. decision to public figures and their non-official but public acts. This includes famous college athletic directors, football coaches and resigned Army generals who "thrust themselves into the limelight" (Curtis Publishing Co. v. Butts (1967)); (Associated Press v. Walker (1967)), a prominent real estate developer involved in a land dispute with a local city council (Greenbelt Cooperative Publishing Association v. Bresler (1970)), candidates for public office (Monitor Patriot Co. v. Roy (1971)), and law enforcement officers even when off duty if their conduct bears on their fitness for office (Smith v. Huntsville Times Co., Inc. (2004)).

What of people who are neither public officials nor public figures but who are caught up in matters of public interest? Should the media have the same constitutional privilege regarding communications about private persons who may be less able to defend themselves against false and defamatory allegations because of less access to the corrective mechanisms of the mass media? In other words, should the focus be shifted from public persons to matters of public interest, regardless of the status of the participants involved? These are extremely important questions. Affirmative answers might so alter the balance between the interest in free speech and press and the interest in individual reputation as to destroy the latter. Whomever the media deemed newsworthy might be regarded by the courts as being bound by the New York Times rule when they sought legal redress.

Initially, a plurality of the Supreme Court in Rosenbloom v. Metromedia, Inc. (1971) answered this question in the affirmative. The Court held the distinction between public and private individuals to be artificial in relationship to the public's interest in a broad range of issues, including, in that case, the arrest of an obscure distributor of nudist magazines on obscenity charges and the confiscation of his magazines as pornographic.

4. The Basic Public Figure–Private Person Distinction of Gertz v. Welch

In Gertz v. Robert Welch, Inc. (1974), however, a majority of the U.S. Supreme Court rejected the plurality decision in Rosenbloom; in Gertz the Court held that the privilege recognized in New

York Times Co. v. Sullivan was applicable only to cases involving defamation of public officials and public figures.

In this case Elmer Gertz, a reputable lawyer not generally known to the public and not then associated with any particular causes, was retained by the family of a youth killed by a police officer to bring a civil suit against the officer. The John Birch Society's magazine American Opinion viciously attacked Gertz and accused him of being a "Leninist," a "Communist-fronter," and of arranging a frame-up of the police officer.

Gertz sued for libel, and the U.S. Supreme Court ruled that despite his prominence in the civil rights area, Gertz was not a public figure for the purposes of this lawsuit. The Court explained that private individuals are more in need of judicial redress, and the state has a greater interest in providing it because they have not chosen to put their reputations at risk by voluntarily inviting public comment. Moreover, the private person will normally have less access to the media to correct the record than will the public person. The High Court delineated two definitions, or two alternative bases, for differentiating between public figures and private individuals: 1) a "pervasive" or "all-purpose" public figure, who is a household name, and 2) a "limited-purpose" or "vortex" public figure who has thrust himself or herself into the forefront of a specific public controversy. These distinctions are discussed in greater detail below.

The Supreme Court stressed the fact that Gertz had not achieved any general fame in the community—the jurors had never heard of him. Moreover, the Court did not think that simply because he was counsel in the civil litigation in question that he had "thrust himself into the vortex" of public controversy.

In Gertz the Court directly modified the common law in two fundamental respects. First, it abolished strict liability for the publication of defamatory material and left to the individual states the determination of the appropriate fault standard of liability for defamatory statements made about private individuals. This means that the states may no longer impose liability on the media where there is no fault in the communication of defamatory material for private individuals. Where there is fault, however, the states have at least three fault standards of liability to choose from (listed in ascending order of protection for the media): 1) unreasonable publication (negligence), 2) extremely unreasonable publication (gross negligence), or 3) knowingly false or reckless publication (New York Times standard).

A few jurisdictions have indicated a preference for the New York Times Company standard. See Walker v. Colorado Springs Sun, Inc. (1975); Aafco Heating and Air Conditioning Co. v. Northwest Publications, Inc. (1974); Sisler v. Gannett Co., Inc. (1986). In none of these cases, however, was the adoption of that standard of fault unanimous. Subsequently the highest courts of most other states considering the question have opted for a simple negligence test. See Phillips v. Evening Star Newspaper Co. (1980) (all state holdings on this issue collected); Triangle Publications, Inc. v. Chumley (1984). New York, however, has chosen to impose liability for defamation only if the defendant "acted in a grossly irresponsible manner without due consideration for the standards of information gathering and dissemination ordinarily followed by responsible parties." Robart v. Post–Standard (1981). This is an intermediate standard between that of New York Times Company and ordinary negligence.

The second modification made in Gertz is that when liability is imposed on the basis of negligence or gross negligence rather than actual malice, recovery is to be limited to compensation for proven actual injury caused by the defamation. Apparently, however, in defamation actions tried pursuant to the New York Times standard, presumed and punitive damages might still be awarded.

This modification of the common law system of damages is clearly designed to protect the media from massive judgments based on the jury's imagination, its ideas of punishment and deterrence, and its prejudices.

5. The Broad Meaning of Gertz

Gertz v. Robert Welch, Inc. set the boundaries of the constitutional privilege established in New York Times Co. v. Sullivan. From here on the privilege of the media negligently to make false and defamatory communications may be limited by the states when it is determined that the complaining party is not a public figure. Beyond this, however, Gertz put an end to the expansion of the absolutist interpretation of the First Amendment that gives primacy to the societal interests in free expression.

As a result the media will have to be more concerned about what they communicate relative to the "unknowns" of our society and will have to review and strengthen verification procedures to avoid the charge of negligence in news gathering, interpretation and dissemination. The other side of the coin minted in Gertz is the greater recognition of the individual's personal worth and dignity.

6. The Public Figure–Private Person Distinction

a. *Narrowing of the Public Figure Classification*

In righting the perceived imbalance in constitutional protection between expression and reputation it was important for the Gertz majority to reduce the range of applicability of New York Times Co. v. Sullivan. This could be accomplished by defining narrowly who was a public figure by the stringent New York Times Company standards.

Gertz thus created the dichotomy between public figures and private individuals and established the framework for distinguishing between two types of public figures: (1) the all-purpose public figure such as Jay Leno, having such great general fame or notoriety that his or her name is a household word, or (2) limited purpose public figures, also known as voluntary or "vortex" public figures, referring to plaintiffs' thrusting themselves voluntarily into the vortex of a specific public controversy.

Within five years of the Gertz ruling, the Supreme Court agreed to hear three more cases to clarify the issue of whether plaintiffs were public figures (who had to prove actual malice) or private individuals (who merely had to prove negligence). These three cases established the truly restrictive nature of the public figure category. The first case, Time, Inc. v. Firestone (1976), involved a highly publicized divorce between Mary Alice Firestone and her husband, an heir to the Firestone tire empire. After a lengthy and spicy public trial the judge granted the husband's request for a complete divorce. Time Magazine reported in its "Milestones" section that Russell Firestone was granted a divorce "on grounds of extreme cruelty and adultery." After her request for a printed retraction was rejected, Mrs. Firestone sued for libel. Time's report was false and defamatory because under Florida law an adulterous wife could not receive alimony, but the Florida court had granted her $3000 per month in alimony.

Time argued that Mrs. Firestone was a public figure, which would require her to show that Time knew the story was false or recklessly disregarded the truth. (Time was innocent of actual malice; its reporter had genuinely misunderstood the grounds for divorce).

In rejecting Time's contention, however, the Supreme Court said that local social prominence is not enough to categorize a plaintiff as a public figure. Divorce is not the sort of "public controversy" referred to in Gertz; rather, it is a private matter.

The Court did not even mention Mrs. Firestone's open air press conferences or her hiring of a press agent designed to tell the public her side of the divorce story. Firestone considerably narrowed the public figure category, given Mrs. Firestone's notoriety. The U.S. Supreme Court further narrowed the public figure category with two cases decided on the same day in its 1978–1979 term.

In Wolston v. Reader's Digest Association, Inc. (1979) the defendant Wolston had been identified as a Soviet intelligence agent. Wolston had been cited for contempt for not complying with a grand jury subpoena 16 years before, but he denied any connection to the Soviet intelligence apparatus and sued the Reader's Digest Association for libel. The U.S. Court of Appeals affirmed the trial court's summary judgment partly on the basis that Wolston was a public figure, but the Supreme Court reversed, ruling that he was not a public figure because he had not thrust himself into a public controversy. Thus, as in Firestone, mere involvement in a matter of public interest is not enough.

This same restrictive view of limited-issue public figures led the Court to reject the Association's other contention that any person who engages in criminal conduct automatically becomes a public figure regarding his trial and conviction. As in the Firestone case, one involved in a public trial (here a criminal one) does not necessarily become a public figure.

In the companion case of Hutchinson v. Proxmire (1979), Senator William Proxmire awarded his uncoveted "Golden Fleece of the Month" awards to NASA and the Office of Naval Research. They had spent almost a half-million dollars to fund Dr. Hutchinson's research on primate aggression with the purpose of finding ways to reduce aggression among humans thrown together in close quarters for extended periods of time. In his speech making the award as well as in a related news release Proxmire described Hutchinson's research as transparently worthless and called for an end to his making "a monkey out of the American taxpayer." Dr. Hutchinson sued Senator Proxmire for libel. As in Wolston, the trial court granted summary judgment for Proxmire because the plaintiff was a public figure, and the United States Court of Appeals affirmed.

As in Firestone and Wolston, however, the Supreme Court reversed on the "public figure" issue, rejecting the view that local newspaper articles on Hutchinson's grants and research made him a limited-issue public figure. In so ruling the Court made the point that those charged with defamation cannot create their own defense by themselves making the victim a public figure. Furthermore, Gertz requires regular and continuing access to the media—not merely access made available to rebut a specific defamatory attack.

Firestone, Wolston and Hutchinson seem to limit "involuntary" public figures to rare cases in which the individual is central to the controversy. Involuntary public figures are rare, but they do exist. See Dameron v. Washington Magazine, Inc. (1985) (air traffic controller on duty when a plane crashed held to be an "involuntary public figure").

In summary, Gertz and its progeny have narrowed the public figure category in these important respects:

    1.   Simply appearing in the newspapers in connection with some newsworthy story or stories does not make one a public figure;

    2.   Social, professional or business prominence does not by itself make one a public figure, except in the case of those who are so famous that their names are household words such as David Letterman or Michael Jackson.

    3.   Forced involvement in a public trial, either civil or criminal, does not by itself make one a public figure;

    4.   Those charged with defamation cannot by their own conduct in making their victims notorious thereby create their own defense;

    5.   Merely applying for, receiving or benefiting from public research grants does not make one a public figure;

    6.   In order to meet the Gertz test of thrusting oneself into the forefront of a public controversy, the controversy must be a real dispute, the out-

come of which affects the general public in an appreciable way. One's conduct must be calculated or clearly be expected to invite public comment respecting that controversy, as for example, the value of a federal investigation into KGB activity in the United States during the McCarthy era.

7.   In order to meet the Gertz test of access to the media the access must be regular and continuing.

All in all, following the Firestone, Wolston and Proxmire decisions, the category of public figures for purposes of New York Times v. Sullivan protection is much smaller than could have been imagined when Gertz was decided.

b.   The Effect of Time Passage on Public Figure Status

In Wolston Justice Blackmun filed a concurring opinion by in which he assumed for purposes of argument that Wolston had been a public figure in 1958. Blackmun then argued that Wolston returned to anonymity with the passage of time until the offending book was published 16 years later. Then Wolston no longer had "significantly greater access to the channels of communication" to defend himself. Consequently, he had lost his public figure status. Justice Blackmun recognized that such analysis implies that a person may be a public figure for purposes of contemporaneous reporting of his activities but not a public figure for purposes of historical commentary on the same activities and events.

Because Justice Blackmun's approach provides less protection for the historical commentator than it does for the contemporaneous journalist, at least one lower court has rejected it. See Street v. National Broadcasting Co. (1981); and compare Brewer v. Memphis Publishing Co., Inc. (1980). Despite these lower court decisions the popular or scholarly historical commentator should be wary because the Supreme Court majority did not reject Justice Blackmun's analysis as a corollary means of narrowing the media's constitutional privilege. Thus, journalists should take special care to achieve factual accuracy in the preparation of the "where are they now"-type features concerning formerly famous or notorious people.

7. The Fact–Opinion Dichotomy

One other major modification of the common law was effected in Gertz to the benefit of the media. By way of dictum Justice Powell stated that "[u]nder the First Amendment there is no such thing as a false idea. However pernicious an opinion may seem, we depend for its correction not on the conscience of judges and juries but on the competition of other ideas." This dictum was reaffirmed in Bose Corporation v. Consumers Union (1984). Justice Powell made clear in his dictum that in distinction from opinion, false statements of fact may be demonstrated to be such and are not protected when made with fault.

The difficulty is in distinguishing between fact and opinion and the dictum in Gertz provides little help with this problem. For awhile, courts had great difficulty with the fact-opinion dichotomy, but received some guidance from the four-part Ollman test outlined in Ollman v. Evans (1984). The Ollman test considers the following:

1) specific language (common or ordinary meaning of the words)

2) verifiability (whether the statement can be proven true or false)

3) journalistic context (when entire article is considered)

4) social context or setting (whether it is a column on an op-ed page or whether it is a political cartoon, for example)

Several years after Ollman v. Evans (1984), the U.S. Supreme Court decided Milkovich v. Lorain Journal Co. (1990). Legal observers assumed at first that Milkovich would supercede the Ollman test, but in fact, the two decisions co-exist. In Milkovich, the Supreme Court ruled that no separate privilege exists protecting statements of opinion. Thus, statements of opinion that can be interpreted as stating or implying false facts may be actionable: in effect, Milkovich returns the media to the common law privilege of fair comment, which still provides a strong defense for those who publish pure opinions.

This case involved an Ohio sportswriter who accused wrestling coach Mike Milkovich and high school superintendent Don Scott of lying at a hearing about a brawl during a wrestling match. "Anyone who attended the meet ... knows in his heart that Milkovich and Scott lied at the hearing after each having given his solemn oath to tell the truth. But they got away with it." When Milkovich sued for libel, the News–Herald claimed that the sports-writer's column was merely his opinion and was thus protected as fair comment. A lower court agreed, but the Supreme Court reversed. The Court explained that the implication that Milkovich com-mitted perjury was factual enough to be proved true or false by simply comparing his testimony at the initial hearing with his subsequent testimony before the trial court. Thus, to say that someone told a lie is a factual allegation that the plaintiff can prove or disprove, whereas to say that someone is "igno-rant" is merely an opinion. The Court remanded the case, and Milkovich ultimately won $116,000 in damages.

Since Milkovich, a number of courts have re-versed summary judgments for media defendants in cases where statements of opinion were factual enough to be proven true or false. See, for example, Unelko Corp. v. Rooney (1990) (Andy Rooney's com-ment that Unelko's Rain–X "didn't work" not pro-tected opinion under Milkovich, although Rooney won summary judgment on other grounds).

The U.S. Court of Appeals for the District of Columbia Circuit wavered between applying Milko-vich or the Ollman test in Moldea v. New York Times Co. I (1994). In Moldea I, the New York Times Book Review published veteran sportswriter Gerald Eskenazi's review of Dan Moldea's book

Interference: How Organized Crime Influences Professional Football. Eskenazi wrote that Moldea's book suffered from "too much sloppy journalism." After the review was published, sales of the book nosedived, and Moldea sued for libel. Although the trial court immediately granted summary judgment for the New York Times, the D.C. Circuit at first applied the narrower Milkovich test and reinstated Moldea's case; the 2–1 majority said that Eskenazi's review "implies certain facts—that Moldea plays fast and loose with his sources." This ruling rejected the Ollman criteria.

The New York Times appealed, and the three-judge panel that had ruled in favor of Moldea took the surprising step of reversing itself, acknowledging that the Ollman test established the importance of considering context. In other words, readers would approach a book review differently from hard news on the front page. Thus, provided that a book review comprises a "supportable interpretation" of the book, it is not defamatory. Moldea v. New York Times Co. II (1994).

8. Specific Problems for the Media Created by Gertz

Gertz raises the pervasive specter of self-censorship, and also presents a number of very specific problems. Distinguishing between fact and opinion or between public figures and private individuals may not be easy for the media, particularly under the pressure of deadlines.

The media must also determine the reasonableness of their publishing procedures in every given case, depending on the standard of liability embodied in the relevant state law. For example, if the source of a media story is a wire service, the media may avail themselves of the "wire service defense" in spite of the republication rule, which would normally hold that a newspaper which repeats a libelous story is also liable for defamation. See Appleby v. Daily Hampshire Gazette (1985).

Journalists are usually on safe ground if their source is a government official or a public document. For example, in Wilson v. Capital City Press (1975), the state police had given a journalist access to a list of people arrested in a drug raid. The list mistakenly included the plaintiff's name, but a Louisiana court ruled that the journalist was not negligent in relying on the state police report. The U.S. Supreme Court has also ruled that there is no First Amendment privilege to protect journalists from testifying about the editorial process if such testimony goes to the heart of a libel plaintiff's case. See Herbert v. Lando (1979), discussed in Chapter VIII.

It was once an unwritten rule for journalists to have two independent sources to verify a story, but if journalists' sources are biased and they make no effort to cover an opposing view, a court may find them negligent. See Richmond Newspapers, Inc. v. Lipscomb (1987), (court ruled that jury could find reporter negligent for writing negative story about a teacher when reporter did not bother to interview anyone who praised teacher). Thus the "two source" rule that Watergate reporters Bob Woodward and Carl Bernstein had popularized does not always preclude a finding of negligence.

Because of the great uncertainties involved in determining the reasonableness of the publisher's conduct prior to trial, the media can expect less favorable treatment on motions for summary judgment against private plaintiffs. Unless the trial judge holds that the publisher's conduct is reasonable beyond question, a jury will have to decide this question. Thus, more protracted litigation can be expected with increasing pressure on media defendants to settle even nuisance claims.

Finally, the problem of large damage awards discussed above will remain a very real concern of the media and may add to the pressure for out of court settlements that can only weaken the financial structure of media organizations.

9. Questions Raised by Gertz

Gertz raised important questions about the existence and operation of common law defenses. Who now has the burden of establishing the truth or falsity of the alleged defamatory communications?

After a number of years of uncertainty, the U.S. Supreme Court answered this question in Philadelphia Newspapers, Inc. v. Hepps (1986). There, the Court ruled, in a case involving a series of newspaper articles linking a private figure to organized crime and his use of those links to influence a state government's decisions, that the *plaintiff* had the burden of establishing the falsity of the articles.

The Court also noted that placing the burden of proof on plaintiffs to establish falsity does not involve undue hardship because plaintiffs already have the burden of establishing fault on the part of the defendant. Also, juries are more likely to find defendants in libel cases at fault if convinced that the statements complained of are false. Publication of truthful information, no matter how damaging, is inconsistent with concepts of negligence and gross negligence.

In Bose Corporation v. Consumers Union (1984), the Supreme Court, by a vote of 6 to 3, gave a strong endorsement to the constitutional principles enunciated in New York Times Co. and its progeny a generation before, suggesting their long-term wisdom. The central issue in Bose was a procedural one involving the scope of a federal appellate court's review of a trial court's determination of actual malice on the part of Consumer's Union, publisher of Consumer Reports magazine. The Supreme Court held that a federal appellate court could do a *de novo* review of a federal district court decision; in other words, the appellate court could make an independent determination of the mixed fact and constitutional law issue of actual malice.

In this case Consumer Reports made an erroneous and derogatory statement about the quality of the sound delivered by the public figure plaintiff's newly designed stereo speaker system. Although a panel of listeners had said that the sound moved along the wall in front of and between the two speakers, Consumer Reports engineer Arnold Seligson wrote that the sound "tended to wander about the room." At the trial, Seligson testified that he believed the two statements meant the same thing. The district court found his testimony ludicrous and said that Seligson clearly knew he had changed the meaning of the statement. This was evidence of actual malice. The court also found the testimony of Monte Florman, Consumer Reports' technical director, to be "wholly untrustworthy and ... not credible."

But the High Court explained: "The statement in this case represents the sort of inaccuracy that is commonplace in the forum of robust debate to which the *New York Times* rule applies;" thus, the Court ruled in favor of Consumer's Union. But see Suzuki Motor Corp. v. Consumers Union of United States, Inc. (2003) (U.S. Court of Appeals for Ninth Circuit permitted product disparagement case against Consumers Union to proceed to trial for rating Suzuki's Samurai vehicle as "not acceptable").

10. An Attempt to "Get Around" New York Times and Its Reaffirmation a Generation Later

Because of the large burden placed upon public officials and public figures in libel cases, some enterprising plaintiffs' counsel have tried to avoid the "actual malice" standard and other requirements of defamation law by changing the designation of their claims. In Falwell v. Flynt (1986), the Reverend Jerry Falwell sued Hustler Magazine publisher Larry Flynt for intentional infliction of emotional distress. Falwell also sued for libel because of a parody of an advertising campaign in which celebrities talked about their "first time," referring, to their first encounter with Campari Liqueur. In Hustler's ad parody, Falwell, in a fictitious interview, allegedly details an incestuous "first time" with his mother in an outhouse. At the bottom of the "ad" is a disclaimer that states "ad parody—not to be taken seriously."

The jury ruled for Flynt on Falwell's libel claim, finding that no reasonable person would believe that the parody was describing actual facts about the minister. On the intentional infliction of emotional distress claim, however, the jury returned a $200,000 verdict for Falwell, and the Fourth Circuit affirmed.

In a unanimous decision, however, the Supreme Court reversed. Writing for the Court, Chief Justice Rehnquist explained that "robust political debate" will often produce caustic comments and vehement attacks. The standard for imposing liability in intentional infliction of emotional distress cases is whether or not the conduct is outrageous. The "outrageousness" requirement is so subjective, however, that imposition of liability would vary from jury to jury. The Court clearly feared that with a standard as subjective as "outrageousness," plaintiffs like Falwell could use the tort of intentional infliction of emotional distress to circumvent the safeguards of New York Times Co. v. Sullivan. Therefore the Court ruled that public officials and public figures who sue for intentional infliction of emotional distress must prove falsity and reckless disregard for the truth, just as in libel cases.

The Court was clearly concerned about the implications of using the intentional infliction of emotional distress tort on the satire and parody of editorial cartoons. "Despite their sometimes caustic nature, from the early cartoon portraying George Washington as an ass down to the present day, ... satirical cartoons have played a prominent role in public and political debate.... From the viewpoint of history it is clear that our political discourse would have been considerably poorer without them." Hustler Magazine, Inc. v. Falwell (1988). Although Hustler's ad parody was at best "a distant cousin of the political cartoons" of Thomas Nast and others, the Court doubted that anyone could establish "a principled standard to separate one from the other." The subjectivity of the "outrageousness" standard could permit plaintiffs like Falwell to recover damages whenever the speech in question had "an adverse emotional impact on the audience," a result which would have an immeasurable chilling effect on speech.

The U.S. Supreme Court thus reaffirmed New York Times v. Sullivan in Bose Corp. v. Consumers Union (1984), Philadelphia Newspapers, Inc. v. Hepps (1986), and Hustler Magazine, Inc. v. Falwell (1988). In view of these decisions, it is unlikely that plaintiffs will be able to make an "end-run" around the tort of defamation by using other torts such as intentional infliction of emotional distress. See Wilkins v. National Broadcasting Company (1999); Steele v. Spokesman–Review (2002). See also Patrick v. Los Angeles County Superior Court (Torres) (1994), (legal newspaper's description of judge as a "despotic twit" and memo purportedly written by said judge declaring "court emergency" and suspending election of judge's successor held to constitute parody and not libel or intentional infliction of emotional distress, even though memo used official court seal and stationery and was distributed at courthouse); New Times, Inc. v. Isaacks (2004) (Texas Supreme Court held that First Amendment protected satirical news report of six-year-old girl arrested and shackled for book report on Maurice Sendak's "Where the Wild Things Are" where purpose of satire was to poke fun at judge who had given harsh sentence to teenage boy for writing threatening Halloween story). But see Murray v. Schlosser (1990) (trial court refused to dismiss action based on extremely insulting "Berate the Brides" radio program in which a disc jockey described a bride as the "dog of the week" and sent her a case of dog food and a dog collar).

11. Non–Media Defendants and Matters of Public Concern

Four decades have elapsed since the landmark decision of New York Times Company v. Sullivan. During this period some have expressed a desire to turn back the clock to the common law way of handling media libel cases. Perhaps the most thoughtful assault on the constitutional privilege developed in New York Times and refined in Gertz was that of Justice White. In his concurring opinion in Dun & Bradstreet, Inc. v. Greenmoss Builders, Inc. (1985) Justice White said, "The New York Times rule ... countenances two evils: first, the stream of information about public officials and public affairs is polluted and often remains polluted by false information; and second, the reputation and professional life of the defeated plaintiff may be destroyed by falsehoods that might have been avoided with a reasonable effort to investigate the facts.... Gertz is subject to similar observations.... I am unreconciled to the Gertz holding and believe that it should be overruled."

Dun & Bradstreet narrowed the scope of Gertz in that it held that the requirement of showing actual malice or negligence in Gertz applies only to issues of public concern, not to libel cases involving discussions of purely private matters. This created a new distinction in the form of a "private matters" test in libel law: courts must now make a public-versus-private matter determination in libel cases. This case began when Dun & Bradstreet, a credit reporting agency, falsely informed some of its clients that the construction company Greenmoss Builders had filed for bankruptcy. The false credit report had resulted from a young worker's negligent (but non-malicious) error in checking records. Even though Greenmoss Builders could not show actual malice, it won a $350,000 libel judgment against Dun & Brad-street. In upholding the judgment against Dun & Bradstreet, the Supreme Court ruled that credit rating reports are not a matter of public concern and should thus not be subject to the actual malice rule established in New York Times v. Sullivan and expanded in Gertz. The Court held that the actual malice requirement from Gertz would still apply to issues of public concern, but not in libel cases involving private matters. The Dun & Bradstreet decision suggests that the pendulum is swinging back toward the common law theory of strict liability, at least for credit reporting agencies. Even if a false credit report is the result of an honest mistake, the agency will be held liable, and a plaintiff may recover presumed and punitive damages without a showing of actual malice.

Dun & Bradstreet also touched on the question of whether the New York Times Co. and Gertz principles that public officials and public figures must prove actual malice applied only to media defendants or extended to non-media defendants as well. In Dun & Bradstreet the Supreme Court said that "the rights of the institutional media are no greater and no less than those enjoyed by other individuals or organizations engaged in the same activities." Dun & Bradstreet v. Greenmoss Builders (1985).

12. Neutral Reportage

The concept of neutral reportage developed as a result of a case in which a New York Times reporter was covering a dispute between the Audubon Society and the chemical industry over DDT's impact on birds. Because annual bird counts were showing increasing numbers, some chemists argued that DDT was not harmful, but the Audubon Society believed that the higher numbers were due to more birdwatchers with better training. An Audubon Society publication warned members that any scientist who argued that the continued use of the pesticide DDT had not taken a serious toll on bird life was "someone who is being paid to lie about it or is parroting something he knows little about." When the New York Times reporter asked an Audubon Society official who was making these arguments, the official gave the reporter a list of five scientists whom the Society believed were being paid by the chemical industry to argue that DDT was not killing birds. The New York Times published the story concerning the bird count with the names of the five scientists. Three of the named scientists filed libel actions against the Audubon Society, Society officials and the New York Times.

In reversing the jury award and judgment against the Times, the U.S. Court of Appeals for the Second Circuit held that the First Amendment protects the accurate and disinterested reporting of charges by a responsible and prominent person or organization, regardless of the reporter's private views regarding their accuracy. The Court of Appeals characterized such protection for journalists as "neutral reportage." Edwards v. National Audubon Society (1977). See also Medico v. Time, Inc. (1981).

Would the Supreme Court deny the constitutional privilege recognized in New York Times Company to one who publishes a damaging charge he or she strongly suspects to be untrue? Would the Supreme Court then substitute another constitutional privilege to protect one who, with reckless disregard for the truth, publishes the charge simply because it came from a reputable and prominent source? If the publisher believes the story is true, he or she will be protected under the New York Times Company privilege if the target of the charges is a public figure in relation to the controversy, without regard to "neutral reportage."

On the other hand, Justice Blackmun has commented favorably on neutral reportage in dicta: "Were this Court to adopt the neutral reportage theory, the facts of [Harte–Hanks] might fit within it." Harte–Hanks Communications v. Connaughton (1989). It is worth noting that Justice Blackmun's positive reference to neutral reportage was made in a case where the Journal News was found guilty of actual malice.

The legal status of the neutral reportage defense remains unresolved. Since 1977, courts have struggled with the question of whether or not to adopt neutral reportage as a constitutional privilege. See Coliniatis v. Dimas, Dimas & Johnston (1997). Courts in Ohio, Florida and the Second and Eighth U.S. Circuit Courts of Appeals have accepted the privilege completely. In contrast, the U.S. Court of Appeals for the Third Circuit has rejected it. Dickey v. CBS Inc. (1978). State courts in other jurisdictions such as New York, Michigan and Pennsylvania have also rejected it. In the jurisdictions that do recognize the privilege, courts appear to require that the charges must be:

1) newsworthy, and associated with a public controversy;

2) made by a responsible and prominent source;

3) reported accurately and with neutrality;

4) about a public official or public figure. See Khawar v. Globe International, Inc. (1998) (press cannot generate false publicity about a private person and then defend itself by claiming that he is a public figure).

With no guidance from the Supreme Court other than Justice Blackmun's dicta in Harte–Hanks, federal and state courts are split on whether neutral reportage is a constitutionally viable doctrine. Courts that have rejected neutral reportage explain that it protects the media more broadly than the actual malice standard would. The neutral reportage privilege came under scrutiny in Norton v. Troy Publishing Co. (2004), however. This case began when the Daily Local News reported that Parkesburg Borough Councilman William Glenn issued a written statement accusing Council President James Norton and Mayor Alan Wolfe of being "queers and child molesters." Glenn also claimed that Norton had made sexual advances toward him. In the same story the Daily Local News included Norton's response: "If Mr. Glenn has made comments as bizarre as that, then I feel very sad for him, and I hope he can get the help he needs."

But when the Daily Local News published the story, Norton and Wolfe sued Glenn for defamation. The trial court ruled that the neutral reportage privilege protected the newspaper, allowing its reporter Tom Kennedy to accurately report Glenn's charges even when Kennedy knew the charges to be false. On appeal, the Pennsylvania Supreme Court refused to adopt the neutral reportage privilege, and reversed the trial court's decision.

Troy Publishing appealed to the U.S. Supreme Court, but it declined to hear the case. Troy Publishing Co. v. Norton (2005). In general, newspersons may find the neutral reportage privilege to be a weak reed to rely on when publishing questionable charges, whether made by irresponsible politicians as in Troy Publishing, or made by responsible sources, as in Edwards v. National Audubon Society (1977).

CHAPTER III

PRIVACY AND THE MASS MEDIA

A. INTRODUCTION

The invasion of personal privacy by government, private organizations and the mass media has reached monumental proportions by the first decade of the twenty-first century. This invasion is almost inevitable given our crowded society and the development of sophisticated electronic devices such as directional microphones, powerful miniature listening devices, telephoto lenses and the all-pervasive computer with its power to store, retrieve and communicate the minutiae of our lives. The problem is exacerbated by the power of the mass media and the Internet to disseminate information about individuals, including their physical images.

The difficulty that confronts the law is to control this invasion without crippling a free society's ability to obtain the information necessary for its proper operation. Thus far, the common law has not been very effective in harmonizing these competing private and societal interests. Perhaps this is because the competing interests are so fundamental yet so difficult to define. It has been said that the right to be let alone and to withdraw from the "madding crowd" is the essence of individualism and that privacy is the first interest to go in a totalitarian state. Nevertheless, the individual lives in a society that may, from time to time, have curiosity about him or her. The mass media may become the instrument for satisfying that curiosity. As difficult as the task is, it is for the law to determine when public interest concerning an individual fulfills a legitimate need of a democratic society and when it does not.

B.　HISTORY AND DEVELOPMENT OF THE COMMON LAW

As common law torts go, invasion of privacy is of relatively recent vintage. Its development is traceable to an article in the Harvard Law Review of December 15, 1890 by Samuel D. Warren and his then law partner Louis D. Brandeis. In it they argued that accepted tort doctrine confirmed the existence of a right to privacy, the violation of which was actionable. 4 Harv.L.Rev. 193 (1890). The Boston newspapers' coverage of Warren's private social affairs apparently precipitated the article. This was of course the era of vicious circulation battles and sensational and often fraudulent press coverage to win readership—the age of "yellow journalism."

The article created great interest in the legal profession but the first test of the theory was unsuccessful. In Roberson v. Rochester Folding Box Co. (1902) a flour mill ordered a woman's portrait lithographed on its boxes without her consent. The woman, who did not relish being referred to as the "Flour of the Family," brought suit for damages for invasion of privacy. In a four-to-three ruling, the New York Court of Appeals held, contrary to Warren and Brandeis' contention, that no right of privacy existed at common law. If interests in privacy were to be protected, the legislatures would have to do it. The New York legislature did just that the following year by enacting a civil rights statute making it both a crime and a tort to appropriate the name or likeness of any person for "trade purposes" without that person's consent.

The first judicial acceptance of the existence of a right to privacy came in Pavesich v. New England Life Insurance (1905), a case very much like Roberson. In Pavesich, a newspaper advertisement for an insurance company contained a photograph of the plaintiff and attributed to him certain words encouraging the purchase of the company's life insurance. He had not consented to such depiction and sued the company. Contrary to the New York court the Georgia Supreme Court found a right of privacy in the common law and reversed the trial court's order dismissing Pavesich's complaint.

C. THE COMMON LAW TODAY

As of 2006 all 50 states and the District of Columbia recognized a right of privacy either by common law, statute or both. Three states, Nebraska, Virginia and New York recognize the right only by statute (and Minnesota did not recognize the claim of invasion of privacy until 1998). Lake v. Wal–Mart Stores, Inc. (1998). The right that is accorded varies to some extent in definition and scope from jurisdiction to jurisdiction, reflecting the immaturity of the tort and its imperfect development to date.

The imperfect development extends to the lack of any articulated theory of liability. This is due in part to the fact that the four privacy torts appear unrelated to each other; furthermore, three of the four privacy torts closely resemble torts from other areas of law, as outlined below. While the tort in several of its forms is suggestive of an intentional civil wrong, it is possible that some aspects of it permit liability without a showing of fault. The uncertainty as to the theory of liability may arise from the fact that the tort has four distinct branches:

1. appropriation of another's name or likeness (similar to copyright infringement)

2. unreasonable intrusion upon another's seclusion (similar to trespassing)

3. publicity which unreasonably places another in a false light before the public (similar to defamation)

4. unreasonable publicity disclosing details of another's private life (the only tort that deals expressly with invasion of privacy but does not mirror a tort from another area of law).

See Cox Broadcasting Corp. v. Cohn (1975); Restatement of Torts 2d 652A–652E; W. Prosser and

W. Keeton, Handbook of the Law of Torts, 851–866 (5th ed. 1984).

1. Appropriation

We have already come across this aspect of the right of privacy in relation to the Roberson and Pavesich cases and the New York statute. What is protected here is the individual's concern for the uses to which his or her name, personality and image are put. The law gives the individual the option to prevent others from trading on his or her name or likeness or to permit such trading for a price.

The news media are rarely sued for appropriation type invasions. It has long been settled that while the media normally disseminate news about individuals in the hope of obtaining a profit from circulation and advertising, this is not such appropriation as would justify the award of damages. For example, Paula Jones, who had accused former President Bill Clinton of sexual harassment, sued Penthouse Magazine for commercialization of her name and likeness when Penthouse published semi-nude pictures of her that it had bought from her former boyfriend. However, the court held the photographs to be newsworthy, and Penthouse prevailed. Jones v. Turner (1995).

Appropriation suits are usually brought in connection with a media outlet's self promotion in which a news or feature story involving the plaintiff is republished to illustrate the media outlet's self-proclaimed excellence in informing the public. For instance, in Booth v. Curtis Publishing Co. (1962), the late actress Shirley Booth (television's "Hazel" of the 1960s) gave consent for her picture to appear in Holiday Magazine. She sued the magazine's publisher, however, when it reproduced her photograph without consent in full-page promotional advertisements for the magazine in two other periodicals. Both advertisements presented a striking photograph of Booth in a large straw hat and up to her neck in water as a sample of the contents of Holiday. Beneath the photograph were the words "Shirley Booth and chapeau, from a recent issue of Holiday." Even here, however, the court refused to award damages under the New York privacy statute because such advertising was only "incidental" to the sale and dissemination of news. The decision turned on the court's construction of the statute and it is uncertain that a similar case would have the same resolution in jurisdictions recognizing a common law right of privacy. Prudence would still dictate, however, that when a media outlet advertises itself by use of antecedent news and feature stories and photographs, it should obtain permission for republication from the individuals involved.

The doctrine of incidental use was expanded in Groden v. Random House Inc. (1995), in which Random House used author Robert Groden's picture without his consent in an ad for Gerald Posner's book *Case Closed* on the assassination of John F. Kennedy. See also Montana v. San Jose Mercury News, Inc. (1995), (picture of Joe Montana in a poster constituted incidental use and was not actionable). Radio shockjock Howard Stern also failed in his attempt to block the use of a photo of himself with bare buttocks on Delphi's web site for debates on Stern's candidacy for governor of New York; again, the court relied on the incidental use doctrine to rule in Delphi's favor. Stern v. Delphi Internet Services Corp. (1995).

The developing law against misappropriation has not answered the question of why celebrities may prevent use of visual and audio images of themselves but cannot stop journalists from writing about them. There is also the question of whether an artist can paint a celebrity and sell prints of the painting. Tiger Woods, who earned $24 million in commercial endorsements in 1997, sued artist Rick Rush for selling 5000 prints of a painting of Woods' 1997 Masters tournament win without Woods' permission. The federal district court held that Rick Rush had not violated Tiger Woods' right of publicity because Woods' likeness was not being used to sell a product. The U.S. Court of Appeals for the Sixth Circuit upheld the ruling for Rick Rush, explaining that the First Amendment protects "art that portrays an historic sporting event." ETW Corp. v. Jireh Publishing, Inc. (2003). One unresolved question for the news media is whether photographs taken at news events can be sold as artwork or memorabilia. It is unclear under current case law, including the ETW Corporation case, whether such photographs would be considered commercial or expressive work.

Courts have also recently encountered questions raised by computerized images of celebrities, as in Hoffman v. Capital Cities/ABC, Inc. and L.A. Magazine, Inc. (2001). In this case actor Dustin Hoffman sued Los Angeles Magazine for including his picture from the film Tootsie, digitally altered to give the illusion that Hoffman was wearing a yellow silk gown currently for sale in Los Angeles rather than the red dress he had worn in the movie. The U.S. Court of Appeals for the Ninth Circuit held that the First Amendment protected the digitally altered image of Hoffman because the article constituted ''news'' about fashion; thus, Los Angeles Magazine prevailed. In contrast, however, the U.S. Court of Appeals for Sixth Circuit held that the rap group OutKast had misappropriated civil rights heroine Rosa Parks' name as a title of one of their songs. Parks v. LaFace Records (2003). OutKast and its label LaFace Records reached an out-of-court settlement with Parks in 2005.

a. Right of Publicity

The traditional tort of appropriation was designed to protect the right to be left alone and not to be exploited for commercial purposes. In contrast, the right of publicity is designed to protect celebrities. It deals only with the question of who should profit from exploitation of the celebrity's name or likeness. It is essentially a property right in one's own personality and image as opposed to a personal right.

The right of publicity has been defined as follows: "The distinctive aspect of the common-law right of publicity is that it recognizes the commercial value of the picture or representation of a prominent person or performer and protects his proprietary interest in the profitability of his public reputation or persona." Ali v. Playgirl, Inc. (1978) (heavyweight boxer Muhammed Ali won injunction to stop distribution of Playgirl Magazine which included drawing of frontally nude black athlete resembling Ali and verses referring to "The Greatest").

More recently ice hockey player Tony Twist won a $15 million judgment against Todd McFarlane Productions for infringing on his right of publicity when Spawn Comics creator Todd McFarlane gave Tony Twist's name to a mafia don in his comic book and an animated movie based on the same character and then bragged that he had modeled the character after the ice hockey player. The Missouri Court of Appeals held that by making the fictional "Tony Twist" an evil character, McFarlane had discouraged potential advertisers who might otherwise have asked the real-life Tony Twist to endorse products in television commercials. Doe v. Todd McFarlane Productions (2006).

Advertisers generally understand that they must have models' written consent to use their name or likeness, but litigation has resulted from the question of whether or not the right of publicity can be passed on to one's heirs. Privacy is a personal right and normally dies with the complaining party. The only apparent qualification is that a deceased person's image or persona may be so desirable for commercial exploitation that a transferable property right in the image is created, as in the case of the actor Bela Lugosi's image as Count Dracula or the Marx Brothers' show business persona.

At present, various courts have taken three different approaches: 1) One is that the right of publicity terminates upon death. Under this approach, when celebrities die, their names and likenesses are available for anyone to use without legal liability. 2) The opposite approach is that death has no effect on the right of publicity. In jurisdictions holding this view, the celebrity's heirs must consent to the use of the deceased celebrity's name or likeness for the period of time set by state law. 3) Between these two extremes is a third approach holding that the right of publicity may survive death only if it had been commercially exploited during the individual's lifetime. In jurisdictions where the right of publicity continues beyond death, state statutes provide for survivability of the right of publicity for periods varying from 10 years after death in Tennessee to 50 years after death in California. As a result, Elvis impersonators, for example, may portray Elvis Presley with impunity in Nevada, but may run into trouble in New Jersey if their portrayal resembles Elvis too closely. In contrast to Tennessee, California courts provide broad protection for the right of publicity of a celebrity's heirs. For example, the California Supreme Court upheld a lower court's

$225,000 judgment against artist Gary Saderup's sale of T-shirts bearing his sketch of the Three Stooges because the sketch was nearly identical to a well-known photograph of the Three Stooges. Comedy III Productions v. Gary Saderup Inc. (2001).

In addition to the question of whether the right of publicity survives a celebrity's death, the use of celebrity "look-alikes" has resulted in litigation. The use of "look-alikes" may not only violate a person's right of publicity; it may also violate Section 43(a) of the Lanham Act, amended in 1988, which holds that anyone who falsely suggests that a celebrity endorses a particular product or service is liable if the suggestion confuses consumers. 15 U.S.C.A. § 1051; 1988 amendments 102 Stat. 3935. Plaintiffs can collect treble damages on Lanham Act claims, whereas right of publicity cases are usually confined to actual damages. The late Jacqueline Kennedy Onassis, Woody Allen and other celebrities have won judgments against advertisers who used models who closely resembled them. Onassis v. Christian Dior–New York, Inc. (1984); Allen v. Men's World Outlet (1988); Allen v. National Video, Inc. (1985).

In addition to allowing celebrities to recover damages against advertisers who used look-alikes, there have been cases allowing singers to recover damages for a "sound-alike" violation of their right of publicity. In one case, Ford Motor Company's ad agency Young & Rubicam approached Bette Midler, asking her to sing her hit song "Do You Want to Dance?" for a commercial. When she declined, the agency hired Midler's backup singer Ula Hedwig to sing the song and asked her to "sound as much as possible like Midler." Although the ad agency had obtained permission to use the copyrighted song, Midler sued, arguing that listeners would believe it was Midler herself singing. Midler ultimately won a jury award of $400,000. Midler v. Ford Motor Company (1988). See also Waits v. Frito–Lay, Inc. (1992), ($2.6 million verdict affirmed for singer Tom Waits for imitation of his distinctive singing voice in his song "Step Right Up;" punitive damages explicitly sustained because commercial was "calculated risk" three months after Midler decision).

In addition to protecting celebrities' right of publicity from look-alike and sound-alike imitations, courts have even protected other aspects of a celebrity's public persona. See Carson v. Here's Johnny (1983)(use of phrase "Here's Johnny" for portable toilets held to violate Johnny Carson's right of publicity), and White v. Samsung (1992)(female robot on Wheel of Fortune set violated Vanna White's right of publicity). A company called Cardtoons did not violate major league baseball players' right of publicity, however, when it distributed unflattering caricatures of well-known baseball players because the caricatures comprised parodies or "social commentary," and thus the First Amendment protected them. Cardtoons v. Major League Baseball Players Association (1996).

b. *Applicability of First Amendment Theory to Appropriation Cases*

The case of Zacchini v. Scripps–Howard Broadcasting Co. (1977) raised the question of the extent of First Amendment protection afforded to news media that invade an individual's right of publicity by appropriating her or her name, image, persona or unique presence. Hugo Zacchini performed a "human cannonball" act in which he was shot into a safety net 200 feet away. Despite Zacchini's objections, a reporter videotaped his entire act at a local county fair and broadcast it on a television news program later the same day. Zacchini sued the broadcasting company for unlawful appropriation of his professional property.

The U.S. Supreme Court ultimately upheld Zacchini's right to seek damages against the defendant. The Court held that the defendant's conduct invaded both Zacchini's right to earn a living as an entertainer and society's interest in encouraging creative activity. The First and Fourteenth Amendments were not designed to protect conduct of a newsgatherer that interferes with an individual's right to earn money by publicizing himself.

The rationale of the Court in refusing First Amendment protection to the newsgatherer who violates an individual's right of publicity is that the individual will make information available to the public but for a price which he or she has a legally protected right to exact. The Court also observed that protecting Zacchini's right of publicity was analogous to enforcing copyright law: just as artists and writers need copyright laws to protect them, Zacchini's right of publicity provided the economic incentive for him to create a performance for which he could charge admission.

Although the media may not broadcast a performer's entire act as in Zacchini, the media may use a trademark in a newsgathering activity. In New Kids on the Block v. News America Publishing, Inc. (1992) the Ninth Circuit held that use of the New Kids' trademark constituted fair use and not misappropriation because the trademark was used in a survey. In this case, USA Today and Star Magazine invited readers to participate in a survey via a 900–telephone number to determine which one of the New Kids was most popular. The New Kids charged that USA Today and Star Magazine had violated their right of publicity, but the court dismissed their claim on the basis of First Amendment protection for newsgathering.

Furthermore, authors and screenwriters may tell a person's life story without violating that person's right of publicity. Kim Wozencraft wrote a book called Rush that was a fictional account of her life as an undercover narcotics agent. Her ex-husband Craig Matthews (who had worked with her as a narcotics agent) sued for infringement of his right of publicity, but the Fifth Circuit U.S. Court of Appeals affirmed a summary judgment in favor of Wozencraft. Matthews v. Wozencraft (1994).

2. Intrusion

a. Common Law

This tort comprises the violation of one's legally protected physical sphere of privacy without one's consent. The intrusion may or may not include the tort of trespass. Often the intrusion itself is not physical but consists of eavesdropping with telephoto lenses or electronic listening devices in areas private to aggrieved individuals such as their homes or offices. Anyone may photograph or record individuals if they are in a public zone, however, without fear of legal action so long as the recording is reasonable.

This particular aspect of invasion of privacy is different in nature from the other three in that no publication regarding the victim need be involved. This distinction is important when the news media learn of matters of public interest through an intrusion and publish them. In this situation, while the publication itself may be privileged on the basis of newsworthiness, the intrusion that made the story possible is not.

An early example of media intrusion occurred in Dietemann v. Time, Inc. (1971). There, a male and female employee of Life Magazine went to the home of Dietemann, a plumber who practiced healing with clay, minerals and herbs. Through misrepresentations of fact they gained entry to the plaintiff's home. Once inside, the female employee complained to Dietemann of a lump in her breast. While examining the breast with an assortment of gadgets, Life's male reporter used a hidden camera to secretly photograph Dietemann. In addition, the woman secretly transmitted her conversation with Dietemann to a tape recorder in a parked car occupied by another Life employee and officials from the local district attorney's office and the California Department of Health. The whole affair was a cooperative venture between Life and the public officials to aid in the crackdown on quackery in Southern California and to allow the magazine to write about it. Life published its story and pictures following Dietemann's plea of nolo contendere to criminal misdemeanor charges.

Dietemann thereafter sued for invasion of privacy and won a trial court judgment for $1000. In contending on appeal that the judgment should be reversed, Time, Inc. took the position that the First Amendment immunized it from liability for its intrusion because quackery was an important public issue. In answer Judge Hufstedler said, "The First Amendment is not a license to trespass, to steal, or to intrude by electronic means into the precincts of another's home or office" simply because such means are used by media representatives in the course of newsgathering. Dietemann v. Time, Inc. (1971). In affirming the judgment for Dietemann, Judge Hufstedler clearly distinguished between the intrusion and the subsequent publication of the story and photographs. A privilege might exist for the publication but it does not extend to the antecedent intrusion.

Dietemann is a troubling case not so much because of its denial of any privilege to intrude in the course of bona fide newsgathering, but because it raises questions as to the extent to which newsgatherers, especially investigative reporters, may go before they are liable for intrusion.

Despite the ruling in Dietemann, using concealed tape recorders is a great temptation to investigative journalists, and has resulted in continued litigation. See McCall v. Courier–Journal and Louisville Times Co. (1981), Cassidy v. ABC (1978), Shevin v. Sunbeam Television Corp. (1977), Benford v. ABC (1980), Boddie v. ABC (1989), and Deteresa v. American Broadcasting Co. Inc. (1997). "Prime Time Live" producers sent "patients" with concealed videocameras to an eye clinic to get evidence of unnecessary cataract operations. When the eye clinic sued, the Seventh Circuit held that there had been no intrusion or actionable fraud because the clinic and two of its surgeons had agreed to allow ABC to videotape a cataract operation. Desnick v. American Broadcasting Company (1995). When a telepsychic company sued ABC after its journalists videotaped an employee with a hidden camera, the Supreme Court of California ruled that there is a "limited, but legitimate" expectation of privacy in a large office where many workers answer telephones in small three-walled cubicles. ABC ultimately paid Sanders $934,000 in damages. Sanders v. American Broadcasting Companies (1999). In contrast to Sanders, however, the U.S. Court of Appeals for the Ninth Circuit ruled that the managers of a medical laboratory did not have a reasonable expectation of privacy in a semi-public laboratory in which non-employees could come in for blood tests and lab work. ABC's "Prime Time Live" reporters, posing as potential clients who might send samples to the lab from other cities, secretly recorded what they heard and saw with regard to how laboratory technicians tested Pap smears for cancer. The court distinguished Sanders, noting that the reporters did not record any personal or private information; thus, there was no intrusion. Medical Laboratory Management Consultants v. American Broadcasting Co. (2002).

b. Federal Legislation

The use of concealed recording devices by both journalists and law enforcement officials has caused Congress to become increasingly concerned with governmental and private intrusions upon individual privacy. In 1968 Congress passed the Omnibus Crime Control and Safe Streets Act, 18 U.S.C.A. §§ 2510–2520. Congress later amended this as the "Electronic Communications Privacy Act of 1986," also known as the Federal Wiretap Statute. This prohibits under criminal penalty the interception of any conversation carried over a wire or a non-wire conversation in a setting where one expects privacy. Congress amended the statute again in 1994 to include cellular and wireless communication within its protection.

Therefore, a journalist who uses a wiretap to record a phone conversation between two other people or "bugs" a room in which a meeting is held could be liable for violating the statute. The United States Attorney General is authorized to initiate civil actions in the United States District Court to enjoin threatened felony violations. Law enforcement personnel and other government officers authorized to engage in electronic surveillance or, as in the case of employees of the Federal Communications Commission, to monitor electronic communications, are generally exempted from the provisions of the legislation when acting within their proper authority.

The same legislation also outlaws unauthorized accessing or tampering with information storage facilities through which electronic communications services are provided, and outlaws the blocking of authorized access to the information while in electronic storage. By this legislation, Congress has recognized the need to protect privacy of communication in our high technology computer age.

Although such incidents may be rare, in one case a Cincinnati Enquirer reporter accessed the voice-mail system of Chiquita Brands International executives by using a secret code which a former Chiquita attorney had given him. The attorney later pled guilty to four misdemeanor charges of attempted unauthorized access to computer systems. The reporter had used the voice-mail messages as background for an investigative report charging that Chiquita's use of pesticides endangered Central American workers' health and that Chiquita ships were used to smuggle cocaine. In 1998 the Enquirer, owned by the Gannett Company, published a front-page apology, agreed to pay Chiquita more than $10 million in damages and fired the reporter. Chiquita Brands International, Inc. v. Gallagher (1999). The reporter later pled guilty to two counts of stealing voice-mail messages; he had violated the

Stored Communications Act in Title B of the Electronic Communications Privacy Act. 18 U.S.C. § 2707(c). (See also Chapter VIII for discussion of the same reporter's betrayal of confidential source's identity.)

There is an important exception, however. The statute expressly permits a participant in the conversation to secretly record it, provided that the participant is not taping it for the purpose of committing any criminal or tortious act. 18 U.S.C. § 2511(2)(d). This exception allows a reporter to secretly record his or her telephone conversations with the person being interviewed because the consent of only one party to the conversation (in this case, the reporter him/herself) is required. Of course, if the reporter's purpose in taping the conversation is to commit a tort such as libel, the reporter would be violating the statute. The question of the reporter's motivation in such cases is generally left to a jury. Thus, it is legal in several jurisdictions for reporters to conceal audiotape recorders while talking to news sources. However, 11 states require that all parties to the conversation must agree to the tape recording. California, Connecticut, Florida, Illinois, Maryland, Massachusetts, Michigan, Montana, New Hampshire, Pennsylvania and South Dakota have outlawed secret recordings, and Nevada and Washington permit them only in emergency situations. Media Law Resource Center, 50–State Survey: Media Privacy and Related Law 2005–06 at 1618–1620.

These states are "all-party consent" states, meaning that all parties to a wire or oral communication must give prior consent before a conversation is tape-recorded. The other states are "one-party consent" states, meaning that participant recording is permitted provided there is no intent to commit a tort.

A grand jury indicted Pentagon employee Linda Tripp on two felony counts in 1999 for taping telephone conversations with Monica Lewinsky about Lewinsky's relationship with President Bill Clinton. Although Tripp's lawyer had advised her that it is illegal to secretly record phone conversations in Maryland, Tripp taped the conversations without Lewinsky's knowledge and then played one tape for a Newsweek magazine reporter. Prosecutors in Independent Counsel Kenneth Starr's office granted Tripp immunity from federal prosecution when she gave them the tape recordings, but whether or not that extended to immunity from prosecution by the state of Maryland was not clear. In May 2000, prosecutors in Maryland dropped all wiretapping charges against Tripp after a judge ruled that Monica Lewinsky could not be compelled to testify about her conversations with Tripp.

In response to increasing complaints of surreptitious videotaping in places such as school locker rooms and department store dressing rooms, Congress passed the Video Voyeurism Prevention Act of 2004. Public Law 108–495, Dec. 23, 2004; 18 U.S.C.A. S 1801. With the proliferation of cell phone cameras, "high-tech peeping Toms" were secretly taking pictures of unsuspecting individuals in compromising positions and posting the photos to Internet web sites. The 2004 law makes it a crime to videotape or photograph the nude or underwear-covered parts of a person without consent when the person has a reasonable expectation of privacy.

In 24 states there is a specific law against hidden video cameras, although many of these laws are limited to attempts to secretly record nudity, as numerous state legislatures have passed laws modeled on the federal Video Voyeurism Prevention Act of 2004. See http://www.rcfp.org/taping. The right to surreptitiously audiotape a conversation is not concomitant with the right to videotape it.

In addition to laws such as the Video Voyeurism Prevention Act of 2004 and the Federal Wiretap Statute, the FCC's "Phone Rule," (47 C.F.R. § 64.501; § 73.1206) requires that before recording a telephone conversation for broadcast, journalists must tell any party to the call that they intend to broadcast the conversation, whether the conversation is being taped or broadcast live. With regard to personal interviews, the FCC states that "No person shall use ... a device ... for the purpose of overhearing or recording the private conversations of others unless such use is authorized by all of the parties engaging in the conversation." 47 C.F.R. § 2.701(a). In Rhode Island, Bruce Clift threatened to commit suicide, but agreed to a taped telephone interview with WPRI–TV reporter Susan Hogan. She broadcast the interview at 6:04 p.m. Clift listened to the news report and then shot himself in the head and died at 6:07 p.m. Clift's wife sued the television station for intrusion and negligence. Although the Rhode Island Supreme Court dismissed the intrusion claim because Clift had consented to the interview, it reinstated her claim for negligence. Clift v. Narragansett Television, L.P. (1996).

Anyone may be the subject of observation, photographing, or even questioning in a public place. The only caveat is that journalists and photographers may not hound or harass anyone. An early example of harassment by a photographer occurred in Galella v. Onassis (1973). Self-styled paparazzi Ron Galella, wanting to profit from selling pictures of the late Jacqueline Kennedy Onassis, followed her so closely that he endangered the safety of her and her children. For example, he nearly ran over her with his motorboat while she was swimming, and he spooked a horse her son was riding. Onassis obtained a court order requiring Galella to stay 25 feet away from her and 30 feet away from her children. Ten years later she felt compelled to sue him for intrusion again because he had ignored the original injunction; this time the court found Galella in contempt, but maintained that he still had the right to photograph Onassis in public provided that he stayed 25 feet away. Galella v. Onassis (1982).

More recently, U.S. Healthcare executives Richard and Nancy Wolfson won an injunction from a federal district court that enjoined broadcast journalists from "Inside Edition" from harassing them and their children. They eventually settled out of court when the journalists agreed to stay away from the Wolfsons' home and families. Wolfson v. Inside Edition (1997).

In 1999 the California legislature passed an "anti-paparazzi" or "stalkerazzi" law after two photographers blocked the car of Arnold Schwarzenegger and his wife Maria Shriver as they drove their son to school. The "stalkerazzi" law creates a new cause of action, permitting lawsuits against individuals who engage in "constructive" trespass by using a "visual or auditory enhancing device" to obtain an image or recording that could not have been obtained without physically trespassing. California Civil Code § 1708.8 (1999). Some legal scholars have questioned the constitutionality of such legislation, but it has remained in effect. Paparazzi use of their automobiles as assault vehicles against celebrities has escalated; for example in 2005 two paparazzi deliberately rammed their cars into vehicles owned by Reese Witherspoon and Lindsay Lohan, and another one used his car to knock down a friend walking with Cameron Diaz and Justin Timberlake. New York Times, June 9, 2005 at A1, A25.

c. Possession of Stolen Material and Intrusion by Journalists on Private Property

Although Dietemann and other recent cases make clear the danger of journalists' intrusive behavior, they are limited to situations in which journalists are directly involved. In situations in which the media merely publicize the fruits of another's intrusion the courts have usually rejected the idea of liability on the part of the media. For instance in Pearson v. Dodd (1969) employees of the late Senator Dodd rifled his files, made copies of some allegedly incriminating documents and turned the copies over to defendant Jack Anderson, who was aware of the manner in which they were obtained, and who subsequently published excerpts from them. The U.S. Court of Appeals held that columnists Jack Anderson and Drew Pearson had not themselves been guilty of any intrusion. If journalists actively encourage or aid and abet others in acts of intrusion, however, they can be held liable for such conduct under ordinary principles of tort law.

The position taken in Dodd makes considerable sense. If the media were required to consider the means by which news is obtained by independent sources out of fear for tort liability, the newsgathering process would be severely hampered. In 1998, however, the Louisiana Supreme Court ruled that two newspapers might indeed be held liable for printing excerpts of transcripts of an unlawfully recorded telephone conversation, despite the fact that the contents of the conversation had been made public at a press conference. Keller v. Aymond (1998). Carol Aymond, an unsuccessful candidate for state trial judge, unlawfully recorded a phone conversation between Avoyelles (Louisiana) Parish Police Juror McKinley Keller and then-state trial Judge Michael Johnson. Aymond then called a press conference to present what he considered to be evidence of corruption and vote-buying within the judiciary. When Aymond provided two newspapers with transcripts of the conversation, Keller and Johnson sued Aymond under the Louisiana Electronic Surveillance Act, which outlaws the recording of a telephone conversation without consent from at least one of the parties to the conversation. The court ruled that because an illegal wiretap was the source of the information, the newspapers' disclosure of the contents of the conversation served no legitimate public interest, and the newspapers' lack of criminal intent did not shield them from liability. The U.S. Supreme Court declined to hear the case. Keller v. Aymond (1998). However, in light of the U.S. Supreme Court's decision in Bartnicki v. Vopper (2001), discussed below, it would appear that Keller is no longer good law.

In contrast to Aymond, the U.S. Supreme Court affirmed the Pearson v. Dodd (1969) precedent in Bartnicki v. Vopper (2001). This case began when Gloria Bartnicki, chief negotiator for the local teachers' union in Wilkes–Barre, Pennsylvania, spoke on her cellular phone with Anthony Kane, president of the teachers' union, about teachers' raises. Kane said, "If [the school board members] are not going to move for three percent, we're going to have to go to their homes [and] blow off their front porches. We'll have to do some work on some of those guys." As Bartnicki spoke with Kane, an unknown person intercepted the call and left a tape recording of it in the mailbox of Jack Yocum, president of the local taxpayers' association. Yocum gave a copy of the tape to radio talk show host Fred Williams (whose legal surname is Vopper) of WILK. Williams aired the tape, which was simulcast over

WILK and WGBI–AM, and local newspapers also published transcripts of the call. Bartnicki and Kane sued Yocum, Williams [Vopper],WILK and WGBI under both federal and state wiretapping laws and the Electronic Communications Privacy Act (ECPA). The federal district court refused the media defendants' request to dismiss the case. On appeal, the U.S. Court of Appeals for the Third Circuit held that the First Amendment protected someone who discloses an innocently received tape recording. Bartnicki and Kane appealed, and the U.S. Supreme Court agreed to hear the case. The High Court affirmed the appeals court ruling for three reasons: 1) the media did not aid and abet the illegal recording, 2) the intercepted conversation was about a matter of public concern, and 3) Kane's comment about blowing up front porches proposed a wrongful act (apparently the humor in Kane's comment was lost on all nine justices). Bartnicki v. Vopper (2001).

In a case that occurred at the same time as Bartnicki, John and Alice Martin intercepted and tape-recorded a cellular phone call between U.S. House Speaker Newt Gingrich and Representative John Boehner. The Martins gave the tape-recording to Representative James McDermott, the ranking Democrat on the House Ethics Committee. McDermott gave copies of the taped conversation to The New York Times and The Atlanta Journal–Constitution, both of which ran front-page news stories about it. The Justice Department charged the Martins with violating the federal wiretapping statute

(18 U.S.C. § 2510 et seq.). They pled guilty and paid a $1000 fine.

Boehner sued McDermott, charging that he had violated the federal wiretapping statute by disclosing the contents of an unlawfully intercepted telephone conversation to the news media. The U.S. Court of Appeals for the D.C. Circuit held that McDermott had violated the civil liability provisions of the Electronic Communications Privacy Act, specifically 18 U.S.C. § 2511(1)(c), which provides sanctions for anyone who "intentionally discloses . . . the contents of any wire, oral or electronic communication, knowing that the information was obtained through the interception of a wire, oral or electronic communication. . . ." Boehner v. McDermott (1999) (Boehner I). On appeal, the U.S. Supreme Court vacated and remanded the case to the appeals court to reconsider in light of its decision in Bartnicki. The appeals court then remanded the case to the federal district court in Washington, D.C. which found that McDermott had "participated in an illegal transaction when he accepted the tape from the Martins; [therefore] he is without First Amendment protection." The difference between Boehner and Bartnicki appears to be that one may receive an illegal tape recording and pass it on to journalists (as in Bartnicki) provided that one knows neither who made the recording nor how it was made. McDermott appealed, but the U.S. Court of Appeals for the District of Columbia Circuit upheld the federal district court's ruling that McDermott had not lawfully obtained the tape recording the Martins had given him. The court ordered McDermott to pay more than $700,000 to Boehner, which included $60,000 in damages. Boehner v. McDermott (2006). (Boehner II).

Property owners may refuse to cooperate with newspersons, particularly television crews, seeking news on their premises. This raises the question of whether media representatives have the right under the First Amendment to go without authorization upon private property or otherwise to utilize such property in the interest of obtaining news. The answer is usually "no." The issue often comes up in connection with private property that is open to the public for business purposes. For example, CBS reporters doing a story on reported health code violations at a New York restaurant entered it without permission, with cameras rolling and bright lights blazing. The restaurant, called Le Mistral, sued CBS for trespass and recovered $1200 in damages. Le Mistral, Inc. v. Columbia Broadcasting System (1978).

In this kind of situation media executives argue that their journalists ought to be able to enter privately owned places of public accommodation along with the rest of the public. If the media are not allowed to enter, the flow of news will be constricted in violation of the First Amendment. Thus far, however, this argument has fallen on deaf judicial ears.

The issue of trespassing was raised in a different context in Food Lion Inc. v. Capital Cities/ABC

(1999). Food Lion charged two ABC producers with "trespassing" when they went undercover for a story. ABC producers Lyn Dale and Susan Barnett landed jobs at Food Lion and used hidden video cameras to record Food Lion's employees selling rat-gnawed cheese, expired beef, aging ham and fish washed in bleach to kill the smell. After ABC's "Primetime Live" broadcast, Food Lion claimed that it lost $2.5 billion when its sales and stock price plummeted. In its lawsuit Food Lion never challenged the truth of the story in court, and it did not bother to sue for intrusion because using hidden video cameras is legal in North Carolina, a one-party consent state. Instead Food Lion sued ABC for trespassing and fraud because Dale and Barnett had misrepresented their employment history when they applied for jobs with Food Lion. Despite a jury award of $5.5 million for Food Lion, the U.S. Court of Appeals for the Fourth Circuit rejected the claim of fraud and struck down the jury's damage awards, but upheld a $2 award for breach of loyalty and trespass. Food Lion, Inc. v. Capital Cities/ABC, Inc. (1999).

The initial Food Lion decision before the total damage award was reduced to $2 may have set a precedent for the initial decision in Veilleux v. NBC (1998). In Veilleux, a jury returned a verdict of $525,000 in compensatory damages against NBC following its broadcast of a Dateline program on the long-distance trucking industry. Free-lance television producer Alan Handel allegedly persuaded trucker Peter Kennedy to allow him to ride along based on promises that Dateline would show "the positive side" of the trucking industry and would not include material from Parents Against Tired Truckers (PATT). Kennedy and his employer Ray Veilleux sued NBC for fraudulent misrepresentation and won at the federal district court level. NBC appealed, however, and the Court of Appeals for the First Circuit reversed the judgments for the truckers on their defamation, "false light," negligent infliction of emotional distress, and invasion of privacy claims. It vacated and remanded for further proceedings the misrepresentation claim based on the promise not to include PATT in the original broadcast. NBC reached an out-of-court settlement with Kennedy and Veilleux in September 2000. Veilleux v. NBC (2000).

Plaintiffs have also charged journalists with trespassing in the context of "ride-along" cases in which members of the press accompany police or rescue workers with cameras rolling. The California Supreme Court ruled that an accident victim being flown to a hospital in a medical helicopter should have a reasonable expectation of privacy. Shulman v. Group W Productions, Inc. (1998). When Ruth Shulman and her son Wayne were lifted into a rescue helicopter after a serious car accident, they did not realize that the flight nurse was wearing a microphone and that a cameraman was videotaping them for the television program "On Scene: Emergency Response." After the broadcast, Ruth and Wayne Shulman sued Group W for intrusion. The California Supreme Court ruled that the Shulmans should have had the same expectation of privacy in the rescue helicopter as they would have had in a hospital room. The case was subsequently settled out of court.

In 1998 the U.S. Supreme Court agreed to hear two "ride-along" cases after two U.S. Courts of Appeal reached conflicting decisions on the issue. The Court of Appeals for the Fourth Circuit ruled that police officers who permitted two Washington Post journalists to accompany them into a private home were entitled to qualified immunity. Wilson v. Layne (1998). However, the Court of Appeals for the Ninth Circuit held that U.S. Fish and Wildlife officers and the Cable News Network (CNN) journalists who accompanied them on a search for illegally poisoned eagles on a Montana ranch could be sued for violating the Fourth Amendment. Berger v. Hanlon (1999).

The U.S. Supreme Court reversed the Fourth Circuit ruling and affirmed the Ninth Circuit judgment. The High Court held that if law enforcement officers permit journalists to accompany them while they enter private homes, they violate the homeowner's right of privacy, and the officers violate the Fourth Amendment. In Wilson the High Court thus ruled against the police but did not order the police officers to pay monetary damages because the law concerning media ride-alongs had not been developed when the original arrests had occurred. Wilson v. Layne (1999). At the same time the High Court remanded Hanlon v. Berger (1999) to the Ninth Circuit, which then held that journalists do not enjoy the kind of qualified immunity that had shielded the police in Wilson. The Ninth Circuit reinstated rancher Paul Berger's Fourth Amendment and trespassing claims against the CNN reporters. In 2001 CNN reached an out-of-court settlement with Berger for an undisclosed amount of money. See, however, Brunette v. Humane Society of Ventura County (2002) (U.S. Court of Appeals for Ninth Circuit found journalist not guilty of Fourth Amendment violation and not liable as state actor because he arrived in his own vehicle to investigate story on animal cruelty after the Humane Society had already begun its search).

In the "ride-along" cases journalists have argued that they should be permitted to enter rescue helicopters and even private homes if the newsworthiness of the events outweighed the offensiveness of broadcasting or publishing them. But these arguments are doubtful for reasons suggested in the analogous case of Lloyd Corp., Ltd. v. Tanner (1972), where the Supreme Court ruled that the private owner of a shopping mall could bar distributors of leaflets protesting the draft and the Vietnam War from the mall. The public's license to enter a private business establishment is limited to engaging in activities directly related to that business and does not normally extend to the pursuit of unrelated business such as newsgathering or propagandizing customers. See Le Mistral, Inc. v. Columbia Broadcasting System (1978), discussed above. Hudgens v. N.L.R.B. (1976) permitted a shopping mall owner to bar from his premises union picketing of a particular store involved in a labor contract dispute.

In contrast to Hudgens, however, the state Supreme Courts of California and New Jersey have both held that their own state constitutions protected the right of protesters to solicit signatures on a petition and to distribute leaflets in privately owned shopping centers. Furthermore, the U.S. Supreme Court upheld the California Supreme Court's decision to adopt "individual liberties more expansive than those conferred by the Federal Constitution." PruneYard Shopping Center v. Robins (1980); New Jersey Coalition Against War in the Middle East v. J.M.B. Realty (1994).

Although California and New Jersey have recognized that regional shopping malls are now like the public fora in downtown commercial districts, in general the press and public do not have a First Amendment right to demonstrate on private property. For example, reporters tried to cover a demonstration by 300 members of the Sunbelt Alliance at the construction site of a nuclear power plant owned by the Public Service Company of Oklahoma, a private corporation. The reporters followed the demonstrators through fences and were arrested, convicted of trespassing and fined $25 each. Stahl v. State of Oklahoma (1983). (Laws against trespassing are laws of general application, meaning that they apply to everyone, including reporters.)

There is thus some uncertainty about the line between legality and intrusion regarding admission to private property. As a result of recent cases, however, we do know that:

(1) outright misrepresentation by newsgatherers to gain initial entry to private or even public property is a very risky business and should not be resorted to except in extremis;

(2) unauthorized entry by newsgatherers onto private or public property constitutes intrusion as to individuals present and trespass as to the property, and that goes for private places of public accommodation as well;

(3) permission from relevant public officials provides the necessary license to gather news in public buildings;

(4) permission by police or fire officials to newsgatherers to accompany the officials onto private property while they conduct official business in the absence of the owner generally does not insulate newsgatherers against tort liability. See Green Valley School, Inc. v. Cowles Florida Broadcasting, Inc. (1976) (television journalists invited to accompany police on midnight raid of school held liable for trespass), and Baugh v. CBS, Inc. (1993) (CBS reporters misrepresented their purpose in order to enter home of battered wife describing her husband's assault; CBS reached out-of-court settlement with battered wife). See also K. Middleton, Journalists, Trespass and Officials: Closing the Door of Florida

Publishing Co. v. Fletcher, 16 Pepperdine Law Review 259 (1989). See also Shulman v. Group W Productions (1998), Hanlon v. Berger (1999) and Wilson v. Layne (1999).

d. *Applicability of First Amendment Theory to Intrusion*

Because intrusion involves no publication in and of itself, the First Amendment is not directly implicated. Because the wrong occurs when the information is gathered rather than when it is published, journalists cannot expect any First Amendment protection if they engage in intrusion.

3. False Light

a. *Nature and Limitations*

Creating a false image for an individual or placing him or her in a false light through publication may be actionable as an invasion of privacy whether or not such falsity involves defamation. The type of invasion of privacy involves publishing material that places an individual in a false light if 1) the false light in which the person finds himself or herself would be offensive to a reasonable person, and 2) the publisher of the material is at fault.

One form of false light invasion of privacy is to ascribe to individuals political or other views which they do not in fact hold or falsely attribute to them authorship of certain writings or remarks. Another dangerous practice is to use a picture or videotape of someone out of context. For example, in Leverton v. Curtis Publishing Co. (1951), a photograph of the plaintiff, a child who had been struck down on a public street by a careless motorist, was properly published in a local newspaper because of its newsworthiness. However, the same news photograph was published several months later in the Saturday Evening Post to illustrate an article entitled "They Ask to Be Killed," dealing with childhood carelessness. The child sued, and the defendant publisher was found liable for placing the child in the false light of being a careless pedestrian.

Similarly, a "voice-over" in a television newscast resulted in liability in Duncan v. WJLA–TV, Inc. (1984). In this case, WJLA–TV had used video footage of people walking down a crowded street in Washington, D.C. as the backdrop for a story on genital herpes. At one point, as the news anchor noted in a voice-over that there is no cure, the camera focused on Linda Duncan as she stood on a corner. Because she had been clearly identified, she sued for defamation and false light invasion of privacy, and won a small damage award from WJLA–TV.

Still another dangerous enterprise is the intentional fictionalization of activities or events involving actual identifiable persons. One book publisher discovered to its sorrow the cost of such a venture when it published a fictionalized biography of the great baseball pitcher Warren Spahn. The book dramatized and fictionalized such matters as Spahn's relationship to his father, his war record, his courtship with his wife and even his thoughts while on the pitching mound. The author even invented long dialogues between Spahn and those with whom he associated. The New York trial court in Spahn v. Julian Messner, Inc. (1964) cast its decision for Spahn in terms of the New York privacy statute, specifically, appropriation of Spahn's image and personality by the defendant for commercial advantage. The New York Court of Appeals enjoined further publication and distribution of the book, however, and awarded substantial damages on a theory of false light invasion of privacy.

In 1997 actor Brad Pitt sued Playgirl Magazine for false light when Playgirl's August 1996 edition contained nude photographs of Pitt and his former fiancee Gwyneth Paltrow, surreptitiously photographed by an unknown photographer while the pair vacationed in the West Indies. Pitt charged that Playgirl had placed him in a false light by implying his consent to the publication. A California judge issued a temporary restraining order barring Playgirl Magazine from further distribution of that issue, although it had already been mailed to subscribers and delivered to newsstands. Pitt v. Playgirl (1997). Five years later Baywatch star Jose Solano won a false light claim against Playgirl magazine for implying that readers would see nude photos of him inside the magazine. Solano v. Playgirl, Inc. (2002).

As in cases of defamation, however, defendants will prevail in false light cases if they can show that their characterization of a plaintiff is true. For example, Deangelo Bailey sued rap music artist Marshall Mathers III (Eminem) for false light invasion of privacy, arguing that Eminem's rap number "Brain Damage" on the 1999 recording "Slim Shady LP" portrayed him as a bully who banged Eminem's head against a urinal, broke his nose and soaked his clothes in blood. Because Deangelo had admitted to bullying or shoving Eminem when they were in fourth grade, however, the Michigan Court of Appeals relied on the "substantial truth" doctrine in affirming the trial court's decision to dismiss the case against Eminem. Bailey v. Mathers (2005).

b.   Relationship to Defamation

Not every false light case involves untruths that injure reputation, but every act of defamation will, while injuring reputation, also place the victim in a false light in the public's mind. Indeed, many actions for defamation are accompanied by actions for invasion of privacy. This raises the intriguing question whether the defamation action might not eventually fall into disuse because of the comparatively greater ease in establishing false light. The plaintiff need not show the defamatory character of false communication and can bypass many technical requirements of defamation actions. Unless and until defamation actions fade away, however, plaintiffs should plead both false light and defamation in appropriate cases.

c.   Applicability of First Amendment Theory to False Light Cases

In marked contrast to the appropriation and intrusion branches, the Constitution does place limits on the reach of the false light tort because of its potential to interfere with publication and restrict the flow of news and information to the public.

When the U.S. Supreme Court handed down its first decision on false light, it emphasized the importance of the journalist's intentions. Local newspapers had made James J. Hill and his wife and five children the involuntary subjects of a front page news story after three escaped convicts held the family hostage in their home for 19 hours in 1952. The convicts released the family unharmed. Hill stressed to newspersons that the convicts had treated his family courteously and had neither molested anyone nor acted violently. After the incident Hill discouraged all media efforts to keep the family in the public spotlight. Less than a year later, however, Joseph Hayes published his novel "The Desperate Hours," depicting the experience of a family of four held hostage by three escaped convicts in the family's home. Unlike the Hill family's experience, the fictional family suffered violence at the hands of the convicts, who beat the father and son and subjected the daughter to verbal sexual harassment.

At this point if Hill had sued Hayes for invasion of privacy, the outcome would have been doubtful because of the difficulty of identifying the fictional family of four with the Hill family of seven. That difficulty was removed when, in conjunction with the production of a play based upon the book, Life magazine published an article indicating that the play "The Desperate Hours," actually mirrored the Hill family's experience. Life photographers even staged photographs taken in the house in which the Hill family had been held captive. The photographs dramatized supposed incidents during the family's ordeal.

Although the Life article and photographs clearly placed Hill and his family in a false light, a closely divided Supreme Court reversed a lower court judgment awarding compensatory damages to Hill because the trial court's instructions to the jury failed to require that Hill establish that Life magazine either knew the facts creating the false light were untrue or that it acted in reckless disregard of the truth. The Supreme Court explained that an innocent mistake or negligence in creating the false light were insufficient bases for liability under the First and Fourteenth Amendments. This ruling is obviously parallel to that in New York Times Co. v. Sullivan (1964), discussed in Chapter II. The analogy with defamation impelled a bare majority of the Supreme Court in Time, Inc. v. Hill (1967) to limit recovery in false light cases to those situations in which the media defendant knew the news story was false or published the story with reckless disregard for the truth. The concern of the majority was to provide a margin for error for the media in gathering and reporting the news.

Although the Hill case was narrowly decided after oral arguments in two successive terms of the Court, a broad majority of the Court confirmed its basic First Amendment thrust in Cantrell v. Forest City Publishing Co. (1974). In Cantrell, a Cleveland Plain Dealer reporter wrote a news story about a bridge that collapsed and killed 44 people, one of whom was Melvin Cantrell. A few months later the reporter drove to the Cantrell home to write a follow-up story on Cantrell's widow and her children, but only the children were home when the reporter arrived. Despite this, the reporter wrote a story giving the impression that he had interviewed Mrs. Cantrell, and she sued for false light invasion of privacy.

In Cantrell, the U.S. Supreme Court held that fabricating an interview constituted actual malice. The Court in Cantrell also raised, without deciding, the question whether, parallel to Gertz v. Welch, Inc. (1974), a state might constitutionally limit Hill by applying a more relaxed standard of liability, meaning negligence, for the communication of false light type statements injurious to private individuals. The High Court's decision Gertz and later private individual defamation cases would suggest that private individuals have to prove negligence but not actual malice in false light cases.

Following Cantrell, at least two state courts have held that private persons merely have to show negligence rather than actual malice to win a false light case. See Crump v. Beckley Newspapers (1983) (West Virginia Supreme Court held that negligence is the standard in false light cases involving private persons; Wood v. Hustler Magazine, Inc. (1984) (applying a negligence standard under Texas law).

The crucial problem with the false light tort is that it covers false but non-defamatory statements.

Defamatory statements raise a red flag, warning editors to carefully verify, modify or delete them, but neutral or even laudatory false statements provide no such warning to editors. Editors must thus double-check *every* asserted fact about an individual at great cost in time and resources or else risk liability. The tension between false light and First Amendment protection for the media was noted in the groundbreaking case of Renwick v. News and Observer Publishing Company (1984). There, an associate dean at the University of North Carolina brought suit for libel and false light against two newspapers for allegedly misreporting that the University had denied admission to about 800 black students over a three-year period. Upon finding no defamation, the North Carolina Supreme Court considered the false light claim, but expressed concern that the false light tort would allow recovery for non-defamatory false statements. The court said it would create "a grave risk [to] ... a free press in a free society if we saddle the press with the impossible burden of verifying to a certainty the facts associated in news articles with a person's name, picture or portrait, *particularly as related to nondefamatory matter.*" Renwick v. News and Observer Publishing Company. Renwick is significant because it is the first appellate decision to wholly and specifically reject the false light tort on the basis that it is redundant of defamation.

By 2006, ten states—Colorado, Massachusetts, Minnesota, Missouri, Ohio, New York, North Carolina, Ohio, Texas, Virginia and Wisconsin—had expressly rejected false light as a viable claim when recovery is sought for untrue statements. In these ten states, plaintiffs must sue for defamation even though the false light tort would better fit the facts of their individual cases. For example in Massachusetts, when Boston Magazine juxtaposed a picture of a student at a high school dance with an article on teenage promiscuity, she could not sue for false light invasion of privacy (although the U.S. Court of Appeals for the First Circuit reversed a lower court's dismissal of her defamation claim). See Stanton v. Metro Corp. (2006), discussed in Chapter II. Some of these ten states, such as Virginia, have statutes that dictate what type of privacy claims may be made, and specifically exclude false light. In other states, the highest courts have determined, as a matter of common law, that they will not recognize false light in their state. See Denver Publishing Co. v. Bueno (2002) (Colorado Supreme Court rejected false light claim after Rocky Mountain News published story about crime family in which 15 of a couple's 18 children had arrest records).

4. Public Disclosure of Private Facts

a. *Nature and Limitations*

Of the four common law branches of the invasion of privacy tort the most troublesome is the unreasonable publication of private facts of an embarrassing and objectionable nature. It is not always easy for reporters and editors to determine when publicity is unreasonable or even when to view facts as private. There is the further problem of determining when a reasonable person of ordinary sensibilities will view private facts as offensive, thus making public disclosure actionable. Then, too, in contrast to false light, truth will not shield the disclosing medium since the gravamen of the tort is the publication of private *facts* that the law deems worthy of protection.

Illustrative of this type of case is Sidis v. F–R Publishing Corp. (1940). William James Sidis was a child prodigy in the field of mathematics and graduated from Harvard College at the age of sixteen amid considerable public attention. A shy and retiring person, Sidis attempted to live down his fame and succeeded quite well until the New Yorker magazine of August 14, 1937, published a brief biographical sketch of Sidis under the title "Where Are They Now?" The sketch recounted Sidis' unusual background, traced his attempts to conceal his identity through the years, described his menial employment far from the field of mathematics and detailed certain bizarre conduct such as his collecting old street car transfers. The facts stated in the article were not alleged to be untrue. Rather, Sidis sued for the destruction of the obscurity he had so laboriously constructed for himself. His suit failed because the court held that the facts disclosed were not of such nature as to be offensive to persons of ordinary sensibilities.

The Sidis case is fairly typical of the result reached in cases brought in this area of invasion of privacy. Although such cases are troublesome, only a handful of plaintiffs have met with success in the years since publication of Warren and Brandeis' article. The reason for this is that the courts recognize a very broad defense for public disclosure of private facts.

b. *The Newsworthiness Privilege*

The common law defense of newsworthiness protects the media in publishing truthful matters of public interest. By and large, the courts have deferred to the media in determining what is of public interest. The motto of the judiciary here might be, "If they publish it, it must be news." This approach has two major virtues, according to Professors Don R. Pember and Dwight L. Teeter, Jr. First, it provides a wide range of freedom of expression and second, it is easy to administer because the judge does not have to act as a social censor, determining what is news and what is not. Pember and Teeter, "Privacy and the Press Since Time, Inc. v. Hill," 50 Wash.L.Rev. 57, 77 (1974).

Given such deference, the media would be protected in the exercise of news judgment in publishing almost anything true about individuals that might interest the public. Under this privilege journalists may publish the content of public records, which almost by definition involve matters of public interest. There are limits to judicial tolerance, however, such as the publication without consent of a photograph showing the plaintiff emerging from a fun house with her dress blown above her waist by a jet of air, as in Daily Times Democrat v. Graham (1964); publication of the intimate details of a hospitalized woman's exotic and embarrassing disease together with a picture of her in her hospital bed taken without consent as in Barber v. Time, Inc. (1942); naming a minor father of an illegitimate child as in Hawkins v. Multimedia (1986); or naming a young man receiving treatment for substance abuse at a hospital, as in Carter v. Superior Court of San Diego County (2002).

Courts in Massachusetts did not at first grant a privilege for newsworthiness in Commonwealth v. Wiseman (1969). This case involved producer Frederick Wiseman's documentary film "Titicut Follies" about patients and conditions at the Bridgewater State Hospital for the criminally insane. The film showed identifiable patients naked, being force-fed, and involved in sexual activity. Although the court permitted mental health professionals to view the film, it upheld an injunction preventing the film's commercial distribution in order to protect the patients' privacy. In 1989 a judge permitted public exhibition of the film, provided that the inmates' faces were blurred, and in 1991 the same judge lifted the 1969 injunction completely, permitting public exhibition of the film provided that names and addresses of the individuals in the film remain confidential. "Follies Can Be Shown," National Law Journal, August 19, 1991 at 6. Aside from cases such as Barber and Wiseman, however, normal judicial deference to media news judgment explains the general lack of success of plaintiffs in this area.

For example, in Virgil v. Time, Inc. (1975), the Ninth Circuit drew a line between public and private information in a judgment for Sports Illustrated. The magazine had published an article reporting that body surfer Mike Virgil liked to put out burning cigarettes in his mouth, burn holes in his wrist with cigarettes, jump off billboards, dive headfirst down flights of stairs and eat live insects and spiders. The Ninth Circuit remanded the case to the district court, which accepted the defendant's argument that reporting Virgil's unusual diet was a legitimate journalistic attempt to explain his daring style of bodysurfing. Virgil v. Time, Inc.

The case of Oliver Sipple provides a second example of judicial deference to media news judgment. Sipple, an ex-Marine, saved the life of President Gerald Ford in 1975 by deflecting the shots of would-be assassin Sarah Jane Moore when he grabbed her arm as she fired. When the San Francisco Chronicle reported that Sipple was an active member of the gay community, his family broke off all communication with him. Sipple sued for invasion of privacy, but the court ultimately dismissed the case on the grounds that Sipple had marched for gay rights and was a leader whose activism had often been reported in the gay press. Therefore, such personal facts were "in the public domain." Sipple v. Chronicle Publishing Company (1984).

In certain circumstances, courts have held even the most intimate details of a person's sexual behavior to be newsworthy. For example, the U.S. Court of Appeals for the Fifth Circuit affirmed dismissal of a suit by a Roman Catholic priest following the broadcast of a videotape of the priest engaged in homosexual activity with two consenting young men. The Fifth Circuit found that the story was newsworthy because it involved the actions of a priest, his collection of child pornography, and the Catholic Church's response. Cinel v. Connick (1994).

Celebrity Pamela Anderson Lee filed a series of lawsuits challenging publication of videotapes of herself and former lover Brett Michaels making love. Although Lee and Michaels sued Penthouse and Hard Copy, the suit was dismissed because the entire videotape was available on the Internet, a fact that the court held to be newsworthy. Lee v. Penthouse International Ltd. (1997). After the videotape had been on the Internet for some time, Lee and Michaels finally won an injunction against further use of the videotape on copyright infringement grounds. Michaels v. Internet Entertainment Group, Inc. (1998). But see Mayhall v. Dennis Stuff, Inc. (2002) (Stuff magazine's publication of photograph of young woman with breasts exposed at rock concert held to be newsworthy; magazine found not liable because a rock concert is a public event).

The North Carolina Supreme Court has refused to recognize the tort of public disclosure of private facts; see Hall v. Post (1988); Miller v. Brooks (1996). In other states, until First Amendment protection is accorded the media in cases like Barber and Hawkins, journalists should approach the intimate and embarrassing facts of an individual's past or even present life with caution and exercise discretion in publishing such material. In this area good taste is the watchword.

Jounalists should be aware that courts will protect plaintiffs' privacy regarding medical records, as in Doe v. New York (1994). In Doe, an individual filed a complaint with the City Commission on Human Rights, charging that Delta Airlines had discriminated against him because he was HIV positive. The Commission arranged a conciliation agreement under which Delta re-hired the man, gave him back pay, seniority and monetary damages. Then, however, the Human Rights Commission issued a press release that, although not identifying the man by name, contained enough detail about him that his Delta colleagues learned that he was HIV positive. He sued the Human Rights Commission for disclosure of private facts, and the Court of Appeals for the Second Circuit ruled that his medical records did not automatically become public records when he filed his complaint. The Second Circuit remanded the case to the district court to determine whether the Commission's press release provided so much detail that it identified Doe.

More recently the widow of a man who died by accident sued for public disclosure of private facts after a newspaper quoted a county police officer as explaining the husband's death as "It looks like it was one of those autoerotic things." The U.S. Court of Appeals for the Tenth Circuit ruled in favor of the police officer, however, finding that the officer's unfortunate comment revealed no information about the widow's former marital relationship. Livsey v. Salt Lake County (2001).

c. Applicability of First Amendment Theory to Public Disclosure of Private Facts

The applicability of First Amendment protection to the invasion of privacy tort seems most compelling in the case of communications involving truthful matters of a private and embarrassing or harmful nature. Without broad constitutional protection here, courts can require the media under existing tort law to pay damages for truthfully informing the public about certain matters which individual plaintiffs consider private. As with false light, the potential threat of damages could have a chilling effect on journalists' enterprise in reporting news about individuals.

(1) Public Disclosure of Private Facts in Cases Involving Sexual Assault

The issue here is whether the First and Fourteenth Amendments mandate the recognition of truth as an absolute defense in invasion of privacy cases. The U.S. Supreme Court considered but did not decide this broad issue in Cox Broadcasting Corp. v. Cohn (1975). There, a clerk of the court gave an Atlanta television reporter the indictments against those accused of the gang-rape and murder of a 17–year–old girl. That day the reporter broadcast a news report naming the girl who was murdered. After the news broadcast, the victim's father brought a civil action for damages against the reporter and Cox Broadcasting, relying on a Georgia statute which made it a misdemeanor for the media to report the name of any woman who was raped.

The trial court entered summary judgment for the plaintiff father, who claimed that the broadcast had invaded his own privacy. When the case reached the U.S. Supreme Court, however, Cox Broadcasting sought a broad holding that plaintiffs cannot hold the press criminally or civilly liable for publishing information that is absolutely accurate, however damaging or embarrassing it may be to individual sensibilities. Cox Broadcasting lost its bid for a sweeping Constitutional privilege for the media, however. Although the Court reversed the trial court, it did so on much narrower grounds. The High Court refused to go beyond ruling that both the common law and the First and Fourteenth Amendments protected mass dissemination of truthful matters contained in public records open to public inspection, including indictments and other judicial papers.

In the decade following Cox Broadcasting, the Supreme Court decided three cases in which journalists had legally obtained and printed the names of juveniles and a judge in violation of court orders or state laws. These three cases taken together set the precedent for a second rape victim identification case that the Supreme Court decided. The three cases were Oklahoma Publishing Co. v. District Court (1977) (Court held that newspaper could publish name of 11 year-old murderer because it learned the boy's name legally); Smith v. Daily Mail Publishing Company (1979) (Court held that two newspapers could publish name of a 15 year-old murderer because his name was legally obtained);

and Landmark Communications, Inc. v. Virginia (1978) (Court permitted newspaper to publish name of a judge whose conduct was under investigation because information was lawfully obtained).

Following this "trilogy" of cases, another case involving state statutes barring publication of a rape victim's name reached the U.S. Supreme Court. This case began when a police officer posted a rape victim's name in the sheriff's press room, where a Florida Star reporter-trainee copied it verbatim. (The sheriff's department admitted they had erred by placing it in the press room.) Although it violated the newspaper's own policy against printing a rape victim's name, the identification got past the editor and the Florida Star published her name. She sued the Florida Star and the sheriff's department (which settled the claim for $2500) for violating a Florida statute similar to the Georgia statute in Cox Broadcasting Corp. v. Cohn (1975), making it a misdemeanor for anyone to publish names of sex offense victims. At trial, the victim testified that after the rapist learned her name from the Florida Star, he made numerous telephone calls to her mother, threatening to rape the victim again.

Although a jury awarded the victim $100,000 in damages, the U.S. Supreme Court reversed in a 6–3 ruling. The High Court relied on Cox, Oklahoma Publishing and Daily Mail, explaining that these cases taken together established that the news media nearly always have the right to publish legally obtained information. The Court explained: "Our holding today is limited.... We hold only that where a newspaper publishes truthful information which it has lawfully obtained, punishment may lawfully be imposed, if at all, only when narrowly tailored to a state interest of the highest order. . . ." The majority cited three reasons for their decision: 1) like the names of the minors in the Oklahoma Publishing and Daily Mail cases, the Florida Star had learned the name of the rape victim lawfully; 2) the Florida statute, § 794.03, swept too broadly because it imposed liability regardless of whether the newspaper intended to publish the name or did so by mistake; and 3) the statute was flawed because it applied only to instruments "of mass communication," but did not apply to a backyard gossip who might tell 50 people. Florida Star v. B.J.F. (1989).

Florida Star might be viewed as a narrow ruling based on a flawed Florida statute that imposed liability with the "broad sweep of a negligence per se standard," meaning that "liability follows automatically from publication." The statute was similar to the flawed statute in Smith v. Daily Mail, that had permitted broadcasters but not newspapers to report names of juvenile criminals. Furthermore, the Florida Star reporter had learned the rape victim's name lawfully from the sheriff's department. See also Star–Telegram Inc. v. Doe (1995) (Fort Worth Star–Telegram reported rape victim's age, address of the travel agency she owned, description of her 1984 black Jaguar and her home address but not her name; Texas Supreme Court dismissed her invasion of privacy suit on grounds that story was newsworthy).

The irony of Florida Star, however, is that the Court failed to address the key fact that the rapist was at large and would not have known the victim's identity if the Star had not published her name: by doing so, the Florida Star endangered her life. Similar situations arose in Tribune Publishing Co. v. Hyde and Times–Mirror Co. v. San Diego Superior Court, discussed below.

In the wake of Florida Star, a number of states passed constitutionally doubtful legislation that would prohibit and in some cases punish publication of sexual assault victims' names. See Dorman v. Aiken Communications (1990); Macon Telegraph Publishing Co. v. Tatum (1993). The effect of the Florida Star decision on "private facts" cases brought under the common law is not clear. Writing for the three dissenters, Justice Byron White complained that the ruling "obliterates" this branch of the privacy tort. If the First Amendment prohibits a private person from recovering for "the publication of the fact that she was raped, I doubt that there remain any 'private facts' which persons may assume will not be published in the newspapers or broadcast on television." Florida Star v. B.J.F. (1989).

Thus the effect of the Supreme Court's decisions in Cox Broadcasting Corp. and Florida Star is to leave uncertain the constitutionality of statutes in Alaska, Massachusetts, Michigan, New York, Pennsylvania and South Carolina insofar as they make punishable the identification of rape victims when such identification is not a matter of public record. The Georgia statute at issue in Cox Broadcasting was declared unconstitutional by the Georgia Supreme Court in Dye v. Wallace (2001). Similarly, the common law rules permitting recovery of damages for the publication of truthful but embarrassing or harmful private information are left in doubt.

In 1994, relying on Florida Star v. B.J.F., the Florida Supreme Court struck down as unconstitutional Florida's statute making it a misdemeanor to publish a rape victim's name. See Florida v. Globe Communications Corp. (1994) in which the state of Florida had criminally charged the tabloid The Globe under its rape shield statute when the tabloid printed Patricia Bowman's name after she said that Ted Kennedy's nephew William Kennedy Smith had raped her.

(2) Public Disclosure of Private Facts in Cases Involving Rehabilitated Ex–Convicts

At one time California courts did not accept the "newsworthiness" defense if the press was dredging up a crime that had occurred many years before and the person who had committed the crime had been rehabilitated. See Melvin v. Reid (1931) (former prostitute prevailed in suit against producers of movie "The Red Kimono"); Briscoe v. Reader's Digest Association (1971) (ex-convict prevailed in suit against Reader's Digest for reporting that he had hi-jacked a truck 11 years before).

A few years ago, however, Melvin and Briscoe were overruled in Gates v. Discovery Communications, Inc. (2004). Steve Gates had pled guilty in 1988 to being an accessory after the fact to a murder-for-hire masterminded by an automobile dealer; Gates served three years in prison. In 2001 the Discovery Channel produced a television series, "The Prosecutors," that re-enacted crimes, including the one involving Gates. Relying on Briscoe, Gates sued for public disclosure of private facts. In deciding Gates, the California Supreme Court turned to the Cox and the Oklahoma Publishing–Daily Mail–Landmark "trilogy" discussed above; the court then added Florida Star v. B.J.F. (1989) and Bartnicki v. Vopper (2001) to the trilogy, affirming that, barring a compelling state interest of the highest order, the news media have a First Amendment right to publish information that they obtain lawfully. Because Gates' 1988 guilty plea had been part of a public judicial proceeding that was never sealed, the news (or entertainment) media could not be penalized for publishing the information. The California Supreme Court thus overruled Briscoe.

(3) Negligent Infliction of Emotional Distress

Although Florida does not recognize the tort of negligent infliction of emotional distress (so that B.J.F. could not have sued the Florida Star under this theory), courts in other states have upheld plaintiffs' right to sue the media for negligent infliction of emotional distress when publication of their names put their lives in jeopardy. In Tribune Publishing Co. v. Hyde (1982), the police gave two local newspapers the name and address of a woman who had escaped from an unknown kidnapper while the assailant was still at large. The man began to terrorize the woman, whose name and address he had not known until the newspapers published them. The Missouri Court of Appeals concluded that the woman's name and address were not newsworthy compared with the high risk to the victim created by their publication. The case was eventually settled out of court when the woman accepted $6000 from the city and nothing from the newspapers.

A California court likewise held that a plaintiff could proceed on a claim for negligent infliction of emotional distress in Times Mirror Co. v. San Diego Superior Court (1988). In this case, a woman returned home just after her roommate had been raped and murdered. As she arrived, she saw the murderer leave. The Los Angeles Times printed her name and said she had discovered the body, but did not say that she had seen the fleeing murderer. She sued for publication of private facts and for negligent infliction of emotional distress, arguing that publishing her name while the murderer was at large endangered her life. Although the Los Angeles Times had taken her name from the coroner's report, which was a public record, the California appellate court ruled that she could proceed on a claim for negligent infliction of emotional distress.

The Los Angeles Times finally settled out of court, paying the woman an undisclosed sum of money.

The Supreme Court has never ruled on the theory of negligent infliction of emotional distress in a case such as Times–Mirror Co. v. San Diego Superior Court. The Court made it clear in Hustler Magazine, Inc. v. Falwell (1988) that plaintiffs cannot use intentional infliction of emotional distress to circumvent defamation law as established in New York Times v. Sullivan (1964). Can one substitute charges of negligent infliction of emotional distress for charges of public disclosure of private facts? If B.J.F. had tried to recover for emotional distress rather than publication of private facts in Florida Star, would she have succeeded? In Tribune Publishing Co. v. Hyde and Times–Mirror Co. v. San Diego Superior Court, courts refused to grant summary judgments for the defendant newspapers when they published the victims' names while the kidnapper and murderer were at large, just as B.J.F.'s name was published when the rapist was still at large. The facts of Florida Star bear enough similarity to Tribune Publishing and Times Mirror to raise the question of whether negligent infliction of emotional distress may circumvent the charge of publication of private facts, but it is a question unanswered thus far by the Supreme Court.

Eventually the Supreme Court will probably have to resolve the issue of whether or not the Constitution mandates truth to be a complete defense in these cases. In Florida Star the Court implied that truth might not be a complete defense if there is a state interest of the highest order; however, it did not elaborate on what might constitute such an interest.

It is worth noting that in contrast with the United States, Great Britain had never recognized a common law tort of invasion of privacy until 2001, when the Court of Appeal, in a case involving the right of publicity of Michael and Douglas and Catherine Zeta–Jones, held that the British Human Rights Act of 1998, Chapter 42, S 8, incorporated the right to privacy in Article 8 of the Convention for the Protection of Human Rights and Fundamental Freedoms of the Council of Europe. Douglas v. Hello! Ltd. (2001). In the United States, some legal scholars argue that the tort of public disclosure of private facts creates too great a burden on the news media. Along with false light, these scholars argue that courts should reject this tort in the twenty-first century.

5. Common Characteristics of the Four Types of Invasion of Privacy

Although it is useful to an understanding of the tort of invasion of privacy to recognize the existence of its four branches, we should also recognize that these branches often overlap in certain cases. For instance, the same act of appropriating a woman's name and photograph for an advertisement endorsing a brand of whiskey may also place her in a false light as a serious drinker of alcoholic beverages. An act of intrusion such as in the Dietemann case may be followed by public disclosure of private facts about the person who suffered the intrusion.

Whatever the invasion, the damages recoverable to the plaintiff are the same: (1) general damages; (2) special out-of-pocket damages, though in contrast to slander or libel per quod they are not required; and (3) punitive damages, upon a showing of malice in the form of ill will, spite or improper motive.

Finally, there are certain defenses common to all four branches. The most obvious is consent. If the plaintiff has consented to the alleged invasion, the defendant's conduct is not actionable. Rarely in these cases will the plaintiff's alleged consent be express and unequivocal. With this defense the question for the trier of fact is normally whether the plaintiff's words or deeds implied consent to the defendant's appropriation, intrusion, false characterization or publication of private information.

The other common defense is that of privilege. The privileges recognized in the law of defamation may often apply in the law of privacy. If the circumstances would protect the publication of false and defamatory material, then the publication of truthful material may also be protected.

D. LEGISLATION DESIGNED TO PROTECT PERSONAL PRIVACY

1. Privacy Act of 1974

In addition to the Federal Wiretap Statute and FCC Phone Rule discussed above, the other important federal legislation in this field is the "Privacy Act of 1974," 5 U.S.C.A. § 552a. Because the purpose of this legislation is to curb abuses by the federal government in the handling and dissemination of information about individuals, it is discussed in the chapter on newsgathering and access to information by the media. See Chapter VII, pp. 324–328, infra.

2. Driver's Privacy Protection Act

With the intention of stopping stalkers like the one who killed actress Rebecca Schaeffer in 1989 or those who broke into David Letterman's farmhouse and rock singer Madonna's English estate, Congress attempted to protect individual privacy by passing the Driver's Privacy Protection Act (DPPA), part of the Violent Crime Control and Law Enforcement Act of 1994. Pub. L. 103–322, § 300002, 108 Stat. 2099–2102 (1994), *codified at* 18 U.S.C.A. § 2721–2725 (West Supp. 1997). The act bars state motor vehicle departments from disclosing to the press and public any personal information about individuals contained in their driver's license records, including pictures, names, addresses, phone numbers and social security numbers if the licensees opt out of disclosure.

Many state motor vehicle departments objected, however, knowing the DPPA would cause a precipitous drop in income from sales of address lists to direct marketers. The Wisconsin Department of Transportation received about $8 million per year from selling such address lists. When South Carolina Attorney General Charlie Condon sued, charging that the DPPA was unconstitutional, the Court of Appeals for the Fourth Circuit agreed, and struck down the DPPA. It held that the law violated the Tenth and Eleventh Amendments to the U.S. Constitution because it forced state officials to perform federal tasks, specifically, the protection of personal privacy. Such an action would exceed Congress' authority under the Commerce Clause and would encroach on state sovereignty. Furthermore, it could not pass Fourteenth Amendment scrutiny because the information covered is not considered confidential; rather, motor vehicle registration information is a public record. Condon v. Reno (1998). The U.S. Supreme Court quickly reversed Condon, however, when it held inter alia that the DPPA did not violate the reserved powers of the states provided in the Tenth Amendment. Rather, the DPPA merely regulates the states as owners of databases in interstate commerce, and it directs the states not to sell the information.

In the meantime Congress amended the DPPA to change the "opt-out" alternative to an "opt-in" requirement so that states must obtain drivers' affirmative consent to disclose their personal information for use in marketing solicitations. Pub. L.

106–69, 113 Stat. 986 §§ 350(c), (d), and (e), Oct. 9, 1999. This law also made adherence to the DPPA by the states a condition of receiving federal highway money.

3. Family Educational Rights and Privacy Act

Another privacy statute that bars media access to information is the Family Educational Rights and Privacy Act (FERPA) of 1974, commonly known as the "Buckley Amendment." 20 U.S.C.A. § 1232g as amended (West 1990 and Supp. Pam. 1996). FERPA bars release of student educational records without written consent of the parents, or of the students themselves if they are 18 or older, by educational institutions that receive funds from the federal government. If a school system or university releases a student's records without permission, it may be denied federal funds. Unfortunately, some university administrators have tried to use this provision to deny reporters access to campus police records in an effort to kill news stories about crime on campus. The administrators argued that crime reports naming students as victims, suspects or even witnesses were educational records and thus inaccessible under FERPA. The courts have rejected this interpretation of FERPA, however. Student Press Law Center v. Alexander (1991).

Also in response to the problem, former President Bill Clinton signed the Omnibus Higher Education Amendments into law in 1998. The amendments include measures that prohibit schools from using secret campus tribunals to hide criminal behavior from the press. The amendments establish that universities can no longer use FERPA to justify closing off information about campus disciplinary proceedings involving violent crimes or sex offenses. The amendments require the use of uniform crime reporting procedures so that students and their families can compare crime rates at different institutions as a factor in choosing which college to attend. See Doe v. Board of Regents of the University System of Georgia (1994). The amendments also contain a "sense of the Congress" provision that First Amendment protections should be extended to students at private schools, but this provision has no force in law and no enforcement mechanism.

University of Maryland administrators invoked FERPA to deny access to student athlete Duane Simpkins' record of $8000 in fines from 200 unpaid parking tickets. When the campus newspaper challenged the denial, the Maryland Court of Special Appeals held that campus administrators had to release Simpkins' records to the campus newspaper. Kirwan v. The Diamondback (1998).

Both Miami University of Ohio and The Ohio State University released students' disciplinary records to the Chronicle of Higher Education following an Ohio Supreme Court decision that FERPA did not cover disciplinary records. (Ohio ex rel. The Miami Student v. Miami University (1997). The U.S. Department of Justice sued both universities seeking to prevent future release of student disciplinary records. In a ruling diametrically opposed to that of the Ohio Supreme Court, the U.S. Court of Appeals for the Sixth Circuit ruled that universities would violate FERPA if they released students' disciplinary records. United States v. Miami University, Ohio (2002).

Recently education major Ru Paster, a student at Gonzaga University in Spokane, Washington, attempted to sue Gonzaga under FERPA when university administrators warned a state teacher certification agency about sexual misconduct allegations made against Paster. The U.S. Supreme Court ruled that FERPA does not permit students a private cause of action if their schools release personal information about them. Gonzaga University v. Doe (2002). The High Court's ruling in Gonzaga could help journalists obtain campus crime reports and records by alleviating universities' concerns about being sued for violating FERPA.

CHAPTER IV

RESTRAINT OF OBSCENE EXPRESSION

A. GENERAL THEORY

1. The Definitional Problem

Western societies generally seem to have a pre-occupation with suppression of explicit public discussion or depiction of sexual matters. English speaking societies are no exception. Censorship and confiscation of sexually obscene materials and even prison sentences may be the lot of the professional or amateur pornographer. There are those in positions of authority who would characterize all public expression concerning sex as obscene and punish it, but the prevailing view in this country is to the contrary; clearly not all sexual expression is condemned.

This view has within it the seeds of confusion because it requires a definition of what is obscene. Because obscenity, like beauty, is in the eye of the beholder, a precise definition seems beyond the reach of the law. Even the 1986 report of the United States Attorney General's commission on pornography fails to define it. It may be that the only honest test for obscenity is the one authored by the late Supreme Court Justice Potter Stewart:

"I know it when I see it." Jacobellis v. Ohio (1964). Because the First Amendment requires more than intuitive reaction to suppress and punish obscene expression, the Supreme Court has spent the last forty years attempting to separate the chaff of obscenity from the wheat of protected sexual expression.

2. Background

Attempts at suppressing obscenity were sporadic in both England and the United States until shortly after the end of the American Civil War. At that time the English judiciary crystallized a standard for suppression which was by and large accepted in the United States. Contemporaneously, Congress enacted certain statutes advocated by the notorious bluenose Anthony Comstock prohibiting, with criminal penalties, the importation or mailing of materials characterized as obscene (now 18 U.S. Code, Sections 1461–1463). Many of the states followed suit with their own criminal obscenity statutes.

The standard set down in the English case of Regina v. Hicklin (1868) was a very broad one: suspect material was to be judged by the effect of isolated passages upon persons particularly susceptible to prurient appeals or lustful thoughts. The combination of the Comstock laws and the Hicklin test provided much work for the censors and the prosecutors. Occasionally, lower federal courts inveighed against the Hicklin test but it remained influential well into the twentieth century.

3. Modern Doctrinal Development

Until 1957 the Supreme Court, while assuming the constitutionality of attempts to suppress obscene expression in Near v. Minnesota (1931), had never definitively held that obscenity was beyond the pale of First and Fourteenth Amendment protection. In Roth v. United States (1957) the Court so ruled, over the strong dissent of Justices Black and Douglas. The Court then considered the appropriate standard for separating protected expression from unprotected obscene expression. The Court affirmed Roth's conviction for sending obscene matter through the mails. The Court rejected the Hicklin standard, however. The Court explained that the Hicklin standard was so concerned with isolated passages and "susceptible individuals" that it would condemn much material covering sexual matters in a serious manner that ought to be protected by the First and Fourteenth Amendments. In its place the Court adopted the test whether to the *average* person, applying contemporary community standards, the dominant theme of the material taken as a *whole* appealed to a prurient interest in sex, and the material is utterly without redeeming social value.

Although the Roth test for obscenity is clearly narrower than the Hicklin test, Roth still permits censorship and criminal punishment for merely inciting impure sexual thoughts even if unrelated to antisocial conduct. In the years since Roth, shifting majorities and pluralities of the Court have shown dissatisfaction with the Roth test because of the uncertainty in (1) gauging the psychological effect of specific material on hypothetical "average" persons; (2) measuring the dominance of obscene themes in large unified works such as books, motion pictures or magazines; (3) determining the relevant community standards to be referred to, such as local, state or national; and (4) protecting against the danger of condemnation of serious expression.

In the celebrated case of the 1749 novel "Fanny Hill," involving the A Book Named "John Cleland's Memoirs of a Woman of Pleasure" v. Attorney General of Commonwealth of Massachusetts (1966), a plurality of the Court announced a basic three-fold formulation to isolate obscenity: (1) a restatement of the Roth standard; (2) a test that the material be patently offensive because it affronts contemporary community standards relating to sexual matters; and (3) a test that the material be *utterly* without redeeming social value. Because the tests were stated in the conjunctive, a censor or prosecutor was required to establish that the expression in question met all three tests. This is extremely difficult to do.

The question inevitably arises in a free society whether almost unrestricted publication, distribution and exhibition of obscenity is too high a price to pay for the protection of serious expression concerning sex. This is a political question as well as a legal one. A year after the "Fanny Hill" case, the justices of the U.S. Supreme Court found themselves reversing convictions for obscenity in cases in which defendants in New York, Kentucky and Arkansas had been convicted for purchasing books or magazines with titles such as High Heels, Spree, Gent or Swank. The justices did not hear oral arguments or provide written opinions; instead, whenever five justices, using their own tests for obscenity, concluded that the material was not obscene, they reversed the convictions. Redrup v. New York (1967).

4. The Last Word on Obscenity: Miller v. California

Finally, in Miller v. California (1973) and Paris Adult Theatre I v. Slaton (1973), the U.S. Supreme Court laid down new and tougher legal standards for dealing with the problem of obscenity. In Paris Adult Theatre I the High Court made it clear that individual states had the right to regulate access even by "consenting adults" to "hardcore" pornography in movie theaters. The following term the High Court elaborated on these rulings in Jenkins v. Georgia (1974). For a fuller understanding of the Court's new position these three decisions are considered together.

In Miller, the petitioner had been convicted of mailing unsolicited sexually explicit material to persons in Orange County, California in violation of a California statute that approximately incorporated the tests for obscenity formulated in the Fanny Hill decision. The trial judge gave these tests to the jury and instructed them to evaluate the materials in light of the contemporary community standards of the state of California. The Supreme Court majority affirmed Miller's conviction and did the following:

1. reaffirmed the holding in Roth that obscenity is not protected by the First and Fourteenth Amendments;

2. rejected important aspects of the tests set out in "Fanny Hill," especially the "utterly without redeeming social value" standard, and substituted its own conjunctive three-fold test to guide the trier of fact (normally the jury):

(a) whether the average person, applying contemporary community standards, would find the material taken as a whole, appeals to prurient interest (a restatement of the Roth test);

(b) whether the work depicts or describes, in a patently offensive way, sexual conduct specifically defined by the applicable state law; and

(c) whether the work, taken as a whole, lacks serious literary, artistic, political or scientific value;

3. indicated that only "hardcore" pornography might be condemned under these tests and included in that classification for the guidance of legislative draftspersons patently offensive representations or descriptions of ultimate sexual acts, normal or perverted, actual or simulated and patently offensive representations or descriptions of masturbation, excretory functions and lewd exhibition of the genitals; and

4. held that hardcore pornography is to be determined by reference to local or state community standards and not national standards.

In the companion case of Paris Adult Theatre, decided the same day, the Court upheld the right of states to enjoin the exhibition of hardcore pornography in movie theaters under the Miller standards, even when the exhibitor makes every effort to limit the audience to consenting adults. In so ruling, the majority recognized that the states, and, by necessary extension, the United States, have a legitimate interest in shielding not only minors but consenting adults as well from obscene material. This legitimate interest encompasses the elevation of the quality of life and the environment in the community, the tone of commerce in the cities and, arguably, the public safety itself. In this connection the majority refused to extend an individual's right of privacy in personal heterosexual intimacies of the home, as upheld in Griswold v. Connecticut (1965), to the viewing of pornography in an adult movie theater. The Court thus avoided the need to balance the state's recognized interest in preventing the exhibition of pornographic films against any individual privacy interest in viewing them.

In Miller, the Chief Justice said all he could to prevent local suppression of serious expressions concerning sex. This did not stop the State of Georgia from convicting Billy Jenkins, the manager of a movie theater in Albany, Georgia for exhibiting the film "Carnal Knowledge," produced by a recognized group of serious movie makers, including director Mike Nichols and actor Jack Nicholson. A divided Georgia Supreme Court had affirmed Jenkins' conviction.

The U.S. Supreme Court, in holding "Carnal Knowledge" not obscene and reversing the conviction, was forced to confront the paradox of differing community standards delimiting the protection afforded by a national constitution. The Court first made clear its commitment to local community standards though indicating its willingness to accept statewide community standards if the states should decide to use them instead.

The Court then turned to the state's contention that the conviction should be affirmed under Miller pursuant to local community standards. In other words, the state of Georgia was arguing that appellate review of the constitutionality of the conviction was precluded so long as the jury was properly instructed pursuant to the three-fold test laid down in Miller. Here the High Court simply held that the scope of protection afforded by the First and Fourteenth Amendments was ultimately for it to decide and substituted its own judgment regarding the nature of the film for that of the local Georgia jury. Jenkins v. Georgia (1974).

The paradox remained troublesome. In Pope v. Illinois (1987), the Court acknowledged that the third prong of the three-fold test of Miller v. California had to be governed by a national standard if the First Amendment were to be complied with. The Illinois state trial courts had instructed the respective juries that in determining whether certain "obscene" magazines, taken as a whole, lacked serious literary, artistic, political or scientific value (the third prong of Miller), the juries were to judge the materials by the standard of "ordinary adults in the whole state." The defendants were convicted and their convictions were upheld on appeal.

The U.S. Supreme Court vacated the convictions and remanded the cases for further proceedings. It ruled that although the first two prongs of Miller should be decided with reference to contemporary community standards, the third or "value" prong is to be judged by whether a reasonable person would or would not find such value in the materials, taken as a whole. The Court reasoned that "just as the ideas a work represents need not obtain majority approval to merit protection, neither, insofar as the First Amendment is concerned, does the value of the work vary from community to community based on the degree of local acceptance it has won." The jury instructions therefore violated the First and Fourteenth Amendments.

In retrospect, it appears that the Court, in a very indirect way, was suggesting in Jenkins v. Georgia (1974) the solution to the national standard-community standard paradox which it finally articulated clearly in Pope.

5. Effects of Miller, Paris Adult Theatre and Jenkins

The effect of Miller and Paris Adult Theatre was to make it easier for prosecutors to win convictions for obscenity. One reason for this was that Miller in effect reversed the "Fanny Hill" Memoirs requirement that prosecutors had to demonstrate that pornographic material was *"utterly"* without redeeming social value; under Miller, prosecutors no longer had to prove this negative. Miller thus affirmed that individual states can regulate obscene material based on "contemporary community standards" as opposed to "national standards." The most important effect of Miller, Paris Adult Theatre and Jenkins was to encourage prosecutors and censors to renew the fight against obscenity. In Atlanta, Georgia, for instance, one zealous prosecutor closed down all of the "adult" movie houses.

Moreover, the Court in Paris Adult Theatre relaxed the evidentiary burden on public officials charged with suppressing obscene expression. The material is now allowed to speak for itself and expert testimony as to its obscene nature is not required. In addition, proof that the material is utterly devoid of redeeming social value is no longer necessary. Now the prosecutor need only show that it is patently offensive and lacks serious literary, artistic, political or scientific value.

Conversely, the burden on the defendant to rebut the claim of obscenity is increased because evidence that the material in question is acceptable by national standards is relevant only to the "value" prong of the three-fold Miller test. As to the first two aspects of the test, the defendant must make out his or her case with expert testimony that it is acceptable locally or, as in Miller, statewide. The sanctioning of local standards also encourages the anti-obscenity forces to shop for the most unsophisticated and intolerant localities within which to seek criminal or civil suppression of material. Of course, the Supreme Court, as it demonstrated in Jenkins and Pope, stands ready to correct the worst abuses arising out of the application of local standards.

The other test in Miller that could have the effect of narrowing the area of unprotected expression is that of patent offensiveness. The Court gave some reasonably explicit examples of what it meant by "hardcore" pornography such as "patently offensive" descriptions of ultimate sexual acts, normal or perverted and "patently offensive" descriptions of masturbation, excretory functions and lewd exhibition of the genitals, as described above. The term "patently offensive" is not well defined, however, and could extend beyond "hardcore" pornography in some local communities.

The Paris Adult Theatre decision has the effect of limiting the area of the consenting adult's constitutional right of privacy to view pornographic material to one's own home. It seems clear that the majority did this to insure the primacy of the state's interest in maintaining and elevating the quality of life and environment particularly in the large urban centers where commercial pornography often flourishes.

6. Difficulties With the New Approach

The Court's new approach perpetuates certain myths regarding control of obscenity. The majority asserted that beyond "knowing it when they see it," as Justice Potter Stewart had said in Jacobellis v.

Ohio (1964), they could define obscenity with sufficient precision to give fair advance warning as to what is forbidden. But clearly the "serious value" test is highly subjective and in the final analysis only a majority of five justices can say, after the fact of publication, what is serious expression and what is not. Even the patent offensiveness-hardcore pornography test will allow for subjectivity unless state legislatures are willing to define in obscene detail the sexual conduct to be suppressed. So far there has been no great trend in that direction.

The other major myth is that obscenity can be constitutionally controlled at the local level using local standards. As the Court was forced to admit in Jenkins and Pope, however, First and Fourteenth Amendment rights and protections are uniform throughout the country. Try as it might, the Supreme Court cannot escape the need to impose national standards and, in the end, to act as a national censorship board.

7. Variable Obscenity Standards

The Supreme Court has developed certain other standards to permit punishment of expression that does not meet the basic obscenity test directed to the average adult set out in Miller. These supplemental tests are designed to prevent pandering of borderline material as the real thing, to suppress expression targeting sexually deviant adults, to shield minors from "adult" materials such as "girlie" magazines, and to protect minors from exploitation and abuse in the production of sexually explicit material. The most important of these supplemental standards are those protective of minor children.

In Ginzburg v. United States (1966), the defendant publisher of a purported sexual autobiography, a hard-cover sex magazine and a sex newsletter, was convicted of sending obscene matter through the mail. The Supreme Court affirmed his conviction for violation of Title 18, Section 1461 of the United States Code because of his open advertising representations that the materials would appeal to the recipient's prurient interest. A majority of the Court ruled that where the purveyor's sole emphasis is on the sexually provocative aspects of his or her publications, that fact may be decisive in determining whether the material is obscene. In other words, in a close case, those who pander material as obscene will be taken at their word.

Because audiences vary as to age and sexual preferences, the Court has also held that the standards for suppression may also vary as to these audiences. In Mishkin v. State of New York (1966), a publisher of sex books for sadists, masochists, fetishists and homosexuals argued that his materials were not obscene because they would not appeal to the prurient interest of average persons but rather would disgust and sicken them. The Court upheld his conviction, however, explaining that where material is designed for a clearly defined deviant group, the prurient appeal test of Roth is satisfied if the dominant theme of the material taken as a whole appeals to the prurient interest in sex of members of that group. In Ginsberg v. State of New York (1968) the defendant was convicted of violating a New York penal statute which prohibited the knowing sale to minors under the age of 17 of any picture which depicts nudity. Ginsberg sold two "girlie" magazines to a sixteen-year-old male. While conceding that the magazines were not obscene for adults, the Court affirmed Ginsberg's conviction, explaining that obscenity varies with the age of the audience and that the state has the constitutional power to restrict minors' access to sex materials. Because of this distinction between minors and adults regarding access to pornography, the High Court has ruled that states may adopt laws known as "variable obscenity" statutes, provided that these laws do not interfere with adults' access to explicit material.

8.   Child Pornography

Whereas the variable obscenity standard focuses on who receives pornographic material, child pornography laws focus on who is pictured in the production of obscene material. In New York v. Ferber (1982), the so-called "kiddie porn" case, the Court held that states may apply more relaxed standards than those in Miller v. California, supra, to obtain criminal convictions in order to protect minors from exploitation and abuse in the production of sexual materials.

To combat the rising tide of sexual exploitation and abuse of minors exemplified by cases such as Ferber, Congress enacted the "Protection of Children Against Sexual Exploitation Act of 1977," P.L.

95–225, 18 U.S.C.A. §§ 2251–2253. This legislation imposed severe fines and penalties upon those convicted of encouraging or coercing minors to engage in sexually explicit conduct for still, motion picture or video cameras. It also made it a federal crime to produce or distribute pornographic materials involving minors, regardless of whether the producer or distributor knows that a performer is under 18.

Congress has substantially strengthened the anti-child pornography law through amendments passed in 1984 (P.L. 98–292, 98 Stat. 204 (1984), codified at 18 U.S.C.A. §§ 2251–2255 (Supp. 1989)), 1986 (P.L. 99–628, 100 Stat. 3510 (1986), codified at 18 U.S.C.A. §§ 2251(c), 2256(5) (Supp. 1989)) and 1988 (P.L. 100–690, 102 Stat. 4485 (1988), codified at 18 U.S.C.A. §§ 2251(c), 2251A, 2252(a), 2257 (Supp. 1989)). The net effect of these amendments has been to increase the number of child pornography convictions.

After the Supreme Court's decision in New York v. Ferber (1982), many child pornography laws were amended to outlaw possession of child pornography in addition to barring its production and distribution. One of these laws was tested in Osborne v. Ohio (1990). In a 6–3 ruling the Supreme Court upheld the constitutionality of an Ohio law that permitted prosecution of anyone possessing sexually explicit materials involving children. (The Ohio law contained an exemption allowing parents to possess nude photographs of their own children).

Congress further attempted to prevent pornographic film producers and photographers from using minors with the 1988 Child Protection and Obscenity Enforcement Act, as amended by the 1990 Child Protection Restoration and Penalties Enhancement Act. This legislation imposes record keeping requirements so that pornographic film producers or photographers must "create and maintain individually identifiable records pertaining to every performer portrayed." 18 U.S.C.A. § 2257(a) (West Supp. 1995).

What if a minor provides false documents, and later it turns out that she was under age when acting in a pornographic film? There have been various legal battles over that question with regard to actress Traci Lords, who used false documents to misrepresent her age when making 49 pornographic videos before she turned 18. Police arrested Rubin Gottesman, owner of X–Citement Video, Inc., for distributing child pornography after he sold them two Traci Lords videos. Evidence at trial indicated that Gottesman had full awareness that Lords was underage when she had acted in the videos. Gottesman argued, however, that the Protection of Children Against Sexual Exploitation Act of 1977 was unconstitutional because it did not include a scienter requirement (meaning knowledge that an actor was under 18 when the pornographic film was produced). 18 U.S.C. §§ 2252(a)(1) and (2) (1988 ed. and Supp. V). Although the Court of Appeals for the Ninth Circuit ruled in Gottesman's favor, the Supreme Court reversed, holding that § 2252 did contain a scienter requirement which included knowledge that a performer was a minor. In other words, if a retailer 1) knows that the video he is shipping contains sexually explicit material and 2) knows that at least one actor was under 18 when it was produced, the retailer is subject to prosecution. U.S. v. X–Citement Video Inc. (1994).

In 1996 Congress attempted to strengthen laws against child pornography so that film producers could no longer claim that a minor deceived them about her age as Traci Lords had. Congress passed the Child Pornography Prevention Act (CPPA) of 1996, which barred not only the use of minors in sexually explicit roles but also barred the production of any images that "appear to depict a minor engaged in sexually explicit conduct." Child pornography is thus defined to include not only actual photos, videotapes or films of children but also computer-generated or "virtual" child pornography created by a process called "morphing." In other words, one would see an image of a child engaged in sex without the need for a photographer to have taken a picture of a real child. The law outlawed possession in addition to production and distribution of such images. See State of Florida v. Cohen (1997). Senator Orrin Hatch, the primary sponsor of this law, explained that computer-generated images are virtually impossible to distinguish from photographs. He further explained that the law is designed to protect children from pedophiles and child molesters, whose criminal behavior may be instigated by such images.

Following constitutional challenges to the Child Pornography Prevention Act (CPPA) of 1996, the U.S. Courts of Appeal for the First, Fourth, Fifth and Eleventh Circuits upheld the CPPA as constitutional. See U.S. v. Hilton (1999), U.S. v. Mento (2000), U.S. v. Fox (2001) and U.S. v. Acheson (1999). In these four cases the U.S. Courts of Appeal held that the CPPA advanced the compelling government interest of preventing child pornography because "virtual" or apparent child pornography is as dangerous as actual images of children in sexually explicit situations. In contrast, in Free Speech Coalition v. Reno (1999), the U.S. Court of Appeals for the Ninth Circuit held that CPPA's statutory language forbidding a "visual depiction that ... appears to be of a minor engaging in sexually explicit conduct" was so vague as to raise constitutional questions. The Ninth Circuit held that "any victimization of children that may arise from pedophiles' sexual responses to pornography apparently depicting children in explicit sexual activity is not a sufficiently compelling justification for CPPA's speech restrictions." With conflicting decisions among five U.S. Courts of Appeal, the Supreme Court agreed to rule on the CPPA's constitutionality. In Ashcroft v. Free Speech Coalition (2002), the U.S. Supreme Court agreed with the Ninth Circuit. Justice Anthony Kennedy wrote that the CPPA was unconstitutional because it "prohibits the visual depiction of an idea—that of teenagers engaging in sexual activity—that is a fact of modern society and has been a theme in art and literature throughout the ages." Thus, the U.S. Supreme Court permitted the use of computer-generated (morphed) images of children having sex provided that no real children were involved.

Congress has also attempted to shield minors from exposure to pornography on the Internet. Congress passed the Communications Decency Act (CDA) of 1996, which the U.S. Supreme Court struck down as unconstitutional in Reno v. American Civil Liberties Union (1997). Congress then passed the Child Online Protection Act (COPA) in 1998, which the U.S. Supreme Court enjoined from enforcement in Ashcroft v. American Civil Liberties Union (2004). Finally Congress passed the Children's Internet Protection Act (CIPA) in 2001. CIPA provides that public libraries must block Internet access to pornographic material considered "harmful to minors" on library computer terminals, and despite a challenge from the American Library Association, the U.S. Supreme Court upheld CIPA as constitutional. United States v. American Library Association (2003). See Chapter XII for further discussion of the CDA, COPA and CIPA.

a. Recent Cases Involving Child Pornography

In 1997 an Oklahoma judge ruled that the 1979 Academy Award winning German film, "The Tin Drum," based on the novel by Gunter Grass, constituted child pornography and was obscene under Oklahoma law because it portrays a young boy having oral sex with a teenage girl. The movie and novel focus on the trauma that the boy suffers in

Nazi Germany during World War II. An anti-pornography organization, Oklahomans for Children and Families, notified police that the R-rated film was in the local public library, several video rental stores, and a few private homes. Despite the fact that no hearing was held, no written order was issued, and there was some doubt about whether the judge who ruled the film obscene had even watched any part of "The Tin Drum," police nonetheless confiscated nine copies of the film. Video Software Dealers Association v. Oklahoma City (1997).

A federal district court intervened, however, and enjoined city officials from withholding the film until an adversarial hearing was held. Ultimately the same court ruled that "The Tin Drum" did not have a dominant sexual theme, had undisputed artistic merit, and therefore did not violate the Oklahoma child pornography statute. Oklahoma ex rel Macy v. Blockbuster Videos, Inc. (1998). In 1999 Gunter Grass won the Nobel Prize for Literature for The Tin Drum and other works.

In 1998 journalist Larry Matthews, a critically acclaimed reporter who has won national awards for his work, sent and received child pornography from his home computer. He claimed to be working on a free-lance article on traffickers in child pornography. The FBI arrested him, and the federal district court judge refused to permit Matthews to assert a First Amendment defense at trial. The judge sentenced Matthews to 18 months in jail. Although Matthews appealed, his conviction was upheld. This case no doubt puts journalists on notice that if they want to research the problem of child pornography, they need to obtain the FBI's permission to do so. U.S. v. Matthews (2000).

9. Feminist Proposals for Statutory Civil Actions to Counter Pornographic Depictions of Women

Two decades ago feminists became concerned that pornography may serve as a "catalyst" to incite real-life violence against women. Social scientists have also gathered evidence that pornography has either incited or legitimized violence against women in real life. There is also a growing body of laboratory and field research supporting the theory that pornography instigates or legitimizes real-life violence against women. Citing such studies, the Attorney General's Commission on Pornography: Final Report, July 1986 (U.S. GPO 0–158–315) concluded that "the available evidence strongly supports the hypothesis that substantial exposure to sexually violent materials ... bears a causal relationship to antisocial acts of sexual violence and, for some subgroups, possibly to unlawful acts of sexual violence" (p. 326). The Commission cited research suggesting that male subjects are more likely to accept "the legitimacy of sexual violence against women" when women are portrayed as enjoying rape or other abuse, a theme that pervades pornography.

One of the Commission's formal recommendations was that "[l]egislatures should conduct hearings and consider legislation recognizing a civil remedy for harm attributable to pornography." This recommendation was a direct reflection of a model anti-pornography ordinance drafted by feminists Andrea Dworkin and Catherine MacKinnon, citing pornography as a violation of women's civil rights. The legislation based on this model ordinance was introduced in several communities, including Los Angeles, Minneapolis, Indianapolis and Cambridge, Massachusetts. The legislation was actually enacted and briefly became law in Indianapolis, but was struck down as unconstitutional, as is discussed below. The legislation had identified pornography as a form of discrimination on the basis of sex. It defined pornography as the "graphic sexually explicit subordination of women." This meant, for example, women "presented as sexual objects enjoying rape, pain or humiliation, being penetrated by objects or animals, ... or in scenarios of degradation or torture in a context that makes these conditions sexual" (Indianapolis–Marion County, Ind., Ordinance 35, ch. 16 (1984). Civil claims for damages would have been created for 1) coercion into pornography, 2) forcing pornography on a person, 3) assault incited by specific pornography, and 4) trafficking in pornography, such as production, sale, exhibition or distribution (Indianapolis–Marion County, Ind., Ordinance 35, § 16–3(g)(4)–(7), (1984)).

The Commission supported this because "the civil rights approach, although controversial, is the only legal tool suggested ... which is specifically designed to provide direct relief to the victims of the injuries so exhaustively documented in our hearings throughout the country" (Report p. 749). The legislation was actually enacted in Minneapolis and Indianapolis. In Minneapolis the Mayor vetoed the ordinance. In Indianapolis its constitutionality was challenged in American Booksellers Association v. Hudnut (1985). The Seventh Circuit accepted the premise of the legislation, agreeing that "depictions of [female] subordination tend to perpetuate [it]." The Seventh Circuit furthermore acknowledged that the "subordinate status of women in turn leads to affront and lower pay at work, insult and injury at home, battery and rape on the streets." The Seventh Circuit nonetheless upheld the district court decision overturning the ordinance because it was "vague and overbroad" and established "a prior restraint of speech." The appeals court pointed out that the definition "graphic sexually explicit subordination of women ..." did not refer to prurient interests, to offensiveness, or to the standards of the community required by Miller v. California (1973). The U.S. Supreme Court summarily affirmed the Seventh Circuit decision in Hudnut v. American Booksellers Association, Inc. (1986). In 1992 Catherine MacKinnon succeeded in persuading the Canadian Supreme Court to ban pornographic material harmful to women. R. v. Butler (Supreme Court of Canada, File No. 22191, filed June 6, 1992). In the United States, however, MacKinnon and other proponents of the anti-pornography ordinances will have to find a definition of pornography that courts will view as "constitutional" before their proposed legislation is adopted as law.

B.   IMPORTANT SPECIAL AREAS OF RESTRAINT OF SEXUAL EXPRESSION

1.   Mail and Customs Censorship

Until recent times the United States Post Office Department carried on a largely futile campaign of administrative censorship of the mails in addition to referring certain cases to the Justice Department for criminal prosecution. Unsuccessful administrative devices have included removal of material from the mail, revocation of the publishers' second class mailing privilege and refusal to deliver mail to alleged commercial pornographers.

Recently a more indirect approach to the problem of obscenity in the mail has proved both workable and less threatening to First Amendment interests. Individual addressees who have received "pandering advertisements" that offer for sale matter that the addressee believes to be erotically arousing or sexually provocative may ask the Postmaster General to issue an order directing the sender to refrain from further mailings to the named addressee. Section 3008, Title 39, U.S. Code. If the pornographer violates the order, the Postmaster General may request that the Attorney General seek a federal court order directing compliance with the Postmaster's order. Violation of the court order will, of course, subject the sender to sanctions for contempt of court. The U.S. Supreme Court upheld the constitutionality of this statute in Rowan v. United States Post Office Department (1970). A postal inspector may not actively solicit orders from a consumer of pornography if the inspector's real intent is to entrap the consumer, however. Jacobsen v. United States (1992).

Customs censorship through seizure and confiscation of incoming materials has had a long history and continues to the present within obscenity standards laid down in Roth and Miller, supra, and pursuant to procedural safeguards required by Freedman v. Maryland, supra.

2. Motion Pictures, Adult Businesses, and Zoning

Police still sometimes seize movies rated NC–17 (meaning no children 17 or under are admitted—previously these movies received an X rating). Some of the leading prior restraint cases have involved motion pictures.

a. Background and Modern Doctrine

Until 1952 the motion picture was not considered a medium of expression protected by the First Amendment, and the censors were free to control film exhibition in any way they saw fit. In that year the Supreme Court in Joseph Burstyn, Inc. v. Wilson (1952) rejected earlier doctrine and held that the First Amendment protects motion pictures. Because local authorities can suppress obscenity under

Roth and Miller, however, prior licensing and confiscation of films as well as subsequent punishment for their exhibition are permissible under certain circumstances. Furthermore, a general constitutional attack on a local ordinance or state statute requiring submission of motion pictures for prior censorship will fail. See Times Film Corp. v. City of Chicago (1961).

One indirect approach to controlling "adult" motion pictures and thereby avoiding the constitutional standards of Roth and Miller is to control land use (zoning) in order to concentrate adult movie houses in so-called "combat zones." Conversely, zoning laws can prevent concentrations of "adult" movie theaters, which have the tendency to destroy commercial and residential neighborhoods. Social scientists have found a positive correlation between the number of adult businesses in a single location and increases in prostitution, assaults, robberies and theft (termed "secondary effects" of adult businesses). Either way, non-proliferation of such establishments is the goal. The U.S. Supreme Court approved this indirect approach, relying on time, place and manner limitations on the exhibition of "adult" films in Young v. American Mini Theatres, Inc. (1976) and City of Renton v. Playtime Theatres, Inc. (1986) because neither case involved total suppression of adult movies or criminal sanctions. More recently the High Court upheld a Los Angeles ordinance that outlawed the establishment of an adult business within 1000 feet of another adult business; thus the city could close two adult businesses located in the same building. City of Los Angeles v. Alameda Books, Inc. (2002).

The following year the U.S. Court of Appeals for the Fifth Circuit held that a San Antonio, Texas ordinance did not apply to a video store that sold adult videos only for viewing at home rather than in the store. The court held that consumers of pornography would not be likely to linger in the area; thus, the city could not demonstrate harmful secondary effects. Encore Videos, Inc. v. San Antonio (2003).

A city may not apply zoning laws to "virtual space," however. A man in Florida installed 30 Internet video cameras throughout a house he called "Voyeur Dorm" and hired several young women to live their lives in front of the cameras for subscribers to his web site. The city of Tampa prosecuted, arguing that this violated its zoning ordinance prohibiting adult entertainment in residential neighborhoods. The U.S. Court of Appeals for the Eleventh Circuit ruled that Tampa's zoning ordinance did not apply because the adult entertainment was dispersed over the Internet rather than into the community; thus, there would not be the harmful secondary effects that the zoning laws were designed to prevent. Voyeur Dorm, L.C. v. City of Tampa, Florida (2001).

b. Procedural Safeguards for Film

After the Times Film Corp. case, supra, it was clear that there could be constitutional as well as unconstitutional prior restraint on motion pictures, and the Supreme Court began to elucidate the rules under which the censors might operate. Freedman v. Maryland (1965) involved a challenge by a film exhibitor to a state statute authorizing certain procedures of the now defunct Maryland Board of Censors, including a lengthy appeal process. The Supreme Court struck down the statute as unduly restrictive of protected expression and set out certain procedural safeguards for regulating the censor's business. Prior restraint statutes and ordinances are now required to:

(a) place the burden of proving that the film in question meets constitutional standards for obscenity (i.e., Roth and Miller) on the censor;

(b) provide that the censor will, within a specified very brief period, either issue a license for exhibition or go into court to seek to restrain exhibition and;

(c) assure a prompt final judicial decision in order to minimize the deterrent effect of an interim refusal to license.

In addition, prior restraint legislation, whether it involves outright censorship or merely mandatory film classification for the protection of minors, as in Interstate Circuit, Inc. v. City of Dallas (1968), must be narrowly drawn, detailed, and precise as to the standards to be employed by the classifier. Anything less will inhibit protected expression and run afoul of the First and Fourteenth Amendments. See FW/PBS, Inc. v. City of Dallas (1990) (Dallas, Texas ordinance overturned for failure to provide prompt judicial review of city restrictions on adult businesses, although basic principle that adult businesses may be regulated was upheld).

Similarly, courts have established procedural safeguards for law enforcement officials to follow before seizing an obscene film. The law enforcement official must obtain a judicial warrant before any seizure. The fact that First Amendment interests are affected by such search warrants does not require a higher probable cause standard for issuing the warrants. New York v. P. J. Video, Inc. (1986). Failure to obtain such warrant will result in the suppression of the film as evidence of obscenity law violations at subsequent judicial proceedings. Roaden v. Kentucky (1973); Lee Art Theatre, Inc. v. Virginia (1968). It is not sufficient justification for the issuance of the warrant that the prospective seizing officer made conclusory assertions of the film's obscene nature. Rather, the magistrate must carefully consider the question of the film's probable nature before issuing the warrant. Ibid. An adversary proceeding at this stage is not required, however. Heller v. New York (1973). If a law enforcement official has a warrant to seize a copy of a film, he or she may do so only with the limited purpose of preserving it as evidence in a subsequent adversary proceeding. Local authorities may not prevent continued exhibition of the film until a prompt determination of its nature is made in that proceeding. If there is only one copy at hand, the film seized must be made available to the exhibitor for copying so that he or she may continue its exhibition. Ibid.

Legislatures and city councils may not bypass these procedural safeguards with indirect prior restraints such as statutes (1) which permit enjoining the operation of adult movie houses as public nuisances because of past exhibition of obscene films; (2) which prohibit the unapproved future exhibition of motion pictures that have not yet been found to be obscene; and (3) which require the judiciary to place its imprimatur on such future exhibitions before the films may be shown to the public without penalty. See Vance v. Universal Amusement Co. (1980).

The focus here has been on the constitutional limitations on prior restraint of motion pictures because prosecutors have fought most of the legal battles over films, but courts have developed parallel safeguards to protect other modes of expression from overzealous censors. See, e.g., Kingsley Books, Inc. v. Brown (1957) (booklets); Marcus v. Search Warrant (1961) (books and magazines). But cf. New York v. P.J. Video, Inc. (1986).

3.   Dial-a-Porn

Although concerns about pornography had traditionally been focused on adult books and NC–17–rated movies, in the 1980s the FCC became concerned with "dial-a-porn" telephone services, in which callers could listen to sexually explicit recorded phone messages or hold an indecent two-way conversation with someone for a fee. In 1988 Congress amended Sections 223(b) and (c) of the

Communications Act of 1934 with the Telephone Decency Act. This amendment banned all dial-a-porn services, including indecent as well as obscene speech. Sable Communications, a dial-a-porn provider, filed suit, and the Supreme Court struck down the provision barring indecent telephone messages, although it upheld the provision barring obscene telephone messages. Sable Communications of California v. FCC (1989). Congress then made another attempt at dial-a-porn legislation by deleting the ban on indecent speech and enacting a revised amendment in 1989 (47 U.S.C. § 223(b)-(c) (Nov. 21, 1989). See also Dial Information Services v. Thornburgh (1991); (U.S. Court of Appeals for the Second Circuit upheld pre-subscription requirement of amendment as constitutional; Supreme Court denied certiorari).

More recently, the Supreme Court has grappled with the issue of indecent programming on broadcast and cable television and the Internet, discussed in Chapters X through XII.

4. Military Bases and Prisons

In 1996 Congress passed the Military Honor and Decency Act, which barred the sale or rental of pornographic magazines and videotapes in the post exchanges on military bases. 10 U.S.C.A. § 2489a (1996). The law created a review board that prohibited the sale of Penthouse, Hustler and Playgirl but allowed the sale of Playboy and Esquire. The U.S. Court of Appeals for the Ninth Circuit upheld the law, however, ruling that because military facilities are not public fora, the government has the right to restrict the content of speech if such speech is at odds with the military's image of honor, professionalism and proper decorum. PMG International Division L.L.C. v. Rumsfeld (2002).

A year after it passed the Military Honor and Decency Act, Congress attached the "Ensign Amendment" to the Omnibus Budget Act of 1997; this amendment prohibited the Federal Bureau of Prisons from allowing prisoners access to any material known to be "sexually explicit or featuring nudity." Three prisoners, along with the publishers of Playboy and Penthouse magazines, challenged the amendment as unconstitutional. The Bureau of Prisons argued that the amendment's purpose was to aid prisoners' rehabilitation by creating a more orderly prison environment. The U.S. Court of Appeals for the D.C. Circuit upheld the constitutionality of the Ensign Amendment, explaining that the "rehabilitative interest" of the government was reasonable "for the custody of those who have already transgressed society's norms." Amatel v. Reno (1998). The Court of Appeals for the Third Circuit likewise found no merit in constitutional challenges brought by two prisoners convicted of raping children. Waterman v. Farmer (1999). The Court of Appeals for the Ninth Circuit also held that prohibiting inmates from possessing "sexually explicit material" was reasonably related to "legitimate penological interests." Mauro v. Arpaio (1999).

5. Sexually Explicit Music Lyrics and Graphic Art

During the past two decades a few prosecutors have expanded their focus on obscenity to include music lyrics and even graphic art on display in art museums. In 1990, a federal district court in Florida ruled that 2 Live Crew's rap recording "As Nasty as They Wanna Be" was obscene; this was the first time in our nation's history that a sound recording had been declared obscene. The Court of Appeals for the Eleventh Circuit reversed, however; it accepted arguments by expert witnesses that the rap music might possibly have serious artistic value. Luke Records, Inc. v. Navarro (1992). See also Soundgarden v. Eikenberry (1994) (Washington State statute barring sale of "erotic" recordings to minors struck down as unconstitutional by Washington Supreme Court).

In addition to concerns about obscene music lyrics, there have been heated debates in Congress over funding for the National Endowment for the Arts (NEA). The question was whether the NEA should provide grant money to artists whose artwork is sexually explicit, sacrilegious or just plain offensive. The controversy began in 1989 when Senator Jesse Helms learned that museum exhibitors used a $15,000 NEA grant to pay for an art exhibition which included artist Andres Serrano's photograph of a plastic crucifix in a jar of his own urine called "Piss Christ." Helms was also angry that museum exhibitors used a $30,000 NEA grant to transport the artwork of the late photographer Robert Mapplethorpe. Two of Mapplethorpe's photographs were of children with their genitals exposed; five of the photographs contained graphic homoerotic or sadomasochistic images. When the Contemporary Arts Center in Cincinnati, Ohio placed 175 of Mapplethorpe's photographs on exhibit, police immediately confiscated the seven photographs described above and charged Dennis Barrie, director of the Contemporary Arts Center, with obscenity. This was the first time in the nation's history that a public art museum was prosecuted for obscenity. An eight-member jury of working-class parents who had never been to a contemporary art gallery found Barrie not guilty of the obscenity charges. Contemporary Arts Center v. Ney (1990).

Responding to the firestorm that the Serrano and Mapplethorpe exhibits ignited, Congress amended the statutory framework of the NEA, providing that NEA funds could not be used to produce works "considered obscene, including ... depictions of sadomasochism, homoeroticism, the sexual exploitation of children, or individuals engaged in sex acts...." Section 304(a), Dept. of Interior and Related Agencies Appropriation Act of 1990; Public Law 101–121, 103 Stat. 701, 741, Oct. 23, 1989. A number of plaintiffs immediately challenged the amendment as unconstitutional. See New School for Social Research v. John Frohnmayer and the NEA (1991) (out-of-court settlement reached with NEA); Bella Lewitzky Dance Foundation v. Frohnmayer (1991) (challenging condition that NEA funding be provided only if artists signed now discredited anti-obscenity pledges; federal district court in California struck down the legislation as unconstitutional).

Congress again amended the NEA's government statute in 1990, this time requiring NEA administrators to "take into consideration general standards of decency" when awarding NEA grants. 1990 Amendments, Public Law No. 101–512, § 103(b), 104 Stat. 1963, codified at 20 U.S.C. § 954(d). Under the new "decency" requirement, the NEA denied funding to four performance artists, Karen Finley, John Fleck, Holly Hughes and Tim Miller, even though the Performance Arts Program Peer Review Panel of the NEA had unanimously recommended that they should receive funding. Finley sued the NEA. Finley v. National Endowment for the Arts (1997). Although she prevailed at the federal district court and appellate court levels, the Supreme Court reversed the Ninth Circuit's judgment and remanded the case. A majority of the High Court justices interpreted the 1990 amendment as containing merely advisory language; in other words, NEA administrators may take general standards of decency into account in awarding grants, but they are not required to do so. The Supreme Court explained that the amendment neither interferes with First Amendment rights, nor is it void for vagueness under the Fifth Amendment. National Endowment for the Arts v. Finley (1998).

The following year Cardinal John O'Connor expressed outrage when the Brooklyn Museum of Art displayed Chris Ofili's painting "The Holy Virgin Mary." The painting portrays an African Madonna with an odiferous clump of elephant dung on one breast and cut-outs of genitalia from pornographic magazines on her blue cloak. Others objected to a display of child mannequins with multiple genitals, a portrait glorifying British child murderess Myra Hindley, a cast of sculptor Marc Quinn's head made with nine pints of his own frozen blood, and dissected animals in tanks of formaldehyde.

New York City's then mayor Rudolph Giuliani was equally outraged, and immediately threatened to cut off $7 million in public financing of the museum. Giuliani also filed suit, asking a judge to evict the museum from its city-owned building in Brooklyn. The mayor charged that the museum had violated a provision in its lease from 1893 requiring it to "enlighten, educate and provide enjoyment" for the public. The Brooklyn Museum of Art retained attorney Floyd Abrams and filed suit against New York City, arguing that Giuliani's suit was punitive and would violate the Museum's First Amendment rights. The federal district court in Brooklyn ruled that Giuliani's actions were a flagrant violation of the museum's First Amendment rights and ordered the mayor to restore city payments and end his effort to evict the museum. Giuliani appealed, but in March 2000 he agreed to drop his suit to evict the museum; in return, the museum dropped its First Amendment lawsuit against Giuliani in a settlement agreement.

6. Nude Dancing

In addition to the question of the extent to which the First Amendment protects offensive music lyrics or graphic art, courts have grappled with the question of the extent to which the First Amendment protects nude dancing as a form of expression. Barnes v. Glen Theatre, Inc. (1991) involved the use of time, place and manner restrictions on nude dancing. The Supreme Court upheld the application of an Indiana public indecency statute to nude dancers in an adult entertainment establishment. Conceding that nude dancing is expressive conduct meriting First Amendment protection, the Court, in a plurality opinion, held 1) that requiring nude dancers to wear pasties and a G-string furthered a substantial government interest in protecting societal order and morality, 2) that this interest was unrelated to the suppression of free expression, and 3) that the restriction was no broader than necessary to further that interest. If the Court had simply held that nude dancing is not expressive behavior, they might have provided lower courts with a clearer precedent, but because the majority had trouble agreeing on a First Amendment rationale for nude dancing, it became necessary for the Court to revisit the issue.

They did so in City of Erie v. Pap's A.M. (2000), but still were not able to arrive at a rationale for upholding public nudity statutes. Five of the six justices who comprised the 6–3 majority agreed that it was appropriate to apply the O'Brien test, which holds that if government regulation of speech "furthers an important or substantial government interest, ... and if the incidental restriction [on expression] is no greater than is essential to the furtherance of that interest," then government regulation of speech is valid. United States v. O'Brien (1968). The Court upheld an Erie, Pennsylvania ordinance requiring nude dancers to wear at least pasties and a G–string, although its fractured majority did not quite explain how that requirement would in fact reduce crime, prostitution, or sexual assaults associated with bars where dancers perform nude. The O'Brien test requires an intermediate level of scrutiny, meaning that the Court directed the City of Erie to balance its efforts to regulate nude dancing against the requirement that the restriction be no greater than necessary to further the city's interest in maintaining social order. In other words, the O'Brien test applies to content-neutral laws that regulate conduct and have only an incidental effect on expression; in this case, the content-neutral laws simply ban all public nudity. As in Barnes, the Court thus held in City of Erie that nude dancing was a form of expression that had at least some minimal First Amendment protection.

C.   SUBSEQUENT CRIMINAL SANCTIONS

The threat of criminal prosecution can have a restraining influence on sexual expression almost as profound as prior censorship. While criminal prosecutions for obscene expression are in general much like other criminal prosecutions and the rights accorded defendants are the same, certain special aspects of criminal obscenity proceedings are particularly significant to the eventual outcome.

Before one can be convicted of violating any criminal statute, the statute must give reasonable notice of the conduct that is prohibited. This has presented substantial difficulties for the drafters of criminal obscenity legislation in the past because of the definitional problem. Courts have reversed convictions because obscenity statutes were "void for vagueness." See Winters v. New York (1948); cf. Interstate Circuit, Inc. v. City of Dallas (1968). Legislatures may alleviate this drafting problem by applying the definition of unprotected obscenity set forth in Miller.

As noted earlier in connection with the discussion of the effects of Miller, Paris, Jenkins and Pope, *where* an obscenity prosecution is brought is of the greatest importance because of the Supreme Court's sanctioning of the application of local standards. Because a prosecutor may file charges for violation of the Comstock Law in any district from, through or into which the mail in question is carried, federal prosecutors will usually have an advantageous choice as to venue. See U.S. v. Thomas (1996), discussed in Chapter XII. Similar options as to venue between counties are often available to state prosecutors.

The burden of proof is always upon the state or federal government and the standard is the same as in all criminal cases: guilt beyond a reasonable doubt. The Supreme Court's ruling in Paris Adult Theatre that the material complained of "speaks for itself" has eased the burden of proof somewhat; thus expert testimony as to its obscene nature is no longer required.

An important element of the prosecutor's burden is scienter or guilty knowledge. It may be difficult in certain cases to establish beyond a reasonable doubt that a book seller, magazine dealer or movie exhibitor knew of the obscene nature and contents of the material he or she was purveying. Neither the states nor the federal government may constitutionally eliminate this mental element in their criminal obscenity statutes, however. Smith v. California (1959).

The Supreme Court has upheld attempts by prosecutors to use the Racketeer Influenced and Corrupt Organizations (RICO) Act to crack down on pornography. Fort Wayne Books, Inc. v. Indiana (1989). Under the RICO laws, the government may seize a defendant's assets after he or she is convicted of racketeering, meaning selling obscene material. Alexander v. U.S. (1993). If the government seizes a pornographer's assets under the RICO statutes, however, there must be some relationship between the gravity of the offense and the value of the property seized; otherwise, the seizure would violate the Eighth Amendment protection against excessive fines. Austin v. United States (1993).

The chief defense in most obscenity prosecutions is that the material is protected expression under the prevailing Supreme Court tests. The defense will normally call expert witnesses to testify that the material has serious literary, artistic, political or scientific value. Perhaps local psychologists or psychiatrists will testify for the defense that the material does not appeal to the prurient interest of the average person in that particular locality. Defense counsel may attempt to establish "tolerant" community standards through expert testimony and the introduction of comparable materials freely available in the local area. This latter defense is meeting with only mixed success before the courts. With the proliferation of pornographic web sites on the Internet, it is likely that prosecutors will turn their attention to virtual obscenity in the coming century as discussed in Chapter XII.

CHAPTER V

RESTRAINT OF THE PRESS FOR PURPOSES OF NA-TIONAL SECURITY

A. THE CONFLICT

Since the founding of the Republic the federal and state governments have laid claim to the right to keep secrets on the ground that disclosures of certain matters would be harmful to the public interest. Obvious examples are troop deployments and diplomatic judgments concerning foreign governments. The working assumption of government officials is that the people would not want to know about sensitive matters if such knowledge would be harmful to their best interest.

Although this assumption may have validity, official judgments as to precisely what knowledge would be harmful to the public interest are coming under increasing challenge. The common theme of the advocates of a freer flow of information is "the people's right to know" or "freedom of information."

The conflict has grown sharper with the growth of governmental activity since the New Deal and the increasing distrust of "big government" engendered in part by the Watergate scandal and by unpopular wars in Southeast Asia and Iraq. Representative of the heightened conflict is the willingness of the media, particularly a once deferential press, to publish material which the government wishes to keep secret and a readiness on the part of governmental officials to retaliate against the media and to seek injunctions against publication of those secrets.

B. LEGAL BACKGROUND

There is no question but that the federal government has an inherent right to keep certain matters secret, especially information relating to national security and diplomatic affairs and that it may invoke executive privilege and may establish a classification system to prevent disclosure. See United States v. Nixon (1974) (the Nixon Tapes case); United States v. Reynolds (1953). Furthermore, the government may enjoin those individuals privy to secret government information from disclosing what they have learned. In certain cases the government may criminally punish these individuals for actually disclosing sensitive information to others. In the process of protecting government secrets, the judiciary will not review the executive's judgment concerning the need for secrecy for the specific material involved because of the separation of powers doctrine.

The problem becomes considerably more complex, however, when the media threaten disclosure. In this situation, of course, First Amendment considerations first raised in Near v. Minnesota (1931) intervene. Although in Near the Supreme Court viewed prior restraint as generally violative of the First and Fourteenth Amendments, the Court did recognize that such restraint might be permissible in extraordinary situations including the threatened publication of military secrets in time of war. This left the door open for the federal government 40 years later to attempt to stop the presses from printing the so-called "Pentagon Papers."

C.   NEW YORK TIMES CO.
v. UNITED STATES

Disillusioned with the war in Vietnam he had once supported, former Defense Department official Daniel Ellsberg arranged for the unauthorized photocopying of a "top secret" Department of Defense study of American involvement in the war between 1945 and 1967. One volume was entitled "History of U.S. Decision Making Process on Vietnam Policy" and the second volume was a "Command and Control Study of the Tonkin Gulf Incident." Ellsberg made them available to selected newspapers throughout the United States. On June 12, 13 and 14, 1971 the New York Times became the first paper to publish summaries and portions of the text of the two studies, popularly known as "The Pentagon Papers." The United States Justice Department sought and obtained a temporary restraining order from the Court of Appeals for the Second Circuit to prevent the Times from continuing publication of the classified material. This restraining order remained in effect until the Supreme Court decided the case, thereby preventing the Times from further publication of the material for 15 days. At the same time the Washington Post began publishing excerpts from the two studies. The government likewise sought to restrain the Post, and succeeded for a short time. However, the U.S. Court of Appeals for the District of Columbia Circuit rejected the temporary restraining order binding the Post before the Supreme Court's resolution of the case, resulting in the anomaly of the Post and New York Times finding themselves in legal limbo until the U.S. Supreme Court resolved the split decision between the two U.S. courts of appeal.

The issue presented to the Supreme Court in the historic case of New York Times Co. v. United States (1971) was very simply whether the press' publication of secret matters relating to the history and past conduct of an ongoing war could be enjoined consistent with the First Amendment. The Court by its judgment freed the Times to continue publication along with the Post. Its per curiam opinion is not, as some at first suggested, a ringing endorsement of a free press, however. The Court stated, " 'Any system of prior restraints of expression comes to this Court bearing a heavy presumption against its constitutional validity.' ... The Government 'thus carries a heavy burden of showing justification for the imposition of such a restraint.' ... The [lower courts] held that the Government had not met that burden. We agree."

The Court thus implied that if the government had sufficient proof of some serious effect on the war effort or national security, the government could enjoin the media from publishing truthful matters of public interest. What saved the press from being permanently gagged by court order for the first time in our history was the government's inability to prove to the High Court's satisfaction that publication of the Pentagon Papers would clearly result in direct, immediate and irreparable damage to our nation or its people.

In addition to the per curiam opinion, the Pentagon Papers case is marked by six concurring and three dissenting opinions. Justice Black and Justice Douglas observed in a concurring opinion that "The Government does not even attempt to rely on any act of Congress. Instead it makes the bold and dangerously far-reaching contention that the courts should take it upon themselves to 'make' a law abridging freedom of the press. . . ." In other words they pointed out that the New York Times and Washington Post had not violated any specific law, and for the courts to fashion a "law" after the fact would be to violate the separation of powers. A close analysis of the other opinions, especially that of Justice White, however, must be considered generally discouraging to those favoring a free press. A majority of the Court did not rule that such prior restraint was unconstitutional—only that the government had not met the heavy burden of proving that such restraint was necessary in this particular case.

Thus, what appeared at first blush to be a great victory for the press was, at best, a pyrrhic one. The Court gave notice that there are limits to the media's right to publish and the people's right to learn government secrets relating to national security. As a result of this case, the media have become more wary of publishing classified material obtained without authorization. At best, the Pentagon Papers case encourages the news media to censor themselves. At worst, it forms the predicate for successful government censorship and prosecutions in the future.

Eight years after the Pentagon Papers case, the Justice Department obtained an injunction to prohibit The Progressive magazine from publishing free-lancer Howard Morland's article entitled "The H–Bomb Secret: How We Got It, Why We're Telling It." United States v. The Progressive, Inc. (1979). Federal district court Judge Robert Penn Warren in Wisconsin issued a preliminary injunction against publication after concluding that some of the information would probably violate the Atomic Energy Act of 1954. The Justice Department contended that Morland's manuscript contained "Restricted Data," defined by the Atomic Energy Act of 1954 as "all data concerning the design, manufacture or utilization of atomic weapons." 42 U.S.C.A. § 2104(y). This law specifically forbids anyone possessing "restricted data" about nuclear weaponry from disseminating it in a way that might be utilized "to injure the United States" or "secure an advantage to any foreign nation." 42 U.S.C.A. § 2274. It also authorizes the attorney general to request a court order to enjoin communication of such restricted data. 42 U.S.C.A. § 2280. Although the Progressive's attorneys attempted to rely on the Pentagon Papers case as precedent, Judge Warren observed that in the Pentagon Papers case there was no statute that barred publication, whereas in The Progressive case the Atomic Energy Act specifically barred publication of "restricted data."

Judge Warren further observed that "a mistake in ruling against The Progressive will seriously infringe cherished First Amendment rights," but "a mistake in ruling against the United States could pave the way for thermonuclear annihilation for us all. In that event, our right to life is extinguished and the right to publish becomes moot."

The Progressive appealed, but three days after the court of appeals heard oral arguments and before it had made a decision, a small Wisconsin newspaper, the Madison Press Connection, published a California computer programmer's letter which contained essentially the same information as The Progressive article. When the Press Connection published the letter, the court of appeals dismissed the case against The Progressive. Journalists expressed relief because numerous legal scholars had speculated that the U.S. Supreme Court would have sustained the injunction against The Progressive.

D.　OTHER INHIBITIONS ON PUBLICATION

1.　Withholding Passports

Aside from direct injunctive restraints on the release of national security information attempted in the New York Times Co., Marchetti, Colby and Progressive cases, the federal government has successfully employed other techniques to discourage disclosure of sensitive diplomatic, military and intelligence information.

The denial or revocation of a passport because of expression that the Government perceives as potentially damaging to national security or foreign policy is one technique for inhibiting the release of undesired information or comment. The U.S. Supreme Court upheld this tactic in Haig v. Agee (1981). This case involved former CIA agent Philip

Agee's attempt to expose existing CIA agents in foreign countries so that anti-CIA groups in those countries would drive them out.

2. Criminal Prosecutions under the 1950 "COMINT" Statute and the 1917 Espionage Act

Under the Reagan administration in 1985 the Justice Department successfully prosecuted former naval intelligence analyst Samuel Morison for furnishing three secret U.S. spy satellite photos to a British magazine. Morison was sentenced to two years for espionage and theft. He was the first person ever convicted of the crime of leaking national security information to the press, and was found guilty under an interpretation of the law that could subject news organizations, as well as their sources, to criminal prosecution. United States v. Morison (1988).

Following Morison's conviction the CIA threatened to prosecute the New York Times, the Washington Post, Time, Newsweek and other news organizations for alleged violation of the 1950 "COMINT" (Communications Intelligence) statute. This statute prohibits publishing classified information about codes, ciphers or "communication intelligence activities of the United States." It also forbids "the divulging of any information" gleaned from code-breaking activities in order "to prevent the indication to a foreign nation that we may have broken their code system." 18 U.S.C.A. § 798 (1953). The stories that triggered the CIA's threats of prosecution dealt with our interception of messages between Tripoli and the Libyan People's Bureau in East Berlin, and the government's prosecution of Ronald Pelton of the National Security Agency who later received a life sentence for selling secrets to the Soviets. When Time magazine's attorney asked the CIA which of Time's articles had violated the law, the CIA refused to identify the article. Washington Post, May 8, 1986 at A3.

More recently government prosecutors have charged lobbyists Steven J. Rosen and Keith Weissman with violating the 1917 Espionage Act by "conspiring to communicate national defense information to persons not entitled to receive it." Rosen and Weissman were lobbyists with the American Israel Political Action Committee (AIPAC), and allegedly provided information about U.S. policy toward Iran to a member of the Israeli government. The federal district court for the Eastern District of Virginia upheld the constitutionality of the Espionage Act of 1917 (18 U.S.C.A. § 793) and extended its reach to individuals outside the government, including, by implication, journalists who are merely doing their jobs. U.S. v. Rosen (2006). This case is likely to reach the U.S. Supreme Court.

3. Prohibition against Revealing Identities of Covert CIA Agents

Perhaps in response to Haig v. Agee, the Reagan Administration persuaded Congress in 1982 to make it a federal crime for anyone to publish anything they have reason to know will disclose the identity of United States intelligence agents, even if their source is public or unclassified information. Intelligence Identities Protection Act, P.L. 97–200, 50 U.S.C.A. §§ 421–426. A survey of news stories written before the act was passed in 1982 turned up more than 80 major books and news articles, the authors of which could arguably have been indicted under the law. A representative sample would include the New York Times' investigation of ex-CIA agents Edwin Wilson and Frank Terpil; revelations that former CIA agents were involved in the Watergate break-in; accounts of illegal domestic spying by the CIA; and disclosures that a CIA employee tried to infiltrate the House and Senate intelligence committees in 1980 at the direction of the KGB. Jay Peterzell, "The Government Shuts Up," Columbia Journalism Review, pp. 31–37 (July–August 1982).

More recently, in October 2005 there was speculation that Vice President Richard Cheney's former chief of staff I. Lewis ("Scooter") Libby may have violated the Intelligence Identities Protection Act when he disclosed the fact that former ambassador Joseph C. Wilson's wife Valerie Plame Wilson was a covert CIA officer. A grand jury indicted Libby for obstruction of justice and perjury, but Special Prosecutor Patrick Fitzgerald did not charge him with violating the Intelligence Identities Protection Act. In fall 2006 former deputy secretary of state Richard Armitage admitted that he had inadvertently disclosed Valerie Plame's identity in conversations with Washinton Post reporter Bob Woodward and columnist Robert Novak in June 2003. Armitage apologized for being the primary source who first leaked Plame's identity to the press. New York Times, September 8, 2006 at A22.

4. Contractual Prohibitions

When agents leave the CIA they are required to sign a secrecy agreement that grants the CIA the right of "pre-publication review," meaning that they must submit every manuscript they write to the CIA for approval for the rest of their lives. In cases touching on national security, the government has had some success in enjoining disclosures by its former employees. More than 30 years ago the government enjoined disclosure of certain CIA secrets in a book by a former agency official (United States v. Marchetti (1972); Alfred A. Knopf, Inc. v. Colby (1975))

The Marchetti case began when former CIA agent Victor Marchetti submitted to Esquire magazine and six other publishers an article in which he reported some of his experiences as a CIA agent. Marchetti had spent 14 years with the CIA, rising to the position of special assistant to the executive director, but left because he had become disillusioned with the CIA's covert actions to destabilize governments considered unfriendly to the United States. The government charged that Marchetti's article contained classified information concerning intelligence sources, methods and operations. The government won a broad injunction to enjoin publication of the article. On appeal, Marchetti argued that the injunction should be barred by the Supreme Court's Pentagon Papers decision because the government had failed to meet the heavy burden against prior restraint of expression. The U.S. Court of Appeals for the Fourth Circuit rejected Marchetti's argument, however, and held that the secrecy agreement Marchetti had signed when the CIA first hired him in 1955 should be enforced. The agreement required Marchetti (and all CIA agents) to submit material to the CIA for approval before it was published. If the material was classified and published without prior review, the CIA could enjoin disclosure. Given this agreement, the court upheld the injunction, except to rule that the CIA could delete only classified information. Marchetti was the first writer in the United States to be subjected to such a censorship order.

Marchetti and a co-author John Marks, a former State Department employee who had also signed an agreement not to disclose classified information learned during his employment, later wrote a book, "The CIA and the Cult of Intelligence," which they submitted to the CIA for prepublication review. The CIA demanded that they delete 339 passages, comprising 15 to 20 percent of the entire manuscript. The CIA required heavy deletions in chapters concerning the Bay of Pigs operation against Fidel Castro, the Vietnam War and the CIA's attempt to prevent Salvador Allende's election as president of Chile. With their publisher Alfred A. Knopf, Inc., the authors sued. Ultimately the CIA permitted 25 of the 26 missing passages to be printed in whole or in part, leaving one to wonder why they had been deleted in the first place. Alfred A. Knopf, Inc. v. Colby (1975).

Five years later, in Snepp v. United States (1980) the government, relying on its claimed contractual rights, got the courts to seize the profits from a book published without CIA prepublication review, causing financial disaster for the author. Frank

Snepp, a former CIA agent, published a book, "Decent Interval," about certain CIA activities in South Vietnam. Snepp did not submit it for prepublication review as expressly required by his employment agreement with the CIA, however. Even though the CIA conceded that "Decent Interval" did not reveal one item of classified information, the government brought suit to enforce the agreement by confiscating all profits that Snepp might earn from publishing the book in violation of the agreement. The district court entered a judgment for the government, giving it the relief it sought, but the United States Court of Appeals refused to approve turning over the profits from the book to the government. The Supreme Court summarily and without benefit of briefs or oral argument on the subject, upheld the government's right to confiscate all profits from the publication—more than $125,000. Thus, the financial burden placed on Snepp to pay off the government was substantial and should give pause to other government employees who are thinking of writing about sensitive official matters.

Perhaps the most chilling aspect of the Marchetti, Colby and Snepp cases is the subordination of First Amendment interests to "boilerplate" contract clauses in CIA employment agreements. In Snepp, the Supreme Court majority relegated First Amendment considerations to a footnote in rigorously enforcing the CIA's secrecy agreement contract against Snepp. See also United States v. Snepp (1990) (Snepp sought but was denied damages after CIA's demand for deletions from a television mini-series script resulted in television deal falling through).

The Snepp opinion also contained broad language that could be interpreted to permit the same prepublication review procedure to be applied to the thousands of non-CIA employees who also have access to classified information. The government had not sought that degree of power in the Snepp case, and it is not clear that the Court intended that result. Citing the Snepp decision, however, in 1983 President Ronald Reagan issued National Security Decision Directive 84, "Safeguarding National Security Information." 9 Med.L.Rptr. 1759, July 5, 1983. This directive would have required thousands of federal employees to submit to lie detector tests if asked; an employee who refused to take such a test could be subject to "adverse consequences." Previously federal employees, except for those in the CIA and certain sections of the Justice and Defense Departments and the National Security Agency—had the right to refuse to submit to such tests without their refusal being held against them or included in their personnel files. The directive also would have required any federal employee with access to classified information to submit for prepublication review any manuscripts containing intelligence information. It would have covered about 128,000 employees who would be bound by the contract for the rest of their lives.

In response to the President's directive, Congress attached a rider to a State Department appropriations bill ordering the administration to delay enforcement of the directive on prepublication review until 1984. The President signed the bill and agreed not to enforce the directive. Despite this promise, however, the General Accounting Office (GAO) reported in 1984 that aspects of the directive had been in effect since 1982. The GAO found that 156,000 employees of the Defense Department had signed the secrecy agreements and that there had been a sharp increase in the number of articles and books being reviewed by the Reagan administration. See FOI Digest, p. 1 (May–June 1984). Furthermore, thousands of government officials were being required to acknowledge in writing that they would face criminal and civil penalties for unauthorized disclosures for the rest of their lives. See Washington Post, p. A16, May 7, 1986. A decade later, however, President Bill Clinton revoked Executive Order 12356 with his own Executive Order 12958, effective April 17, 1995.

More recently, former CIA operations officer Gary Berntsen sued the CIA, charging that the CIA's prolonged pre-publication review of his manuscript "Jawbreaker" constitutes an unlawful prior restraint. In his manuscript Berntsen alleges that the United States knowingly allowed Osama bin Laden to escape from Tora Bora during the war in Afghanistan. The CIA is required to issue its decision wtihin 30 days after receiving a manuscript for prepublication review, but after more than 60 days, Berntsen filed suit in the U.S. District Court for the

District of Columbia, and the case is pending. Berntsen v. Central Intelligence Agency (2005).

5. Balancing National Security against Access to Combat Zones before September 11

Journalists have accompanied American military forces in every war since at least the Mexican–American War of 1848. Although reporters did accede to censorship in both world wars and the Korean War, they were always allowed on the scene to cover the fighting. Journalists even accompanied Allied forces when they invaded Europe in 1944 on D–Day, one of the most secret military operations of all time. There was little censorship, however, during the Vietnam War, and many in the military had developed an intense distrust of the press, blaming the press in part for the United States having lost the war in Vietnam.

In reaction to the lessons of Vietnam, the Reagan Administration exercised a form of prior censorship when it ordered an unprecedented 48–hour news blackout of the American invasion of Grenada in the Caribbean Sea in 1983. About 400 journalists were denied transportation to Grenada, and the military stopped and threatened to shoot a few reporters who tried to reach Grenada by boat from nearby islands. Pentagon officials argued that they had banned journalists for 48 hours because they needed absolute secrecy to launch the invasion, and they were also concerned for the journalists' safety. The press scoffed at both reasons. Hustler magazine publisher Larry Flynt filed suit against Defense Secretary Caspar Weinberger for declaratory and injunctive relief, but the U.S. Court of Appeals for the District of Columbia dismissed his suit, holding that it was moot because the military operation in Grenada was over. The appellate court did not rule on whether or not it was constitutional for the government to ban the press from covering military actions. Flynt v. Weinberger (1985).

Following severe criticism of the administration and the military for its exclusion of the press from the early aspects of the Grenada operation, Defense Secretary Caspar Weinberger asked retired army Major General Winant Sidle to form a panel on press-military relations. The Sidle panel recommended that a small pool of reporters should accompany the military on all future missions, secret or not, and should share the information obtained with others in the press. The pool, formed in 1984, was activated for the U.S. bombing of certain targets in Libya in 1986. Eight reporters and photographers boarded a U.S. aircraft carrier in the Mediterranean and got first-hand reports of the bombing from the pilots and others.

Subsequent uses of this pool arrangement have been heavily criticized. During the U.S. invasion of Panama, the media complained that reporters were not allowed where the real action was taking place. See "Panning the Pentagon," Editor & Publisher, March 31, 1990 at 11. The Persian Gulf War also led to extensive criticism. Media pools were not even called until U.S. troops had been in Saudi

Arabia for almost a week. Once there, the media complained that the pools were often taken to unnewsworthy locations and that the military sometimes selected the soldiers to be interviewed. Other complaints concerned the required "security review" of press stories.

In January 1991, several publications sought an injunction prohibiting implementation of many of these press policies. Several months later, after the hostilities had ceased, a federal district court held that the issue was moot even though the situation was capable of repetition. Because the military lifted the restrictions on press access at the end of the war, the court held that there was "no longer any presently operative practice" for the court to enjoin. The Nation Magazine v. Department of Defense (1991).

Under guidelines issued by the Pentagon and approved by the American Newspaper Publishers Association and the American Society of Newspaper Editors, only Pentagon-accredited journalists may report on military operations and they may report only "releasable information" as defined by the Pentagon. Accreditation is lost if the ground rules are violated. The releasable information list does not include estimates of enemy strength (the issue in Westmoreland v. CBS, Inc.) and the "information not releasable" list prohibits such things as "cancelled operations," as in the Carter Administration's failed Iranian hostage rescue mission.

In the wake of the Persian Gulf War, Defense Department officials worked with media executives to create new policies in order to improve the press' access to information in subsequent conflicts. Although they agreed not to use press pools after the initial stages of any military operation, there was deep disagreement on whether there should be any official "security review" to determine what was "releasable information." Whereas the news media executives argued that such review is unwarranted, Pentagon officials insisted on having the right to "pre-publication review" of news stories, and this disagreement was never resolved. New York Times, May 22, 1992 at A15.

In the early 1990s Pentagon officials appeared to encourage broad press coverage of American and NATO troops as peacekeepers in Bosnia and Yugoslavia. See Jacqueline Sharkey, "The Shallow End of the Pool." American Journalism Review, Dec. 1994 at 43. When NATO bombed Yugoslavia in April 1999, however, the press once again charged that NATO and Pentagon officials provided minimal information or none at all about the number of attack missions against Yugoslav forces or what targets were hit. When U.S. editors protested, the Pentagon slowly began providing more information about air attacks. New York Times, April 18, 1999 at A11.

6. Balancing National Security against Access to Combat Zones in Afghanistan and Iraq

Soon after the September 11 attacks, the Bush administration sent troops to Afghanistan (dubbed

Operation Enduring Freedom), and journalists complained that the Pentagon was denying them access to American troops in the field. Hustler magazine publisher Larry Flynt again filed suit in 2002, attempting to stop the Pentagon from interfering with journalists' right of access to American ground troops in Afghanistan. Recalling the rulings in Flynt v. Weinberger (1985) and The Nation Magazine v. Department of Defense (1991), the U.S. Court of Appeals for the District of Columbia Circuit again rejected Flynt's claim, ruling that there is "no constitutionally based right for the media to embed with U.S. military forces in combat." Flynt v. Rumsfeld (2004). The two cases that Flynt filed, along with The Nation Magazine case, together raise a recurring question regarding the right of the press to cover military actions, especially in view of the fact that courts held the earlier two cases to be moot.

When the Bush administration sent troops to invade Iraq in March 2003 (Operation Iraqi Freedom), the Pentagon announced that it would permit 500 reporters to accompany military units into battle and report on what they saw, with only limited restrictions. Journalists would thus be "embedded" with the troops as they covered the fighting. Pentagon officials stressed that any journalist who violated their ground rules could be expelled from the combat zone.

In April 2004 someone leaked photographs taken by American soldiers involved in abuse of prisoners at Abu Ghraib prison in Iraq. When Joint Chiefs of

Staff Chair General Richard B. Myers argued that the photographs were classified, the American Civil Liberties Union filed an FOIA suit against the Department of Defense seeking the release of 87 photographs and four videotapes from Abu Ghraib. The Department of Defense at first refused to release the photographs and videotapes (known as the "Darby photos"), arguing that it would instigate Moslems to retaliate against American troops in Iraq, but federal district court Judge Alvin Hellerstein ordered release of the images. The Pentagon appealed, but ultimately withdrew its appeal in March 2006, a few months after the British Broadcasting Corporation had broadcast disturbing video footage of prisoners being tortured in Abu Ghraib. American Civil Liberties Union v. Department of Defense (2005). (See Chapter VII for further discussion of the FOIA and the Abu Ghraib prison scandal.)

7. Legislative Restraints on the Press after September 11, 2001

a.   USA PATRIOT Act

On September 11, 2001, Al Qaeda terrorists flew passenger planes into the World Trade Center and the Pentagon, killing more than 3000 Americans. Congress responded six weeks later by passing a law entitled the United and Strengthening America by Providing Appropriate Tools Required to Intercept and Obstruct Terrorists Act of 2001) (USA PATRIOT Act, Public Law 107–86, 115 Stat. 272, October 26, 2001). Under Section 215 of the USA PATRIOT

Act, the FBI can search a newsroom without having to prove that the owner of the documents in question is under criminal investigation. Section 215 amended the Foreign Intelligence Surveillance Act (FISA) by lowering the level of proof required for an FBI agent to search business records. The person receiving the order to search is forbidden from telling anyone that the FBI is engaged in the search. A secret FISA Court grants a type of administrative subpoena known as a "national security letter," and it is essentially impossible to appeal this order. Unlike a regular subpoena, a national security letter cannot be challenged in court; in this sense it more closely resembles a search warrant. To get a national security letter, FBI agents merely need to show that it is "for an authorized investigation...to protect against international terrorism." In other words the FBI can execute a search of bookstores, libraries, newsrooms and an individual's use of the Internet and then impose a gag prohibiting the person involved from reporting that he or she has just been searched.

It is unclear how Section 215 interacts with the Privacy Protection Act of 1980, which prohibits newsroom searches without a search warrant but permits newsroom searches with a subpoena, although the Privacy Protection Act does have an exception for offenses "relating to the national defense." (See Chapter VIII for a discussion of the Privacy Protection Act.) The USA PATRIOT Act also provides FBI agents with greater authority to trace telephone numbers, tap computers and intercept packages if they consider a journalist's sources suspicious. The law also allows FBI agents to examine the books an individual bought or checked out of a library.

The American Library Association reported that law enforcement officials had made more than 200 formal or informal inquiries about libraries' internal records since 2001. New York Times, Aug. 26, 2005 at A12. The FBI demanded library records from the Library Connection, a consortium of 26 Connecticut libraries, and the American Civil Liberties Union (ACLU) filed suit on the Library Connection's behalf, challenging the FBI's Section 215 request. New York Times, Sept. 1, 2005 at A20. The FBI had used a national security letter to demand library records without a judge's approval. The ACLU's lawsuit was filed under seal, referring to four librarians on the board of the Library Connection only as "John Doe" because the PATRIOT Act provides that FBI requests remain confidential. In June 2006 the FBI dropped its request for a library patron's computer records, explaining that the patron in question had not posed a serious threat to national security after all. Associated Press, June 27, 2006.

A federal district court judge in California struck down a provision of the USA PATRIOT Act as unconstitutionally vague in July 2005. The lawsuit involved challenges from the Kurdistan Workers Party in Turkey and the Liberation Tigers of Tamil Eelam in Sri Lanka, both of which the State Department has designated as "terrorist" groups. The

plaintiffs wanted to provide humanitarian aid to the
two movements, including relief to Sri Lankans left
homeless by the December 2004 tsunami, but they
feared prosecution under the USA PATRIOT Act.
The federal district court judge ruled that the PA-
TRIOT Act's language making it illegal to give
"expert advice" or "training" to foreign terrorist
organizations was impermissibly vague, but the
judge upheld a provision of the PATRIOT Act that
prohibits giving "material support" to terrorist organizations. Humanitarian Law Project et al. v.
Alberto Gonzales (2005).

Congress renewed the USA PATRIOT Act in
March 2006. USA PATRIOT Improvement and
Reauthorization Act, Pub. L. No. 109–177, 120 Stat.
192 (2005). There were a few slight changes; for
example, those who receive subpoenas for information now have the right to challenge the requirement that they refrain from telling anyone, and
those who receive a National Security Letter (a
demand for records or documents) are no longer
required to provide the FBI with the name of their
lawyer if they consult one. Associated Press World-
stream March 8, 2006.

In addition to journalists' concerns about the
USA PATRIOT Act, journalists have charged that
the "War on Terrorism" has subjected them to an
information blackout with regard to suspected terrorists detained but not charged with a specific
crime. For example, the Immigration and Natural-

ization Service (INS) would not release the names of about 1200 mostly Arab men detained for months without charges after September 11. Center for National Security Studies v. Department of Justice (2003), cert. denied (2004). In January 2002 Alberto Gonzalez (before becoming Attorney General) advised George W. Bush that detainees in U.S. custody do not qualify as prisoners of war and therefore are not subject to the 1949 Geneva Convention's prisoner-of-war guidelines. Facing allegations that it authorized the use of torture to obtain information from Al Qaeda and Taliban detainees, the Bush administration released certain documents related to this question in June 2005.

b. Department of Homeland Security

In January 2003 the Bush administration established the Department of Homeland Security, a new law enforcement and investigatory agency which was a consolidation of 22 other federal agencies, including the Federal Emergency Management Agency (FEMA). The Homeland Security Act criminalized leaks of unclassified "critical infrastructure information" provided to the government by companies that in turn are promised immunity from prosecution if they share with Homeland Security what they know. This new law raises a host of new Freedom of Information Act (FOIA) questions, discussed further in Chapter VII.

c. Leaks to Journalists Related to the War on Terrorism

During George W. Bush's second term there were increasing tensions between his administration and the press regarding publication of information related to national security. For example, the press reported that the CIA was interrogating al Qaeda captives in secret prisons known as "black sites" in Eastern Europe. Washington Post, November 2, 2005 at A1. In 2004 New York Times reporters became aware that President Bush had secretly authorized the National Security Agency (NSA) to eavesdrop on Americans and others inside the United States without warrants required by a court established by the 1978 Foreign Intelligence Surveillance Act (FISA). After the White House asked the New York Times not to publish its story about warrantless eavesdropping, arguing that it could alert terrorists that they might be under scrutiny, the New York Times delayed publication for a year until late 2005. New York Times, December 16, 2005 at A1, A22. President George W. Bush acknowledged the existence of its effort to monitor the content of telephone calls and argued that he has inherent authority as president to order wiretaps without warrants. Bush also cited a resolution that Congress had passed a week after the September 11 attacks; he claimed that the resolution, called the Authorization for the Use of Military Force (115 Stat. 224, n.f. 50 U.S.C.A. S 1541) gave him the power as commander-in-chief to engage in eavesdropping without a warrant. New York Times, December 20, 2005 at A–25; Department of Justice, Legal Authorities Supporting the Activities of the NSA Described by the President, January 19, 2006.

Despite the Bush administration's defense of the program, the American Civil Liberties Union (ACLU) filed suit against the NSA, charging that the NSA's wiretapping of telephone calls without warrants was unconstitutional; furthermore, the NSA's wiretapping had interfered with journalists' First Amendment right to speak by telephone with people in the Middle East. American Civil Liberties Union v. National Security Agency (2006). After several months of resistance, the White House agreed to permit the FISA court to rule on whether or not the NSA's program of warrantless eavesdropping is constitutional, although the FISA court's ruling could remain secret. New York Times, July 14, 2006 at A1, A16. The Office of Professional Responsibility (OPR), an internal affairs office of the Department of Justice, had also begun to investigate the warrantless eavesdropping program in response to requests from members of Congress in January 2006, but several months later President George W. Bush blocked the investigation by refusing to give security clearances to the attorneys who were attempting to conduct the probe. As a result the OPR abandoned its investigation. New York Times, July 19, 2006 at A–14.

In May 2006 USA Today broke the news report that the NSA had compiled a huge database of billions of calls inside the United States (not the content of the calls, but a record of to which phone numbers the calls were made and for how long).

AT&T, Verizon and BellSouth relinquished their phone records to the NSA, although Qwest, a smaller phone company based in the Rocky Mountain states, refused to give the NSA its phone records because its executives had legal doubts about the NSA's request. Newsweek, May 22, 2006 at 26. Tash Hepting and the Electronic Frontier Foundation (EFF) filed suit against AT&T in the federal district court in San Francisco, charging that AT&T had violated its customers' privacy by turning over its telephone records to NSA. Federal district court Judge Vaughn Walker ruled that Hepting's suit against AT&T could proceed. Hepting v. AT&T Corp. (2006).

A number of individuals including journalist Studs Terkel joined the American Civil Liberties Union (ACLU) of Illinois in a similar suit against AT&T, charging that AT&T had illegally given information about its customers to NSA. The plaintiffs cited the Electronic Communications Privacy Act (ECPA) which holds that "the provider of electronic communication service to the public shall not . . . divulge information pertaining to a customer to any governmental entity." 18 U.S.C.A. § 2702 (a)(3). In response, AT&T and the government argued that the case should be dismissed based on the state secrets privilege. The state secrets privilege is a common law evidentiary privilege that permits the government to block discovery of information that, if disclosed, "would adversely affect national security." United States v. Reynolds (1953). In asking that the case be dismissed, director of national intelligence John Negroponte refused to confirm or deny that AT&T had in fact turned over the telephone records of its customers to the NSA; instead, he argued that the plaintiffs' claims were not "justiciable" because "the very subject matter of their lawsuit is a state secret." In contrast to the decision in Hepting, the federal district court in Chicago accepted the arguments made by AT&T and the government, and dismissed the case. Terkel v. AT&T Corp. (2006).

A month after the general public learned that NSA was amassing records of its telephone calls, the New York Times published a story about a classified CIA program that tracks records of the global banking industry, the Belgian cooperative called the Society for Worldwide Interbank Financial Telecommunication (SWIFT). SWIFT has permitted CIA, FBI and Treasury Department officials to examine thousands of financial transactions in order to find clues to money trails of terrorists. The program led to the capture of Al Qaeda operative Riduan Isamuddin, known as Hambali, who had masterminded the 2002 bombing of a Bali resort. Treasury Department officials do not seek individual court-approved warrants or subpoenas to analyze specific transactions; instead, they rely on broad administrative subpoenas for millions of records from SWIFT. New York Times, June 23, 2006 at A1, A10. The Bush administration had asked the New York Times not to publish any information about SWIFT. The New York Times' decision proved controversial among both the media and the government.

CHAPTER VI

THE FREE PRESS–FAIR TRIAL CONFLICT

A. THE PROBLEM

1. Introduction

The Sixth Amendment guarantees that in criminal prosecutions the accused shall be entitled to a speedy and public trial "by an impartial jury." This constitutional mandate implies that jurors must not be influenced in their determination of the guilt or innocence of the accused by forces outside the courtroom or by information or material not admitted into evidence at the trial.

If journalists report on a defendant's past criminal record or the fact that he or she has made a confession, the impartiality of individual jurors may be compromised. Because accused persons are entitled only to "impartial" juries and not favorably biased ones, the constitutional requirement binding on the states through the Fourteenth Amendment may also be violated by publicity adverse to the prosecution.

In addition, the criminally accused may not be deprived of life, liberty or property without due process of law, as guaranteed by the Fifth Amendment. Journalists can impede due process by generating pressure on the trial judge through editorial content. Journalists can also disrupt the repose of the courtroom, making fair procedure and calm deliberation difficult if not impossible.

The problem for the courts in attempting to safeguard an accused's Fifth and Sixth Amendment rights arises out of the potentially conflicting guaranty of the First Amendment that Congress shall make no law abridging freedom of the press. This guaranty is interpreted to include court orders. Thus, if a judge issues an order designed to assure a fair and impartial trial but which restricts the press, the order may run afoul of the First Amendment. Some restrictive orders, particularly those that bar newspersons from the courtroom, may also violate the "public trial" requirement of the Sixth Amendment itself.

While most of the potential conflicts between fair trial and free press might be avoided by the exercise of restraint and common sense by the media, judiciary, trial participants and law enforcement officials, these qualities are sometimes in short supply, especially in criminal cases of great public interest. Then the conflict becomes real and troublesome. One example will suffice to illustrate the extreme bounds of the problem.

2. A Case Study: Sheppard v. Maxwell

The classic case of abusive pretrial and trial publicity and improper courtroom behavior by the media is Sheppard v. Maxwell (1966). Correlatively, it is a classic case of the judge's abdication of responsibility and his failure to safeguard the rights of the accused.

In 1954 in a suburb of Cleveland, Ohio, someone slipped into Marilyn Sheppard's bedroom and bludgeoned her to death. Police charged her husband Dr. Samuel Sheppard with her murder, although he steadfastly maintained his innocence. Before and during his trial there were many egregious instances of highly prejudicial publicity. Recounting only a few of them will suggest the environment in which the jurors decided Sheppard's fate.

During the trial, a Cleveland police officer gave testimony that contradicted portions of Sheppard's written statement made to the police. Two days later, in a broadcast over WHK, Robert Considine, Hearst feature writer and radio personality, likened Sheppard to a perjurer and compared the episode to Alger Hiss' confrontation with Whittaker Chambers. Defense counsel asked the judge to question the jury to determine how many had heard the broadcast, but the judge refused and overruled a motion for a continuance based on the same incident. Later a story dealing with the defendant's temper appeared under an eight column headline reading "Sam Called A 'Jekyll–Hyde' By Marilyn, Cousin To Testify." The prosecutor never produced this testimony at trial. Two weeks later a police captain not at the trial and never called as a witness denied certain trial testimony given by Sheppard under the headline " 'Bare–Faced Liar,' Kerr says of Sam."

The judge did not sequester the jurors until after the case was finally submitted to them. After the jury found Sheppard guilty, however, defense counsel discovered that the jurors had made telephone calls every day and no one kept a record of the calls. The trial judge had failed to instruct the bailiffs to prevent such calls. Defense counsel moved for a new trial. The motion was overruled. Sheppard's initial state appeals were unsuccessful and review by the United States Supreme Court was denied. He served ten years in the Ohio penitentiary before obtaining a review of his conviction in the federal courts under a habeas corpus application. Sheppard was re-tried and acquitted in a second trial.

The miscarriage of justice in Sheppard's case became evident in 1997 when DNA tests of 43 year-old blood samples from Sam Sheppard's home pointed to Richard Eberling as the man who in fact murdered Marilyn Sheppard. The Sheppards had hired Eberling as a window-washer. Eberling later served a life sentence for murdering another woman. He once told a nurse that he had murdered Marilyn Sheppard, but refused to make a formal confession before his death in jail in 1998. Sheppard's son, Sam Reese Sheppard, filed a civil suit against the state of Ohio for the wrongful imprisonment of his father, but the jury rejected his claim that his father had been wrongfully imprisoned. Sam Reese Sheppard then filed an appeal with the Eighth District Ohio Court of Appeals and later the Ohio Supreme Court, both of which declined to hear his appeal on the grounds that the statute of limitations on the estate's claim had expired. Murray v. Ohio (2002).

During the ten years Sam Sheppard had spent in jail, the Supreme Court's attitude toward trial and pretrial publicity had been changing. In Marshall v. United States (1959), the Supreme Court, exercising its supervisory authority over the lower federal courts, reversed a conviction for unlawfully dispensing drugs because jurors had seen newspaper stories indicating that the defendant had two prior convictions, one of which was for practicing medicine without a license. The Court ordered a new trial despite assurances from the jurors that they would not be influenced by these stories. Then in Irvin v. Dowd (1961), the Supreme Court held for the first time that jurors' exposure to massive and highly inflammatory pretrial publicity (including news stories that the accused had confessed to six murders) violated the accused's right to a fair trial guaranteed by the due process clause of the Fourteenth Amendment. Again, in Rideau v. Louisiana (1963), a conviction was reversed because of pretrial publicity undermining a fair trial, this time in the form of a televised "interview" of the accused by the local sheriff during which the accused admitted to bank robbery, kidnapping and murder. Finally, in Estes v. Texas (1965), a conviction for large-scale fraud was reversed because pretrial and trial proceedings were televised and filmed. The Court held that such coverage denied to the accused a fair trial because the television and film crews distracted the judge, jurors, witnesses and the accused himself.

In requiring a new trial in Sheppard's case, the Supreme Court signalled its determination to end free-wheeling media coverage of important criminal cases. Its decision intensified the conflict between the judiciary and the media. The High Court recognized in Sheppard that inflammatory press reports could bias jurors, especially when these reports contained prejudicial information never introduced in evidence at trial. The Court then ruled that the defense counsel could presume (without having to prove) that jurors were biased against the defendant following exposure to inflammatory media reports. The Court held that the ubiquitous pretrial publicity calling for Sheppard's conviction made Sheppard's case one of those in which the presumption of juror bias (resulting in an unfair trial) would apply.

The Court further stated that the trial judge compounded the problem of undue publicity in the case by acting as if he lacked the power to control it in any way. The Court catalogued a number of approaches and tactics that the judge might have utilized to guarantee Sheppard a fair trial without imposing restrictions or sanctions *directly* against the press. These will be discussed shortly.

Courts do not automatically assume that massive trial and pretrial publicity always results in the denial of a fair trial. Otherwise, the more notorious the crime, the less the likelihood of obtaining a valid conviction in this age of mass communication. For example, had Lee Harvey Oswald lived, he could not have been convicted for the assassination of President Kennedy because a fair trial would have been impossible anywhere. However, the judicial system will not allow itself to be paralyzed. If the presumed prejudice is rebutted on voir dire examination of the prospective jurors and the circumstances surrounding the trial do not betray inflamed community sentiment, there is no denial of a fair trial merely because of the publicity. In Irvin v. Dowd, the judge excused 268 of the 430 veniremen, as compared with only 20 of the 78 potential jurors questioned in Murphy v. Florida (1975). In Murphy, unlike the Sheppard, Rideau and Estes cases, the conduct of the trial and atmosphere in the courthouse were proper. In such circumstances, the Supreme Court held that the defendant had indeed received a fair trial. Murphy established that courts will consider claims of prejudicial publicity on a case-by-case basis, and will carefully scrutinize the circumstances surrounding the trials. Courts will not automatically reverse convictions because of substantial publicity. See Patton v. Yount (1984), and Mu'Min v. Virginia (1991).

More recently the U.S. Court of Appeals for the Sixth Circuit, sitting en banc, affirmed the trial court's ruling that a defendant had received a fair trial despite the fact that local newspapers had published the transcript of a videotape of his murder confession. In this case Lawrence DeLisle drove his wife and four children into the Detroit River in the family's station wagon. DeLisle and his wife survived, but their four children drowned. DeLisle told police that he had purposely driven his family into the river and that he had attempted to blow up his home eight years earlier. Even though the Wyandotte, Michigan district court ruled that DeLisle's statements would not be admissible at trial, the Michigan Court of Appeals ordered police to play videotapes of DeLisle's confession for the press, and local newspapers published DeLisle's incriminating comments. When DeLisle sought to recant his confession and suppress the statements, the appellate court held that the trial court had adequately safeguarded DeLisle's right to a fair trial through an exhaustive voir dire, after which seven of the 12 empaneled jurors did not know that DeLisle had even confessed. The appellate court thus refused to grant DeLisle a new trial. DeLisle v. Rivers (1999). See also Florida v. Lopez (1993) (broadcast of confession held not to prevent defendant from receiving fair trial).

Even when judges work to allay the effects of pretrial publicity, there is still a serious free press-fair trial problem created when the media cover criminal proceedings. Prosecutors and defense counsel who violate their code of professional responsibility by trying their cases in the news media, law enforcement officials seeking glory for their agencies, judges who cannot resist the limelight, prominent uninvolved parties such as Presidents of the United States who pass judgment on accused in advance of trial and, of course, media representatives who aid, abet and encourage these sources all share the blame for unfair pre-trial publicity.

B.   APPROACHES TO THE PROBLEM

1.   Resort to Judicial Procedural Devices

It is the judge's responsibility to maintain strict control over the courtroom and courthouse environment to ensure that neither the media nor the public interfere with a defendant's fair trial. Judges have a number of procedural devices available to neutralize prejudicial publicity and reporters' behavior without *direct* limitation on them. These include 1) postponing the case until the danger of prejudice abates (granting a continuance), 2) transferring it to another county if the publicity has not saturated the entire state (granting a change of venue), or importing jurors from another county instead of exporting the trial, a rarely used but legal alternative (granting a change of venire), 3) supervising the voir dire to ensure that veniremen with pre-conceived opinions on the defendant's guilt or innocence do not become jurors, 4) sequestering the witnesses or at least admonishing them not to follow the proceedings in the media until they have testified, 5) sealing off or sequestering the jury as soon as it is empaneled to shield the jurors from trial publicity, and 6) issuing a restrictive order prohibiting all parties involved in a case from making prejudicial statements to the media (a gag order). The latter two devices are last resorts; issuing a restrictive order constitutes a prior restraint which is presumed to be unconstitutional except in the most extreme of circumstances, as is discussed below. The other measures may not always be fully effective in insuring a fair trial, however. For instance, postponements and venue changes will have little effect if the publicity is dramatic and pervasive, and sequestration does not shield the jurors from prejudicial publicity before they are selected.

The various means of ensuring a fair trial listed above are designed to protect defendants' rights after they have been arrested and formally charged with a crime. Most of the options listed above would not apply in a situation where the media identify someone as a suspect, but the person is never charged with any crime. For example, when an FBI source leaked Richard Jewell's name as a suspect in the 1996 Olympic Centennial Park bombing in Atlanta, Georgia, Jewell sued for libel. A few weeks after Jewell filed suit, the Society of Professional Journalists amended its Code of Ethics to suggest that the press "be judicious about naming criminal suspects before the formal filing of charges." (Eric Rudolph pled guilty to the Olympic Centennial Park bombing and was sentenced to life in prison in August 2005).

2. Limiting Access of the Media to Information on Pending Legal Matters

Various groups have favored limiting journalists' access to information about pending criminal trials. Some of the means by which judges can limit access are discussed below.

a. *Guidelines for Attorneys on Releasing Information to the Press*

The Judicial Conference of the United States, the agency responsible for formulating policy for the federal courts, has recommended that the United States District Courts firmly regulate both the physical courtroom environs and the release of information by members of their bars and by federal court personnel, but it has rejected the use of the contempt power to prevent unwanted publicity. See Judicial Conference Fair Trial–Free Press Guidelines, 6 Med.L.Rptr. 1897 (1980).

The ABA's Code of Professional Responsibility establishes standards for all attorneys. Consistent with its Reardon Report, ABA Code disciplinary rule DR 7–107 provides guidelines for prosecutors and defense counsel alike regarding the release of information concerning pending criminal cases roughly parallel to the Katzenbach Rules. Guidelines are also provided for professional disciplinary proceedings, juvenile justice proceedings, civil cases and administrative proceedings. In those states that have adopted DR 7–107 by statute or court rule, judges may discipline attorneys for violating its precepts. Although the ultimate sanction of disbarment has yet to be invoked for violation of DR 7–107, harsher disciplinary penalties can be expected in the future. See Gentile v. State Bar of Nevada (1991) (U.S. Supreme Court found Nevada Supreme Court Rule prohibiting lawyers from making extrajudicial statements to be void for vagueness).

b. Exclusion of Camera Operators and Equipment from the Courtroom and Environs

The American Bar Association vigorously opposed cameras in the courtroom for decades through its ABA Canon of Judicial Conduct No. 3A(7). In Chandler v. Florida (1981), however, the U.S. Supreme Court in effect reinterpreted Estes v. Texas (1965), ruling that the Constitution neither mandates nor prohibits cameras in the courtroom. The High Court thus held that states could permit cameras in the courtroom, even in criminal cases and even if the defendants objected. As a result of this change of judicial attitude in Chandler, the American Bar Association, bowing to the inevitable, revoked Canon 3A(7) in 1982 and in its place adopted a guideline stating that judges should be able to authorize unobtrusive camera use under carefully devised local court rules.

Proponents of cameras in the courtroom realized that the backlash against the media following O. J. Simpson's criminal trial in 1995 would discourage the use of videocameras in courts. Indeed, after O. J. Simpson's trial, California's Judicial Council created a new rule which granted trial court judges more authority to ban videocameras from the courtroom. However, after Timothy McVeigh's trial for the 1995 Oklahoma City bombing was moved to Denver, Congress voted to have McVeigh's 1997 trial videotaped and sent back to the families of the victims in Oklahoma City via closed circuit television. Even though the public could not see it, at least the court permitted videotaping for the family members who could not travel to Denver for the trial. Later, when an Internet network asked to videotape McVeigh's execution, a federal district court ruled that the law forbids the recording of federal executions. Entertainment Network Inc. v. Lappin (2001).

By 2005, 49 states permitted cameras in state courtrooms, and 17 states offered webcasts of their state supreme court proceedings as well. See 29 News Media and the Law 2:32–33 (Reporters Committee for Freedom of the Press, Spring 2005). Only the District of Columbia and the state of New York maintain a total ban on video cameras.

Despite this ban, individual judges in New York have occasionally defied the ban. For example, in 2000, the New York Supreme Court in Albany County ruled that banning video cameras from the courtroom violated the First Amendment. When the case of four police officers who killed an unarmed African immigrant by firing 41 bullets into him went to trial, the Court TV Network sought permission to cover the proceedings but was barred by New York's Civil Rights Law § 52. The court, however, held that Section 52's absolute ban on all audio-visual coverage of trial court proceedings was anachronistic. Thus, it granted Court TV's motion and permitted video coverage of the trial in People v. Boss (2000). In 2005 Rensselaer County Judge Patrick McGrath permitted television cameras in his courtroom during a murder trial, but when the defendant objected, the Supreme Court of New York granted the defendant's petition for a new trial, and barred Judge McGrath from permitting "audiovisual coverage" of the new trial. In the Matter of Heckstall v. McGrath (2005). A few months later

Court TV lost its civil suit in which it had argued that Section 52 comprised an unlawful "restraint on the press." The New York Court of Appeals unanimously upheld Section 52, however, explaining that the state legislature had allowed Judiciary Law S 218 (permitting cameras on an experimental basis) to sunset in 1997. Thus the court ruled that banning cameras from the courtroom does not violate the First Amendment. Courtroom Television Network LLC v. State of New York (2005).

With regard to federal courts, the Judicial Conference of the United States voted in 1994 to continue to ban video cameras from federal district courts but voted to permit judges in each of the 13 federal circuit courts of appeal to decide whether to permit cameras in their own circuits. In 1996 the U.S. Court of Appeals for the Ninth Circuit announced that it would permit electronic media coverage of its civil proceedings, and the Second Circuit now permits video cameras to cover civil cases also. The U.S. Courts of Appeal for the Seventh and Ninth Circuits and the U.S Supreme Court permit audio webcasts of archived recordings, the latter made available through the National Archives ten months after the end of each term.

Judges may also ban cameras from the courtroom in high-profile cases, no matter which state the trial is in. For example, judges banned cameras from the trials of Michael Jackson (charged with molesting a child), Kobe Bryant (charged with rape), Martha Stewart (charged with insider trading) and Scott

Peterson (charged with murdering his pregnant wife).

In addition to covering trials, broadcasters have sometimes asked to videotape jury deliberations. Although a few courts in Arizona and Wisconsin have permitted the videotaping of jury deliberations in rare cases, the vast majority of courts have refused to permit cameras in the jury room, citing the concern that cameras could have a distorting effect on the jurors. See State ex rel. Rosenthal v. Poe (2003).

Whereas courts had traditionally been concerned with effects of television coverage of their proceedings, in the 1990s courts had to confront the obverse problem resulting from the proliferation of camcorders and amateur videotapes introduced as evidence. One example occurred in the first Rodney King case, which involved the original criminal prosecution and subsequent acquittal of four police officers accused of using excessive force on Rodney King. There is also the concomitant problem of whether the repeated broadcast of such "home videos" over national television will interfere with a defendant's right to a fair trial. Powell v. Superior Court (People) (1991). Do programs such as "Eyewitness Video," which show actual scenes of alleged crimes, interfere with the defendant's right to a fair trial? The popularity of Court TV on cable television also raises questions about its effects: Does Court TV educate people about the court system or does it acculturate the public to watch trials as merely another form of entertainment like made-for-television movies? Do pseudo-courtroom programs such as "Judge Hatchett" and "Judge Judy" lead the general public to expect resolution of legal conflicts during a half hour time slot? These are questions that remain to be answered.

c. *Sealing Arrest and Other Public Records*

The judiciary can also restrict media access to information about criminal prosecutions by sealing arrest records, either pursuant to statute or under the inherent power of the court. The premier example of this latter approach is the trial of the Watergate defendants in which Judge Sirica sealed many of the documents and tapes in the case from public view. When officials of the Reporters Committee for Freedom of the Press wrote Judge Sirica a letter requesting that the material be unsealed, the letter itself was ordered sealed. See, however, Ashcraft v. Conoco, Inc. (2000) (U.S. Court of Appeals for Fourth Circuit reversed lower court ruling holding reporter and her newspaper in contempt for disclosing terms of a confidential settlement agreement after clerk of court inadvertently gave it to her in a judicially sealed envelope).

More recently, when a woman accused basketball player Kobe Bryant of rape, the trial court held an in camera pretrial hearing to determine whether the woman's previous sexual conduct was relevant. The court reporter accidentally e-mailed a transcript of this hearing to the Associated Press and several other media companies. The judge immediately issued a restraining order prohibiting the media from publishing any information in the transcript. When the case reached the Colorado Supreme Court, it narrowed the judge's gag order, ruling that the media could publish those parts of the transcript that were admissible at trial. The court added that the restraining order did not apply to information that journalists acquired through their own investigative reporting. People v. Bryant (2004). Nevertheless, the Colorado court's narrow holding forbidding publication of the erroneously distributed transcript constituted a prior restraint of the press.

Although secrecy in judicial proceedings is increasing, the press is beginning to attack the practice of sealing public records and removing them from public inspection. The media are now recognized as having legal standing to assert the public's right to be informed about judicial proceedings when individual judges (or statutes) would otherwise shield those proceedings.

d. *Closing the Courtroom*

Parallel to the sealing of public records is the exclusion of the public and the news media from the courtroom during trial and pretrial proceedings, usually in sensational criminal cases. American courts had rarely resorted to this device (see In re Oliver (1948)). It became increasingly popular, however, after the U.S. Supreme Court imposed strict limits on trial courts' power to issue injunctive orders preventing publication of news concerning pending criminal trials in Nebraska Press Association v. Stuart (1976), discussed in Chapter VII. See, however, Press–Enterprise Co. v. Superior Court (1984), discussed in Chapter VII (voir dire proceedings held to be presumptively open to the press and the public unless there is an overriding interest in closing them). The problems engendered by judicial resort to the court-closing device are considered in detail in Chapter VII.

e. *Judicial Protection of Juror Anonymity*

Judges can protect juror anonymity as a means of preventing jury tampering, intimidation, harassment, threats of physical harm and invasion of privacy of the jurors both during and after a trial. Anonymous juries are a fairly new phenomenon. The first anonymous jury empaneled in the United States was in the 1977 trial of drug trafficker Leroy Barnes in New York City. The judge feared that Barnes posed a real danger to the jurors, and took the extraordinary precaution of keeping their identities secret. United States v. Barnes (1979). The problem of press access to jurors' names and identities is discussed further in Chapter VII.

3. Prior Restraint of the News Media

The devices discussed above are employed to prevent the news media from obtaining information about judicial proceedings that the judiciary believes would prejudice such proceedings. An even more difficult legal question than restricting access to news is posed when the judiciary restrains the media from publishing news that they have already obtained. The media's pejorative term for such judicial conduct is "gag order" and, indeed, the effect of judicial restrictive orders is prior restraint of the press.

a. *Problems Engendered*

Once the news media obtain information about pending judicial proceedings which, if published, might seriously affect their conduct and outcome, the courts must choose between previously discussed procedural devices designed to minimize the impact of publication and the issuance of restrictive or "gag" orders directly against the news media. In some cases journalists have refused to obey constitutionally invalid orders enjoining publication of the news. For example, in United States v. Dickinson (1972), a black civil rights worker in Louisiana became the subject of an allegedly baseless prosecution for conspiracy in a murder. Two reporters were assigned by their news service to cover a federal hearing challenging the legality of prosecuting the civil rights worker on the grounds that law enforcement officials were trying to harass or frame him. When the reporters defied the judge's order not to report details of evidence given in open court, they were each fined $300 for criminal contempt. On appeal of the contempt convictions, the United States Court of Appeals for the Fifth Circuit held that the restrictive order violated the First Amendment, but it further held that the news media must obey even constitutionally invalid injunctive orders until they are successfully challenged on appeal.

This means that reporters, editors and publishers may properly be prosecuted for ignoring restrictive orders that violate the First Amendment while such orders are in effect.

The Dickinson case thus held that journalists must, under threat of criminal penalties, obey unconstitutional judicial orders until they are dissolved. State courts have generally followed the Dickinson principle, although there have been exceptions. See State ex rel. Superior Court of Snohomish County v. Sperry (1971) (criminal contempt convictions of two reporters for violation of patently unconstitutional restrictive order vacated on appeal).

The Washington Supreme Court relied on Sperry in overturning a contempt judgment against KHQ–TV after it violated a restraining order barring it from broadcasting a tape recording which had been played in court during the trial of MaymeRuth Coe. Coe's husband Gordon Coe was managing editor of the Spokane Chronicle newspaper, which had offered a reward for information leading to the arrest of a serial rapist. When the "South Hill rapist" was caught, it turned out he was Kevin Coe, Gordon and MaymeRuth Coe's son. After Kevin Coe was convicted, MaymeRuth Coe attempted to pay a hitman $4000 to murder the judge and prosecutor who had convicted her son. It was her conversation with the "hitman," actually an undercover police officer, that KHQ–TV broadcast in defiance of the restraining order, for which it was fined $2000 for contempt. The Supreme Court of Washington reversed

the contempt conviction, however, finding that the
trial court's prior restraint order was patently invalid and void because the tape recording was lawfully obtained and was a matter of public record
because it had been presented in open court. State
v. Coe (1984).

As in Sperry and Coe, a case that the U.S. Court
of Appeals for the First Circuit decided suggests
that the force of Dickinson may be weakening. In
Matter of Providence Journal Co. (1987), the Providence Journal had sought to publish a story based
on FOIA material about a deceased alleged organized crime boss, but the district court had granted
a temporary restraining order in an action brought
by the dead man's heirs. The newspaper appealed
the temporary injunction but also published the
story before the appellate court could decide the
appeal, and the district court found its executive
editor guilty of contempt.

The First Circuit reversed his conviction, specifically distinguishing the Dickinson principle. The
crime boss' "privacy" rights were not sufficient to
lay the basis for a prior restraint and, even if they
could, the district court had not demonstrated that
less extreme measures were unavailable.

Then the appeals court, in an en banc modification of its opinion, made clear that news organizations covered by what they believe to be transparently invalid restraining orders must exhibit good
faith when they publish restrained material by
seeking emergency relief from the appropriate ap-

pellate court first. If timely access to the appellate court is not available or if a timely decision is not forthcoming, the publisher may then proceed to publish and challenge the constitutionality of the order in the subsequent contempt proceeding. The U.S. Supreme Court granted certiorari, but then the petition was dismissed because the court-appointed special prosecutor did not have the authority to appeal on the State of Rhode Island's behalf without the solicitor general's authorization; in other words, the government of Rhode Island had not followed its own procedures. United States v. Providence Journal Co. (1988).

Dickinson and Providence Journal can, of course, be reconciled by noting that in Dickinson the prior restraint was not "transparently" invalid, whereas the Providence Journal restraint was held to be so. Journalists and their editors must realize, however, that judges may permit an asserted right of privacy to be the basis for some types of prior restraint. All a news organization can do to reduce the risk of contempt sanctions is build a record of good faith action if it decides to publish.

b.   *Nebraska Press Association v. Stuart*

Fortunately for the news media, the U.S. Supreme Court finally halted the indiscriminate issuance of restrictive orders in Nebraska Press Association v. Stuart (1976). There the Court unanimously reversed restrictive orders by Nebraska courts barring newspersons from (1) reporting testimony and evidence presented in an open preliminary hearing concerning a ghastly multiple murder case; (2) reporting the existence of any confessions that the accused made to law enforcement officers; and (3) reporting any other facts "strongly implicative" of the accused. This was the first time the High Court had considered the question of judicial restrictive orders aimed directly at the press. It took the opportunity to make clear that its distaste for prior restraints on the press first expressed in Near v. Minnesota (1931) had not abated.

Terming prior restraints on expression "the most serious and the least tolerable infringement on First Amendment rights," the Court reaffirmed the idea expressed in the "Pentagon Papers" case (discussed in Chapter V) that every form of prior restraint comes to the Court with a strong presumption of its unconstitutionality. A majority of the justices, however, explicitly rejected the idea that the First Amendment (at least at this time) absolutely bars all prior restraints of the press when First and Sixth Amendment interests are in conflict. Instead the majority set out certain considerations to aid trial courts in determining whether, in a given case, judges might meet their heavy burden of justifying prior restraint of the media on Sixth Amendment grounds.

First, the courts must determine whether there is "a clear and present danger" that pretrial publicity will impinge upon the defendant's right to a fair trial.

Second, the courts must examine alternatives to prior restraint of publication that may be available to them, such as change of venue or postponement of the trial, and then make findings supported by probative evidence that alternatives short of prior restraint orders will not be effective.

Third, even where the courts believe that they can establish that less drastic alternatives will not work, they must also assess the probable effectiveness of prior restraint on publication as a method of safeguarding the accused's right to a fair trial. If, as a practical matter, a prior restraint order will not safeguard the accused's rights, it should not be entered. In the Nebraska Press Association case the facts militated against entry of such orders. Among other things, the issuing courts could not obtain jurisdiction over all news media organizations and persons reporting on the murder case, and thus might not be able to enforce their orders uniformly and effectively. Furthermore, because the murders occurred in a small community of 850 persons, mouth-to-mouth rumors would saturate the community anyway and might be more prejudicial to a fair trial than reasonably accurate news accounts.

Fourth, trial courts must consider whether proposed restrictive orders would prevent the reporting of events transpiring in open court. To the extent they have this effect, such orders are constitutionally invalid.

Finally, the courts must consider carefully the terms of such orders. The prohibitions on the media must be precise and not overbroad. In Nebraska Press Association, one restriction on the news media was that they not disseminate information "strongly implicative of the accused as the perpetrator of the slayings." This language was held to be vague and overbroad.

Regarding this last consideration, a restrictive order to be valid must be appropriately narrow and precise and yet must also be effective in safeguarding the accused's Sixth Amendment rights. Walking this constitutional tightrope will not be easy. It is safe to say that the matters that must be considered before a prior restraint order may be entered will severely curtail resort to such orders in the future. For this reason and because of the Supreme Court's unanimous reaffirmation of its attitude of hostility toward prior restraints, Nebraska Press Association v. Stuart was an important victory for the press, but not the last word on the subject. See also Gentile v. State Bar of Nevada (1991), mentioned above.

The relative security that Nebraska Press Association had provided was called into question in Cable News Network, Inc. v. Manuel Noriega (1990). After the U.S. invasion of Panama, the Panamanian dictator Manuel Noriega was captured and brought to Miami to stand trial for drug trafficking. Federal prison officials (violating their own policy against monitoring attorney-client conversations) recorded several of Noriega's telephone calls to his attorneys. The Cable News Network (CNN) obtained seven of these tapes from an unidentified source and broadcast one of the tapes. A federal district court judge ordered CNN to turn over all the Noriega tapes so that he could determine whether anything in the tapes presented an immediate and irreparable danger to Noriega's right to a fair trial. The judge also enjoined CNN from further broadcasting privileged communications in the tapes. The U.S. Court of Appeals for the Eleventh Circuit denied CNN relief from the restraining order and directed CNN to relinquish the tapes. The U.S. Supreme Court denied certiorari a week later. The district court judge ultimately lifted the restraining order against CNN after reviewing the tapes and concluding that CNN's broadcast of them would not interfere with Noriega's right to a fair trial. In 1994, however, the U.S. Attorney's office in Miami filed criminal contempt of court charges against CNN, and a federal judge fined CNN for the original broadcast. United States v. Cable News Network (1994). At present no other jurisdiction has chosen to follow the Eleventh Circuit decision.

c. *Gag Orders on Trial Participants Following Nebraska Press Association v. Stuart*

Since Nebraska Press Association, judges have understood that they should not impose restraints on the press. Instead, they impose gag orders on the sources of information, making an end-run around the Constitution's presumption against prior restraint. Judges have apparently concluded that prior restraints on individual trial participants are somehow less offensive than prior restraints on the press. Most (but not all) courts accept the principle that media organizations have standing to challenge a gag order imposed on trial participants. Journal Publishing Co. v. Mechem (1986). See, however, Ireland v. Smith (In re Detroit Free Press) (2000) (Supreme Court of Michigan denied standing to Detroit Free Press unless it could identify a specific "willing speaker").

As in the Detroit Free Press case, a trial court judge in South Dakota issued a gag order on all trial participants in a case in which a 14 year-old girl was found dead following a forced run at a state juvenile detention center. When former Governor William Janklow and former Senator James Abour-ezk sparred publicly about the guilt or innocence of two women charged with manslaughter in the 14 year-old girl's death, the trial court judge barred journalists from conducting interviews or broadcast-ing inside the courtroom. The judge also ordered all participants not to discuss the case with the media. The South Dakota Supreme Court upheld his gag order on the grounds that it was necessary to en-sure a fair trial for the two defendants. Sioux Falls Argus Leader v. Miller (2000).

Similarly, when prosecutors charged Louisiana Insurance Commissioner James Harvey Brown with insurance fraud, the judge placed a gag order on all trial participants. Brown himself, the criminal de-fendant, challenged the gag order as unconstitution-al, claiming that it violated his First Amendment right to free speech. The U.S. Court of Appeals for the Fifth Circuit upheld the gag order, however, basing it on a "substantial likelihood" that publicity could adversely influence the court's ability to conduct a fair trial. U.S. v. Brown (2000).

In contrast to Sioux Fall Argus Leader and Brown, a federal district court struck down a Florida state court's gag order on all participants in a civil suit against tobacco companies because the order was overbroad. The federal district court held that the state court must first make some findings that participants' out-of-court statements would jeopardize the defendants' right to a fair trial. Dow Jones & Co. v. Kaye (2000).

4. Subsequent Criminal Punishment of the News Media

Subsequent criminal punishment of the news media may be just as harmful to the media's ability to inform the public about judicial matters as prior restraints or "gag orders." In Landmark Communications, Inc. v. Virginia (1978) the U.S. Supreme Court struck down as unduly restrictive of press freedom a Virginia statute making it a crime to divulge information regarding proceedings before a state judicial review commission that was hearing complaints alleging the incompetence or misconduct of sitting judges. In this case the Virginian Pilot was convicted of violating the statute when it accurately reported on a pending commission inquiry and identified the judge involved.

In reversing the conviction, the High Court made it clear that subsequent punishment of the press for publishing accurate information can be just as dangerous a violation of the First and Fourteenth

Amendments as judicial and legislative attempts to prevent publication in the first instance. Compare the media contempt cases of Bridges v. California (1941); Pennekamp v. Florida (1946); Craig v. Harney (1947); Wood v. Georgia (1962). But see Kamasinski v. Judicial Review Council (1994), (U.S. Court of Appeals for Second Circuit upheld as constitutional Connecticut's statutory ban on disclosure of facts that a complaint had been filed with the state's judicial review council).

A case similar in effect to the Landmark decision is Smith v. Daily Mail Publishing Co. (1979). In this case, a 15–year-old boy shot and killed a 14–year-old classmate. Two newspapers published his name, violating West Virginia statutes (W.Va. Code § 49–7–3, 20 (1976)) making it a misdemeanor for a *newspaper* (but not a radio or television station) to publish, without the written approval of the juvenile court, the name of any youth charged as a juvenile offender. (See pp. 173–176 in Chapter III for a discussion of Landmark and Smith with regard to invasion of privacy.) The West Virginia Supreme Court of Appeals ruled that the statute under which the newspapers were indicted violated the First and Fourteenth Amendments, and the U.S. Supreme Court affirmed.

Both Landmark and Smith require a balancing of the media's interests in freely disseminating information against the state's interests in maintaining confidential judicial proceedings. In Landmark, the Supreme Court held that the state's interests in confidentiality of investigations of members of the judiciary simply did not outweigh First Amendment interests. In Smith the High Court held that a criminal statute permitting broadcasters but not newspapers to disclose the names of alleged juvenile offenders did not further the state's interest in maintaining confidentiality of juvenile proceedings.

CHAPTER VII

FREEDOM TO GATHER NEWS AND INFORMATION

A. INTRODUCTION

The freedom of expression guaranteed by the First Amendment would have little meaning if there were nothing to express. The First Amendment assumes that the citizenry will have access to information, particularly concerning their governance, as the grist for meaningful expression in a democratic society. As James Madison wrote, "A popular Government, without popular information, or the means of acquiring it, is but a Prologue to a Farce or a Tragedy; or, perhaps both. Knowledge will forever govern ignorance: And a people who mean to be their own Governors, must arm themselves with the power which knowledge gives." Letter to W.T. Barry, August 4, 1822, quoted in Environmental Protection Agency v. Mink (1973) (dissenting opinion of Douglas, J.).

Nevertheless, since the time of George Washington, the federal and state governments have claimed the right to withhold information about their activities and operations in the "public interest" and to restrict journalists' access to certain sources of information. It is clear, however, that not all government secrecy and restrictions on the gathering of information are justified.

In the 1950s the media began a movement to reverse the trend toward secret government. By the late 1970s they had won some notable successes in the fight for open government, such as the federal Freedom of Information Act (FOIA) and federal and state open meetings legislation. The 1980s saw a pendulum swing in the opposite direction with the introduction of a comprehensive package of amendments to FOIA which could only be described as constricting the flow of information from the government to the press and public. The pendulum swung back toward an open government again during the Clinton administration when former Attorney General Janet Reno sent a memorandum calling for "maximum responsible disclosure." Memorandum for Heads of Departments and Agencies from Attorney General Janet Reno, Oct. 4, 1993. The pendulum swung back toward less openness a month after the September 11 terrorist attacks in 2001, when former Attorney General John Ashcroft issued a memo telling federal agencies that the Justice Department would support agency decisions to withhold information if they had a "sound legal basis." In 2002 former White House Chief of Staff Andrew Card ordered federal agencies to withhold "sensitive" information to protect national security even if it was not classified.

It is clear, then, that ease of access to government data cannot be taken for granted but depends to a large extent on the good will and grace of the legislative and executive branches of government.

B.   THE FEDERAL FREEDOM OF INFORMATION ACT (FOIA)

1.   Historical Background

In 1966 Congress passed the Freedom of Information Act (FOIA), 5 U.S.C.A. § 552. It requires federal executive and independent regulatory agencies to publish indexes in the Federal Register and make documents and records available to anyone who requests them if they are not specifically exempted from disclosure by the Act itself. The language of the Act is affirmative in requiring disclosure; nowhere does it require nondisclosure. Documents generated by Congress and the Office of the President are not subject to FOIA, but those of federal agencies are. An agency may, if it chooses, refuse to release information under a claim that the information is covered by one or more of the nine enumerated exemptions discussed below. If an agency refuses to release information, it may be required to defend its refusal in federal court where the burden of justification is on the withholding agency, not on the person or organization seeking disclosure. With Congress' bestowal of jurisdiction upon the federal courts to hear complaints of alleged FOIA violations, agency officials are no longer the sole judges of what information should and should not be made available to the public.

2.   Operation of the Original Act

a.   *In the Courts*

Results of litigation under the original FOIA were mixed. Although the courts placed the burden on the agencies to justify withholding information and exercised the injunctive jurisdiction to force disclosure when deemed appropriate, they also construed certain of the exemptions broadly.

3.   Early Amendments to FOIA

After experience with the operation of FOIA over several years, Congress amended it in 1974 and again in 1986 to increase and expedite governmental disclosure. The amendments were both substantive and procedural. One substantive amendment defined a federal agency to encompass any executive or military department, including the Executive Office of the President itself, government corporations, and any independent regulatory agency. These amendments were needed because in the past some administrative units had tried to avoid responding to FOIA requests by claiming they were not "agencies."

The procedural amendments were designed to speed the release of information and reduce the costs to those who request it. The amendments required the agencies to establish uniform fee schedules and limit fees to reasonable charges for document searches and duplication. The 1986 amendments provided for limited fee waivers for the news media, educational and scientific institutions.

4. The Electronic Freedom of Information Act

Because some federal agencies had contended in the early 1990s that the FOIA did not apply to electronic records, Congress finally passed the Electronic Freedom of Information Act (EFOIA) in 1996. Pub.L. 104–231, 110 Stat. 3048 (1996), codified in 5 U.S.C.A. § 552, as amended (West Supp. 1998). The EFOIA requires that federal agencies apply the same standards of disclosure to electronic records that they have always applied to "hard copy" paper documents, including all e-mail messages as well as letters or notes. The amendment also requires agencies to publish an on-line index of the documents they have, and to set up "electronic reading rooms" in which their documents are available online. If an agency determines that certain information is likely to be requested more than once, the agency must put that information in the "electronic reading room" where the public has routine access to it. The EFOIA gives agencies 20 working days rather than 10 (as had been the rule up to 1996) to respond to FOIA requests. If the agency cannot comply within 20 days, it must notify the person who requested the information and give an estimated time of compliance. If redactions are made to protect against unwarranted invasions of personal privacy, agencies must, if technically feasible, indicate the places in their documents where the deletions occur.

a. *Expedited Review*

When Congress passed the EFOIA in 1996, it included a provision allowing journalists and the public to seek expedited review when there is a compelling need for the public to have government information. For example, Mohamed Al Fayed, whose son Dodi Al Fayed died in the 1997 car crash with Princess Diana, sought expedited review for 21 FOI requests after someone tried to sell him supposed CIA papers detailing a British government plot to murder Princess Diana, but the U.S. Court of Appeals for the District of Columbia Circuit denied expedited review. Al Fayed v. CIA (2001).

b. *Fees for Processing FOIA Requests*

Although litigation or the threat of it is very important to the operation of FOIA, the proof of the legislation is in its day-to-day administration by the agencies themselves. Litigation is costly and time consuming. The media need information quickly and at reasonable cost. At the administrative level, too, the results have been mixed. Some agencies such as the Department of Justice (excluding the FBI) have promulgated fair and reasonable regulations for the expeditious release of information and are generally following them. Some agencies have not been as conscientious. Journalists have too often faced exorbitant charges for searches and copying and extensive delays in release of information.

For example, when Hartford Courant reporter Jack Dolan requested an electronic copy of all criminal conviction records in Connecticut, the Department of Public Safety calculated the fee for his request at $20.4 million. Connecticut's Freedom of Information Commission and a superior court judge upheld the $20.4 million fee. Hartford Courant Company v. Freedom of Information Commission (2002). And in 2002 the California Department of Forestry and Fire Protection charged the Environmental Protection Information Center (EPIC) $40,000 for a CD–ROM with data on logging operations in California. Despite this type of "fee abuse," vast amounts of information that the government would have kept from view before the FOIA was passed have been made routinely available to the public and the media.

The FOIA provides that a plaintiff should recover attorney's fees if the plaintiff has "substantially prevailed." A civil rights case involving the Americans with Disabilities Act, however, set a precedent permitting federal agencies to avoid paying attorney's fees in FOIA litigation by releasing documents and settling cases at the last minute. Buckhannon Board and Care Home, Inc. v. West Virginia Department of Health and Human Resources (2001).

In 2005 President George W. Bush signed Executive Order 13,392 (70 Fed. Reg. 75,373, December 14, 2005), entitled Improving Agency Disclosure of Information. This executive order outlines steps that each federal agency must take regarding FOIA processing, including designating a chief FOIA officer and establishing a requester service center, but there are no provisions for enforcement of time limits on fulfilling requests, penalties for noncompliance or for Congressional oversight.

5. Litigation Involving the FOIA's Nine Exemptions

The discussion below covers the nine exemptions that agencies may invoke to avoid disclosure, as well as examples of litigation and judicial construction of the exemptions.

(1)(a) specifically authorized under criteria established by an executive order to be kept secret in the interest of national defense or foreign policy and (b) are in fact properly classified pursuant to such executive order.

In Environmental Protection Agency v. Mink (1973), the Supreme Court held in effect that the executive branch had some authority to determine under Executive Order 10501 (setting up the present government classification system) what information was to be kept secret in the interest of national defense or foreign policy. The Court ruled that Exemption 1 as originally adopted in 1966 permitted no challenge whatsoever to the classification of a document. It would not allow a federal district court to study in closed chambers classified documents concerning an underground nuclear test on Amchitka Island in order to isolate non-secret portions and order their release. A classified stamp on a file meant that the information in the file could not be disclosed unless a government employee first redacted sensitive or classified information. The Mink case became the catalyst for Congress to amend FOIA in 1974 to give courts the power to inspect classified documents in closed chambers to determine whether they are properly classified, and order their release if they are not. P.L. 93–502, 88 Stat. 1561. (Part (b) in Exemption 1 above, exempting properly classified documents, was added as part of the 1974 amendments.)

The current system of classification has three tiers: 1) "confidential," (information which could harm national security if released), 2) "secret" (information which could cause serious damage to national security if released), and 3) "top secret" (information which could cause exceptionally grave damage to national security if released). In 1995 former President Bill Clinton issued Executive Order No. 12958, entitled "Classified National Security Information," (3 C.F.R. 333, 1996) that would require federal agencies to declassify most documents after 25 years and make them available to the public. Clinton's executive order exempted CIA documents that would reveal names of its "intelligence sources" (spies) as well as Department of Defense documents regarding strategies for war, for example.

Executive Order No. 12958 would have declassified about 600 million documents. After Los Alamos National Laboratory scientist Wen Ho Lee was accused of giving nuclear secrets to China, however, Congress suspended the automatic declassification for records after 25 years when it passed the National Defense Authorization Act for 1999 and again for 2000 (Public Law 106–65). One provision mandated that all 600 million documents declassified since 1995 must be reviewed again to ensure that none of them contained any data on nuclear weapons.

President George W. Bush amended Clinton's executive order with a new executive order in which government officials are allowed to classify information even if they doubt that classification is necessary. Bush also postponed until December 31, 2006, the time at which documents classified for 25 years would be automatically declassified. Unlike Clinton, Bush allowed public documents to be re-classified if the director of an agency thought it necessary. Executive Order No. 13292, 68 Fed. Reg. 15315, Mar. 28, 2003. A group of historians discovered in 2006 that documents they had photocopied decades ago had disappeared from open files. Apparently the CIA, the Defense Intelligence Agency, the Air Force and other agencies had removed more than 55,000 pages of information from the National Archives because officials of these agencies believed that the documents should not have been declassified. The documents removed from open files included intelligence estimates from the Korean War, reports on Communism in Mexico in the 1960s and Treasury Department records from the 1960s, for example. New York Times, March 3, 2006 at A1, A18.

In past years the FBI has also invoked Exemption 1 in denying access to files on unlikely subjects ranging from race relations and unionization efforts among Chicago slaughterhouse workers in the 1930s to African–American author James Baldwin. British historian Eric Halpern had requested files on the slaughterhouse workers and British author James Campbell had requested the FBI's file on James Baldwin, but the FBI refused in both cases. After the U.S. Court of Appeals for the Second Circuit remanded Halpern's case for a further explanation of how releasing files on unionization in the 1930s would threaten national security, the federal district court upheld the FBI's refusal under Exemption 1 after the FBI argued that releasing the requested documents would impair the relationship between the United States and a foreign government. Halpern v. FBI (2001). The U.S. Court of Appeals for the D.C. Circuit likewise remanded Campbell's case for a better explanation of how releasing files on James Baldwin would threaten national security, but the federal district court likewise ruled that the FBI could continue to invoke Exemption 1 and withhold the requested documents. Campbell v. United States Department of Justice (2002).

(2) related solely to the internal personnel rules and practices of an agency.

There has been a question concerning Exemption 2 with regard to whether it applies to agency staff manuals. When a citizen sought access to a Bureau of Alcohol, Tobacco and Firearms (BATF) staff manual titled "Surveillance of Premises, Vehicles and Persons," the U.S. Court of Appeals for the District of Columbia Circuit upheld the Bureau's decision to release all but 20 pages, which described its internal practices. Crooker v. Bureau of Alcohol, Tobacco & Firearms (1981). See also Audubon Society v. United States Forest Service (1997). (U.S. Court of Appeals for Tenth Circuit ordered U.S. Forest Service to disclose maps of location of Mexican spotted owl; maps were held to be unrelated to personnel practices).

After the terrorist attacks of September 11, 2001, former Attorney General John Ashcroft issued a memo to FOI officers instructing them to use Exemption 2 to deny any agency records which might be useful to terrorists. Attorney General's Memorandum of October 12, 2001. Under Exemption 2, the Federal Energy Regulatory Commission (FERC) has the right to avoid disclosure of "sensitive information contained in vulnerability assessments." This would allow the FERC to avoid public disclosure of information relating to internal weaknesses in the "critical infrastructure" of a company that supplies energy. For example, if a natural gas pipeline explodes and kills people, journalists and the public would need to know whether the company maintaining the pipelines was keeping them in proper working order, but if the FERC invokes Exemption 2, the press and public would be denied this information.

   (3) matters specifically exempted from disclosure by statute (other than [the Privacy Act]), provided that such statute (a) requires that the matters be withheld from the public in such a manner as to leave no discretion on the issue, or (b) estab-

lishes particular criteria for withholding or refers to particular types of matters to be withheld.

This exemption is designed to prevent disclosure of information required or permitted to be kept secret by numerous other federal laws. An example of a statute which would exempt information from disclosure is the National Security Act of 1947, which Congress amended in 1984, exempting entire systems of CIA files from search and review. The law provides for judicial review of whether the files are classified, but judicial review has not been effective because judges are reluctant to second-guess the executive branch on classification of national security materials.

The courts' willingness to defer to Exemption 3 in the interests of national security is illustrated by the case of CIA v. Sims (1985). From 1953 to 1966, the CIA financed a research project code-named MKULTRA in which 185 researchers at more than 80 universities received funding to study the effects of mind-altering substances on people. Several MKULTRA subprojects involved experiments in which researchers surreptitiously administered dangerous drugs such as LSD to unwitting human subjects. At least two people died as a result of the MKULTRA experiments, and others may have suffered impaired health. In 1963 the CIA's inspector general investigated the project and reported that researchers were using people as guinea pigs without their knowledge. CIA files on MKULTRA were declassified in 1970. The Public Citizen Health Research Group and a private attorney filed an FOIA request asking for the names of universities and individuals who had conducted the experiments. The CIA refused to disclose names of the researchers and 21 of the institutions involved, saying that they had been promised confidentiality. The CIA argued that their names were exempt from disclosure under the National Security Act of 1947, which states that "the Director of Central Intelligence shall be responsible for protecting intelligence sources . . . from unauthorized disclosure." The Supreme Court agreed with the CIA that Exemption 3 of FOIA, providing that an agency need not disclose matters specifically exempted from disclosure by statute, was applicable, and the CIA could withhold the information. The Court added that the CIA Director's decisions, because he "must of course be familiar with the whole picture, as judges are not, are worthy of great deference given the magnitude of the national security interests and potential risks at stake." CIA v. Sims (1985). The Court has thus given the CIA an indeterminate degree of latitude in making disclosure decisions within the context of intelligence gathering. The Court's "great deference" standard may encourage the CIA to assert national security justification in an effort to hide improvident or incompetent behavior. In effect, CIA v. Sims expanded permissible Exemption 3 nondisclosure in a manner that could virtually exempt the CIA from FOIA coverage. L. Good and D. Williams, "Developments under the Freedom of Information Act—1985," 1986 Duke L.J. 384, at 433.

For the past two decades the CIA has also invoked the "Glomar response" (named after a secret underwater vessel, the Glomar Explorer), meaning a refusal to confirm or deny the existence of records requested under FOIA. To complicate matters further, several months after the terrorist attacks of September 11, 2001, Congress passed the CIA Information Act. 50 U.S.C. 431 (2002). The CIA Information Act expressly exempts from disclosure CIA files labeled "operational." Since its passage in 2002, the CIA has used the CIA Information Act to place large amounts of material outside the reach of FOIA.

(4) in the nature of trade secrets and commercial or financial information obtained from a person and privileged or confidential.

The so-called "reverse FOIA case," Chrysler Corp. v. Brown (1979), gives an expansive interpretation to FOIA to permit federal agencies to release certain classes of information required to be submitted to these agencies by private businesses, including their trade secrets and confidential statistical data. In so ruling the Court repeated the idea that FOIA is exclusively a disclosure statute and that the exemptions in it, particularly the one dealing with trade secrets, permit agencies to withhold records but do not require them to do so. This ruling has created problems for the government in collecting privately held confidential business information. The business community has called for amendment of the Act to require agencies to withhold certain records in order to prevent harm to businesses that make disclosures of information to the government.

In 1982 two federal agencies did release information that hurt some companies. The EPA mistakenly disclosed the formula for one of Monsanto's most profitable products, an herbicide, to one of its major competitors in response to the latter's FOIA request. Washington Post, Sept. 18, 1982, p. A1. The Food and Drug Administration (FDA) released "the ingredients and molecular structure of a new drug about to be marketed by a major pharmaceutical company" to that company's competitor. 4 Gov. Disclosure Rep. Bull. No. 2, Para. 2.2 (Feb. 8, 1983). These two incidents contributed to corporations' long-standing fears that the commercially sensitive data that they are compelled to disclose would inadvertently be made available to competitors through FOIA.

Possibly in response to these incidents and Chrysler v. Brown, Congress passed the National Cooperative Research Act of 1984, P.L. 98–462, 15 U.S.C.A. § 4305(d). This law limits antitrust liability for companies embarking on joint research projects if they notify the Federal Trade Commission (FTC) and the Attorney General about their joint projects. The Research Act qualifies as an Exemption 3 statute of the FOIA by mandating nondisclosure by the FTC. Because it permits no agency discretion regarding disclosure, the Research Act limits the effect of the pro-disclosure interpretation in Chrysler v. Brown.

Several years ago the Federal Aviation Administration tried to use the "financial information" arguments in Exemption 4 to deny the Chicago Tribune documents on in-flight medical emergencies because the emergencies "occurred while the aircraft were in revenue-producing operations;" thus the FAA argued that the Tribune was requesting financial information. A federal district court disagreed, however, ruling that the FAA must provide data on flight and aircraft tail numbers of flights on which mid-air emergencies had occurred. Chicago Tribune v. Federal Aviation Administration (1998).

To the alarm of some researchers, in 1998 Congress passed a one-sentence amendment to an appropriations bill requiring that anyone can make an FOIA request for "all data produced" when researchers publish a study paid for with any public funds. The FOIA request would cover everything from a summary of findings to scientists' notebooks, e-mail messages or even information about human subjects. Scientists who opposed this amendment argued that it would allow lawyers from private companies to harass scientists collecting data on controversial issues such as environmental health, pollution and global warming. Other opponents observed that the amendment applies to nonprofit groups receiving government grants but not to private corporations doing research through government contracts; in other words, the amendment would cover a YMCA receiving federal grant money but not to Boeing's research, paid for with government contracts.

The one-sentence amendment had not taken effect in late 1999, so the Public Citizen Health Research Group could not rely on it in its request to the Food and Drug Administration (FDA) for data on drug testing that had resulted in deaths or serious injuries to human subjects. The FDA cited Exemption 4 in denying the watchdog group's request. Although three drug companies ultimately consented to the FDA's disclosure of their data, Schering Corporation objected, arguing that disclosure of five files could facilitate a competing drug company's development of three anti-fungal agents, a hypertension drug and a drug to suppress asthma. The Court of Appeals for the D.C. Circuit upheld the FDA's decision not to release the files, finding that the public's interest in knowing why Schering had abandoned tests on these drugs did not outweigh Schering's proprietary interests in the data. Public Citizen Health Research Group v. FDA (1999).

> (5) in the nature of inter-agency or intra-agency memoranda or letters which would not be available by law to a party other than an agency in litigation with the agency.

This exemption is designed to protect working papers, studies and reports prepared within an agency or circulated among government personnel as the basis of an agency's final decision. Communication between an agency and its legal counsel is also shielded from disclosure.

This exemption is also called the executive privilege exemption. Executive privilege is a common law privilege which presidents beginning with George Washington have invoked to keep records and documents of the executive branch and the administrative agencies secret. In United States v. Nixon (1974), Richard Nixon argued that executive privilege protected his White House tapes when the special prosecutor subpoenaed them. The Supreme Court, however, ruled that the president has an absolute executive privilege only when the material in question consists of military or diplomatic secrets. Because the White House tapes did not contain such secrets, there was only a limited privilege, and the High Court ordered Nixon to surrender the tapes. When Nixon tried to take his White House papers with him upon leaving office, he encountered a great public outcry. In response to public pressure, in 1974 Congress passed the Presidential Records and Materials Preservation Act, 44 U.S.C. § 210 (1989), to prohibit destruction of records related to the Watergate scandal or otherwise of historical significance. Insisting that the papers were his personal property, Nixon sued for compensation. In 1992 the U.S. Court of Appeals for the District of Columbia Circuit ruled that the papers had indeed been Nixon's private property, and directed the federal district court to determine how much money Nixon should receive as compensation. Nixon v. United States (1992).

Many years after the Watergate scandal, officials of the Reagan and Bush administrations attempted to erase all electronically stored information when they left office. Director of the National Security Archive Scott Armstrong obtained a temporary injunction to prevent the Reagan administration from destroying its electronic files, and then asked the court to extend the order to prevent the first Bush administration from destroying its computer tapes four years later. Armstrong v. Bush (1992). On appeal, the U.S. Court of Appeals for the District of of Columbia Circuit ruled that the first Bush administration could not destroy the electronic records created by the Executive Office of the President and by the National Security Council during the Bush and Reagan administrations; e-mail messages are also records under the Federal Records Act (44 U.S.C.A. § 2100). Armstrong v. Executive Office of the President (1993).

In 1995 the National Archives and Records Administration authorized government agencies to erase e-mail messages and electronic files after they had been copied to paper. The watchdog group Public Citizen immediately filed suit, however, arguing that the directive General Records Schedule 20 (GRS 20) regulation permitting destruction of electronic files was too broad. Public Citizen argued that John Carlin, the Archivist of the United States, had ignored Armstrong v. Executive Office of the President (1993) in which the court held that electronic records must be managed under the Federal Records Act (44 U.S.C.A. § 2100). The Court of

Appeals for the D.C. Circuit ruled in favor of Carlin, however, holding that Congress intended to reduce unnecessary retention of records when it passed the Records Disposal Act, and GRS 20 provided a means of accomplishing this. Furthermore, federal agencies may determine for themselves how to maintain their record-keeping systems. Public Citizen v. Carlin (1999).

The Court of Appeals for the D.C. Circuit expanded Exemption 5 in a case dealing with the Department of Justice's Office of Special Investigations' report on former United Nations Secretary–General Kurt Waldheim. The report detailed Waldheim's involvement in Nazi massacres of Yugoslav partisans and Jews and deportation of 60,000 Jews from Greece. The court held that the report was exempt from disclosure as an internal memorandum in the form of an "attorney work product" because former Attorney General Edwin Meese used the report to place Waldheim on a list of aliens to be barred from the United States. Mapother v. Department of Justice (1993). See also Linder v. Department of Defense (1998) (finding that CIA properly invoked privilege in refusing to release documents on death of a mechanical engineer allegedly murdered by Contras in Nicaragua).

Following the expanded interpretation of Exemption 5 in Mapother, the Court of Appeals for the Ninth Circuit also read Exemption 5 broadly in Kasza v. Browner (1998). The appellate court held that Exemption 5 barred discovery and trial in a case brought by workers and deceased workers' widows at the Groom Dry Lake Air Force base. The workers claimed that they had suffered respiratory distress, cancers and bleeding skin lesions as a result of the Air Force's burning of hazardous waste in open trenches. The Air Force, however, argued that Exemption 5, also known as the common law "state secrets privilege," barred disclosure of "security sensitive environmental data." Despite the fact that the EPA had filed a report on the toxic emissions at Groom Dry Lake, and the Resource Conservation and Recovery Act requires revelation of environmental hazards, President Clinton invoked Exemption 5 to bar the EPA report from disclosure. The appellate court held that the state secrets privilege is absolute; furthermore, once invoked, this privilege does not require the President to explain why a requested document affects national security. Although the workers appealed, the Supreme Court declined to review the case.

In 2001 the U.S. Supreme Court narrowed the scope of Exemption 5. The High Court held that the Department of the Interior's Bureau of Indian Affairs had to release copies of its correspondence with Native American tribes to farmers who wanted to use water from the Klamath River for irrigation. Although the Bureau of Indian Affairs had argued that its trustee relationship with the Native American tribes made its correspondence with them privileged and invoked Exemption 5, the High Court held that the tribes were an "interested party" in a Department of the Interior decision-making process. Furthermore, and the correspondence did not fall within the inter-or intra-agency exception because the documents were not "internal." Department of the Interior v. Klamath Water Users Protective Association (2001).

(6) in the nature of personnel and medical files and similar files the disclosure of which would constitute a clearly unwarranted invasion of personal privacy.

There have been numerous attempts to invoke Exemption 6 during the past several years. A few of the cases in which courts have not permitted the government to invoke Exemption 6 are Lissner v. U.S. Customs Service (2001) (U.S. Customs Service ordered to disclose information about police who smuggled steroids into California from Mexico); Perlman v. U.S. Department of Justice (2002) (Immigration and Naturalization Service ordered to release files on sham investments under its EB–5 program).

On the other hand, courts have upheld the use of Exemption 6 to deny information in other cases such as Kallstrom v. City of Columbus (2001) (release of private information about undercover narcotics officer would result in risk of serious harm); Forest Guardians v. U.S. Federal Emergency Management Agency (FEMA) (2005) (digital version of FEMA flood maps in New Mexico not released because it could compromise privacy of residents in area); News–Press v. United States Department of Homeland Security (2005) (government did not have to release names of 605,000 people who received $5.3 billion from FEMA, some of which paid for 300 funerals even though Florida hurricanes killed only 125 people in 2004).

In a case involving gun purchases, the Bureau of Alcohol, Tobacco and Firearms (BATF) invoked Exemption 6 when the City of Chicago attempted to learn the identities of individuals who buy more than one gun within five days; Chicago police were trying to learn who bought and who sold the guns used in committing murders. When the City of Chicago sued under FOIA, BATF claimed that it would not release any data about gun buyers and sellers because to do so would invade their personal privacy. Although the U.S. Supreme Court affirmed the orders of two lower courts and ordered BATF to release firearms purchasing data to the City of Chicago, Congress then passed a rider to the Consolidated Appropriations Act of 2005. This rider barred any spending of federal funds by the BATF to process FOIA requests for disclosure of gun purchase data, including the names of the owners and sellers of guns used to commit murders. Thus, the rider had the effect of insulating firearms laws from legal challenges. The U.S. Court of Appeals for the Seventh Circuit finally ruled that the BATF's gun-tracking databases are no longer public because of the Consolidated Appropriations Act of 2005, which makes the gun-tracking data "immune from the judicial process" and therefore exempt from FOIA. As a result, neither journalists nor the public are permitted to tap into the BATF's statistics that trace gun ownership. Thus, the City of Chicago lost its seven-year battle to find out who is buying the guns used to commit the hundreds of murders in Chicago each year. Chicago v. U.S. Department of Treasury (2005).

The Pentagon invoked Exemption 6 when it refused to release photographs of the flag-draped coffins arriving at the Dover Air Force Base in Delaware. University of Delaware professor Ralph Begleiter filed suit under FOIA for these pictures in 2004 after receiving no response to his FOIA request for six months. Only when Begleiter filed suit did the Department of Defense release photographs on a compact disc, but at first it covered the faces of the honor guard soldiers with black rectangles, claiming that it was protecting their privacy. (Later the Pentagon provided pictures of the honor guards without their faces blacked out.) Begleiter v. Department of Defense (2004).

The Department of Defense also invoked Exemption 6 when the Associated Press (AP) requested the names of the "enemy combatants" held in captivity in Guantanamo Bay for several years. Although the Pentagon claimed that releasing the prisoners' names would be a "clearly unwarranted invasion of their personal privacy," federal district court Judge Jed Rakoff nonetheless ordered the government to ask the prisoners their names. In March 2006 the Pentagon released more than 5000 pages of transcripts of hearings that included some but not all of the Guantanamo Bay detainees' names. Of the 490 prisoners held at Guantanamo Bay since 2001, only 10 have been charged with crimes. Associated Press v. United States Department of Defense (2005).

The Department of Defense again invoked Exemption 6, arguing that it had the right to withhold graphic photographs and videos (known as the Darby pictures after military policeman Joseph Darby turned over the pictures to the Army Criminal Investigative Command) of the torture of detainees at the Abu Ghraib prison in Iraq in order to protect their personal privacy. When the American Civil Liberties Union (ACLU) sued under FOIA, Chairman of the Joint Chiefs of Staff Richard Myers argued that insurgents in Iraq would use the pictures to incite riots and violence against U.S. troops in Iraq. Despite this argument, federal district court Judge Alvin Hellerstein explained: " ... my task is to interpret and apply ... the Freedom of Information Act ..." and he ordered the Pentagon to release the pictures and videos, redacted or pixilated to protect the privacy of the detainees. American Civil Liberties Union v. Department of Defense (2005).

(7) in the nature of investigatory records compiled for law enforcement purposes, but only to the extent that the production of such records would (a) interfere with enforcement proceedings, (b) deprive a person of a right to a fair trial or an impartial adjudication, (c) could reasonably be expected to constitute an unwarranted invasion of personal privacy, (d) disclose the identity of a confidential source and, in the case of records compiled by a criminal law enforcement authority

314 THE FIRST AMENDMENT Pt. 1

in the course of criminal investigation, or by an agency conducting a lawful national security intelligence investigation, confidential information furnished only by the confidential source, (e) disclose investigative techniques and procedures, or (f) endanger the life or physical safety of law enforcement personnel.

Congress tightened disclosure under this exemption in 1986. Under the 1986 amendments, informant files are no longer disclosable under FOIA. The 1986 amendments also changed the wording in Exemption 7 from "will interfere with [law] enforcement" to "could reasonably be expected to interfere with [law] enforcement." In addition, the FBI need no longer confirm or deny the existence of documents in counter-intelligence and terrorism files if the files are classified. P.L. 99–570, amending 5 U.S.C.A. § 552. The FBI had argued that those who were targets of its investigations were using the FOIA to determine whether the FBI was compiling files on them.

The threshold test of Exemption 7 is whether the requested documents are "compiled for law enforcement purposes." 5 U.S.C.A. § 552(b)(7) (1988). The Supreme Court ruled in John Doe Agency v. John Doe Corporation (1989), that the term "compiled" covers materials put together at different times and without regard to the original purpose of the collection. The effect of this decision is that routine records that were available at one point will become unavailable when put into an investigative file. Thus, the Court expanded Exemption 7 to shield from public scrutiny any information collected for a law enforcement purpose.

When the Center for National Security Studies sued the Department of Justice under the FOIA to request the identities of all individuals detained after the September 11 terrorist attacks, the U.S. Court of Appeals for the District of Columbia Circuit ruled that the Justice Department could keep secret the names of foreign detainees under Exemption 7(A), finding that release of the detainees' names would interfere with law enforcement proceedings. Center for National Security Studies et al. v. U.S. Dept. of Justice (2003). But see Associated Press v. United States Department of Defense (2005) (federal district court judge held that Department of Defense could not invoke Exemption 6 as reason to refuse disclosure of names of Guantanamo Bay prisoners, discussed above).

Nearly 20 years ago the Supreme Court expanded Exemption 7(C) in U.S. Department of Justice v. Reporters Committee for Freedom of the Press (1989). In this case, CBS news correspondent Robert Schakne and the Reporters Committee for Freedom of the Press asked the FBI to disclose its rap sheets on Charles Medico and three other members of his family. The FBI's rap sheets contain information indicating arrests, indictments, acquittals, convictions and sentences on about 24 million people in the United States. These computerized files are compilations of what are usually public records held by law enforcement agencies across the country. The Justice Department has simply compiled all the information about an individual from various police agencies into a single computerized file. Medico, a defense contractor, was allegedly connected to organized crime. His company, Medico Industries, had allegedly obtained a number of defense contracts through an improper arrangement with a corrupt congressman. Schakne argued that a record of Medico's financial crimes would be a matter of public interest; furthermore, Medico could not assert a privacy claim because the criminal process is public. The Department of Justice denied Schakne's request, however, citing the personal privacy factor in Exemption 7(C).

When the case reached the Supreme Court, it upheld the Department of Justice's denial in a unanimous decision, ruling that Exemption 7(C) protected rap sheets in the FBI's computerized database of criminal history information. The Court held that individuals' privacy interests in their rap sheets outweighed the public interest in disclosure, even though a diligent search of public records throughout the country could uncover the same information held in the rap sheets. The Court explained that rap sheets do not shed any light on government activities, however, and therefore Exemption 7(C) protects them. It is worth noting the difference in phrasing between Exemption 6, referring to "a clearly unwarranted invasion of person privacy," and Exemption 7(C), referring to information which "could reasonably be expected to constitute an unwarranted invasion of personal privacy." Exemption 7(C) permits withholding of information if there is merely a reasonable expectation rather than a certainty that privacy would be invaded as in Exemption 6. Thus, Exemption 7(C) provides a more relaxed standard by which the Court found that Medico's privacy outweighed public interest in disclosure of the rap sheets.

The Reporters Committee standard broadened the protection of personal privacy interests under FOIA. Although the Supreme Court's decision protects individual privacy, its narrow interpretation of the public interest failed to ensure the FOIA would continue to serve its main purpose of providing open access to government-held information. S.E. Wilborn, "Developments under the Freedom of Information Act—1989," 1990 Duke L.J. 1113, at 1125.

Despite the expansion of Exemption 7(C) in Reporters Committee, the Court of Appeals for the Ninth Circuit ruled in 1995 that the FBI could not rely on this exemption in withholding 6600 pages of documents on the University of California at Berkeley's 1964 Free Speech Movement. (The Free Speech Movement had challenged the administrations regulations barring all political activities on campus.) Journalist Seth Rosenfeld requested the files in 1981, but the FBI refused to release the documents for 15 years. The appellate court held that Exemption 7(C) did not apply because the FBI had no legitimate law enforcement purpose in its probe of the Free Speech Movement. The FBI's monitoring of participants in the Free Speech Movement continued from 1965 through 1974, despite the fact that the FBI itself had concluded in 1965 that there was no subversive threat whatsoever from the Free Speech Movement. Although the FBI argued that releasing the documents could invade the privacy of those who were monitored, the Ninth Circuit ordered the FBI to release the files. Rosenfeld v. U.S. Department of Justice (1995).

More recently the U.S. Supreme Court has extended Exemption 7(C) to cover the privacy rights of survivors of a deceased government official. When California lawyer Allan Favish requested 10 death-scene photographs of Vincent Foster, who had been deputy counsel to President Clinton, the High Court held that the government could withhold the photographs under Exemption 7(C) because disclosure would have resulted in an unwarranted invasion of the privacy of Foster's close relatives. National Archives and Records Administration v. Favish (2004).

Although the Supreme Court expanded Exemption 7(C) in Reporters Committee, it was somewhat more cautious in a case involving Exemption 7(D). In claiming Exemption 7(D), federal agencies must show that the information provided by confidential sources was given in confidence. If there is no provable express promise of confidentiality, then the government must demonstrate an implied assurance of confidentiality. In Department of Justice v. Landano (1993), the Supreme Court rejected the FBI's argument that all sources who give information to federal agents during a criminal investigation are confidential sources. Rather than having an automatic right to withhold information on its sources, the FBI must consider such requests on a case-by-case basis. Justice O'Connor explained: "A source should be deemed confidential if the source furnished information with the understanding that the FBI would not divulge the communication, except to the extent the Bureau thought it necessary for law enforcement purposes."

(8) contained in or related to examination, operating or condition reports prepared by, on behalf of, or for the use of any agency responsible for the regulation or supervision of financial institutions.

This exemption is designed to prevent disclosure of sensitive financial reports or audits that if made public could undermine public confidence in banks and other financial institutions. It has seldom been litigated, even when the savings and loan industry collapsed in the 1980s. There were widespread allegations of wrongdoing and misfeasance by government officials and owners of savings and loans. Despite these allegations, however, Exemption 8 has remained a serious obstacle to any attempts by journalists and the public to fully understand why American taxpayers were left to pay nearly half a trillion dollars to cover the losses resulting from the theft, corruption and irresponsibility of those in power. Even historians may be unable to write an intelligible history of the fiasco. Only if the supervisory and regulatory agencies involved in oversight of failed savings and loans should decide to release financial reports will they become available to the public. In deciding whether to release such information, agencies will consider the embarrassment such release may cause their past and present officials. See Gregory v. Federal Deposit Insurance Corporation (1980).

(9) in the nature of geological and geophysical information and data, including maps, concerning wells.

This exemption protects the valuable proprietary information of oil companies and mining companies from disclosure.

6. Assessment of FOIA

There is some criticism regarding the uses to which FOIA is put. However, journalists have used the FOIA to expose the following abuses:

—disclosures about nuclear bomb testing and danger of the radiation to Utah residents

—details of America's role in the Bay of Pigs invasion of Cuba

—the litany of FBI and CIA excesses during the 1960s and 1970s, such as illegal spying on ordinary United States citizens, leaders such as the Rev. Dr. Martin Luther King, Jr. and Beatle John Lennon

—organized crime's infiltration of the coal industry

—Navy admirals with $14,000 sofas and $41,000 carpets on their destroyers

—the Pentagon permitting military contractors to charge the Department of Defense for the costs incurred in lobbying Congress for appropriations for their weapons systems. See New Statesman, Jan. 10, 1986, at 12–13.

—the CIA's efforts to overthrow the government of Salvador Allende in Chile, ending with Allende's assassination in 1973

—information about Ford Pinto gas tanks, which exploded and burned upon impact

—the dangers of Agent Orange to Vietnam War veterans

—tests on biological warfare conducted by the U.S. Army in open air over an Alabama city

—a nuclear accident near Albuquerque, New Mexico

—illegal drug use by an Air Force security unit assigned to guard a nuclear weapons storage depot

—a 1996 government public relations cover-up on "mad cow disease"

—operations errors by air traffic controllers

—pharmaceutical research on human beings

—declassified CIA training manuals released in 1997 disclosing techniques of torture used by CIA against suspected subversives in Latin America

—Food and Drug Administration (FDA) reports of appalling squalor on a Mexican onion farm whose scallions wound up at Chi Chi's, a restaurant chain that suffered a hepatitis outbreak in one of its Pennsylvania restaurants

—the U.S. Department of Education's spending of $9.4 million on public relations under the George W. Bush administration, including paying columnist Armstrong Williams for favorable press for the "No Child Left Behind" program

—the Fish and Wildlife Service's granting of hundreds of permit exemptions to the Endangered Species Act allowing miners, loggers and hunters to harm, injure or kill animals that are nearly extinct

—the declassified Presidential Daily Briefing (PDB) of August 6, 2001, in which the CIA warned President George W. Bush of an impending al-Qaida attack involving passenger planes in the United States

—no-bid contracts to rebuild Iraq granted to prominent campaign contributors to the Bush administration such as Bechtel and Halliburton, whose subsidiary Kellogg, Brown & Root overcharged the Army Corps of Engineers by as much as $61 million for fuel

—photographs of American soldiers torturing Iraqi prisoners at Abu Ghraib Prison in Iraq

—FBI documents describing detainees in U.S. custody being shackled in the fetal position without food or water for 24 hours at a time

In short, despite its problems and limitations, FOIA provides the American people and the media that serve them with an instrument for holding their government somewhat accountable.

C. LEGISLATION LIMITING ACCESS IN THE NAME OF NATIONAL SECURITY

A year after the terrorist attacks of September 11, 2001, President George W. Bush signed into law the Homeland Security Act of 2002, creating the cabinet-level Department of Homeland Security. Public Law No. 107–296. One of the more controversial provisions of this law (Section 214) is known as the Critical Information Infrastructure Act (CIIA). This law provides that if a corporation voluntarily submits information involving vulnerabilities in its critical infrastructure to the Department of Homeland Security (DHS), that information is exempt from disclosure under both FOIA and also state and local disclosure laws. For example, if privately operated nuclear power plants, bridges, dams, ports or chemical factories voluntarily submit to DHS any information that includes potential dangers to health and safety, this information is exempt from disclosure. Furthermore, the corporation that submits the information about its vulnerabilities or potential dangers is granted immunity from any civil action after it voluntarily submits the information. The law also provides for criminal penalties against anyone who discloses the information submitted. Legal scholars and journalists fear that Section 214 will permit corporations to dump embarrassing or even criminal information on DHS with the assurance that DHS will never disclose this information to the public. For example, Section 214 could bar the federal government from disclosing information about chemical spills, fires and explosions unless it first receives written consent from the company that causes the accident. Due to the civil immunity guaranteed by the CIIA, if a company submits information that its factory is leaking arsenic into ground water, that information cannot be given to public health authorities to use in any enforcement proceeding, nor could the general public receive access to this information through FOIA in a civil tort action. See Kristen Uhl, "The Freedom of Information Act Post–9/11: Balancing the Public's Right to Know, Critical Infrastructure Protection, and Homeland Security," 53 American University Law Review 261 at 296 (October 2003).

D. LEGISLATION LIMITING ACCESS IN THE NAME OF PERSONAL PRIVACY

In contrast to the movement toward disclosure embodied in FOIA, Congress has also passed legislation to prevent public scrutiny of government-assembled information about individuals. In 1974, Congress passed the Privacy Act, 5 U.S.C.A. § 552a, to curb government abuses in handling of personal information about individual citizens. The idea behind the federal statute has spread to the states and by 2006 about half of the states had enacted some kind of privacy act covering, for example, information about an individual's criminal history and whether it may be released to the press and the public. At least 40 states have legislation providing for expungement of nonconviction arrest records.

See U.S. Department of Justice, Bureau of Justice Statistics, Criminal History Record Information: Compendium of State Privacy and Security Legislation: 2002 Overview: Current Status of Law and Summary of State Statutes (available at http://www.ojp.usdoj.gov/bjs/abstract/cspsl02.htm). Because of privacy claims, the press has less access to government records, especially arrest records.

When Congress passed the Privacy Act, it attempted to avoid confusion about whether Exemption 3 of FOIA (matters exempt from disclosure by statute) referred to the Privacy Act. Congress thus tried to clarify in the 1974 amendments to FOIA that Exemption 3 was not applicable to the Privacy Act; in other words, FOIA should take preference over the Privacy Act if there is a question about whether to release information or not. A government official who refuses to disclose information merely faces a vague threat of disciplinary action under FOIA, whereas if the same official discloses too much information about an individual, he or she faces monetary penalties under the Privacy Act. This in itself creates a subtle pressure on government agencies to give the Privacy Act a higher priority than FOIA, even though this was not the intent of Congress.

After various conflicting lower court decisions, Congress tried to partially resolve the conflict between FOIA and the Privacy Act (5 U.S.C.A. § 552a(q)(1)) with a 1984 amendment to the National Security Act of 1947 (50 U.S.C.A. § 431) which declared that the Privacy Act is not an Exemption 3 statute. If the Privacy Act had been declared an Exemption 3 statute, it would have protected all information within its scope from disclosure under FOIA; entire systems of records could have been withheld. The Privacy Act clearly states that "no agency shall disclose any record . . . unless disclosure of the record would be required [under FOIA]."

The Privacy Act was intended to prohibit the government from keeping files on individuals because of how they exercise their First Amendment rights. For example, when former J. Roderick MacArthur Foundation president Lance Lindblom learned that the FBI was maintaining a file on him with no reason to believe he had engaged in any criminal activity, he sued, hoping to force the FBI to expunge its files. The Court of Appeals for the D.C. Circuit ruled in favor of the FBI, explaining that the FBI may maintain files on how individuals exercise the right of freedom of association without violating the Privacy Act if the file was compiled as part of a legitimate law enforcement activity. J. Roderick MacArthur Foundation v. FBI (1996).

The Court of Appeals for the D.C. Circuit has also ruled that like civilian agencies, the military can be liable for damages under the Privacy Act. Former Navy lieutenant Mary Louise Cummings successfully sued the Navy for leaking an unfavorable evaluation of her ability to fly a Strike Fighter Attack F–18 "Hornet" aircraft. Cummings v. Department of the Navy (2002).

Former FBI contract translator Sibel Edmonds sued the Department of Justice under the Privacy Act when it insinuated that she had done unsatisfactory work that led to the FBI firing her. In fact Edmonds claimed that she was a whistleblower whose supervisor kept telling her to slow down and let the cases pile up in order to argue for a larger budget for translators. When Edmonds sued, however, the Department of Justice retroactively classified information relevant to the suit, also barring Edmonds' testimony in lawsuits brought by families of September 11 victims. In 2005 the U.S. Court of Appeals for the District of Columbia closed oral arguments in her case after the FBI argued that it could withhold information related to Edmonds' claim because producing the information would jeopardize national security. Edmonds argued that she had blown the whistle on FBI misconduct and possible espionage. Edmonds appealed to the U.S. Supreme Court, but it declined to hear the case. The U.S. Court of Appeals for the District of Columbia held that the FBI could withhold the information under Exemption 1 because the information she sought had been classified. Edmonds v. Department of Justice (2005).

Like Sibel Edmonds, nuclear scientist Wen Ho Lee and anthrax expert Steven Hatfill have both sued the government under the Privacy Act, claiming that certain government agencies disclosed personal information about them to the media. Lee v. Department of Justice (2005); Hatfill v. Ashcroft

(2005). Because Lee and Hatfill's cases involved attempts to use the Privacy Act to circumvent the reporter's privilege, their cases are discussed further in Chapter VIII.

E. LEGISLATION LIMITING ACCESS TO AN INDIVIDUAL'S MEDICAL RECORDS

In 1996 Congress passed the Health Insurance Portability and Accountability Act (HIPAA) (Pub. L. No. 104–191, 110 Stat. 1935 [1996]), designed to protect private information in an individual's medical files. Pursuant to Congress' mandate in HIPAA, the Department of Health and Human Services (HHS) promulgated final regulations called the "Privacy Rule" in 2001, and hospitals and health care professionals were given until 2003 to comply. 42 U.S.C.A. S 1320d–4 through S 1320d–6[b]. Doctors, hospitals and other health care professionals must obtain a patient's written consent before disclosing the patient's personal health information. Any health professional who discloses a patient's health information without consent can be fined up to $250,000 or imprisoned up to 10 years for knowingly misusing such information. As a result of this law, journalists are finding that hospital officials are withholding more information than necessary to avoid any risk of penalties, even in cases where journalists are requesting aggregate data rather than information about a specific individual.

F.   OPEN MEETINGS–OPEN RECORDS
LEGISLATION

1.   The Federal Government in the "Sunshine"

Parallel to the Federal Freedom of Information Act are federal and state "government in the sunshine" statutes which require federal, state and local governmental units to conduct their business in the open. In 1976 Congress passed the Government in the Sunshine Act, the federal open meetings law. P.L. 94–409, 5 U.S.C.A. § 552b. This statute affects about 50 federal boards, commissions and agencies that are required to conduct their business meetings in public. The law also prohibits informal communication between officials of an agency and representatives of companies with whom the agency does business unless this communication is recorded as part of the public record. The only officially reported case of a news organization successfully invoking the federal Sunshine Act is Philadelphia Newspapers, Inc. v. Nuclear Regulatory Commission (1984). In this case the Court of Appeals for the D.C. Circuit held that the Nuclear Regulatory Commission could not close a meeting regarding Three Mile Island in Pennsylvania after the nuclear accident there. The Nuclear Regulatory Commission (NRC) kept its meetings open for the next 15 years, but in 1999 decided to close its meetings. The Natural Resources Defense Council (NRDC) filed suit under the Sunshine Act. The NRC cited Federal Communications Commission v. ITT World Communications (1984), however, in which the U.S. Supreme Court had ruled that FCC commissioners could have preliminary discussions among themselves that did not fall under the definition of "meeting" under the Sunshine Act. The High Court had decided that meetings that do not result in actual deliberations can be closed, the NRC argued. The U.S. Court of Appeals for the D.C. Circuit ruled in favor of the NRC, holding that NRC commissioners were permitted to have preliminary discussions among themselves before the disposition of official NRC business. Natural Resources Defense Council v. Nuclear Regulatory Commission (2000).

Congress also passed the Federal Advisory Committee Act (FACA), 5 U.S.C.A. App. 2 § 10 (West Supp. 1993), which requires advisory committees to open their meetings. The U.S. Supreme Court has held that a committee of the American Bar Association which rated the competence of candidates for federal judiciary appointments was not an advisory committee subject to the requirements of FACA. Public Citizen v. Department of Justice (1989). In the 1990s courts ruled that meetings on health care reform, use of laboratory animals, and old growth forests should be open. See Association of American Physicians and Surgeons v. Hillary Rodham Clinton (1997); Animal Legal Defense Fund v. Shalala (1997); California Forestry Association v. U.S. Forest Service (1996).

More recently journalists and public interest groups such as Judicial Watch and the Sierra Club sought information under FACA about meetings of

Vice President Dick Cheney's national task force on the energy industry. The citizens' groups wanted to learn the extent to which oil companies and other private energy corporations influenced federal energy policy. After the Enron Corporation filed for bankruptcy, Cheney told reporters a little about Enron executives' role in advising the task force, but he refused to respond to requests for task force records from the General Accounting Office (GAO), the investigative agency of Congress. Judicial Watch v. National Energy Policy Development Group (2002). The U.S. Supreme Court remanded the case, now called Cheney v. U.S. Dist. Court (2004), to the U.S. Court of Appeals for the D.C. Circuit. The appellate court dismissed the case, ruling that Cheney's task force was exempt from FACA's disclosure requirements because President Bush officially named only government employees to the task force, and because the energy company executives who participated were not voting on task force decisions. In re Richard B. Cheney (2005).

2. State Open Meetings and Open Records Laws

Statutes similar to the federal Government in the Sunshine Act are now in force in a large majority of states, but vary considerably, and journalists and lawyers must acquaint themselves with the provisions in their particular jurisdiction if the legislation is to be effectively utilized.

Some states limit their "sunshine" legislation to the final stages in the decision-making process such as meetings at which final votes are taken. The spirit of open government may be easily avoided by agencies making the real decisions behind closed doors and then ratifying their decisions in the "sunshine." One problem is that the growing use of e-mail has made it possible for members of government boards or commissions to hold "virtual" meetings online. Whether or not e-mail discussions constitute a meeting subject to state open records laws has yet to be resolved. See State ex rel. Wilson–Simmons v. Lake Cty. Sheriff's Department (1998); see also Beck v. Shelton (2004) (Virginia Supreme Court reversed trial court decision that e-mail messages among some, but not all, city council members had constituted a "public meeting").

The "sunshine" statutes of most states provide specific exemptions from the public meeting requirement to ameliorate unwarranted disclosure. These exemptions are generally similar to those in the federal Sunshine Act.

Many state Sunshine or "open records laws" do have teeth: a Florida judge sentenced Escambia County Commissioner Wyon Dale Childers to 60 days in jail and fined him $500 plus $3600 in costs for violating the state's open meetings law. Childers v. State (2006). In another case, a Tennessee court held that the state open records law trumped the confidentiality clause in a settlement agreement signed by city officials of Memphis. Contemporary Media, Inc. v. City of Memphis (1999). And several years ago the Tennessee Supreme Court ruled unanimously that private companies that perform functions once done by state government must open their books to public scrutiny. It made this ruling after two Cherokee Children & Family Services daycare workers left two toddlers in closed vans in 90–degree heat, killing the children. The state supreme court ruled that reporters and the public had a right to know how Cherokee was spending millions of dollars the state of Tennessee was funneling to it. Memphis Publishing Co. v. Cherokee Children & Family Services, Inc. (2002).

California had an open records provision that made public general information about individuals who were arrested, but in 1996 the legislature amended this provision so that only journalists and scholars could receive access to the addresses of arrestees. Cal. Govt. Code § 6254(f)(3). The purpose of this amendment was to protect arrestees from lawyers' solicitations, but United Reporting immediately sought an injunction, claiming that the amendment was unconstitutional. United Reporting publishes a newsletter, "The Register," containing lists of arrestees' names and addresses, and its subscribers use the information to solicit business. Although the Los Angeles Police Department insisted that the amendment's purpose was to protect arrestees' privacy. When the U.S. Supreme Court ultimately ruled on the case, it found in favor of the Police Department. Although United Reporting Publishing argued that it had lost prospective clients and sales and would be put out of business, the High Court held that the amendment merely restricted access to government information, but did not restrict protected speech. Los Angeles Police Department v. United Reporting Publishing (1999).

In a case involving access to the names and addresses of everyone with driver's licenses, the Supreme Court upheld the Drivers Privacy Protection Act of 1994 as constitutional in January 2000. Reno v. Condon (2000). Pub. L. 103–322, S 300002, 108 Stat. 2099–2102 (1994), codified at 18 U.S.C.A. §§ 2721–2725 (West Supp. 1997). See Chapter III for a discussion of Reno v. Condon (2000).

More recently the New York Court of Appeals and the Kansas Supreme Court have held that their state transportation authorities could not use the federal Hazard Elimination Program law as an exemption to state open records laws when the person requesting information is a journalist. Under the Hazard Elimination Program, states may receive federal funds for improving safety at dangerous railroad crossings, bridges and intersections if they submit reports to the federal government identifying such hazards. Such reports cannot be used in discovery or admitted as evidence in personal injury cases, however; in other words, these hazard reports are subject to an "evidence ban" in personal injury litigation. New York's highest court ruled, however, that if journalists want to find out why a chunk of the Tappan Zee Bridge breaks off and falls into the Hudson River, they should have access to state hazard reports. See Newsday v. Department of Transportation (2005); Telegram Publishing Co.,

Inc. v. Kansas Department of Transportation (2003).

G. MEDIA ACCESS TO GOVERNMEN-
TALLY RESTRICTED PLACES
AND INSTITUTIONS

A field in which the freedom to gather news and information has not expanded in recent years is that of access to governmentally restricted institutions such as military bases and penitentiaries and geographic areas such as unfriendly foreign countries. Although the Supreme Court recognized in the abstract in Branzburg v. Hayes (1972), that "without some protection for seeking out the news, freedom of the press could be eviscerated," the Court in that very case appears to have restricted First Amendment protection for newsgathering to those areas accessible to the general public.

Such an approach to access assures that the government will not discriminate against the media in the gathering of information. A security conscious government may further curtail both public and media access to sources of information, however.

1. Access to Prisons

Initially it was thought that because Branzburg involved a claim of indirect restriction on newsgathering (see pp. 380–382, infra for a discussion of the case), the limitation on protection for newsgathering might not be applicable to direct governmental restrictions on media access. This has not proven to be the case. In Pell v. Procunier (1974) and Saxbe v. Washington Post Co. (1974) the California Department of Corrections and the Federal Bureau of Prisons had by regulation barred representatives of the media from interviewing specifically designated penitentiary inmates.

The U.S. Supreme Court reaffirmed this view of the Constitution in Houchins v. KQED, Inc. (1978). Houchins is significant, however, because of Justice Stewart's concurring opinion in which he emphasized that, although journalists had no more right of access to prisons than the general public, they should be allowed to use their "tools of the trade," including videocameras and tape recorders. Twenty years later in 1998 the California legislature passed legislation that would have permitted journalists to videotape interviews with selected prisoners. Governor Gray Davis vetoed the legislation, however, arguing that it would create "celebrity criminals" and cause additional pain for victims and their families. However in 1999 the Sullivan Correctional Facility in New York permitted journalists Maxine Paul and Amy Kalafa to videotape interviews with serial murderers such as Artie Shawcross and "Son of Sam" killer David Berkowitz for a Court TV documentary.

With regard to the death penalty, the Department of Justice prohibits videotaping executions in federal cases and limits access to inmates during the week before the death sentence is carried out. Implementation of Death Sentences in Federal Cases, 58 Fed. Reg. 4898 (1993), codified at 28 C.F.R. § 26.

In 1999 the Florida Supreme Court posted photographs of the electrocution of murderer Allen Lee Davis on the Internet at the request of Florida Supreme Court Justice Leander Shaw. Shaw wanted to spark debate on whether Florida should change from electrocution to lethal injection as a more humane form of execution. In 1999 the U.S. Supreme Court agreed to hear a case regarding this question, but in January 2000 the Florida legislature passed a law changing the means of electrocution to lethal injection, so the case before the High Court was dismissed as moot.

A few years later the U.S. Court of Appeals for the Ninth Circuit held that the public does indeed have "a First Amendment right of access to view executions from the moment the condemned is escorted into the execution chamber." Thus the citizens of California are permitted to view executions if they choose to. California First Amendment Coalition v. Woodford (2002).

2. Access to Proceedings Related to Suspected Terrorists

a. *Access to Immigration and Naturalization Service Proceedings*

In the weeks following the terrorist attacks of September 11, 2001, federal agents detained more than 1000 people for questioning or for violating immigration laws. In November 2001 the Department of Justice revealed the nationality of 548 detainees and the nature of their immigration violations, but it referred to each detainee by number rather than by name. The Department of Justice did, however, release the names of 93 persons charged (in contrast with those detained but not charged) with federal crimes in connection with the September 11 attacks.

Immigration and Naturalization Service (INS) proceedings are handled by INS administrative courts rather than by regular federal district courts. The INS regulations provide that the proceedings should be open to the public, but allow for closure if necessary for reasons of national security or of privacy. 8 CFR 240.10(b). If detainees are being held in an INS facility, then a reporter must obtain permission from the INS to interview individual detainees. If an INS detainee is held in a local jail, then a reporter needs permission from the local sheriff to interview that detainee.

In 2002 a New Jersey Superior Court judge ruled that jailers in Hudson and Passaic Counties should release the names of more than 300 federal detainees held under contract with the INS. Despite the judge's ruling, the INS ordered all jailers not to release the names of the mostly Arab men detained after the September 11 attacks, notwithstanding a federal FOIA request for their names. American Civil Liberties Union of New Jersey v. County of Hudson (2002). But see Turkmen v. Ashcroft (2006) (federal district court judge held that INS can detain non-citizens indefinitely without specific charges).

b.   The Material Witness Statute

If the government has a warrant in the form of an affidavit (from an FBI agent, for example), it may detain a material witness to a crime if there is a risk that the witness will flee or is in danger. Material witnesses are expected to testify at grand jury proceedings or trials. Grand jury proceedings are normally closed to the public, but other court proceedings, such as a hearing to determine whether the witness should be detained, are ordinary court proceedings, presumed to be open to the press and the public. Judges may close the hearing or seal records in some circumstances, however. Many of those detained at first after the September 11 terrorist attacks were brought in as material witnesses, although as the investigation continued, some were released and others faced criminal charges.

3.   Access to Accident Sites

The principle that journalists are not accorded special access to news sources by the First Amendment is a broad one and would seemingly apply to any situation in which the state or federal government limits public access reasonably and in a nondiscriminatory way. A common situation is the setting up of police lines to seal off a geographic area in the interest of public safety. By definition police lines are designed to keep the public out of even public areas for limited periods of time, and if there exists a reasonable basis for the lines it would seem to follow that the media could also be excluded. In practice, police often permit accredited journalists to cross the lines. If such permission is given, however, it must be extended on a nondiscriminatory basis to all journalists with proper credentials and the credentials must be issued in a fair and nondiscriminatory manner.

If police officers order everyone except rescue workers to leave the scene of an accident, however, courts are usually unsympathetic to journalists who defy such orders. For example, in State v. Lashinsky (1979), a news photographer refused to leave the scene of an accident after a policeman had ordered him to do so. The photographer wanted to take pictures of a car that had run off the Garden State Parkway, crashed down an embankment and overturned. A badly injured girl was trapped inside the car under her mother, who had been killed. Because the car might catch fire, the police officer ordered everyone not involved in rescue efforts to leave the scene. The photographer was convicted for violating the policeman's order and the New Jersey Supreme Court affirmed his conviction. The photographer argued that the policeman's order should not apply to him because he was a member of the press, but the court held that the needs of journalists must yield in some circumstances so that police can take care of those who are their immediate responsibility. State v. Lashinsky (1979).

Similarly, in City of Oak Creek v. Ah King (1989), a television cameraman defied a police officer's order not to enter the closed-off site of a plane crash. A four-member crew from a Milwaukee television station drove through a police roadblock to get to the scene of the crash. Although three of them left when a detective advised them to, cameraman Ah King refused, and police charged him with disorderly conduct. The Wisconsin Supreme Court affirmed his conviction, ruling that he did not have a First Amendment right of access to the scene of the plane crash when the public had been reasonably excluded. See also Kinsey v. City of Opp, Alabama (1999) (no clearly established constitutional right to take pictures at accident site).

Although the prevailing judicial view refuses to mandate constitutional protection for the media in their newsgathering function beyond that afforded the general public, special consideration may still be accorded the media by legislative or administrative grace. For example, under California Penal Code § 409(d), a police officer may permit access to a closed off disaster scene to a "duly authorized representative of any news service," meaning anyone with a press card. In addition to such examples of credentialed newspersons being permitted to cross police lines, there are Department of State regulations giving professional journalists special authorization for travel to restricted foreign areas if the purpose of the travel is to make information available to the public concerning these areas. Of course, what is given at the government's discretion may also be withdrawn at its discretion.

Journalists may not trespass on government property such as a prison or a military base (termed non-public-forum public property) to cover a news story. For example, reporters illegally entered the Camp Garcia Naval Installation in Vieques, Puerto, Rico in order to cover a demonstration against the Navy's use of the area as a bombing range. The U.S. district court in Puerto Rico found the journalists guilty of trespassing, explaining that there is no journalists' privilege to trespass. The U.S. Supreme Court has not ruled on whether the news media have the right to follow a news story onto private property, but lower courts have ruled against reporters in such cases. Arizona v. Wells (2004); United States v. Maldonado–Norat (2000). See also Stahl v. Oklahoma (1983).

Ironically, however, journalists have also been sued for cooperating too closely with law enforcement agents, as in the so-called "ride-along" cases in which reporters accompany police as they execute search warrants, arrest fugitives or investigate leads. See Wilson v. Layne (1999), Hanlon v. Berger (1999), and Brunette v. Humane Society of Ventura County (2002), discussed in Chapter III.

Journalists may also run into trouble when they use hidden videocameras or misrepresent themselves on job applications in order to gain access to information. Food Lion, Inc. v. Capital Cities/ABC (1999); Wolfson v. Lewis (1996); Veilleux v. National Broadcasting Co. (2000). See Chapter III for a discussion of Food Lion, Wolfson and Veilleux.

H.   MEDIA ACCESS TO COURTS AND JUDICIAL RECORDS

1.   Access to Trial Proceedings

Another major source of concern is media access to governmentally generated information, this time in relation to the courthouse. (See Chapter VI for more in-depth coverage of the free press–fair trial issue.) It had long been our history that the doors of American courtrooms were open to the public and press (see Justice Black's opinion in In re Oliver (1948)). In the 1970s, however, a trend toward closing the courtroom developed as a judicial response to the threat to fair trials allegedly posed by publicity surrounding those trials. By the end of that decade the Reporters Committee for Freedom of Press had documented several dozen cases in which pretrial and trial proceedings across the country had been closed to the public and press by judicial order. This movement to deny media access to judicial information and news reached its zenith with the decision in Gannett Co. v. DePasquale (1979). In a 5–4 decision, the Supreme Court ruled in Gannett that judges may close pretrial hearings.

The four dissenters in Gannett warned that secret judicial proceedings would be a menace to liberty. More than 75 percent of federal criminal prosecutions never reach a full trial. Serious plea bargaining often takes place, perhaps because a prosecutor realizes that the case is not as strong as desired. When such plea-bargaining takes place, there are no public proceedings after the pretrial hearing, which then is the last point for the public to learn what happens to the defendant. An example of abuse during plea-bargaining in a closed pretrial hearing occurred in Chico, California in 1979. When three white hunters were unable to find deer to shoot, they went looking for "dark meat," as they put it. They maliciously shot and killed a deaf and mentally handicapped black man. The judge closed the preliminary hearings. He allowed the three hunters to plead guilty in return for lesser sentences and placed a gag order on the press for a year. Detroit Free Press, Feb. 24, 1980, pp. 1B, 4B. The local media assumed that the black man's death was a random hunting accident, and did not learn that the murder was premeditated and racially motivated. Thus, they did not bother to challenge the gag order. Such abuses of plea-bargaining during closed pretrial hearings were a source of concern to the four dissenters in the Gannett decision.

Fortuitously, a case was already in the judicial system of the State of Virginia that squarely raised these questions and would quickly give the Supreme Court an opportunity to clarify what it had decided in Gannett. In Richmond Newspapers, Inc. v. Virginia (1980), a murder trial was closed to the public and the press on the motion of the defendant, who had already gone through three previous mistrials of the same case. When the court ordered the trial to proceed "with the press and public excluded," Richmond Newspapers appealed to the Virginia Supreme Court and finally to the U.S. Supreme Court.

The U.S. Supreme Court granted a petition for certiorari to review the case.

In his opinion reversing the judgment of the Virginia Supreme Court, Chief Justice Burger noted at the outset that the Richmond Newspapers case involved exclusion from a trial and not from a pretrial proceeding. The Chief Justice explained that while the Sixth Amendment provided the press with no right of access to trials, the First Amendment, as applied to the states through the Fourteenth Amendment, did. "We hold that the right to attend criminal trials is implicit in the guarantees of the First Amendment; without the freedom to attend such trials, which people have exercised for centuries, important aspects of freedom of speech and 'the press could be eviscerated.' " Chief Justice Burger relied on both an historical and a functional analysis of public access to trials. He found an historical presumption of openness, noting that criminal trials had been open to the public dating back to thirteenth century England. Justice Brennan concurred and expanded on the "structural" or functional view of the First Amendment, referring to the importance of informed debate in a democracy and the need for the media to function as surrogates for the public.

Chief Justice Burger made clear that the First Amendment right of access to trials was not absolute. If the trial court could find, as the Virginia trial court did not, that there was a specific overriding interest in closing a trial, then an occasional courtroom closure might pass constitutional muster.

However, he did not state the precise constitutional standards that litigants would have to meet to obtain such closures or whether different standards might be applied to the closing of pretrial proceedings permitted by Gannett. The Court avoided reversing Gannett. Pretrial proceedings pose greater risks of generating publicity prejudicial to a fair trial because prospective jurors may be influenced by the news stories arising out of such proceedings before they are even selected, and the judicial devices to prevent potential prejudice in such cases are limited.

There has been, however, a clear trend toward upholding access to courtrooms for press and public in nearly all situations since the Richmond Newspapers decision. In Globe Newspaper Co. v. Superior Court (1982), the state of Massachusetts closed a rape trial involving minor victims because of a state law requiring that trials be closed without exception when juvenile victims of a sexual assault testified. The Supreme Court struck down the statute, holding that it violated the First Amendment right of access to court proceedings. Even the compelling interest of the state to protect minor victims of sex crimes from further trauma and embarrassment was held insufficient to justify mandatory exclusion of the press and public from those portions of criminal trials during which the victims testify. See, however, Austin Daily Herald v. Mork (1993) (permissible to close trial during testimony of minor victims of sexual assault).

In recent years courts have ruled in favor of closing specific portions of a trial when an undercover officer is testifying in order to protect the officer's safety. See New York v. Martinez (1993), New York v. Rivera (1997) and Ayala v. Speckard (1997) for example, (but see Pearson v. James (1997) (testimony of undercover officer cannot automatically result in closing that portion of trial)). In a case related to the 1993 bombing of the World Trade Center, a New York court closed a trial on grounds of national security. U.S. v. Doe (1999). In a case related to the September 11, 2001 bombing of the World Trade Center, the court also closed portions of the trial on grounds of national security. United States v. Moussaoui (2004), cert. denied (2005).

Whereas a juvenile was the victim of a crime in Globe Newspaper, when juveniles are the perpetrators rather than the victims of crime, there is no guarantee of access to juvenile proceedings under the Federal Juvenile Delinquency Act (FJDA) (18 U.S.C. §§ 5031–5042). Rather, federal courts may grant access to juvenile proceedings and records on a case-by-case basis. See U.S. v. A.D. (1994) and U.S. v. Three Juveniles (1995) (Court of Appeals for First Circuit held that FJDA created presumption that juvenile proceedings were closed but did not mandate closure in case where three juveniles vandalized Jewish temples and harassed African–Americans).

The U.S. Supreme Court has never ruled on whether the public has a constitutional right of access to juvenile court proceedings. A few courts in the United States have opened juvenile delinquency files and in some cases juvenile proceedings, especially when a minor is charged with a violent crime inciting community outrage. For example, under the New York Court of Appeals' Uniform Rules for the Family Court § 205.4 (1997), family courts are now presumptively open to the press and public, despite the fact that historically family courts had routinely operated in secret. See In re Terrell (1996) (Rule 19.1 of Arizona Supreme Court opens certain juveniles' files). See also People v. Saechao (1999) (press granted access to interview juvenile in detention center).

The U.S. Supreme Court has never decided whether the public has a First Amendment right to access to civil trials. The U.S. Court of Appeals for the Third Circuit extended the qualified right of access to attend criminal trials, outlined in Richmond and upheld in Globe, to civil trials in Publicker Industries, Inc. v. Cohen (1984). In spite of Publicker Industries, courts in other jurisdictions still permit closure of civil proceedings. See Virmani v. Presbyterian Health Services Corp. (1999)(medical peer review proceedings closed); West Virginia ex rel. Garden State Newspapers, Inc. v. Hoke (1999), and Pierce v. St. Vrain Valley School District (1999). In 1999 the California Supreme Court became the first state supreme court to rule that the First Amendment provides a right of access to ordinary civil trials and proceedings. NBC Subsidiary (KNBC–TV), Inc. v. Superior Court of Los Angeles County (1999) (public had right to attend trial in which actress-producer Sondra Locke sued actor-producer Clint Eastwood).

2. Access to Trial Proceedings in the United States Senate

Until 1929 the Senate had debated all treaties and nominations in secret, and until 1979 many Senate committees met behind closed doors. In the 1990s Senate committees held closed sessions only when discussing classified information such as the debate on the Chemical Weapons Convention in 1997, for example. After the House of Representatives impeached President Bill Clinton in January 1999, the Senate closed its doors to press and public as it deliberated key aspects of the impeachment proceedings such as 1) the motion to dismiss the articles of impeachment, 2) the question of whether to call witnesses, and 3) the final debate on whether to convict or acquit the President of the charges against him. Most Democrats favored open sessions whereas most Republicans voted for closed proceedings. Republicans relied on historical precedent to justify closure. The Senate deliberations in the 1868 impeachment trial of President Andrew Johnson had been closed, as are the impeachment proceedings against federal judges.

When the Senate doors swung shut during the 1999 impeachment proceedings, the Cable News Network (CNN) filed a brief requesting public access. CNN had no court to which to submit the brief, however, because the Senate makes its own rules on impeachment proceedings. Instead, CNN delivered its brief to all 100 Senators. In re Impeachment of William Jefferson Clinton, President of the United States, Application of Cable News Network for a Determination that the Closure of these Proceedings Violates the First Amendment to the United States Constitution, filed January 29, 1999; reprinted in Joseph Steinfeld and Robert Bertsche, ''Recent Developments in the Law of Access—1999,'' Communications Law 1999, Practising Law Institute 1999. Despite CNN's arguments, the Senate kept its doors closed during the debate.

More recently Senator Harry Reid invoked Senate Rule 21 to bring the Senate into a closed session in November 2005; the session dealt with the Bush administration's use of intelligence to declare war on Iraq.

3. Access to Pretrial Proceedings

The right of access to criminal trials is well established. However, because the Supreme Court did not clearly resolve the question of access to pretrial hearings in Gannett Co. v. DePasquale, supra, some confusion remained in the lower courts during the five years following Gannett concerning the openness of both criminal and civil proceedings.

Then in 1984 the Supreme Court issued the first of three decisions that helped resolve the issue. The Press–Enterprise in Riverside, California protested the exclusion of reporters from nearly six weeks of jury questioning (voir dire) at the trial of Albert Greenwood Brown, who was later convicted and sentenced to death for the rape and murder of a 13 year-old girl. In a unanimous opinion, the Supreme Court ruled that voir dire proceedings should be open to press and public unless those wishing to close the proceedings can demonstrate that 1) there is an overriding interest that would be prejudiced by open proceedings, 2) the closure is no broader than necessary to protect that interest, 3) reasonable alternatives to closure have been considered, and 4) the trial court made findings adequate to support closure. Press–Enterprise Co. v. Superior Court (1984).

In the second case signalling a trend toward increased access to pretrial proceedings, Waller v. Georgia (1984), the state of Georgia tried to close the pretrial hearing in one case so that the prosecutor might use the same wiretap evidence against other people not yet charged. However, Waller, the defendant, wanted the hearing to be open. The Supreme Court unanimously upheld his position, ruling that hearings are presumptively open and cannot be closed against the defendant's wishes unless there are compelling reasons to do so. The Court held that the defendant's Sixth Amendment right to a public trial extends to pretrial hearings except where the party seeking to close the hearing meets the four-part test outlined above in Press–Enterprise.

Finally, in Press–Enterprise Co. v. Superior Court (II) (1986), the same newspaper that had won ac-

cess to the voir dire two years before won a Supreme Court ruling that the public and media have
a qualified First Amendment right to attend pretrial proceedings in criminal cases. The case began
when a California court closed a pretrial hearing at
the request of a nurse accused of murdering 12
elderly patients at a nursing home by injecting
them with lethal doses of the heart drug lidocaine.
The Press–Enterprise protested the closure.

When the case reached the Supreme Court, the
first question to be addressed was whether there
was a presumption of openness attached to the jury
selection. To answer this question, the court applied
a two-part test involving 1) an historical analysis
(referring to a tradition of public access), and 2) a
functional analysis (referring to whether openness
serves a positive function such as enhancing both
the fairness of a criminal trial and the appearance
of fairness essential to public confidence in the
judicial system). Having determined that a presumption of access to jury selection existed, the
Court then applied the same analysis as in Press–
Enterprise I: "The presumption [of openness] may
be overcome only by an overriding interest based on
findings that closure is essential to preserve higher
values and is narrowly tailored to serve that interest." Press–Enterprise Co. v. Superior Court (II).

Thus the Supreme Court ruled that a pretrial
hearing may be closed only if 1) there is a substantial probability that publicity will prejudice the defendant's right to a fair trial, and 2) a judge cannot
find reasonable alternatives to closure to protect the

defendant's fair trial rights. Mere risk of prejudice does not automatically justify refusing public access to pretrial hearings. If judges find a "substantial probability" of prejudice, they may order closure only in the narrowest manner that will be effective. For instance, if three hours of testimony during a four-day pretrial hearing might cause prejudice, the hearing may be closed only during those three hours. The Supreme Court has thus made it extremely difficult for those wishing to close pretrial hearings, although judges are still tempted to do so. See U.S. v. Simone (1994) (judge erred in closing post-trial questioning of jurors; release of transcript 10 days later was not sufficient); Vermont v. Koch (1999) (judge erred in closing "non-hospitalization" hearing of mentally ill man who killed another man). See also Commonwealth of Pennsylvania v. John Theodore Howell (2003) (pretrial hearing closed to no avail).

Although the Court's opinion in Press–Enterprise II is directed to pretrial hearings in California, the question arises whether the 7–2 decision tacitly overrules the Court's earlier decision in Gannett Co. v. DePasquale that criminal pretrial hearings may be closed to press and public. The majority opinion relied heavily on historical analysis, however, arguing that if pretrial hearings have generally been open in the past, there is a presumptive First Amendment right of access. In any case, the Court avoided a blanket ruling that pretrial proceedings must be open to the public and press.

Courts may still close pretrial proceedings in those rare instances in which they cannot find reasonable alternatives to closure. During the wire fraud trial of boxing promoter Don King, the Court of Appeals for the Second Circuit upheld the trial court judge's decision to close voir dire proceedings because he had been concerned that potential jurors would not express their views honestly if they were afraid their views would be publicized in the press. U.S. v. King (1998).

The Press–Enterprise test applies to documents as well as to hearings. Journalists covering the trial of Timothy McVeigh and Terry Nichols, charged with killing 168 people in the 1995 federal building bombing in Oklahoma City, sought copies of Nichol's motion to suppress certain evidence and copies of both defendants' motions for separate trials. The Court of Appeals for the Tenth Circuit found no right of access to a law enforcement officer's notes, however, because his notes were held inadmissible; the court also denied access to the motions for separate trials. U.S. v. McVeigh (1997).

To summarize, the Supreme Court has consistently ruled that the First Amendment creates the right for the public to attend criminal trials and related judicial proceedings, except in the most extraordinary circumstances. These four cases, Richmond Newspapers, Inc. v. Virginia (1980), Globe Newspaper Co. v. Superior Court (1982) and Press–Enterprise I (1984) and Press–Enterprise II (1986) are termed "the quartet" of First Amendment access cases.

a. *Access to Grand Jury Proceedings*

Just as there is no access to inadmissible evidence, grand jury proceedings and documents are traditionally secret under federal rules of criminal procedure. In 1998 the press sought access to Independent Counsel Kenneth Starr's grand jury proceedings involving Whitewater and the Monica Lewinsky/Bill Clinton affair. Journalists also sought access to documents related to Clinton's request to invoke executive privilege and his motion to show cause against Starr for allegedly leaking secret grand jury information to the news media. The Wall Street Journal and other media organizations argued that because there were open hearings on issues involving the grand jury inquiry in the Watergate investigation of Richard Nixon, the press should have access in this case as well. The Court of Appeals for the D.C. Circuit ruled that there was no First Amendment or common law right of access to grand jury proceedings or documents, however, and the Supreme Court declined to hear the case. In re: Motions of Dow Jones & Co. (1998).

Clinton later asked the Department of Justice to prosecute Starr's office for contempt of court. Clinton's request came after the New York Times (January 31, 1999) reported that Starr intended to seek an indictment against Clinton on charges of perjury and obstruction of justice even after Clinton was impeached by the House of Representatives but not convicted by the Senate in early 1999. However, the Court of Appeals for the D.C. Circuit ruled later that year that Starr's office did not violate the requirement for grand jury secrecy by revealing that it intended to seek an indictment against Clinton. In re: Sealed Case No. 99–3091 (1999).

In a lower profile case than that involving Clinton and Lewinsky, the press in California sought access to grand jury transcripts of an investigation of Merrill Lynch's potential liability for Orange County's bankruptcy. When the security company agreed to pay Orange County $30 million after one of its brokers had sold the county derivative securities, the investigation was terminated. Even though California courts possess the inherent power to authorize disclosure of grand jury transcripts, the California Supreme Court refused to disclose any documents on the Merrill Lynch investigation. This was a loss for proponents of access. In re Request for Transcripts (1998). See also San Jose Mercury News, Inc. v. Criminal Grand Jury of Santa Clara County (2004) (admonition to all witnesses not to discuss their testimony held not to be an unconstitutional prior restraint on the press).

b. *Access to Jurors' Identities*

In an effort to protect jurors from fear of reprisals should they find a defendant guilty, and to shield jurors from harassment by the media, some judges have refused to disclose names and addresses of jurors even after a trial has concluded. Courts are divided on the question of whether there is a right of access to information about jurors' identities. The Court of Appeals for the Fourth Circuit has stated explicitly that this right exists. In re Baltimore Sun (1988). The Court of Appeals for the Third Circuit ruled that a federal district court judge should not have sealed a voir dire transcript in order to bar reporters from learning jurors' names and addresses. U.S. v. Antar (1994). See also People v. Mitchell (1999) (Michigan Court of Appeals held that press always has qualified right to names and addresses of jurors post-verdict). In contrast, the Court of Appeals for the Fifth Circuit has ruled that there is no right of access to names and addresses of jurors. U.S. v. Edwards (1987). See also U.S. v. Cleveland (1997) (upholding restriction on press interviews of jurors in order to protect jury from harassment).

By the 1990s, the use of anonymous juries had become more prevalent. Most courts base the decision to empanel an anonymous jury on factors such as 1) whether the defendant was involved with organized crime or some other group that could harm jurors, 2) past attempts by the defendant to tamper with a jury, and 3) publicity that could expose jurors to intimidation or harassment from members of the public.

In 1998 the Director of State Courts in Wisconsin proposed a Supreme Court Rule that would have required complete juror anonymity in all criminal and civil cases brought in Wisconsin courts. Petition 98–09; Proposed Supreme Court Rule 73.04—Juror Confidentiality (1998). The Wisconsin Supreme Court rejected the proposed rule on the grounds that it is jurors' public status as citizens known to the community by name that gives the judicial process its integrity.

As in Wisconsin, in some state courts, the list of jurors' names is put into the case file and becomes public record after the trial ends. In the federal system, each federal district court has a "jury plan" for selecting jurors, and the law provides that each court determines when the names of jurors will be made public 28 U.S.C. S 1863 (b)(7). In 2004, however, the Judicial Conference changed its policy in order to protect jurors' privacy. Its new policy provides that identifying information about jurors or veniremen is no longer included in the public case file and is unavailable to the press and public, either in electronic form at at the courthouse. The administrative Office of U.S. Courts is advising federal district courts to review their jury plans in light of the Judicial Conference's new policy. Despite this new policy, the press is supposed to have access to jurors' identities after a trial is over.

Even after a trial is over, however, judges sometimes protect post-verdict anonymity, as in cases in which subsequent trials of other defendants might involve the same crime. If jurors comment on their deliberations they could influence the subsequent trial. Furthermore, there is always the potential for a retrial if a defendant who was convicted files an appeal or if there is a hung jury, resulting in a mistrial.

For example, the first trial of former Rabbi Fred Neulander, accused of hiring a hitman to murder his wife, ended in a mistrial. The trial court judge barred the media from interviewing or identifying jurors, fearing that jurors' comments in the mistrial case might influence jurors participating in the re-trial. The New Jersey Supreme Court upheld this order on the grounds that if juror interviews from the mistrial revealed "some insight into the jury's deliberative process, it might give the prosecution an unfair advantage in the re-trial and would violate Neulander's Sixth Amendment right to a fair trial. State of New Jersey v. Neulander (2002), cert. denied (2003).

In a case involving the frequently prosecuted former Louisiana governor Edwin W. Edwards, federal district court Judge Edith Brown Clement ordered that the jury remain anonymous in order to prevent tampering, which was rumored to have occurred in an earlier prosecution of Edwards. When the media challenged her order, the U.S. Court of Appeals for the Fifth Circuit grudgingly acknowledged that Judge Clement's orders to the media "not to interfere with" or "circumvent" her decision to empanel an anonymous jury constituted an unconstitutional prior restraint on newsgathering. The ambiguity of the terms "interfere" and "circumvent" rendered the orders overbroad. U.S. v. Brown (2001). Thus, journalists may use time-honored strategies such as attending jury selection and writing down the names called out, or waiting until the trial is over and approaching jurors in the courthouse parking lot. The Fifth Circuit added, however, that the court itself could try to maintain post-verdict juror anonymity by declining to provide jurors' names to journalists, and it reaffirmed this decision in a subsequent appeal from Edwards and his co-defendants. United States v. Edwards (2002).

Some legal scholars argue that secret juries violate the First Amendment rights of the press. More than a decade ago the U.S. Court of Appeals for the First Circuit explained that "Knowledge of juror identities allows the public to verify the impartiality of key participants in the administration of justice, and thereby ensures fairness, the appearance of fairness and public confidence in that system." In re Globe Newspaper Co. (1990). Without knowing who is serving on a jury, people might suspect that only those with certain social or political connections are chosen as jurors. Furthermore, public knowledge of juror identities might deter veniremen from intentionally misrepresenting themselves during jury selection. For example, the U.S. Court of Appeals for the Second Circuit ruled the trial court judge's decision to ban the press from attending jury selection in Martha Stewart's trial was unconstitutional. ABC v. Stewart (2004).

c. *Access to Secret Dockets*

Journalists check court dockets to learn when complaints are filed in cases across the United States. The docket contains the case number the court assigns, the parties' names, and a brief entry of each document filed or of action taken in the case. Court dockets are public records, available from the clerk of the court or through an Internet-

based case management system, Case Manage-
ment/Electronic Case Files (CM/ECE) and from an
electronic public access service called Public Access
to Court Electronic Records (PACER). In recent
years, however, at least 46 federal district courts
and some state courts have permitted cases to remain secret, never appearing on the court docket or
hidden with pseudonyms such as "Sealed v. Sealed"
or "John Doe v. Jane Doe." Some prosecutors favor
secret dockets in gang-related or organized crime
cases because they have discovered that criminals
were using public dockets to find cases in which
nothing has happened after an arrest. The criminals, suspecting that defendants in such cases were
cooperating with prosecutors, would silence the defendants by killing them. When prosecutors keep a
case off the docket, it can proceed through the court
system without the press or public's knowledge.
Such a system makes it nearly impossible for the
press and public to learn what types of cases are
being "super-sealed" or to challenge the constitutionality of the sealing orders.

For example, U.S. authorities secretly detained
the Algerian-born Mohamed Kamel Bellahouel and
jailed him for five months at the Krome Detention
Center in Miami because FBI agents thought he
might have served meals to two of the September
11 hijackers when he had worked as a waiter at a
Middle Eastern restaurant in Delray Beach, Florida.
Bellahouel's case did not appear on the court docket
except briefly by accident when a clerk for the U.S.
Court of Appeals for the Eleventh Circuit inadver-

tently allowed Bellahouel's name and case number to appear on the court's oral argument calendar. Ultimately the government concluded that Bellahouel was harmless and released him on $10,000 bond. While still in prison, however, Bellahouel had filed a legal challenge to his custody. Bellahouel appealed to the U.S. Supreme Court, but it declined to hear his case. M.K.B. v. Warden (2003).

In addition to keeping the Bellahouel case secret, the federal district court in Miami also kept secret the docket in which Columbian defendant Fabio Ochoa–Vasquez was convicted on drug trafficking charges. He appealed to the U.S. Court of Appeals for the Eleventh Circuit, arguing that the federal district court's practice of maintaining secret dockets had violated his right of due process and violated both the First and Sixth Amendments. For example, the government's case against Ochoa–Vasquez' co-conspirator Nicholas Bergonzoli had been kept off the public record entirely. The docket contained no proceedings involving Bergonzoli, but Ochoa–Vasquez argued that Drug Enforcement Agency (DEA) agents had "sold" a sentence reduction to Bergonzoli, who was secretly convicted and sentenced to only three years in prison. Ochoa–Vasquez rebuffed an alleged deal that would have shortened his prison sentence if he paid a $30 million bribe to a DEA informant; this information was crucial to Ochoa–Vasquez' defense. Ochoa–Vasquez' attorneys pointed out that the Eleventh Circuit had already ruled against secret dockets in United States v. Valenti (1993). Despite its earlier ruling in the Valenti case, and despite the fact that the government admitted to a corrupt sentencing program, the Eleventh Circuit affirmed Ochoa–Vasquez' conviction and sentence, ruling that he had failed to show that his trial was unfair as a result of the secret docketing system. United States v. Ochoa–Vasquez (2006).

As in the Ochoa–Vasquez case, government prosecutors had kept secret the docket in their case against Iyman Faris, who pled guilty in May 2003 to assisting al Qaida. Indeed, the public might never have heard of Faris except for the work of Newsweek reporters Michael Isikoff and Mark Hosenball, who learned of Faris' existence through intelligence documents. After Newsweek published their June 18, 2003 article, former Attorney General John Ashcroft confirmed that Faris had pled guilty to terrorist charges. The U.S. Supreme Court granted certiorari and then remanded the case to the U.S. Court of Appeals for the Fourth Circuit, which upheld Faris' conviction. United States v. Faris (2005).

Since 2001 the federal district court in Washington, D.C. has heard 469 cases (18% of its 3000 cases from 2001–2005) that were on secret dockets, so that the press and public did not know that these cases existed, and could not challenge the secret dockets. The News Media & the Law 30:1 (Winter 2006) at 4.

Although the U.S. Supreme Court has not ruled on whether or not secret dockets are constitutional, the U.S. Courts of Appeal for both the Eleventh and Second Circuits have ruled that the press and public have a qualified First Amendment right to see docket sheets in both civil and criminal cases. After the Hartford Courant sought access to an estimated 10,000 cases that had been concealed from the public during the past 40 years, its reporters found that Connecticut courts had "selectively" sealed divorce, paternity and other cases involving judges, celebrities and wealthy corporate chief executive officers. Judge Robert Katzmann of the Second Circuit emphasized that docket sheets have historically been available to the public, and remanded the case "for proceedings consistent with this opinion." Hartford Courant Co. v. Pellegrino (2004). Although Connecticut's Superior Court judges finally ruled against the use of secret dockets, judges may still seal cases if they give notice and provide the public with an opportunity to challenge their decision to seal a case.

4. Access to Judicial Documents and Discovery Materials

In Seattle Times Co. v. Rhinehart (1984), the Supreme Court ruled that the news media do not have a First Amendment right of access to discovery materials. See U.S. v. Rahman (1994) (barring disclosure of discovery materials held not to be a prior restraint in prosecution related to 1993 World Trade Center bombing). Despite the Seattle Times ruling, however, subsequent lower court decisions suggest that discovery materials are available to the public once they have been filed with the trial court. For example, in Public Citizen v. Liggett Group, Inc. (1988), Public Citizen and the Wall Street Journal won access to a tobacco company's discovery documents in a lawsuit by survivors of a smoker. See also In re Agent Orange Litigation (1987).

Judges sometimes request psychiatric reports as part of discovery, as in the case of Theodore Kaczynski, the "Unabomber" who killed three people and injured two. When the San Francisco Examiner and CBS Broadcasting requested access to Kaczynski's sealed psychiatric competency report, the trial court ordered a redacted version of the report unsealed. Kaczynski appealed, asserting a privacy interest. The Court of Appeals for the Ninth Circuit affirmed the trial court's decision, recognizing the media's common law right of access to judicial documents, although it declined to address the media's First Amendment claim. United States v. Kaczynski (1998).

The U.S. Court of Appeals for the D.C. Circuit ruled that depositions taken in antitrust litigation as part of pretrial discovery in the Department of Justice's lawsuit against Microsoft had to be available to press and public under the Publicity in Taking of Evidence Act of 1913. 15 U.S.C. § 30. Although the trial court had barred the media from attending the deposition of Microsoft's chairman Bill Gates, the appellate court held that the media must have access to the transcript and videotape of Gates' deposition. The appeals court further held that the Federal Rule of Civil Procedure 26(c), authorizing a court to issue a protective order barring the press and public from attending discovery proceedings if good cause (such as protecting trade secrets) is shown, did not supersede the 1913 Act. United States v. Microsoft Corporation (1999).

More recently the New Jersey Supreme Court upheld the principle that the public has no right of access to discovery materials in a case involving the safety record of Goodyear's Load Range E tire. Frankl v. Goodyear (2004). Despite the fact that the Federal Rule of Civil Procedure 26(c) specifies that judges should grant protective orders only "for good cause," as mentioned above, federal judges are generally reluctant to second-guess the confidentiality designations of litigants.

5.   Access to Sealed Documents

A serious obstacle to access for the press and public is the growing trend in which parties to litigation agree to seal their settlement agreements and all related court papers. Plaintiffs are often willing to agree to confidentiality in order to obtain more money in the settlement. When the news media and public interest groups request that court documents be unsealed, the courts have split on whether to make the documents available. Compare Bank of America v. Hotel Rittenhouse Associates (1986) (affirming right of access to sealed settlement agreements), with Holland v. Eads (1993) (denying access to records of a plaintiff's settlement with a car dealership in order to protect trade secrets).

In one of the worst cases of a judge turning his gavel into a sledgehammer, U.S. District Court Judge John Feikens barred Business Week magazine from publishing an article it had prepared based on a sealed settlement agreement between Procter & Gamble and Bankers Trust. Procter & Gamble (P&G) had sued the bank for failing to advise P&G of the risks of derivatives (financial contracts whose value is linked to some underlying asset such as stocks and bonds), causing P&G to lose nearly $200 million. After the settlement agreement was reached, a P&G employee made an off-the-record phone call to a Business Week editor, suggesting that some of the documents might be of interest. The editor had a contact with a lawyer at the firm representing Bankers Trust; the lawyer apparently did not realize that the documents were under seal, and provided Business Week with copies. Three hours before Business Week was going to press with the story, Judge Feikens faxed an order enjoining Business Week from publishing the news article.

McGraw–Hill, owner of Business Week, appealed, but the U.S. Court of Appeals for the Sixth Circuit doubted that it had jurisdiction and instead returned the case to the district court for a fact-finding hearing. McGraw–Hill Companies v. Procter & Gamble Co. (1995). After six months, the Court of Appeals for the Sixth Circuit finally vacated the permanent injunction and held that Judge Feikens never should have sealed the documents in the first place. Nonetheless, Judge Feikens had gagged Business Week for six months, apparently not understanding what the Press Clause of the First Amendment requires. Procter & Gamble Co. v. Bankers Trust Co. (1996).

At the same time that Business Week was waiting for the Sixth Circuit to grant relief regarding documents under seal, the Court of Appeals for the Second Circuit was creating a balancing test designed to help trial courts weigh factors governing the presumption of access to judicial documents. United States v. Amodeo (1995). In Amodeo, Judge Mary Shannon Little filed a sealed report on corruption in the Hotel Employees & Restaurant Employees International Union in which she mentioned attorney Harold Ickes of Meyer, Suozzi, English & Klein because Ickes had represented the Union. Ickes was appointed to Deputy Chief of Staff to President Clinton, at which point New York Newsday asked the federal district court in New York to unseal the document. The district court directed Little to redact the document and release it, but Meyer, Suozzi appealed, citing privacy interests. The Court of Appeals for the Second Circuit held that the presumption of access should be balanced against 1) the danger of impairing law enforcement, 2) judicial efficiency and 3) the privacy interests of those resisting disclosure. The appellate court concluded that "Part 1" of the report, containing accusations against Ickes, should not be released because the accusations were unsworn and were "of doubtful veracity." Newsday did not file an appeal.

A federal district court judge applied Amodeo's balancing test in United States v. Glens Falls Newspapers, Inc. (1998) and denied access to drafts of settlement documents in a case in which the Environmental Protection Agency charged that General Electric had negligently poisoned an aquifer. When Glens Falls Newspapers appealed, the Second Circuit upheld the district court decision to deny access on the grounds that negotiation itself is a private matter, and publicity would impede settlement of the case, which had dragged on for 10 years.

Reporters who disclose the terms of settlement agreements under seal can face serious consequences. A clerk mistakenly gave reporter Kirsten Mitchell a copy of the sealed settlement agreement between Conoco Oil and residents of a trailer park in Wrightsboro, North Carolina, after the residents sued Conoco because a gas leak had contaminated their drinking water. A confidential source had told Mitchell's colleague Cory Reiss that Conoco had paid $36 million to Wrightsboro residents; Mitchell then verified the amount from court documents and published an article with the details. She and Reiss were both held in contempt of court, and Reiss was sentenced to jail until he disclosed the identity of his source. Mitchell and her newspaper, the Wilmington (North Carolina) Morning Star were jointly fined $500,000. Ashcraft v. Conoco Inc. (1998).

Although courts have shown a propensity for sealing settlement agreements, which has been discouraging to proponents of access, the Court of Appeals for the Ninth Circuit recently held that the media have the right by mandamus to intervene to seek access to court records in civil cases. The appellate court added that under both common law and the Federal Rules of Civil Procedure, a pre-judgment right of access to judicial records exists in civil cases. San Jose Mercury News, Inc. v. District Court (1999) (media should have access to expert's report in an employment sex discrimination case against a California police department).

With regard to sealed records in criminal rather than civil cases, journalists have had varying degrees of success in persuading judges to unseal court records of sexual abuse by Roman Catholic priests, in some cases occurring many years ago. In many cases involving pedophile priests, attorneys for church officials persuaded judges to seal arrest warrants, while the clergy covered up evidence of lawsuits and transferred the pedophile priests to distant parishes. For example, an appellate court in Connecticut reversed a trial judge's order to release documents from 23 cases involving sexual abuse of children by priests; thus, the Catholic Church managed to keep the documents under seal. Rosado et al. v. Bridgeport Roman Catholic Diocesan Corp. (2003). Rules for gaining access to sealed court records vary according to state law and the type of record requested.

6. Access to Videotapes, Audiotapes or Still Photographs

The presumption that journalists have access to court records does not always extend to making copies of audio or videotaped evidence used during a trial. For example, in Maryland a television station asked to copy a videotape played in open court during a murder trial. The video showed murder victim Pamela Basu and her daughter getting into their car; in the background are two men whom police later charged with Basu's murder. The defendants were being tried separately. A television station asked to broadcast the videotape after the first trial, but the Maryland Court of Special Appeals affirmed a lower court ruling that the videotape could not be aired until after the second trial, in order to ensure a fair trial for the second defendant. Group W Television Inc. v. Maryland (1993).

Courts are of course more willing to grant access to audio and videotapes if the tapes have already been introduced into evidence. The Courts of Appeal for both the D.C. and Third Circuit have ruled that there is a strong presumption in favor of access to videotaped material. In re Application of NBC (1981); U.S. v. Martin (1984). The Court of Appeals for the Fifth Circuit disagreed, however, explaining that there is no absolute right to copy judicial documents and that it could not find a basis for the presumption of access to audio and videotaped material. Belo Broadcasting v. Clark (1981).

The Court of Appeals for the Eighth Circuit ruled that neither the press nor the public had a First

Amendment or common law right of access to President Bill Clinton's videotaped deposition in the criminal trial of Susan McDougal in Arkansas. The court held that the videotaped deposition was not a court record within the meaning of the common law right of access to judicial records, and even if it were, the presumption of access had been overcome. Furthermore, there was no First Amendment right of access because the court had provided a full transcript and access to the trial to both press and public. U.S. v. McDougal (1996). But see KNSD Channels 7/39 v. Superior Court (1998) (California appellate court ruled that audiotape of conversation between defendants, admitted as evidence at trial, is judicial record to which press has common law access).

Courts in Pennsylvania and Virginia have held that audiotapes of 911 calls are not public records subject to disclosure under state FOIA laws. See North Hills News Record v. Town of McCandless (1999); Tull v. Brown (1998). In contrast, however, the New York Supreme Court ruled that New York's Freedom of Information Law (FOIL) required the New York City Fire Department to release audiotapes and transcripts of the 911 calls from the World Trade Center during the September 11 terrorist attacks. Before releasing the tapes in March 2006, New York City officials redacted the voices of the callers so that only the voices of the 911 dispatchers could be heard. In the Matter of the New York Times Company v. City of New York Fire Department (2005).

CHAPTER VIII

NEWSPERSONS' PRIVILEGE, SUBPOENAS, CONTEMPT CITATIONS AND SEARCHES AND SEIZURES

A. SUBPOENAS VERSUS CLAIMS OF PRIVILEGE

1. The Contemporary Problem

Until the late 1960s it was rare for agencies of federal, state and local governments to subpoena newspersons to testify about their sources. Through the 1950's there had been only a handful of cases involving government attempts to force disclosure from unwilling members of the press. As late as the advent of the Nixon administration the problem was not one of major concern.

Then a number of social and political forces combined to embolden prosecutors, judges, legislators and other government officials to seek unpublished information of interest to them in the hands and minds of newspersons. Mutual distrust and even enmity between public officials and reporters began to grow, particularly in large urban areas. The distrust was fueled at least in part by the Vietnam war, a troubled economy, widespread graft and corruption at all levels of government, leaks of secret

government information, doubtful media coverage
of government and its personnel and what some
might characterize as anti-establishmentarianism
by some elements of the media. Then too, the press
became more interested in writing stories about the
drug and sex subcultures and violence-prone anti-
government organizations. As a result, reporters
were made privy to information concerning violations of law that prosecutors wanted and could not
obtain through traditional means. In addition, "law
and order" concerns began to grip the land in the
wake of an ever-increasing crime rate. The 1970s
engendered a widespread attitude among government officials that if reporters had unpublished
information concerning crimes and anti-establish-
ment conduct, they had the same legal duty as
anyone else to disclose it.

This attitude has persisted into the twenty-first
century, and poses special problems for newspersons. First, the ethics of their profession require
that they not divulge information obtained in confidence. Second, any disclosure of sources or other
information obtained in confidence will mark reporters as "unreliable" in the view of those from
whom they are obtaining information. This will
inhibit their ability to gather and disseminate news.
Third, reporters think of themselves as "professionals" like lawyers or doctors. This gives them a basis
for claiming protection from disclosure of their non-
published work product. News media personnel
thus insist that the law must accord them a privilege not to testify or produce materials under com-

pulsion of subpoena when their testimony would run counter to their ethical obligations or have an adverse effect on their ability to gather the news.

The professional status of newsgatherers is difficult to define, however. Whereas physicians and attorneys cannot practice medicine or law without licenses, to require a journalist to have a license before writing would constitute prior restraint. The question of who is a journalist is also complicated by new technologies such as the Internet in which anyone can post a web log ("blog"). For example, the California Court of Appeal ruled that Jason O'Grady, publisher of an online news site called PowerPage, did not have to disclose the identity of his confidential source who leaked trade secrets about an upcoming Apple product. O'Grady v. Apple Computer, Inc. (2006). Furthermore, in 2006 the Federal Election Commission (FEC) issued new rules regulating campaign ads under the Bipartisan Campaign Reform Act of 2002 (P.L. 107–155, 116 Stat. 81, March 27, 2002). The FEC's new rules specifically exempted blogs from regulations regarding political advertising. These new rules effectively treated blogs like news media, holding that they fell under the news media exemption. 11 C.F.R. Part 109 [Notice 2006–10], Coordinated Communications, Effective July 10, 2006. See also Shays v. FEC (2005).

Whereas bloggers may join the ranks of "journalists," however, some individuals or even corporations who are not journalists might find it convenient to claim the reporter's privilege despite tenuous connections to gathering news. For example, the credit rating agency Fitch, Inc. tried to quash a subpoena under New York's shield law. Fitch's attorneys argued that it conducted "research, fact-gathering and analytical activity that is directed towards matters of ... public concern, just like any journalist." The U.S. Court of Appeals for the Second Circuit rejected this argument, however, explaining that Fitch reported only on the specific transactions of its clients whereas a business newspaper or magazine would cover any transactions deemed newsworthy. In re Fitch, Inc. & American Savings Bank, FSB v. UBS Paine-Webber, Inc. (2003). The problem of how to define a professional journalist has been one of the obstacles confronting Congress in trying to pass a federal shield law.

Not having professional status might be an advantage to journalists with regard to making them eligible for collective bargaining, but it is disadvantageous to the extent that courts do not accord them an absolute privilege against being compelled to testify, in contrast, for example, with physicians, attorneys or priests. Whether the courts consider them professionals or not, in many cases today, newspersons are refusing to obey subpoenas and choosing to face jail for contempt when the claimed privilege is denied.

There is now a serious and growing confrontation between those who would gather the news and those who would use these newsgatherers to provide information for government purposes. What makes the problem especially difficult is that both sides to the dispute may say with some justification that by their actions they are serving the public interest. Journalists who write stories on organized crime, for example, would obviously want to promise confidentiality to their sources; if the source's identity were revealed, the source's life could be in danger. On the other hand a prosecutor would want to know whom the journalist had interviewed in order to protect society from someone who might be a dangerous criminal.

2. Legal Background

a. *Common Law Privilege*

The common law, while recognizing testimonial privileges for the attorney-client, doctor-patient and marital relationships, has never accorded a like privilege to the newsperson-news source relationship or any other aspect of the newsgathering process. A strong policy argument can be made that a newsperson's privilege is at least as necessary to the public welfare as the recognized privileges are because of its societal benefit in encouraging a freer flow of news and information to the public. The law has accepted the strong opposing policy, however, that the public, in the words of Dean Wigmore, "has a right to every man's evidence." The more testimonial privileges that are recognized, the less evidence will be available to those who must attempt to reconstruct the truth in a judicial proceeding or establish public policy in the halls of a legislature or in an executive office. Not surprisingly, then, the common law courts have consistently refused to expand the number of recognized privileges in order to cover newspersons.

b. Newspersons' Shield Statutes

An alternative to persuading the courts to fashion a newsperson's privilege is to convince legislatures to enact statutes embodying such a privilege. The first so-called newspersons' shield law was enacted in Maryland in 1898 to protect the confidentiality of news sources. It remained unique for more than three decades before New Jersey adopted a similar statute. Thereafter, lobbying campaigns by the newspaper industry have resulted in the enactment of shield statutes of one type or another in just over half the states. These acts are analyzed below.

Though such legislation is now widespread, the statutes at best provide uncertain protection for newspersons because they are subject to interpretation and application by the state courts, which have generally been hostile to their aim. They are, with few exceptions, narrowly construed and sharply limited as to the protection they afford. One reason that state courts have been hostile toward shield statutes is that a reporter's privilege to keep sources confidential can conflict with a criminal defendant's Sixth Amendment right to have compulsory process to obtain witnesses in his or her favor, or to confront the prosecution's witnesses.

The first federal shield statute was proposed in 1929, but though numerous bills have been introduced in Congress since then, Congress has never enacted a federal statute extending a testimonial privilege to newspersons. Perhaps this is because no consensus has ever developed within the media regarding either the necessity for such legislation or its proper scope.

c.   *Claims of Privilege under the First Amendment*

A relatively recent claim of newspersons to immunity from testimonial compulsion is based on the Constitution. The argument is that compelling reporters to testify in judicial and other proceedings will have a detrimental effect on their access to sensitive and confidential news sources and will consequently restrict the flow of news to the public in violation of the First Amendment.

This argument was first raised in Garland v. Torre (1958). Judy Garland had brought an action against the Columbia Broadcasting System alleging, inter alia, that the network had fostered the publication of false and defamatory statements about her to the effect that she was refusing to rehearse a show for CBS. New York Herald Tribune radio-TV columnist Marie Torre had written the allegedly defamatory statements, and attributed them to an unnamed CBS executive. When Garland's attorney deposed Torre she refused to disclose the name of the executive, asserting that to do so would violate a journalistic confidence. Court proceedings were initiated to compel her to disclose the name. Again Torre refused to make disclosure. She was held in criminal contempt and sentenced to ten days imprisonment. On appeal she raised the constitutional issue. Judge (later Justice) Potter Stewart affirmed her conviction, and Ms. Torre was forced to leave her newborn child and her toddler and serve the

10–day sentence. Judge Stewart, while recognizing that compulsory disclosure of a journalist's confidential sources might entail an abridgment of press freedom, held that such abridgment had to be balanced against the obvious need in the judicial process for testimonial compulsion. Where, as here, the need for the testimony sought went to the heart of the plaintiff's claim, the Constitution conferred no right on Torre to refuse to answer.

In his opinion Judge Stewart had noted that the judicial process was not being used to force wholesale disclosure of a news source or to discover the identity of a source of doubtful relevance or materiality. He thereby implied that there might be situations in which the First Amendment would provide the newsperson with a qualified privilege not to testify under compulsion of legal process.

Yet state court decisions after Garland and before 1972 held that the First Amendment provided no testimonial privilege of any kind. See In re Taylor (1963); State v. Buchanan (1968). Thus, the existence of even a limited First Amendment testimonial privilege for the newsgatherer was in doubt and the U.S. Supreme Court would have to decide the issue.

3.   The Branzburg–Pappas–Caldwell Trilogy

The U.S. Supreme Court eventually combined three different cases, which were Branzburg v. Hayes, In re Pappas and United States v. Caldwell

(1972). The Court held that "the First Amendment does not guarantee the press a constitutional right of special access to information not available to the public generally." Furthermore, it denied newsgatherers a testimonial privilege to refuse to appear before grand juries to testify about 1) possible criminal activities they might have witnessed in the course of their professional responsibilities, and 2) the identity of those who engaged in such activities.

a. What the Supreme Court Decided

What the Court decided in the trilogy of newsperson privilege cases is not entirely clear because of the failure of Justice White, the author of the majority opinion, to relate his lengthy reasoning to the three cases at hand and to make distinctions among them. The issue is further confused by the presence of what appears to be a conflicting concurring opinion of Justice Powell, a member of the five-person majority. The confusion results in part because Justice Powell seems to suggest that conferring the reporter's privilege should be determined on a case-by-case basis; in this call for ad hoc balancing, Justice Powell seems to agree with the dissent.

It is clear that the majority recognized no basis for a newsperson to refuse to appear and answer some questions when summoned by a grand jury. It is also clear that the majority held that members of the news media may be compelled to provide information if they witness criminal activity. It also seems to follow that the appearance and testimony of newspersons would be compelled in criminal and civil trials. If immunity against compelled testimony is denied in a closed and freewheeling grand jury proceeding, it would be difficult to justify allowing such immunity in open public trials controlled by strict evidentiary rules. The Court clearly rejected the idea that the First Amendment confers an absolute privilege upon newspersons not to appear and testify in judicial proceedings.

In contrast, dissenters Stewart, Brennan and Marshall would have required ad hoc balancing *before* the reporter was required to appear before a grand jury. Under their approach the government, in a proceeding to quash the subpoena, would have to: (1) show that there is probable cause to believe that the newsperson has information that is clearly relevant to a specific probable violation of law; (2) demonstrate that the information sought cannot be obtained by alternative means less destructive of First Amendment rights; and (3) demonstrate a compelling and overriding interest in the information. In the years following Branzburg, many federal and state courts have applied Justice Stewart's three-part test in deciding whether to compel journalists to testify or not. The strength and clarity of the dissenters' three-part test may explain the continued interest of these courts in determining the scope of a qualified constitutional privilege for newspersons.

b. The Legal Situation After Branzburg

(1) Civil and Criminal Cases and Grand Jury Proceedings

Many lower federal and state courts have limited the application of Branzburg. In the leading civil case of Baker v. F & F Investment (1972), plaintiffs, alleging racial discrimination in the sale of houses to blacks in Chicago, sued certain local real estate organizations and sought before trial to depose Alfred Balk, a writer and editor, as to the true identity of the fictitiously named "Norris Vitchek," a real estate agent and the main source for Balk's article published in the Saturday Evening Post on "blockbusting" in Chicago. Balk and his publisher had previously promised Vitchek that they would not reveal his true identity. Consequently Balk, while highly sympathetic to the plaintiffs' cause, refused to provide Vitchek's true identity, claiming First Amendment protection. The plaintiffs sought an order from the federal district court directing Balk to provide the information. The order was denied and the Second Circuit handed down a decision after Branzburg affirming that denial. Recognizing that to compel disclosure of newspersons' confidential sources has a "chilling effect" on the flow of news to the public, the court of appeals balanced the competing interests along the lines Justice Stewart had suggested in his dissent in Branzburg, thereby de facto recognizing a qualified constitutional privilege in civil cases. See Silkwood v. Kerr–McGee Corp. (1977) (documentary film-maker treated as a reporter when making film about mysterious death of Karen Silkwood after she found she had been contaminated by plutonium radiation at processing plant run by Kerr–McGee); Loadholtz v. Fields (1975) (disclosure of unpublished background materials sought and refused); Democratic National Committee v. McCord (1973) (disclosure of unpublished background materials sought and refused).

Of course, the balance may be struck in favor of compelling the newsperson to reveal confidential sources and to provide unpublished background materials and work product. See Caldero v. Tribune Publishing Co. (1977) (reporter refused to reveal name of source of libelous story; court inferred that no source existed); Matter of Farber (1978) (reporter found to be in criminal contempt for refusing to give up his notes); Ashcraft v. Conoco, Inc. (1998) (reporter found in contempt for refusing to identify confidential sources who may have violated gag order); Lee v. U.S. Department of Justice (2005) (reporters held in contempt for refusing to identify confidential sources in Department of Justice who leaked information about nuclear scientist Wen Ho Lee, discussed below); and In re Special Proceedings (2004) (broadcast journalist James Taricani sentenced to six months' home confinement after refusing to reveal source of secret FBI videotape, discussed below). With the exception of Matter of Farber and In re Special Proceedings which were criminal cases, the other cases cited above involved only the claim of the reporter's privilege at the pretrial discovery or motion stage in civil proceedings. At that stage the relevance and materiality of the journalist's information may not be as clear, and the person suing the reporter will probably not have thoroughly explored alternative sources for the same information.

It is not yet clear whether the newsperson will be protected as regularly and to the same degree at the *trial* of a civil case when a litigant seeks confidential information from a journalist which will likely make or break his or her case. In such situations the interests of the individual litigant in fair and peaceable settlement of private disputes comes into direct confrontation with the public's First Amendment interest in the free flow of information.

The courts are not likely to be very sympathetic to a reporter defendant sued for libel or invasion of privacy who asserts the qualified privilege to prevent allegedly wronged plaintiffs from proving their cases. In this context Garland v. Torre (1958), discussed earlier, states the applicable principle: the balance is to be struck in favor of disclosure if the information sought goes to "the heart of the plaintiff's claim."

This principle has taken on increased importance with the advent of the New York Times v. Sullivan line of defamation cases requiring the plaintiff, if a public official or public figure, to establish knowing falsity or reckless disregard for the truth on the part of the defendant. This may be impossible to prove unless the plaintiff can see the defendant's notes and background materials and examine his or her sources for the defamatory message. The Supreme Court expressed such a concern in Herbert v. Lando (1979). In that case, admitted public figure Army Col. Anthony Herbert sued Lando, an editor-producer for CBS' "Sixty Minutes." Lando claimed a privilege under the First Amendment not to divulge his thought processes or the state of mind he possessed when he was editing and producing the program segment complained of. The Supreme Court, in rejecting the claimed privilege, ruled that to give Lando the privilege would make it far more difficult for Herbert to establish actual malice as required by New York Times Co. v. Sullivan. It appears then that if a newsperson has evidence relevant to the actual malice issue in a libel suit brought by a public figure, and if the evidence cannot be otherwise obtained and goes to the "heart of the case," the courts will not grant a qualified privilege.

More recently, a federal district court issued an order requiring five journalists to reveal the identities of confidential sources after they had reported on the FBI's espionage investigation of Wen Ho Lee, a former Los Alamos nuclear scientist who was later cleared of all but one of the 59 charges against him. Lee had filed suit to learn the identities of government personnel who had violated the Privacy Act (discussed in Chapter VII) when they leaked personal information about Lee to the five reporters. The federal district court judge balanced the need for a reporter's privilege against Lee's need for evidence, but after Lee's attorneys deposed 21 government officials, the judge concluded that Lee had "exhausted every reasonable alternative source of information." He held the five reporters in contempt of court, ordering them to pay a fine of $500 a day until they divulged their sources or until the trial was over and they could no longer testify. The U.S. Court of Appeals for the District of Columbia upheld the contempt charges and fines. Lee v. U.S. Department of Justice (2005).

Turning from civil to criminal proceedings, the lower federal and state courts generally follow the narrow holding of Branzburg and deny the privilege when newspersons assert it before grand juries to protect (1) the identity of sources who may have engaged in criminal activity and (2) reporters' unpublished notes, information and background materials which might lead to the discovery of the criminals. See Lewis v. United States (1974) (claim of privilege by radio station manager to withhold original document of Weather Underground and tape recording of Symbionese Liberation Army from federal grand jury rejected). See also In re Grand Jury Proceedings (Scarce v. United States) (1993) (graduate student found in contempt for refusing to testify before grand jury about his acquaintance, suspected of vandalism and animal liberation at a university research laboratory); United States v. Cutler (1993) (reporters compelled to testify about conversation with Bruce Cutler, suspected of violating court order not to talk to press about Cutler's client, mob boss John Gotti); and In re Grand Jury Subpoena

American Broadcasting Companies, Inc. (1996) (ABC compelled to provide outtakes of "Prime Time Live" interview with Whitewater defendant Susan MacDougal); In re Special Counsel Investigation (2004) (Time Magazine and New York Times reporters held not to have any First Amendment privilege to refuse to disclose sources who leaked status of CIA employee Valerie Plame as a covert agent). Because the grand jury has evolved by and large into a prosecutorial device, prosecutors have been quite successful both before and after Branzburg in having claims of constitutional privilege rejected during the preliminary stages of criminal investigations.

Most worrisome to journalists is the recent trend in which federal and state courts in criminal proceedings declare flatly that there is no First Amendment privilege, either absolute or qualified, for journalists, harkening back to Justice White's opinion for an apparent majority in Branzburg v. Hayes, In re Pappas and United States v. Caldwell (1972).

In Leggett v. United States (2002) for example, Vanessa Leggett, a free-lance writer, was working on a book about the murder of a Houston woman found shot to death. Police charged the woman's husband, a wealthy bookmaker, and his brother with her murder. Leggett interviewed the brother before he committed suicide. The case against the husband went forward. The grand jury issued a subpoena for nearly all of Leggett's confidential work product, including notes of her interviews. She refused to comply, claiming the qualified privilege to protect her sources. A federal district court judge held her in contempt. The judge closed the hearing on the contempt citation and sealed the order sending Leggett to jail for 168 days. Continuing the secrecy of the proceedings, the U.S. Court of Appeals for the Fifth Circuit sealed the briefs filed in the appeal, closed the oral argument to the press and public, and refused to publish its opinion justifying its action in upholding the contempt citation and affirming its earlier decision in United States v. Smith (1998) rejecting a qualified privilege for journalists and other writers who disseminate news and information to the public.

What little of the Fifth Circuit's rationale has leaked out comes from an unofficial report of the opinion, contemporary newspaper accounts, media organization press releases and Internet reports. The Bureau of National Affairs and the Associated Press reported that the Fifth Circuit unanimously found that "the journalist's privilege is ineffectual against a grand jury subpoena, absent evidence of governmental harassment or oppression." Furthermore, the court said, "This court takes a narrow view of the journalist's privilege in criminal cases, particularly in grand jury proceedings." See also United States v. Smith (1998); In re Special Counsel Investigation (2004).

A year after Vanessa Leggett went to jail, federal district court Judge Ernest Torres appointed a special prosecutor to find out who had given broadcast journalist James Taricani a secret surveillance videotape of an FBI informant giving a $1000 cash bribe to a Providence, Rhode Island city official. Taricani worked for NBC-affiliate WJAR–TV, which aired an excerpt of the secret tape. Prosecutor Marc DeSisto interviewed nearly 20 potential witnesses over two years, but could not identify the source of the leak. When Taricani refused to name his source, Judge Torres ruled that even if there was a qualified reporter's privilege, DeSisto had overcome it by interviewing the potential witnesses. Judge Torres thus held Taricani in civil contempt and fined him $1000 per day. WJAR–TV paid $85,000 in fines for Taricani, at which point Judge Torres concluded that the fine was not working. He suspended the fine, found Taricani guilty of criminal contempt and sentenced him to six months' home confinement (Taricani served four of the six months). Judge Torres accused Taricani and WJAR–TV of airing the videotape to get higher ratings, not to expose corruption, because the district attorney's office had already discovered the corruption (various city officials including the mayor were convicted in a scandal known as "Operation Plunder Dome"). The U.S. Court of Appeals for the First Circuit upheld Judge Torres' ruling that Branzburg applies not only to grand jury proceedings but also to cases involving special prosecutors. In re Special Proceedings (2004).

In a case that drew far more national attention than the cases of Vanessa Leggett and James Taricani, the U.S. Court of Appeals for the District of Columbia Circuit held that Time magazine correspondent Matthew Cooper and New York Times reporter Judith Miller had no First Amendment privilege to refuse to disclose the source who leaked the information that CIA employee Valerie Plame was a covert agent. In re Special Counsel Investigation (2004). (It is a violation of the Intelligence Identities Protection Act (50 U.S.C.A. SS 421 35 seq.) to reveal the name of covert CIA agents, and the Department of Justice had appointed a special prosecutor, U.S. Attorney Patrick Fitzgerald, to conduct a grand jury investigation into who leaked Plame's name to Cooper and Miller.) The court relied on Branzburg for its holding, and said "The Supreme Court decided in Branzburg that there is no First Amendment privilege protecting journalists . . . from testifying before a grand jury or otherwise providing evidence to a grand jury. . . . The Highest Court has spoken and never revisited the question. Without doubt, that is the end of the matter." In re Special Counsel Investigation (2004). Thus Cooper and Miller faced contempt citations and jail time.

The consequences of the District of Columbia Circuit's ruling and the U.S. Supreme Court's subsequent denial of certiorari were immediate. Time magazine's editor-in-chief Norman Pearlstine announced that Time would turn over the documents and e-mail messages in its possession concerning Cooper's confidential sources to the grand jury investigating who leaked the identity of Valerie Plame. This prevented Cooper from serving a jail term. New York Times, July 1, 2005 at A1, A12. Although New York Times reporter Judith Miller had not published any articles naming Valerie

Plame, she had taken notes indicating that she had discussed Plame's identity with an unnamed source. When Judith Miller was taken into custody, special prosecutor Patrick J. Fitzgerald acknowledged that he already knew the identity of Miller's source. Furthermore, he added that her source had already relieved her of her duty to protect his anonymity. Fitzgerald commented that ''Miller's views may change over time if her irresponsible martyrdom is later viewed by her . . . colleagues as hurting rather than helping reporters' efforts to protect their sources. Washington Post, July 6, 2005 at A1. Miller served nearly three months in jail, from July 6 to September 29, 2005. In re Grand Jury Subpoena (2005). (Although the general public learned a month later that Miller's source was Vice President Richard Cheney's chief of staff I. Lewis ''Scooter'' Libby, the following year former deputy secretary of state Richard Armitage admitted that he had been the original source of the leak. In June 2003 Armitage had inadvertently disclosed Valerie Plame's identity to Washington Post reporter Bob Woodward and columnist Robert Novak. New York Times, September 8, 2006 at A22.)

Miller's jail term served as a reminder that the qualified privilege is unlikely to stand in cases involve testimony before a grand jury. Compare New York Times Co. v. Gonzales (2005) (U.S. Department of Justice rebuffed in seeking telephone records of two reporters from third party telephone company on First Amendment grounds). On the other hand, in cases not involving grand jury testimony, a majority of the U.S. courts of appeal have at least at one time explicitly accepted the idea of a qualified privilege protecting reporters when they are subpoenaed to testify about confidential matters.

On the other side of the ledger from the government's grand jury proceedings, reporters cannot successfully claim the privilege in every case involving a criminal defendant, however, especially if disclosure of an informer's identity is relevant to the defense of an accused person. In Matter of Farber (1978), the court rejected New York Times reporter Myron Farber's claim of privilege not to disclose sources and documents he used in his articles leading to prosecution of Dr. Mario Jascalevich for poisoning five patients. In Kansas v. Sandstrom (1978), in which a woman was charged with killing her husband, reporter Joe Pennington testified at the trial that a confidential source had told him that one of the state's witnesses had threatened to kill the husband shortly before the murder. Pennington said the informant had heard about the threat from someone who had attended a party at which the state's witness made the threat, but Pennington refused to identify the informant, claiming a privilege. Noting that after Branzburg, courts had generally tried to balance the need of the defendant for a fair trial against the reporter's need for confidentiality, the Kansas Supreme Court ruled that the constitutional privilege did not apply in this case because the informant's identity was critical to the defense and there was no other way to get the information.

At least one court has held that the prosecution has no right comparable to a defendant's Sixth

Amendment rights that may trump the privilege. Florida v. Wade (1995). However, a California court held recently that the interests of the prosecution may overcome the reporter's privilege as guaranteed by the state shield law, despite the fact that the shield law is part of the California Constitution. Art. 1, § 2 (1993). When KOVR–TV reporter Tom Layson videotaped an interview with a prison inmate who had confessed to a murder, prosecutors issued a subpoena, and KOVR immediately gave them the videotape which had been broadcast. When KOVR's news director Ellen Miller refused to provide the outtakes, however, she was held in contempt. The California Court of Appeal ruled against KOVR, finding that the press interests protected by California's shield law can yield to the interests of the prosecution in a criminal trial. The Supreme Court of California reversed, however, ruling that California's shield law provides for absolute rather than qualified immunity from contempt for journalists who decline to reveal unpublished information obtained in the newsgathering process. Miller v. Superior Court of San Joaquin County (1999).

(2) Cases Involving Non–Confidential Information

Although U.S. courts have permitted journalists to protect confidential sources and information, there have been conflicting decisions when non-confidential information is involved. Whereas the Court of Appeals for the Ninth Circuit has formalized the balance to be struck between First Amendment concerns and the need to compel testimony regarding non-confidential information, the Courts of Appeal for both the Second and Fifth Circuits have refused to grant a qualified privilege for non-confidential information. The Ninth Circuit case involved author Ronald Watkins' book Birthright about a bitter family feud between Leonard Shoen, founder of U–Haul, and two of his sons, whom the father accused of brutally murdering a daughter-in-law. Shoen v. Shoen (I) (1993). Although a lower court had found Watkins in contempt when he refused to relinquish his notes and tapes from the interview of a non-confidential source, the Ninth Circuit vacated the contempt order in a strong affirmation of journalists' rights. Shoen v. Shoen (II) (1995). Both the Florida Supreme Court in Kidwell v. Florida (1998) and Georgia Supreme Court in In re Keith Paul (1999) have held that reporters who conducted jailhouse interviews with accused murderers did not have to disclose unpublished notes despite the facts that both reporters had published news stories based on the interviews and that the identities of their sources were non-confidential. As in Shoen II and Kidwell, the U.S. Court of Appeals for the Second Circuit held that a qualified reporter's privilege exists under federal common law or the First Amendment for non-confidential information. Gonzales v. National Broadcasting Company (1999) (NBC's unedited videotape from "Dateline NBC" held to be protected by qualified reporter's privilege).

In United States v. Smith (1998), when WDSU–TV reporter Taylor Henry videotaped an interview with Frank Smith a few days before Smith was arrested on arson charges, federal prosecutors subpoenaed WDSU's outtakes. Although a federal district court quashed the subpoena, federal prosecutors appealed, and the U.S. Court of Appeals for the Fifth Circuit held that no privilege exists for non-confidential information unless the purpose of the subpoena is to harass the media; thus, WDSU turned over its outtakes. See also Wilson v. Amoco Corp. (1998) (Wyoming newspaper compelled to provide non-confidential but unpublished photographs of sheens of oil downstream from Amoco oil refinery).

More recently free-lance journalist Robert Young Pelton interviewed John Walker Lindh, called the "American Taliban," who was indicted for joining terrorists in Afghanistan in 2002. Lindh's attorneys subpoenaed Pelton to testify, and a federal district court judge in Virginia denied Pelton's motion to quash. Pelton had to concede that his source (Lindh) was non-confidential, and the judge held that Pelton could not invoke a First Amendment privilege on the basis of protecting a source's identity. A few days later, however, Lindh pled guilty to charges of aiding the Taliban; thus Pelton never had to testify. United States v. Lindh (2002).

The following year, when defendant Michael McKevitt was extradited to Ireland and prosecuted for directing terrorism, he asked for tape recordings of reporters' interviews with David Rupert, a key witness for the prosecution. Because McKevitt's request was for non-confidential information, the federal district court ordered the journalists to turn over the tapes to McKevitt, and the U.S. Court of Appeals for the Seventh Circuit affirmed. Writing for a unanimous three-judge panel, Judge Richard A. Posner questioned whether a federal reporter's privilege should exist at all in a case involving non-confidential source. In other words, if the reporter is not protecting a source's identity, it is difficult to see how the First Amendment is related to the question of compelled disclosure. He also wrote that "some cases that recognize the [reporter's] privilege essentially ignore Branzburg ... and some [cases] audaciously declare that Branzburg actually created a reporter's privilege.... The approaches that these decisions take to the issue of privilege can certainly be questioned." McKevitt v. Pallasch (2003). Judge Posner further surmised that the journalists' real motive was to protect their intellectual property in the recordings because they had a contract to write Rupert's biography. McKevitt v. Pallasch (2003).

Despite Shoen II, Kidwell, Gonzales, and In re Keith Paul, U.S. courts in general have been far more reluctant to grant a qualified privilege when non-confidential information is involved, as in Smith, Wilson and McKevitt. Because of the conflicting approaches of the Second and Ninth Circuits compared with the Fifth and Seventh Circuits toward non-confidential information, the U.S. Supreme Court may eventually need to resolve the issue.

(3) In Summary

Although generalization in the field of reportorial privilege is risky, the following principles and rules are suggested for states that do at least recognize some form of the privilege:

(1) There is no absolute First Amendment newspersons' privilege. A qualified or common law privilege is recognized in 48 of the 50 states (Courts in Hawaii and Wyoming have not fully considered or ruled on a qualified privilege.)

(2) The recognition by the courts of a qualified newspersons' privilege depends to a great extent on the legal context in which the claim of privilege is made, and there are some states in which the privilege is not available at all in criminal proceedings.

(3) The courts will not honor the claim of privilege made before grand juries and trial courts when it would protect sources if the reporter has seen these sources engaging in the suspected criminal activity under investigation.

(4) The courts will not honor the claim of privilege made before grand juries when the reporter is asked to produce physical evidence in his or her possession of suspected criminal activity under investigation such as tape recordings and documents.

(5) The courts will not honor the claim of privilege at a criminal trial or collateral hearing when

the prosecutor seeks evidence relevant and material to his or her case.

(6) Some courts will honor the claim of privilege at a criminal trial or collateral hearing when the criminal defendant seeks confidential information or evidence but it is not critical to his or her defense.

(7) The courts will generally honor the claim of privilege in civil pretrial proceedings and trials unless the information or evidence sought by the litigant goes to the heart of his or her case and there is no alternative source for that information.

(8) When the newsperson is a defendant in civil litigation (usually defamation or invasion of privacy actions), the courts are more likely to find that the information or material sought to be protected under the privilege goes to the heart of the plaintiff's case and cannot be obtained from alternative sources.

(9) When the newsperson is a plaintiff in civil litigation and claims the qualified privilege to prevent the defendant from obtaining information relevant to his or her defense, the claim of privilege will be denied. See Anderson v. Nixon (1978).

(10) If the newsperson's claim to a qualified privilege in the particular context is not accepted, he or she will have to choose between revealing confidential information or material and accept-

ing the consequences of disobedience of a lawful court order.

c. The Practical Effect of Branzburg on Newsgatherers

Despite the well-meaning efforts of lower federal and state courts to carve out a qualified privilege, particularly in civil cases, the holding in Branzburg has had a serious effect on newsgatherers. The majority's rejection of an absolute privilege has left journalists to guess whether and to what extent the courts will protect promises of confidentiality which journalists make to their sources. At the time assurances of secrecy are given to sources, reporters will often be unable to determine in what legal context they will be asked to breach such confidences. Thus, even assuming the rules of the game to be clearly established after Branzburg, reporters cannot always be sure which rule or rules will be applicable when their testimony is sought to be compelled. It should be clear, however, that journalists cannot have it both ways, either claiming the privilege or disclosing a source's identity depending on whichever suits them. See Cohen v. Cowles Media Co. (1991), discussed below.

(1) Confrontations with Congress

Journalists have occasionally been served with subpoenas to testify or provide outtakes to Congress and have likewise asserted the reporter's privilege. In 1848 reporter John Nugent of the New York

Herald sent his editor a confidential draft of a proposed treaty to end the Mexican–American War. The U.S. Senate, which had been debating the treaty in secret, subpoenaed Nugent and demanded to know his source. When Nugent refused to answer, he was held in contempt of Congress and jailed. Ex parte Nugent (1848).

More than a century later, in 1971, a House subcommittee subpoenaed Frank Stanton, then president of CBS, and demanded that he turn over all outtakes and other materials CBS had used in producing the documentary The Selling of the Pentagon, which dealt with Defense Department expenditures for public relations and propaganda during the Vietnam era. Stanton refused, taking the risk of being held in contempt of Congress. In a rare disavowal of one of its own committees, however, the House voted 226–181 to return the contempt resolution back to committee, thus ending the attempt to punish CBS for its award-winning documentary. In 1976 then-CBS reporter Daniel Schorr refused to tell Congress his source for the Pike Committee's report on CIA activities; Schorr narrowly avoided a contempt citation from the House Ethics Committee. Daniel Schorr, Clearing the Air, 1977.

In 1991 the Senate appointed special counsel Peter Fleming to investigate news leaks regarding influence-buying by savings and loan owner Charles Keating, and leaks of an FBI report revealing that law professor Anita Hill had accused Supreme Court nominee Clarence Thomas of sexual harassment. Fleming subpoenaed four reporters to testify about their sources and two news organization officials for company records, notes and outtakes. Fleming argued that the press had no right to resist subpoenas in criminal investigations and added that the leaks probably violated 18 U.S.C.A. § 641, which outlaws the theft of government property. In other words, Fleming tried to argue that information is property, just like a desk or a paperclip. None of the reporters or news organization personnel would disclose their sources or any materials. Fleming then asked for subpoenas for the records of the reporters' long-distance phone calls. The House Rules Committee refused to issue the subpoenas, and after six months of interviews of nearly 400 people and the expenditure of $200,000 of taxpayers' money, Fleming concluded that he would not be able to identify the sources of the leaks. See 16 News Media & the Law 3–5 (Spring 1992).

B.   NEWSPERSONS' SHIELD LAWS

In Branzburg Justice White wrote that Congress and the state legislatures were free to write laws extending to journalists a privilege against being forced to testify so long as such "shield" legislation did not run afoul of the First Amendment. Since Branzburg, 32 states have added shield statutes, with the most recent being Connecticut in 2006. Numerous bills have been introduced in Congress to provide some kind of protection for newsgatherers. No federal statute has been enacted to date, and the federal judiciary does not recognize state shield law protection of journalists in its courtrooms. Thus, if a qualified First Amendment privilege is not recognized in a federal court proceeding, reporters are likely to be held in contempt when they refuse to provide evidence in response to a subpoena.

1. State Shield Laws

a. *Statutory Analysis*

More than half the states have enacted some form of shield legislation, and one state—California—has adopted a constitutional provision protecting newspersons. Although they vary somewhat in their language and provisions, these statutes usually address the following essential questions: (1) who should be protected against testimonial compulsion (reporters only or others communicating to the public and those aiding and abetting in such communication); (2) which kinds of media should be covered (newspapers only or radio, television, motion pictures); (3) what information should be protected (the identity of confidential sources or other unpublished matter as well); (4) at what types of government proceedings and at what stages in these proceedings is the privilege against testimonial compulsion available (judicial proceedings alone or legislative, executive and administrative proceedings); (5) whether there are any exceptions or conditions to the availability of the privilege (such as the need for regular publication and general circulation, thereby excluding many non-establishment publications); and (6) whether the reporter waives the privilege by disclosing the identity of a source to third persons.

These are the issues that determine the availability and scope of the privilege afforded in local shield legislation.

State shield statutes are divided into three main groups, according to a study of the Freedom of Information Center of the University of Missouri School of Journalism. 1) The first group of statutes provides for the unqualified protection of reporters against having to divulge the source of information obtained in the course of their employment, but most statutes in this group only refer to sources and do not expressly cover the reporter's work product or unpublished information and materials. Given the propensity of the courts to construe shield statutes narrowly, it is not safe for reporters to assume that these matters are also protected by such statutes. 2) The second group of shield laws provides a privilege against disclosure of the source of information actually published or broadcast. Although absolute in their terms, statutes in this group are very weak in protecting sources because neither the source nor the reporter can be certain at the time the information is given that the information will actually be published or broadcast. Moreover, like the statutes in the first group, these statutes do not protect the information itself. 3) The third group includes statutes which are conditional in their grant of privilege to newspersons or which provide a basis for the waiver of the privilege. The statutes in this category are also narrow in scope, protecting only sources. Even when a privilege in this category appears to cover a particular reporter's situation, there is no certainty that the courts will uphold it when the reporter actually invokes it.

To summarize, the degree of protection that the First Amendment provides against compelled disclosure of sources and unpublished information increases from the least protection in (1) to the most protection in (3) in the three situations below:

(1) Criminal case where a grand jury, prosecutor or defendant wants information (least protection);

(2) Civil case where reporter is defendant (slightly more protection than in criminal cases);

(3) Civil case where reporter is not a party to suit (greatest protection).

b. Judicial Treatment

Despite explicit acceptance of a qualified privilege by most of the twelve U.S. Courts of Appeal and the existence of shield laws in 32 states and the District of Columbia, journalists are meeting with increasing resistance regarding a reporter's privilege in lower state and federal courts.

Thus, journalists cannot rely with confidence even upon the plain language of their jurisdiction's shield law, but must also be aware of the case law construing such statutes. Even then, journalists should assume that in sensitive cases the courts will not uphold their claims to the statutory privilege and they should act as cautiously as possible consistent with "getting the story."

2. Administrative Protection for the News-person: Department of Justice Guide-lines

Though no federal shield legislation has ever been enacted, the Department of Justice has adopted a set of guidelines that define when and how a U.S. attorney can obtain a subpoena against a working reporter. 28 C.F.R. § 50.10. In striking a balance between free dissemination of information and effective law enforcement, Department of Justice personnel must consider the following: (1) there should be reasonable belief based on non-media information that a crime has occurred: (2) there should be reasonable ground to believe that the information sought is essential to a successful investigation—particularly with reference to directly establishing guilt or innocence; (3) the government should have unsuccessfully attempted to obtain the information from alternative non-media sources; (4) except under exigent circumstances subpoenas should be limited to verification of published information; (5) even the appearance of harassment of media personnel should be avoided if at all possible; (6) subpoenas should, wherever possible, be directed at material information regarding a limited subject matter, should cover a reasonably limited period of time, and should avoid requiring production of a large volume of the newsperson's unpublished material. In 1980 the guidelines were extended to afford similar protection in civil actions and to telephone toll records of journalists.

Although the guidelines reflect the Department's sensitivity to the problem of compelling testimony from newspersons, they provide only minimal and uncertain protection because they are limited in scope to federal criminal prosecutions and are construed by government officials whose main concern must, of necessity, be for effective law enforcement. Moreover, the protection afforded is by administrative grace and that protection can be modified or withdrawn by the Department of Justice almost at will.

C.   LAWSUITS BY NEWS SOURCES

Journalists who promise confidentiality to a source will normally go to great lengths and even to jail to keep that promise. In rare cases, however, journalists or their editors may decide that a source's identity is so important to a story that they will name the source even when the source had been promised anonymity.

Such a situation led to the landmark Supreme Court decision of Cohen v. Cowles Media Co. (1991). By a 5–4 vote, the Court ruled that if a promise of confidentiality to a source is broken, the First Amendment does not protect the media from a common law action by that source, no matter how newsworthy the source's name is.

The case began in 1982 when Dan Cohen, a public relations aide to Republican gubernatorial candidate Wheelock Whitney, gave several reporters documents revealing misdemeanors committed many years earlier (an arrest at a protest rally in the 1960s and a six dollar shoplifting conviction later set aside) by Marlene Johnson, the Democratic candidate for lieutenant governor. Without knowledge or approval from Whitney's campaign, Cohen leaked the information to the press just before the Minnesota gubernatorial election.

When Cohen's name was used, he was immediately fired from his advertising agency job. He sued for breach of contract, arguing that the promise of confidentiality was an enforceable contract under Minnesota law. A jury awarded him $700,000 in damages. On appeal, the Minnesota Supreme Court held that a contract cause of action was "inappropriate for these particular circumstances," but the court suggested that Cohen might proceed on a theory of promissory estoppel, although neither party had argued this theory to the jury. "Promissory estoppel" is a doctrine of state law which, in the absence of a contract, creates obligations that are not explicitly stated (as in a written contract).

When the case reached the Supreme Court, it held that the First Amendment protects the media's right to publish truthful information, but only if it is lawfully obtained. Writing for the majority, Justice Byron White said Cohen's information was not lawfully obtained because of the broken promise of confidentiality: "[T]he First Amendment does not confer on the press a constitutional right to disregard promises that could otherwise be enforced under state law...." Cohen v. Cowles Media Co. (1991).

The Court observed that since journalists have insisted for more than a century that they should have the same privilege not to reveal a source as that enjoyed by physicians and priests, the refusal by editors and reporters to keep promises of confidentiality damages the credibility of journalists' claim to a constitutional privilege. Furthermore, the doctrine of promissory estoppel is a law of general application; hence, a newspaper publisher is subject to it just as everyone else is. The Court thus remanded the case for further proceedings on the question of whether Cohen had a valid claim of promissory estoppel.

Four justices dissented, arguing that using Cohen's name was justified because voters had a right to know that the Republican gubernatorial candidate's public relations aide was leaking stories to the press about a Democratic candidate. In a dissenting opinion, Justice David Souter wrote: "There can be no doubt that the fact of Cohen's identity expanded the universe of information relevant to the choice faced by Minnesota voters ... [and] the publication ... was thus of the sort quintessentially subject to strict First Amendment protection." On remand, the Minnesota Supreme Court awarded Cohen $200,000 in damages. Cohen v. Cowles Media (1992).

See also Ruzicka v. Conde Nast Publications, Inc., (1990) (upholding judgment in promissory estoppel action against Glamour Magazine when reporter promised to mask source's identity but provided so many details that source was identifiable and suffered such severe emotional distress that she lost her job as a result of being identified).

In the wake of Cohen, several courts have permitted causes of action based on disclosure of a source's identity. See Anderson v. Strong Memorial Hospital (1991); Multimedia WMAZ, Inc. v. Kubach (1994). Other courts, however, have rejected suits based on disclosure of a source's identity. See Morgan v. Celender (1992); O'Connell v. Housatonic Valley Publishing (1991); Steele v. Isikoff (2000).

After former Cincinnati Enquirer reporter Michael Gallagher was convicted on two felony charges for stealing internal voice mail messages from the Chiquita Brands International banana company, Gallagher disclosed the identity of his confidential source, former Chiquita attorney George Ventura, who had provided Gallagher with the access codes to the voice mail of two Chiquita lawyers. Ventura attempted to suppress tapes and other evidence by invoking Ohio's shield law. The Cincinnati trial judge ruled, however, that only reporters can assert the shield law; the shield law gives no protection to the sources themselves. In 1999 Ventura filed suit against the Cincinnati Enquirer for breach of contract and promissory estoppel, based on the breach of confidentiality which Gallagher had promised him. The trial court granted summary judgment to the Cincinnati Enquirer, and the U.S. Court of Appeals for the Sixth Circuit affirmed. The Sixth Circuit explained that Ventura was in effect asking the court to enforce an agreement he had made with Gallagher to withhold evidence of Ventura's crimes; thus public policy should preclude Ventura from being permitted to enforce Gallagher's promise to conceal Gallagher's criminal activity. Ventura v. Cincinnati Enquirer (2005).

Journalists charge that cases such as Cohen and Ruzicka (if not Ventura) force them to choose between defending a lawsuit for revealing a source, or going to jail for not revealing a source when subpoenaed. Some media attorneys had warned that Cohen could encourage news sources who are not pleased with how they appear in the news to sue the media, contending that they were promised confidentiality. Cohen and Ruzicka should remind journalists not to make a promise of confidentiality unless they are certain that they will not be compelled to testify, or unless they are willing to go to jail to protect a source's identity. Journalists must also realize that if they abuse the privilege as in Cohen and Ruzicka, neither the courts nor the public will take them seriously.

D.   CONTEMPT FOR UNPRIVILEGED REFUSAL TO TESTIFY

1.   The Real Importance of the Privilege

The existence of a privilege is important in shielding a newsperson from the sanctions associated with the contempt power of courts and legislatures. Without a privilege to refuse to comply with a judicial or legislative subpoena, the journalist will almost surely be held in contempt if the information sought is deemed relevant and material to the work of the government unit seeking the information. Depending on the type of contempt involved, the sanctions may include jail sentences, criminal fines and civil payments to parties injured by the contemptuous conduct.

2. Types of Contempt

Traditionally, contemptuous conduct is categorized in two ways. First, there is the distinction between direct and indirect contempt. Direct contempt involves misconduct in or near the courtroom. For example, if a reporter without privilege refuses to testify at a trial or if someone violates the decorum of court or shows disrespect for the legal process, the judge may cite him or her for direct contempt.

If, on the other hand, the refusal to testify occurred in a grand jury proceeding, this would be an indirect contempt outside the presence of the court. Before a sanction could be imposed by the court, the reporter would be entitled to some notice as to what was complained of together with a hearing on the matter before the appropriate judge.

The other major distinction is between civil and criminal contempt. This dichotomy is based on the purpose for which the sanction is imposed. If the sanction is designed to force the contemnor to testify, the sanction is viewed as coercive and non-punitive and hence civil in nature. Civil contempt is intended to compel a future act, not to punish a previous act. The time period for sanctions for civil contempt is indeterminate because the sanctions for civil contempt end upon compliance with the order. For example, when New York Times reporter Judith Miller was jailed for civil contempt, the judge explained to Miller that her jail term would end if she revealed her source; in other words, she "held the keys to her own prison." See In re Special Counsel Investigation (2004), discussed above. In contrast, if the sanction is imposed to uphold the dignity and authority of the court and its orders without concern for coercion, it is deemed punitive in nature; thus, the contempt is criminal. For example, a union leader could be held in criminal contempt for calling an illegal strike. If reporters violate a judge's gag order, the judge may find them guilty of criminal contempt because the transgression has already occurred; the reporters cannot undo something that they have already done.

3.   The Impact of Contempt on Newspersons

The number of contempt citations issued against newspersons for refusal to testify before or otherwise cooperate with government units has increased dramatically in the last decade. Although the number of newspersons actually languishing in jails around the country is not yet great, the potential for such a situation is. The courts know that imposing fines or civil payments is not likely to intimidate reporters who, on principle, refuse to cooperate in a grand jury or judicial proceeding.

Only imprisonment is at all likely to have the desired effect. Thus journalists who dig in their heels must be ready to accept incarceration of either determinate or indeterminate duration. The only comforting note from the newsperson's perspective is that if the contempt is treated as criminal the likelihood of a sentence in excess of six months is remote because of the burden on the judicial system of granting the newsperson a jury trial.

4. Alternatives to Contempt Citations and Jailing of Newspersons

Courts are learning that even imprisonment for contempt is rarely effective in achieving the goal of disclosure by newspersons of confidential information. The courts are slowly changing tactics and choosing alternatives to contempt in an effort to enforce their disclosure orders.

In cases where reporters refuse to reveal the name of a source in libel proceedings, some courts have declared that such a refusal may allow an inference that no source exists. This is tantamount to saying the story was fabricated, making it much easier for the plaintiff to prove malice or reckless disregard for the truth. Courts have used this tactic in Caldero v. Tribune Publishing Co. (1977); Greenberg v. CBS Inc. (1979); Downing v. Monitor Publishing Co. (1980); DeRoburt v. Gannett Co. (1981); and Ayash v. Dana–Farber Cancer Institute (2005).

Another device to force reporters' compliance with judicial disclosure orders employed by at least one state trial court is to strike the newspaper defendant's pleadings and to enter a default judgment for plaintiffs in their libel actions. Because this device raises a serious question of deprivation of due process, courts must be very careful to employ it only when the information sought is absolutely essential to the plaintiff's case and cannot be obtained by less drastic means. For example, when the Twin Falls, Idaho Times–News refused to disclose confidential information, the trial judge ruled it in default and awarded $1.9 million to the plaintiff. The Idaho Supreme Court reversed this ruling, noting that the plaintiff's inability to discover the reporter's sources had not been shown to obstruct the plaintiff's ability to prove the story false. Sierra Life Insurance Co. v. Magic Valley Newspapers, Inc. (1980).

In another case, Jerry Plotkin, one of the Americans held hostage during 1980–81 in Iran, filed a $60 million lawsuit against the Los Angeles Daily News and two of its reporters, Adam Dawson and Arnie Friedman, when they published an article headlined: "Plotkin May Be Questioned in Drug Probe." When the two reporters refused to disclose their sources, Judge Sara Radin entered a default judgment against the defendants. The Daily News then ordered Dawson and Friedman to disclose their sources (sparking a storm of criticism from other journalists). The reporters refused and hired separate attorneys to defend themselves. The default order was later vacated, but Judge Radin said that if no sources were named within 20 days, it would be "established as a matter of law" that no sources existed. One of the reporters finally identified two sources, both of whom were Drug Enforcement Administration (DEA) agents. "News Notes," Med.L.Rptr. (Jan. 17, 1984).

More recently the Supreme Judicial Court of Massachusetts affirmed a default judgment against the Boston Globe after its reporter Richard Knox mistakenly reported that Dr. Lois Ayash had countersigned an order for an overdose of a highly toxic chemotherapy drug at the Dana–Farber Cancer Institute (Boston Globe reporter Betsy Lehman died as a result of the overdose). Although the Boston Globe published a correction three months later in which it apologized for Knox's error, Knox refused to identify a confidential source who had provided him with information about an internal investigation within the hospital. Ayash suspected that Knox's source was deliberately trying to make her a scapegoat, even though a different doctor had accidentally prescribed the overdose; however, Ayash could not proceed with her defamation case without knowing who was trying to "scapegoat" her. After the court found the Boston Globe and its reporter Knox in contempt, a jury awarded Ayash more than $2 million in damages against the Boston Globe and Richard Knox. Ayash v. Dana–Farber Cancer Institute (2005).

Despite the fact that some reporters may be too trusting of sources with ulterior motives, the importance of source protection becomes apparent when one considers the fact that if Washington Post reporters Robert Woodward and Carl Bernstein could not have guaranteed confidentiality to their source "Deep Throat" (finally identified in 2005 as former

FBI officer W. Mark Felt), the American public might never have learned the extent of the corruption involved in the Watergate scandal. In sum, it is important for courts to grant reporters the privilege not to reveal their sources because:

(1) The reporter's privilege encourages the free flow of information to the public; reporters' sources could dry up if they could not promise confidentiality;

(2) corruption in government might go unreported if whistle-blowers are afraid of being identified by reporters who are forced to reveal their identities;

(3) the physical safety or economic security of sources might be jeopardized by revelation of their identities if they are providing reporters with information about organized crime.

E.   THE EFFECT ON NEWSGATHERING OF SEARCHES AND SEIZURES IN THE NEWSROOM

1.   Zurcher v. Stanford Daily

Searches and seizures in the newsrooms of the nation by law enforcement officers pursuant to properly issued search warrants have been rare in American history. Normally, prosecutors seeking evidence of crimes documented in newsroom files have simply subpoenaed someone associated with the news operation to bring the evidence, if any, to court. This procedure avoids the disruption of a search of the newsroom, avoids the chilling effect on the gathering of sensitive news and information and gives the subpoenaed party an opportunity to move to quash the subpoena.

In Zurcher v. Stanford Daily (1978), however, a local district attorney obtained a search warrant issued on a judge's finding of probable cause to believe that the Stanford Daily, a student newspaper, possessed photographs and negatives revealing the identity of demonstrators who assaulted and injured police officers who were attempting to quell a riot at the Stanford University Hospital. Police searched the paper's newsroom but found no incriminating evidence. Thereafter, the paper and certain staff members sought a judicial declaration that the search had deprived them of their constitutional rights and an injunction against further searches.

The case ultimately reached the U.S. Supreme Court, where the Stanford Daily argued that such searches of newspaper offices for evidence of crimes committed by others seriously threatened the ability of the press to gather news, thereby violating the First Amendment. The newspaper argued that (1) searches are physically disruptive to orderly publication; (2) confidential sources of information will dry up and access to various news events will be denied because of fear that press files will be readily available to law enforcement authorities; (3) reporters will be dissuaded from recording their recollections for verification and future use; (4) the processing of news and its dissemination will be chilled by the prospect that searches will disclose internal editorial deliberations; and (5) the press will resort to self-censorship to conceal its possession of information of potential interest to the police.

A majority of the Court led by Justice White held that searches and seizures in newsrooms pursuant to warrant did not violate First Amendment guarantees because 1) the drafters of the Constitution had not forbidden search warrants directed to the press under the Fourth Amendment, 2) the Fourth Amendment did not require special showings that subpoenas would be impractical before warrants could be issued to search a newsroom, and 3) if a press organization was named in a search warrant, the police would not have to show first the organization's complicity in the alleged offense being investigated.

Justice White argued in support of his conclusion that if law enforcement officers and the courts properly administer search warrants, the preconditions for their issuance—probable cause, specificity with respect to the place to be searched and the things to be seized, and overall reasonableness in searches and seizures—should afford sufficient protection against infringement of First Amendment interests. Further, Justice White doubted, in the face of numerous press organization affidavits to the contrary, that confidential sources would dry up or that the press would suppress news because of fears of warranted searches.

2.   Federal Legislation in the Wake of Zurcher

Less than three years after the decision in Zurcher, a Congress less sanguine than Justice White about the dangers posed by searches and seizures in newsrooms enacted P.L. 96–449, the Privacy Protection Act of 1980, 42 U.S.C.A. § 2000aa–1 et seq. This act substantially restricts the situations in which a newsroom search and seizure may legally occur: generally law enforcement personnel must have a subpoena rather than merely a search warrant. In very limited circumstances the law allows searches and seizures of documentary materials such as photographs or videotapes with only a search warrant if 1) the person with the information is suspected of a crime, 2) law enforcement officers believe the materials must be seized immediately to prevent someone's death or injury, 3) there is reason to believe that giving notice with a subpoena would result in the materials being destroyed, changed or hidden, or 4) the materials were not produced pursuant to a court order that has been affirmed on appeal. A journalist's "work product" such as notes or rough drafts cannot be seized unless 1) the journalist is suspected of a crime, or 2) such seizure is necessary to prevent someone's death or injury. See Steve Jackson Games, Inc. v. U.S. Secret Service (1994) (Secret Service ordered to pay damages to individuals after launching raid with a warrant but without subpoena). But see Citicasters v. McCaskill (1996) (Eighth Circuit upheld police seizure with only a warrant of broadcaster's videotape of abduction of woman who was later murdered).

Police in East Lansing, Michigan, made a successful "end-run" around the Privacy Protection Act by avoiding a newsroom search. When a riot broke out after Michigan State University lost a basketball game to Duke, a Lansing State Journal photographer took numerous photographs of the riot until he was attacked by a rioter who wanted to avoid being identified by police. Police seized photographs of the riot from a department store photo processing lab and posted the photos on the Internet, asking the public to identify the individuals. Within a few days, police arrested 27 people involved in the riots. Although the Michigan Supreme Court ruled that the lower courts should have issued investigative subpoenas, similar to search warrants, rather than discovery subpoenas, the ruling came too late for the press because the police had already posted the photographs on the Internet. In re Subpoenas to News Media Petitioners (1999).

CHAPTER IX

REGULATION OF COMMERCIAL SPEECH

A. CONSTITUTIONAL HISTORY

First Amendment protection for commercial speech—particularly commercial advertising—has had a checkered history in the Supreme Court. First the Court refused to recognize any such protection. Then, after recognizing some protection utilizing the language of ad hoc balancing, the Court appeared to move toward absolutist protection of such speech qualified only by time, place and manner considerations. Next the Court, settled upon a seemingly well-defined balancing approach that nevertheless left the Court great latitude in its specific application. Most recently, the Court appears to be moving back towards stronger protection for commercial speech.

The chronology begins with Valentine v. Chrestensen (1942), in which the Court unanimously sustained an ordinance which banned the distribution of commercial handbill advertising. After being prohibited by local authorities from distributing a handbill announcing the exhibition of a submarine, the promoter had printed on the reverse side of the handbill a protest against an official refusal to allow him to use city wharfage facilities for such exhibition. The court found this supposed political protest to be a mere subterfuge to evade the ordinance and suggested that "purely commercial advertising" was not protected by the First Amendment. In short, the government could constitutionally regulate product or service advertising without abridging the First Amendment.

This distinction between types of expression has been a controversial one. In Cammarano v. United States (1959), Justice Douglas said that the Chrestensen opinion was "casual, almost offhand" and "has not survived reflection." But thereafter the Court reiterated the distinction between purely commercial advertising and all other expression in New York Times v. Sullivan (1964).

This was the state of commercial speech until Bigelow v. Virginia (1975). Jeffrey C. Bigelow was the managing editor of the Virginia Weekly, a newspaper published in Charlottesville, Virginia. The Weekly ran a referral service for an abortion clinic in New York City. Bigelow was convicted for violating a Virginia statute which made it a misdemeanor for any person by advertisement to encourage or promote the procuring of abortions. His conviction was reversed by the Supreme Court which held that merely because an advertisement is labeled commercial speech does not mean that it is stripped of all First Amendment safeguards, as had been implied in Valentine v. Chrestensen. Such speech retains some degree of constitutional protection which must be weighed against the state's interest in regulating the particular advertisement. Justice Blackmun, writing for the Court, then found some value in the abortion referral ad as a vehicle for conveying information of potential interest to Virginia Weekly readers. According to Justice Blackmun, the ad did more than fulfill Bigelow's profit motive. His interest coincided with the constitutional interests of certain of his audience who might need the service offered, or who were concerned about New York's laws or who were seeking abortion law reform in Virginia. Justice Blackmun noted that the availability of legal abortion in New York was information of value to the public and that, as previously decided, the right to early term abortion itself involved a woman's constitutional right to privacy. See Roe v. Wade (1973) and Doe v. Bolton (1973).

On the other side of the balance, Virginia contended that abortion referral agencies breed practices such as fee splitting that tend to decrease the quality of medical care and that advertising these agencies would encourage women to seek abortions from those interested only in financial gain and not in providing professional medical service. Virginia, however, made no claim that this advertisement would in any way affect the quality of medical care within its own boundaries, and the Court reasoned that the state was actually asserting an interest in regulating what Virginians hear or read about another state's services. This interest, in the Court's view, was entitled to little, if any, weight. Consequently, the state's interest was not sufficient to permit it to punish Bigelow for running the ad and his conviction was reversed.

Bigelow seemed to say that if First Amendment protection was to be accorded to commercial speech, it would be on an ad hoc balancing basis. In Virginia State Board of Pharmacy v. Virginia Citizens Consumer Council, Inc. (1976), however, the Court appeared to adopt an absolutist approach to the protection of commercial speech in a case where the state statutorily prohibited pharmacists from advertising the prices of prescription drugs which they offered for sale—advertising which, unlike that in Bigelow, was *purely* commercial in nature.

In striking down the Virginia statute, Justice Blackmun, speaking for the Court, appeared to reject the balancing process when he said, "There is no claim ... that the prohibition on prescription drug price advertising is a mere time, place, and manner restriction. We have often approved restrictions of that kind provided that they are justified without reference to the content of the regulated speech, that they serve a significant governmental interest, and that in so doing they leave open ample alternative channels for communication of the information.... Whatever may be the proper bounds of time, place, and manner restrictions on commercial speech, they are plainly exceeded by this Virginia statute, which singles out speech of a particular content and seeks to prevent its dissemination completely." To similar effect are Linmark Associates, Inc. v. Township of Willingboro (1977) (local ordinance forbidding display of "for sale" signs in front of houses struck down); Carey v. Population Services International (1977) (statute prohibiting advertisement of contraceptives struck down).

B. THE FOUR–PART COMMERCIAL SPEECH ANALYSIS OF CENTRAL HUDSON

Following Bigelow, Virginia Pharmacy Board, Linmark and Carey, the issue was no longer whether purely commercial speech is protected expression but rather what First Amendment philosophy and analysis would govern the extension of such protection. That question appeared to be answered in Central Hudson Gas and Electric Corp. v. Public Service Commission (1980).

There, a regulation promulgated by the New York Public Service Commission banned electric utilities in the state from engaging in advertising which promoted the increased use of electricity. In striking down the regulation as violative of the First and Fourteenth Amendments, a bare majority of the Court enunciated a four-part test for determining the availability of constitutional protection for commercial speech. The test emphasizes the balancing of state interests in the regulation of commercial speech against individual free speech interests.

In short, the four-part test includes first a determination whether the expression is at all protected by the First Amendment. Commercial speech which involves or advertises unlawful activity or is false or misleading is *not* protected. For examples of this idea see Pittsburgh Press Co. v. Pittsburgh Commission on Human Relations (1973) (ordinance prohibiting newspapers from carrying help wanted ads categorized by gender upheld); Princess Sea Industries, Inc. v. Nevada (1981) (statute prohibiting advertising of prostitution service in Nevada counties in which such service is illegal upheld); Friedman v. Rogers (1979) (statute prohibiting practice of optometry under a trade name upheld because ill-defined association of trade name with price and quality could be manipulated by user of trade name to mislead the public).

If the commercial speech does not involve illegality and is neither false or misleading, then the second part of the analysis comes into play. The test here is whether the asserted governmental interest in regulation or prohibition of certain commercial speech is substantial. If the state's interest is substantial, then regulation or complete prohibition of the particular commercial expression may be permitted, depending on the results of the third and fourth parts of the test.

The third part asks whether the state's regulation directly advances the asserted governmental interest. Such regulation will not be upheld unless it is actually effective in advancing the state's interest directly. Indirect or speculative advancement of the state's interest will not suffice.

The final part of the test and the one the New York Public Service Commission failed in the Central Hudson case is whether the state's regulation is only as broad as is necessary to serve the state's substantial governmental interest. In Central Hudson, the Court's five-member majority was not persuaded that the Commission's complete suppression of promotional advertising by New York electric utilities was necessary to further the State's interest in energy conservation. The majority pointed out that the Commission had made no showing that a more limited restriction on the content of promotional advertising would have been inadequate to serve the state's interests.

The second and third parts of the Court's four-part test clearly call into play the ad hoc balancing of First Amendment interests against conflicting legitimate state interests while the fourth part attempts to limit the degree of conflict and the extent of intrusion into the First Amendment area posed by the second and third parts.

In his concurring opinion Justice Blackmun pointed out the contradictions of the four-part balancing test with the more absolutist approach taken earlier in Virginia Pharmacy, Linmark and Carey. He noted that such test would permit a complete ban on utilities advertising, for instance, the advantages of air conditioning, assuming that a more limited restriction on such advertising would not effectively deter members of the public from cooling their homes.

Because the Central Hudson four-part test leaves each justice great latitude to insert personal views on the degree of protection to which specific commercial speech is entitled, subsequent decisions have not followed a clear direction or rationale. For example, in Metromedia, Inc. v. San Diego (1981), the Court struck down a city ordinance banning almost all off-site billboards. The decision featured five separate opinions, causing Justice Rehnquist to term it "a virtual Tower of Babel."

Three years later, in City Council v. Taxpayers for Vincent (1984), the Court was faced with another sign ordinance, this time a ban on posting signs on public property. By a 6–3 vote, the ordinance was found directly to advance the city's interest in limiting "visual clutter and blight." "By banning these signs, the City did no more than eliminate the exact source of evil it sought to remedy."

Although limiting visual clutter and blight is a sufficient government interest to justify restricting commercial speech, protecting people from offensive material is not. In Bolger v. Youngs Drug Products Corp. (1983), the Court unanimously struck down a postal regulation prohibiting the mailing of unsolicited advertisements for contraceptives. In addition to the offensiveness assertion, the government argued that the regulation was necessary to help parents control "the manner in which their children became informed about sensitive and important subjects such as birth control." The regulation there was deemed more extensive than necessary to accomplish the latter goal.

The seeming inconsistency of some of these cases illustrates the true ad hoc nature of the Central

Hudson four-part test. The weight given the asserted state interest appears to depend more on the
personal views of the justices and less on the degree
of evidence offered by the government. A majority
of the Court seems willing to defer to the legislative
or administrative body's judgment, except where a
justice personally disagrees with that judgment.

That view was again evident in Posadas de Puerto Rico Associates v. Tourism Company of Puerto
Rico (1986). By a 5–4 vote the Court upheld a
Puerto Rico statute prohibiting advertising of casino gambling directed at residents of Puerto Rico,
while permitting similar advertising aimed at tour-
ists.

Justice Rehnquist, writing for the majority, found
that the speech in question met the first part of the
four-part test because the advertising concerned a
lawful activity and was not inherently false or misleading. He then accepted the government's contention that the substantial government interest
served by the regulation was the reduction of casino
gambling by the residents of Puerto Rico as well as
the claim that casino gambling leads to increases in
corruption, prostitution, local crime and organized
crime. The application of the advertising ban solely
to casino gambling was also seen as reasonable
because other forms of gambling such as cockfight-
ing, horse racing, and the lottery might be "traditionally part of the Puerto Rican's roots."

The government's assertion that the advertising
ban directly advanced that interest was also accept-

ed without much scrutiny. Justice Rehnquist observed that the Puerto Rico legislature believed that banning advertising would reduce demand and that in his opinion such a belief was reasonable.

Finally, the ban, in Justice Rehnquist's view, was no more extensive than necessary. He rejected an argument that counterspeech, speech aimed at reducing casino gambling, was a less First Amendment intrusive way to accomplish the same ends. Whether counterspeech would be effective in accomplishing the same end was a decision for the legislature, not the Court.

One of the more disturbing aspects of Justice Rehnquist's opinion was its extreme deference to the legislature. Essentially he seemed to be saying that as long as the government's assertions are plausible they will be accepted even though there is no direct evidence to support the assertions. Justice Brennan, in his dissent, argued that, at least where the government's asserted purpose is to influence citizen behavior, a stricter standard is needed. He would have required the government to show that casino gambling had serious harmful effects, that banning advertising would reduce the demand for casino gambling and that neither counterspeech nor strict regulation of casino gambling itself would accomplish the same end. He found no showing that the government had evidence for any of these assertions.

However, in Board of Trustees, S.U.N.Y. v. Fox (1989) the Court interpreted Posadas differently. In an opinion written by Justice Scalia, the Court held that the fourth part of the Central Hudson test merely requires a means narrowly tailored to achieve the desired objective, as opposed to the least restrictive means available. Thus, Justice Scalia viewed Posadas as holding that the legislature had only to show a reasonable fit between the means chosen by the legislature and the goal the legislature sought to achieve. He did emphasize, however, that the burden is on the government affirmatively to establish that reasonable fit.

The change from a least restrictive means test to a reasonable fit test did nothing to reduce the ad hoc nature of the Central Hudson test. A 1993 case illustrates the degree to which the Court is fragmented on this issue. In Cincinnati v. Discovery Network (1993), the Court struck down the city's prohibition against the use of newsracks to distribute "commercial handbills," while permitting the use of newsracks to distribute newspapers.

The majority, in an opinion written by Justice Stevens, held that the ban failed the reasonable fit test. The city argued that the ban served its interests in safety and esthetics. First, the ban affected 62 newsracks, while allowing between 1,500 and 2,000 newspaper newsracks. Thus, the ban only minimally advanced the city's asserted interests. Second, the distinction between those newsracks banned and those permitted was totally unrelated to the city's asserted interests. In Justice Stevens' view one requirement for a "reasonable fit" is that the distinction between regulated and unregulated speech must be related to the interests the regulation is designed to advance. Unless the commercial speech is being regulated because of its content or adverse effects stemming from its content, it cannot be singled out for restrictions that are not placed on other speech.

In his dissent Chief Justice Rehnquist flatly rejected this interpretation of reasonable fit. According to Rehnquist the city, in its quest to improve safety and esthetics had decided to burden low value speech without imposing a similar burden on high value speech. By restricting the ban to commercial handbill newsracks, Rehnquist argued that the city was advancing First Amendment interests.

In the last decade the Court has seemingly moved to a more exacting examination of the government's asserted interest and the availability of less restrictive means. For example, in Rubin v. Coors Brewing Co. (1995)), the Court voted unanimously to strike down a federal ban on disclosure of the alcohol content of beer on labels or in advertising. Not only was the asserted interest in combatting alcohol strength wars contradicted by requirements that wines stronger than 14 percent disclose alcohol content on labels, but there were less restrictive means available such as limiting alcohol content of beers or banning marketing campaigns emphasizing high alcohol content.

Similarly, in 44 Liquormart, Inc. v. Rhode Island (1996), the Court struck down two restrictions on advertising the retail price of alcoholic beverages.

The state claimed that the absence of advertising would result in higher prices which in turn would reduce consumption, promoting the state's interest in temperance. The Court found that not only had the state failed to adequately show that the lack of advertising would promote temperance, but also less extensive means, such as mandating higher prices, taxing alcoholic beverages more heavily, or limiting per capita purchases, were available.

C.   ATTEMPTS TO BAN ADVERTISING OF LEGAL PRODUCTS

In Posadas the Court finally addressed another important commercial speech question. Can the government consistent with the First Amendment ever ban advertising for a legal product? The question has received increased attention in the past decade with the proposals by SMART (Stop Marketing Alcohol on Radio and Television) to ban broadcast advertising for beer and wine and the American Medical Association to ban all advertising for tobacco products.

In response to arguments that it was unconstitutional to ban advertising of a legal product, Justice Rehnquist stated that whenever the state has the authority to ban an activity it has the right to take the less intrusive step of banning advertising for that activity. He thought it would be "strange" to hold the state can ban an activity outright, but not reduce demand for that activity by banning advertising. He also cited with approval several lower court cases upholding advertising bans on legal activities or products. See Dunagin v. Oxford, Mississippi (1983) (Mississippi ban on alcoholic beverage advertising held constitutional under the Central Hudson test.); Capital Broadcasting Co. v. Mitchell (1971) (Federal ban on cigarette advertising on electronic media found constitutional).

Justice Brennan strongly disagreed. He argued that the advertising ban was not less intrusive than a prohibition of the actual activity. "The 'constitutional doctrine' which bans Puerto Rico from banning advertisements concerning lawful casino gambling is not so strange a restraint—it is called the First Amendment."

The reach of Posadas was debated for more than a decade before it was apparently put to rest in 44 Liquormart. All the Justices other than Scalia specifically rejected the deferential Posadas approach and Scalia declined to address the question because he believed the regulation failed even under that approach. Justices Stevens, Kennedy, Thomas and Ginsburg also rejected the proposition, voiced in Posadas, that the right to regulate the conduct includes the right to regulate speech concerning the conduct.

However, 44 Liquormart did not focus on what is becoming one of the most commonly asserted justifications for restricting speech–protecting children. This trend can be seen in many areas beyond commercial speech including the V-chip and limiting broadcast indecency to night-time hours (both discussed in Chapter X), as well as the Child Online Protection Act and the Children's Internet Protection Act (discussed in Chapter XII). It is also being used to justify banning advertising for lawful products that are seen as harmful to children, most commonly alcohol and tobacco. For example, the Fourth Circuit upheld Baltimore ordinances restricting outdoor advertising of alcohol and tobacco. The asserted state interest was promoting the "welfare and temperance" of children. Initially, the Supreme Court granted certiorari and then remanded with instructions to reconsider the case in light of 44 Liquormart. The appeals court affirmed its earlier decision, 2–1. The court treated the ordinances as time, place and manner restrictions distinguishable from the ban at issue in 44 Liquormart. A second petition for certiorari was denied. Anheuser–Busch, Inc. v. Schmoke (1997); Penn Advertising of Baltimore, Inc. v. City of Baltimore (1997).

In contrast, in Lorillard Tobacco Co. v. Reilly (2001) the Court struck down Massachusetts regulations prohibiting outdoor advertising or inside advertising visible from outside of tobacco products within 1,000 feet of a school or playground and requiring all point of sale advertising in those areas to be a minimum of five feet from the floor. The Court found that the regulations, as applied to cigarettes, were preempted by the Federal Cigarette Labeling and Advertising Act. As applied to cigars and smokeless tobacco products, the Court held that the regulations failed the fourth part of the Central Hudson test. The areas where the advertising was prohibited constituted a substantial, and in some cases almost complete, portion of major metropolitan areas. In addition, the regulations even covered oral communications regarding these products. Thus, there was no evidence of narrow tailoring.

D. DEFINING COMMERCIAL SPEECH

As noted in Chapter 1, a major difficulty with definitional balancing is defining the speech in question. In his Central Hudson concurrence, Justice Stevens noted that the Court was using two definitions of commercial speech. The first, which he found too broad, was "expression related solely to the economic interests of the speaker and its audience." The second, which he argued was too narrow, was "speech proposing a commercial transaction."

A too narrow definition does not present major First Amendment problems, but an overly broad one does. Commercial speech is afforded less constitutional protection than many other types of speech. Improperly classifying speech as commercial increases the chances that it can be suppressed.

A controversial case exemplifying this problem is Kasky v. Nike (2002). Nike, in response to public allegations that it was mistreating workers at its foreign facilities, issued press releases and wrote letters to newspapers, university presidents and university athletic directors, all denying the allegations. Marc Kasky, a California resident, filed a lawsuit under California's Unfair Competition Law,

Cal. Bus. & Prof. Code Ann. § 17200 et seq. (West 1997), and False Advertising Law, § 17500 et seq., alleging Nike made numerous "false statements and/or material omissions of fact" regarding the issue "in order to maintain or increase its sales." The trial court dismissed on the grounds the statements were protected by the First Amendment and the appeals court affirmed.

However, the California Supreme Court reversed and remanded the case for further proceedings, holding that Nike's speech was commercial. The court examined three factors in reaching this conclusion: the speaker, the intended audience and the content of the message. "Because the messages in question were directed by a commercial speaker to a commercial audience, and because they made representations of fact about the speaker's own business operations for the purpose of promoting sales of its products, ... [the] messages are commercial speech." The Supreme Court granted certiorari, but then voted to dismiss it as improvidently granted. The parties then settled.

E. THE SPECIAL PROBLEM OF PROFESSIONAL ADVERTISING

Advertising by professionals had been generally frowned upon in the twentieth century and individual members of a number of the learned professions such as law and medicine were prohibited by the states at the behest of professional organizations such as the ABA and the AMA from advertising their services, ostensibly because such advertising was unseemly and unprofessional but more realistically because such bans reduced economic competition within the professions.

1. Advertising by Lawyers: A Case Study

After the Supreme Court's decisions in Bigelow and Virginia Pharmacy Board according First Amendment protection to commercial speech, it was inevitable that bans on professional advertising would come under attack. As might be expected the first legal challenges came from members of the legal profession.

As the legal profession began to change and develop new forms of delivery systems for legal services such as legal clinics for the less affluent in society, advertising became an important tool in achieving volume business to sustain lower fee schedules. The use of such a tool was in direct conflict with established law, however.

In Bates v. State Bar of Arizona (1977), two Phoenix legal clinic attorneys, in seeking business from persons of modest income in need of legal services, placed an ad in the Arizona Republic, a daily general circulation newspaper saying "Do You Need a Lawyer? Legal Services at Very Reasonable Fees" and listing the services available, the charges for such services and the name of the clinic, the address and the telephone number. The ad clearly violated the American Bar Association Disciplinary Rule 2–101(B), embodied in Rule 29(a) of the rules of Arizona Supreme Court. The president of the state bar immediately filed a complaint with the Arizona Supreme Court and ultimately that court censured the two attorneys.

By a 5–4 vote, the United States Supreme Court reversed that portion of the state court order which had upheld the total ban on advertising. In so ruling the majority emphasized the consuming public's First Amendment interest in receiving truthful information about available services and products. Justice Blackmun, writing for the majority, noted that the ABA itself had reported that the middle 70 percent of the population on the economic scale was not being reached or adequately served by the legal profession. According to Justice Blackmun, advertising could help solve that problem.

In holding that lawyer advertising could not under the First Amendment be subjected to blanket suppression, however, Justice Blackmun made clear that such advertising was too risk-filled not to be regulated. Regulation would be permitted to insure truthful advertising by lawyers for the protection of the public. Reasonable restrictions on the time, place and manner of advertising would be permitted, as would the suppression of false and misleading information and even accurate advertising concerning illegal transactions. In addition, advertising via electronic broadcast media might warrant special consideration and control. Justice Blackmun expected that the organized bar would have "a special role to play in assuring that advertising by attorneys flows both freely and cleanly."

Emphasizing cleanliness over freedom, the American Bar Association responded to the Bates decision by promulgating two alternative substitutes for the now dead letter DR 2–101(B). "Plan A"—the preferred alternative—listed 25 categories of information that a lawyer could include in his or her advertising. Nothing more could be included. The less restrictive "Plan B" simply permitted advertising that did not run afoul of a small number of general guidelines designed to prevent fraud, deception or the misleading of the public.

Despite warnings from legal scholars that "Plan A" was too restrictive to pass constitutional muster, a majority of the states that considered the ABA's alternative proposals adopted "Plan A" or some variation of it.

Missouri was one of them. The Missouri Supreme Court's Rule 4 listed only ten categories of information that could be included in newspaper, periodical and telephone directory ads. When attorney R_____ M. J_____ placed ads in local newspapers and the St. Louis telephone directory containing material not included in Rule 4 such as the fact that he was licensed in Illinois and had been admitted to practice before the United States Supreme Court, the Advisory Committee of the Missouri Bar filed a complaint in the Missouri Supreme Court seeking the imposition of sanctions. Following a hearing the attorney was officially reprimanded by the Missouri Supreme Court and required to pay the costs of the action despite his contention that his advertising was protected speech.

On appeal the United States Supreme Court, reflecting the principles laid down in Central Hudson and Bates, voted unanimously to reverse the judgment of the Missouri court. First Amendment protection was accorded the lawyer's advertising because none of the information contained therein was shown to be misleading nor did the Missouri Supreme Court identify any substantial state interest in so sharply limiting lawyer advertising that would outweigh the lawyer's or the public's interest in such advertising. In the Matter of R.M.J. (1982). As a result of this decision the constitutionality of state bar advertising rules based upon restrictive "Proposal A" of the American Bar Association is now in doubt.

A slightly different question was presented in Peel v. Attorney Registration and Disciplinary Commission (1990). Attorney Peel had placed on his letterhead a notation that he was a "Certified Civil Trial Specialist By the National Board of Trial Advocacy," as well as one that he was licensed in Illinois, Missouri and Arizona. The Illinois' Attorney Registration and Disciplinary Commission held that this violated an Illinois prohibition on attorney's holding themselves out as "certified" or "specialists." On appeal the Illinois Supreme Court found that the letterhead was inherently misleading, that it implied that the state had authorized this certification, and that there was an implied claim of superiority of the quality of the lawyer's services.

The United States Supreme Court reversed. Justice Stevens, joined by three other Justices found that the letterhead was not actually or inherently misleading. Even if there was a danger of confusion, less restrictive means such as screening certifying organizations or requiring disclaimers regarding the certification would be sufficient to prevent such confusion. Justice Marshall concurred in the judgment finding the state rule unconstitutional as applied to attorney Peel, but expressed concern that placing certifications on letterhead could be potentially misleading.

One of the special problems of professional advertising is that at some point it shades off into personal solicitation of business. The prohibition of these personal attempts by professionals to generate business has been upheld by the Supreme Court in the face of First Amendment claims because of the inherent dangers of fraud, undue influence, intimidation, overreaching and vexacious conduct. See Ohralik v. Ohio State Bar Association (1978).

In Zauderer v. Office of Disciplinary Counsel (1985), an attorney had been disciplined for running a newspaper advertisement stating that he was available to represent on a contingent fee basis women injured through use of the Dalkon Shield, an intra-uterine contraceptive device. The advertisement stated that there would be no legal fees unless there was some recovery. The advertisement was accompanied by a drawing of the Dalkon Shield. The Ohio Supreme Court held that the advertisement violated Ohio Disciplinary Rules prohibiting self-recommendation and banning the use of illustrations in lawyer advertising.

By a 5–3 vote the United States Supreme Court struck down the self-recommendation prohibition as overbroad because it applied even to nondeceptive advertising. The Court distinguished Ohralik as applying to face-to-face solicitation, which in its view posed a much greater threat of undue influence and intimidation. Using the same reasoning the Court also struck down the ban on all illustrations. The Court did, however, find one aspect of the lawyer's ad misleading in that he stated no legal fees would be charged without some recovery, but failed to mention that court costs could be charged. The Ohio court's finding that this violated a full disclosure requirement for contingency fee rates was therefore upheld.

Similarly, in Shapero v. Kentucky Bar Association (1988), the Court struck down a total ban on targeted direct mail solicitation. The Court distinguished targeted direct mail from in-person solicitation in two ways. First, direct mail did not present the same potential for "overreaching, invasion of privacy, the exercise of undue influence, and outright fraud." Second, there are means of ensuring public scrutiny of direct mail that are not applicable to in-house solicitation. For example, submission of a sample letter for screening could be required.

However, in Florida Bar v. Went For It, Inc. (1995), the Court upheld a rule banning targeted mail to accident or disaster victims or their families for 30 days after the event. The Court distinguished Shapero on the special vulnerability of victims.

The separation between protected commercial speech and prohibited solicitation appears to be at the point where the expression is so immediate and personal that danger exists that the potential client's privacy may be invaded or the potential client may not be able to exercise his or her free will in deciding whether to accept a particular professional's services.

2. The Effect of the Lawyer Advertising Cases on the Other Professions

The principles espoused in the lawyer advertising cases seem generally applicable to restraints on advertising imposed on the other professions. Responding to these cases, the American Dental Association, for instance, has entered into a consent decree with the Federal Trade Commission agreeing not to engage in unfair competition by unduly restricting the advertising of its members. This agreement was contingent upon the success of the FTC's litigation with the American Medical Association to eliminate the AMA's restrictions on price advertising and advertising of the availability of individual and alternative medical services. The FTC prevailed in American Medical Association v. FTC (1980).

Not all the restrictions on lawyer advertising have been upheld when applied to other professions. For example, in Edenfield v. Fane (1993), the Supreme Court struck down a Florida statute prohibiting personal and telephone solicitation by CPAs.

The Court distinguished Ohralik on the basis both of the difference in training for the two professions and the type of clients each has. First, lawyers serve as advocates and are trained in the art of persuasion. CPAs' training emphasizes independence and objectivity. Also, lawyers' potential clients are often injured, distressed or unsophisticated. A CPA's potential clients are most often sophisticated and experienced business executives. Thus, the potential for harm to the people solicited by CPAs is much less than in the case of lawyers.

Overall, there has been a decided loosening of strictures on professionals advertising their services. This trend was given fresh impetus by the Supreme Court's affirmance of the FTC's victory over the AMA in the Second Circuit and the Court's decision in Edenfield v. Fane.

F.   ACCESS OF THE PUBLIC TO THE PRIVATE ADVERTISING MEDIA

Thus far in this chapter the thrust of discussion has been the constitutional protection afforded to individual and corporate commercial speech. It is important to remember, however, that the First and Fourteenth Amendments are directed only to governmental action and do not compel private media interests to communicate commercial expression. Indeed, the Supreme Court has held that those Amendments do not require newspapers and broadcasters to accept paid editorial messages let alone purely commercial advertising. See CBS, Inc. v.

Democratic National Committee (1973); Miami Herald Publishing Co. v. Tornillo (1974).

Thus, while the Constitution limits governmental regulation of commercial speech, there is no guarantee that it will be heard if the speaker is dependent on private means of communications controlled by others. The exception occurs where the media outlet in question has monopoly power and refuses advertising for the purpose of furthering that monopoly. For example, in Home Placement Service, Inc. v. Providence Journal Co. (1982), the Providence Journal refused to accept advertising for a rental referral service. Because the newspaper was the only daily newspaper in the city and Home Placement was a direct competitor for real estate advertising, the court held that the refusal to accept Home Placement's advertising violated § 1 and § 2 of the Sherman Act.

───────

The fact that until recently commercial speech generally was not accorded First Amendment protection, and false and misleading speech specifically has never been constitutionally protected accounts, at least in part, for the rise of statutory and administrative controls on advertising at both the state and federal levels designed to protect the public from commercial loss. In the remaining sections of this chapter we consider the agencies that exercise these controls, the nature of the controls, available sanctions against commercial wrongdoers and limitations on the imposition of these sanctions.

G. STATE STATUTORY REGULATION

As manufacturing began to dominate the early American agrarian economy and the frontier pushed westward, the distances between the manufacturers and their markets constantly expanded, making regional and national advertising increasingly necessary. Gradually the use of brand names, trademarks, magazine advertising and even advertising agencies grew to fulfill this need. Along with this dramatic growth of advertising use came flagrant advertising abuses. The patent medicines were the epitome of this advertising era, with elixirs such as Dr. J. W. Poland's White Pine Compound, claiming to cure "sore throat, colds, coughs, diphtheria, bronchitis, spitting of blood, and pulmonary afflictions generally." Flamboyant misleading copy writing, false testimonials, slogans, jingles and trade characters quickly became the rule in local and national advertising. Advertisers could, and did, promise anything and everything.

Common law and early state statutory remedies proved inadequate to curb advertising abuses. See E. Kintner, A Primer on the Law of Deceptive Practices: A Guide for the Businessman 7–8, 405–407. Today a majority of the states have added legislation similar to the Federal Trade Commission Act, discussed below, to encourage criminal prosecutions and to provide civil remedies for aggrieved consumers.

Companies whose products have been denigrated by competitors can bring product disparagement or trade libel suits. These actions require plaintiffs to prove false disparagement, identification, publication and special damages. In addition, some states require proof of intent to injure, while others only demand proof of negligent disparagement. Note that the constitutional privilege in defamation (discussed in Chapter 2, supra) does not apply to trade libel.

H. FEDERAL STATUTORY AND ADMINISTRATIVE REGULATION

1. The Federal Trade Commission

a. *Nature and Jurisdiction*

The original Federal Trade Commission Act was not directed toward false advertising but rather toward the prevention of monopolistic and unfair methods of competition in interstate commerce. Despite the absence of a clear congressional mandate in the advertising area, the early commissioners regulated deceptive ads by labeling them "unfair methods of competition." They took the position that exaggerated or misleading claims for an advertiser's product gave him or her an inequitable competitive advantage over those sellers who told the truth. This position was affirmed by the Supreme Court in Federal Trade Commission v. Winsted

Hosiery Co. (1922). Justice Brandeis, speaking for the Supreme Court, upheld an FTC determination that when a manufacturer labels its underwear "Natural Wool" and "Natural Worsted" the product must be all wool, not merely 10 percent wool. The Court agreed that when misleading ads are marketed in competition with truthful ads, potential customers are unfairly diverted from the honest advertiser's products. By 1925 three quarters of the Federal Trade Commission's orders concerned false and misleading advertising.

All of the Federal Trade Commission's orders of this period were tied to the concept of unfair competition. The question remained whether the Commission could protect the public from false advertising directly, without having to demonstrate economic injury to a business competitor. Finally, in Federal Trade Commission v. Raladam Co. (1931), the Supreme Court answered that question in the negative. In a unanimous decision the Court held that the Commission had no authority to ban purely false advertising unless it could be shown to be an unfair method of competition. The Raladam decision prompted Congress in 1938 by the Wheeler–Lea Act to amend the Commission's enabling act to permit regulation of "unfair or deceptive acts or practices in commerce" that injure the consumer. Congress also provided for substantial civil fines for violations of Commission orders to "cease and desist" from proscribed advertising practices and for criminal penalties for and injunctions against the dissemination of false advertising pertaining to cosmetics, therapeutic devices and drugs.

b. *Organization and Enforcement*

The Federal Trade Commission is an independent regulatory agency with five commissioners appointed by the President for renewable seven-year terms. No more than three members can belong to the same political party. It has more than 1200 employees divided primarily among four bureaus. The one most concerned with advertising is the Bureau of Consumer Protection. Through this bureau the Commission may institute an investigation upon the receipt of even a single letter of complaint from a member of the public. Unfortunately, because of its large work-load and reduced budget, investigations often take a considerable length of time to start and complete, if begun at all.

If, as a result of the investigation, the Commission feels a formal hearing is necessary to determine the issues, it will draft a detailed complaint specifying the alleged false or deceptive practices and will hold a hearing. At the hearing an administrative law judge will make an initial decision after both sides present their respective positions. The judge's decision is final unless it is reviewed by the Commissioners. If the decision is unfavorable to the advertiser the Commission may issue a cease and desist order which, if violated, will subject the advertiser to an action in a federal district court for civil fine. The advertiser may seek review of the cease and desist order in the United States Court of Appeals.

Because of the delays inherent in such formal proceedings, the Commission has developed faster, less expensive methods of halting or preventing deceptive advertising. Indeed, the general policy has been to avoid litigation if possible by offering some form of settlement to offenders. This settlement can be effected through an "assurance of voluntary compliance" wherein the advertiser merely signs an affidavit that it will discontinue the practices involved. A second and more common approach is the use of the consent decree. Under this procedure the Commission drafts a proposed complaint together with a cease and desist order and attaches them to a notice of intent to commence formal proceedings. This package is sent to the alleged offender who must advise the Commission within 10 days if it is willing to forego a formal hearing and have the issues resolved by consent decree. Once a settlement is negotiated and accepted by the parties, it has the same effect as an order issued after a formal proceeding.

These settlement methods are made palatable to the businesses involved because they do not have to admit any violations of law. Another individualized approach, involving anticipatory regulation, is the advisory opinion. This is simply an informal non-binding statement of advice from a responsible member of the Commission staff to assist the businessperson in determining in advance the legality of proposed conduct such as a future advertising campaign. The request must anticipate the act; the Commission will not give advice concerning current business practices.

The Commission also employs certain industry-wide approaches to illegal advertising and other business practices. One generalized method the Commission utilizes to promulgate its views on advertising is the publication of practical manuals or "Guides." The Guides, in pamphlet form, are disseminated to both industry and public to inform them of the Commission's position on certain business practices such as bait and switch advertising, testimonial advertising and deceptive pricing. These Guides reflect the view of the Commission as to what might be considered illegal practices. Violation of a guideline is not itself a violation of law. Rather, where a guideline has not been followed, the Commission must plead and prove that the accused business violated a provision of the Federal Trade Commission Act itself. For litigation purposes, it is as if the Guide did not exist.

This is in marked contrast to cases involving violations of Commission Trade Regulation Rules which state the types of conduct that will be deemed unfair or deceptive by the Commission under the Federal Trade Commission Act. In these cases the Commission need only show that its Trade Regulation Rules have been violated. Thus, these Rules are treated as having the force of law and their violation may result in civil penalties of up to $10,000 for each offense.

c. *The Federal Trade Commission Improvement Act of 1974*

Another major grant of power to the Commission was effected by the Magnuson–Moss Act, 15 U.S.C.A. § 2301 (1975). The 1938 amendments to the Federal Trade Commission Act had placed deceptive advertising squarely within the Commission's jurisdiction, but the advertising was required to be "in commerce." In most other areas of federal regulation the quoted phrase, drawn from the Constitution, has been expanded by court decision to allow federal regulation of matters which merely "affected" interstate commerce. This liberal interpretation was denied to the Commission in Federal Trade Commission v. Bunte Brothers (1941). The Bunte Brothers decision declared that only a congressional amendment could expand the scope of the Commission's powers to permit regulation of local business activity "affecting" interstate commerce. Thirty-three years later that amendment was made in the Magnuson–Moss Act. Accordingly, the Commission now has clear regulatory power over advertising reaching down to the local level and may, of course, control local advertising by Trade Regulation Rule, if necessary. In addition, as a result of a "rider" attached to the Trans–Alaskan Pipeline Act of 1973, violations of Commission rules outlawing certain trade practices can now be enjoined. See 15 U.S.C.A. § 53 (Cum.Supp.1976).

Industry claims that the FTC was abusing its powers by using the unfairness standard to regulate truthful, nondeceptive advertising led Congress in its 1980 FTC reauthorization bill to remove the FTC's authority to use that standard to initiate any new rulemakings. For years the House and Senate were unable to agree on an FTC authorization bill, but instead have included the unfairness prohibition in the Continuing Resolutions providing operating funds for the FTC. Finally, in 1994 Congress amended the Act to provide that "before an act or practice can be found to be unfair, the FTC must first find that (1) the act or practice causes or is likely to cause substantial injury to consumers; (2) which is not reasonably avoided by consumers; and (3) is not outweighed by countervailing benefits to consumers or to competition."

d. Constitutional Limitations on the Federal Trade Commission's Power to Impose Sanctions

Even before the Central Hudson case, supra, it was accepted constitutional doctrine that no protection was afforded false or deceptive advertising. Nevertheless, several United States Courts of Appeal have held that the First Amendment limits the *remedies* the Federal Trade Commission can fashion to protect the public against the risks created by such advertising. Thus it is not correct to assume that the FTC (and state agencies as well) are free to wield unlimited power against fraudulent or misleading advertising. These courts, while mindful that the First Amendment does not shield false or deceptive commercial speech from governmental control, insist that the Commission's exercise of that control be no greater than necessary to protect the public.

For example, in Beneficial Corp. v. FTC (1976), the Commission ordered a combined loan and income tax preparation company to stop using the words "Instant Tax Refund Plan" or "Instant Tax Refund Loan" in its advertising because such terms mislead the public as to the nature of the transaction by which consumers received amounts of money from the company equivalent to their prospective tax refunds (actually loan transactions with a substantial interest charge). While not questioning the correctness of the Commission's findings that Beneficial's ads were misleading, the Court refused to approve the Commission's complete ban on the use of the delineated phrases. Rather, the court permitted advertising with the inclusion of those phrases provided they were sufficiently qualified so as not to mislead the audience. The Court said, "The Commission, like any governmental agency, must start from the premise that any prior restraint is suspect, and that a remedy, even for deceptive advertising, can go no further than is necessary for the elimination of the deception."

Similar rulings modifying FTC remedial orders were made in National Commission on Egg Nutrition v. FTC (1977) (FTC order requiring a trade association whose advertising on the risks of egg consumption was misleading to present arguments in its future advertising in opposition to its own position disapproved); Warner–Lambert Co. v. FTC (1977) (FTC order requiring corrective advertising to counteract previous false claims that a mouthwash prevented or moderated the common cold modified so as to delete the prefatory phrase "Contrary to prior advertising").

2. The Federal Communications Commission

The Federal Communications Commission licenses radio and television broadcasters to operate in the "public interest, convenience and necessity." This includes broadcast advertising, but historically the FCC has relied on self-regulation by the broadcasters to avoid the specter of government censorship forbidden by Section 326 of the Federal Communications Act of 1934. For a long time there was an absence of any clear boundary between the FCC's authority over advertising through commercial broadcasting facilities and the FTC's general authority over advertising. This issue was finally resolved by agreement between the two agencies. The FCC has responsibility for assuring that commercials are neither objectionably loud nor excessive in number and that a separation is maintained between advertising and programming, especially during children's programs. Misleading or deceptive advertising on radio or television is to be controlled by the FTC.

*

PART TWO

REGULATION OF THE ELECTRONIC MASS MEDIA

CHAPTER X

REGULATION OF BROADCASTING

From the beginning, the electronic media have been regulated differently than the print media. As we will discuss in the next two chapters, these differences range from requiring government permission to operate (in the form of licenses or franchise agreements) to a reduced level of First Amendment protection. However, as we will discuss in the final chapter, recent technological developments are raising questions regarding this approach to the electronic media.

A. THE FEDERAL COMMUNICATIONS COMMISSION

The most important government agency involved in regulation of the electronic media is the Federal Communications Commission. The existence of the Commission is, in effect, a typical American reac-

459

tion to a practical and scientific problem. Government regulation of radio began in 1910 at a time when radio was perceived primarily as a safety device in maritime operations and as a potential advance in military technology. The government's primary concern was to assure itself of efficient use of this safety and defense technology, and its role was roughly analogous to that played by the police in registering automobiles. Persons desiring to use radio frequencies would register with the Department of Commerce and frequencies would be assigned to them. Pervasive regulation of the type we have come to accept as routine did not exist because there was no need.

Radio technology made quantum leaps during World War I and the commercial possibilities of radio began to be recognized by entrepreneurs. By the mid–1920's there were hundreds of radio stations operating for commercial use, and frequencies were set aside by the Secretary of Commerce for commercial application. However, the powers of the Secretary to regulate such broadcasting were questionable, particularly the Secretary's power to require a radio applicant to broadcast on a particular frequency at a particular power. Two opinions, one by the courts (United States v. Zenith Radio Corp. (1926)) and one by the Attorney General, (35 Ops. Atty.Gen. 126 (1926)), concluded that the legislation then in force did not permit the Secretary to limit applicants in the use of power and frequencies. The Secretary could only record the applications and grant frequencies, but he did not possess the expansive powers required to regularize radio operations.

These decisions threatened to throw the emerging radio industry into chaos and led to repeated requests by the industry itself for a government agency with greater power than had been possessed by the Secretary of Commerce—an agency which could assign applicants to specific frequencies, under specific engineering rules and with the power to enforce these rules through its licensing function. These efforts culminated in the Radio Act of 1927, which established the Federal Radio Commission and which transformed licensing from a ministerial act to a judgmental one, empowering the Commission to create and enforce standards for the broadcasters' privilege of using the public's airwaves.

The Federal Radio Commission created by the Radio Act of 1927 to supervise broadcasting was, pursuant to the Communications Act of 1934, merged into what is today the Federal Communications Commission. The 1934 Act, modeled largely after the Interstate Commerce Commission Act, and embodying much of the law that had already been made by the 1927 Radio Act, remains the organic legislation which controls American commercial and non-commercial ("Public") broadcasting. The Communications Act prescribes the basic task of the Federal Communications Commission to be that of "regulating interstate and foreign commerce in communication by wire and radio so as to make available, so far as possible, to all the people of the United States a rapid, efficient, nationwide and world-wide wire and radio communication service with adequate facilities at reasonable charges for the purpose of the national defense, for the purpose of promoting safety of life and property through the use of wire and radio communication ..." 47 U.S.C.A. § 151. The standard to which the Commission must conform in carrying out this responsibility is that of action "consistent with the public interest, convenience [and] necessity." 47 U.S.C.A. § 307. The courts have repeatedly emphasized that the standard is sufficiently broad to allow the Commission to act dynamically in areas of changing or emerging technology while, at the same time, sufficiently precise to prevent the Commission from acting in a wholly arbitrary, unreasonable or capricious manner.

1. Scope of the Commission's Power

It is important at the outset to recognize that the Commission's jurisdiction and power are strictly limited in scope to that which is granted by its enabling legislation, the Communications Act of 1934. It can only act in those areas in which it is specifically empowered to act.

There are many areas which might be considered part of the "communications realm," but over which the Commission has no jurisdiction. Perhaps most important, and least known, is that the Commission does *not* have jurisdiction and power over the entire radio spectrum space available to the United States under international treaty. In fact, the Commission has jurisdiction of only approximately one-half of this available radio space. Section 305 of the Communications Act exempts from the Commission's power or jurisdiction all "radio stations belonging to and operated by the United States." The United States government, through its various agencies, offices and departments (military and civilian), operates a host of radio services occupying approximately one-half of the total available frequency space. Allocation of spectrum space among the various governmental branches is made through a governmental coordinating group which is now housed in the National Telecommunications and Information Administration (NTIA), a division of the Department of Commerce. The FCC coordinates with this group but exercises no jurisdiction over the government's stations. It is only that part of the spectrum allocated to non-federal government use over which the FCC exercises jurisdiction. It is instructive to recall this fact when the concept of a "scarcity" of frequency space is discussed. At least in part, the scarcity of frequency space for commercial broadcasting is man-made and its dimensions are initially defined by the Executive Office of the White House.

Even with those frequencies over which the FCC clearly possesses jurisdiction, there are large areas in which the FCC is forbidden to or has chosen, as a matter of policy, not to exercise power. Thus, for example, the Commission is not empowered by the Act to enforce or decide antitrust issues as embodied in the Clayton and Sherman Antitrust Acts; it has been explicitly forbidden to do so by the courts.

United States v. Radio Corp. of America (1959). Although the Commission may, and sometimes must take into consideration, as part of its public interest standard, economic considerations involving such matters as competition, merger, market share, and the like, it is nevertheless free to ignore the policies favoring competition underlying the Sherman and Clayton Acts if to do so would be in the public interest, convenience and necessity. Federal Communications Commission v. RCA Communications, Inc. (1953).

Similarly, the Commission does not determine whether a particular advertising message is "false and misleading." That question has been delegated by law to the Federal Trade Commission. Of course, the FCC would act where a licensee continues to broadcast an advertisement which has been finally adjudicated by the FTC to be false and misleading. But the Commission regularly refuses to make the initial determination as to the nature of the advertising. See FTC–FCC Liaison Agreement, Current Service, Pike and Fischer Radio Reg., p. 11:212 (hereafter cited as R.R.).

The FCC does not ordinarily become involved in civil or contractual litigation between broadcasters. It does not set advertising rates or oversee ordinary and usual business practices such as production charges, commission arrangements, and salaries of artists. It does not regulate rates which may be charged the public by pay television. It does not regulate closed circuit television or radio. It does not license radio or television networks. There are many other areas which might appear to fall within its power but which do not.

The reason is at once simple and complex. The American system of broadcasting is an attempt to introduce state regulation of the radio spectrum while, at the same time, allowing as much free market play as possible. The Commission sets the ground rules by which stations can be licensed. It will choose between applicants for conflicting licenses, set up a framework which attempts to insure some competition, and then allow the free market to determine, as well as possible, such matters as advertising costs, expenses, cost of equipment and, perhaps most important, choice of programming by broadcasters. The simplicity of the system breaks down at those points where free market considerations may not work well. A free marketplace may not automatically serve up programming for minority, ethnic or cultural groups. At a number of points (many of which are discussed later), the government has chosen to intervene; more recently (as the number of media types and outlets have grown) the government has "deregulated" many areas and given market forces more scope. Much of communications law cannot be understood unless it is recognized that the basic bias of our communications system is toward allowing, where possible, the free market to determine matters. See Report and Order, Deregulation of Radio, 46 Fed.Reg. 13888 (1981). Government regulation is, in essence, a last resort, to be used when the free market cannot deliver.

2. Structural Organization of the Commission

Having been delegated broad powers to make rules and regulations necessary to carry out the mandate of its enabling legislation, the Commission faces the task, first, of attempting to satisfy the differing demands for communications frequency space in a modern industrial (indeed, post-industrial) economy. Although most familiar to the public in the role of a regulator of commercial and "public" broadcasting, the Commission has the equally demanding responsibility of regulating non-broadcast use of communications facilities such as interstate common carrier systems, radio systems for industrial use such as truck-to-truck communications, taxi cab networks, communications between central plant and repairmen or servicemen, communications between hospital and doctor, marine and ship radio, aviation frequencies, citizen band radio, international "ham" communications, police and fire communications networks, computer-to-computer communications, and emerging technologies such as cable, pay television, satellite communications, computer networks, cellular telephones, personal communications networks, etc. In the case of common carriers, the FCC acts as a rate-making agency for interstate common carriage in a manner similar to state public utilities commissions. The reach of its jurisdiction is quite remarkable.

The Commission itself is composed of five commissioners, appointed by the President with the advice and consent of the Senate. The President designates the chairman. Not more than three members of the Commission can be members of the same political party. Commissioners are appointed for a term of five years on a staggered basis. See 47 U.S.C.A. § 154(a).

To meet its responsibilities, the Commission established a number of bureaus, each of which governed a different service. The most important of these bureaus were Mass Media, Cable Services, Common Carrier and Private Radio.

In an era of technological convergence coupled with the removal of legal barriers to provision of multiple services by individual companies (e.g. cable delivery of both phone and video services), this technology-based organizational structure came under increasing criticism. The Commission responded with a 1999 proposal for a radical reorganization plan.

Noting that "the advent of Internet-based and other new technology-driven communications services will continue to erode the traditional regulatory distinctions between different sectors of the communications industry," the FCC began shifting to a function-based organizational structure. The first step in this process was to "consolidate currently dispersed enforcement functions into a new Enforcement Bureau and currently dispersed public information functions into a Consumer Information Bureau." Subsequently, the remaining functions were divided among four additional bureaus, International, Media, Wireless Telecommunications, and Wireline Competition.

The new structure is also based on the assumption that "U.S communications markets [will] be characterized predominately by vigorous competition that will greatly reduce the need for direct regulation." Thus, additional goals of the proposed reorganization include eliminating barriers to entry in domestic markets, deregulating as competition develops, enforcing the rules so that businesses compete fairly, and promoting competition in international communications markets.

3.   Juridical Basis for Commission Regulation of Broadcasting

Government regulation of broadcasting is anomalous. We accept a depth and type of regulation over broadcast facilities which we do not, as a Constitutional matter, tolerate with respect to print media. The most obvious example is governmental licensing of broadcast stations. The First Amendment flatly forbids any such licensing requirement for newspapers, books or magazines. See Near v. Minnesota (1931); New York Times Co. v. United States (1971). Yet the licensing of radio stations has long been upheld. Federal Radio Commission v. Nelson Brothers Bond and Mortgage Co. (1933). Broadcasters at one time operated under the constraints of the Fairness Doctrine, requiring them to air controversial issues of public importance, and to do so in a manner allowing presentation of contrasting views. See Red Lion Broadcasting Co. v. Federal

Communications Commission (1969). No such requirement could constitutionally be enforced against the print media. Moreover, "indecent" (though not obscene) material, which would be protected under the First Amendment if seen in a movie or magazine, may nevertheless be channelled into certain hours for broadcast over the air. The Supreme Court has noted that " ... of all forms of communication, it is broadcasting that has received the most limited First Amendment protection." Federal Communications Commission v. Pacifica Foundation (1978).

Although the courts have justified these apparent contradictions on the ground that different media present different First Amendment considerations, they do not often explain in any rigorous analytical detail how the differences in media result in constitutional distinctions. It is even rarer for a court to test the breadth or scope of its holding against the constitutional justification for differences in regulation. For example, the United States Supreme Court in Miami Herald Publishing Co. v. Tornillo (1974) struck down a Florida "right-of-reply" law that applied to newspapers, without ever mentioning or attempting to distinguish the cases that allow precisely such regulation in the broadcast area.

The justification for broadcast regulation has been stated in terms of the "scarcity" of broadcast frequencies. The leading case discussing this point (National Broadcasting Co. v. United States (1943)) set the formulation:

The plight into which radio fell prior to 1927 was attributable to certain basic facts about radio as a means of communication—its facilities are limited; they are not available to all who may wish to use them; the radio spectrum simply is not large enough to accommodate everybody. There is a fixed natural limitation upon the number of stations that can operate without interfering with one another. Regulation of radio was therefore as vital to its development as traffic control was to the development of the automobile.

Use of the term "scarcity," however, to describe the legal rationale for broadcast regulation has caused much unnecessary confusion. The confusion derives from the fact that the term can be used in two quite different senses: "numerical scarcity," on the one hand, and "allocational scarcity," on the other. "Numerical scarcity" simply means measuring the government's power to regulate the broadcast media by gauging the number of broadcast and other competing media facilities which exist at any one time. The smaller the number of media facilities, the greater the government's power to regulate and, conversely, the government's regulatory power shrinks as the number of media outlets increases.

Although the Supreme Court failed to discuss the broadcast cases in Miami Herald, its decision made clear that numerical scarcity was not an adequate justification for restricting First Amendment rights. There are far more broadcasting stations than daily newspapers in the United States and it is more difficult (from an economic point of view) to start a newspaper than a radio station. By numerical standards, newspapers are "scarcer." The FCC itself has noted that cable broadcasting, multipoint distribution services using microwave frequencies, satellite transmission direct to privately owned satellite reception dishes and a host of other new technological innovations all demonstrate that broadcasting is, indeed, no longer a numerically "scarce" resource. See FCC Report: General Fairness Doctrine Obligations of Broadcast Licensees, 50 Fed.Reg. 35418 at 35421 (Aug. 30, 1985); 58 R.R.2d 1137. Yet the Commission has never suggested that this lack of scarcity has deprived it of regulatory jurisdiction, nor can anyone seriously argue that the relative scarcity of newspapers vis-a-vis broadcast media would allow the government to regulate the press. The difference between broadcasting and print media lies not in numerical scarcity, but rather in the other use of the term, i.e., "allocational" scarcity.

Justice Frankfurter in *NBC* grounded the regulatory distinction between broadcasting and other media not upon numerical scarcity, but rather, upon the fact that broadcasting imposes a duty upon the government which it does not face in the print media—the duty of making choices between two or more potential broadcasters wishing to utilize the same broadcast space. Two newspapers can, without governmental intervention, physically operate in the same community at the same time; their survival would depend on competitive market forces. In broadcasting, however, if there is but one frequency available for use in a particular community, then, by the laws of physics, two stations cannot physically operate on it, for to do so would result in neither being heard. Broadcasting is unique because it is the only communications medium which requires some type of governmental intervention as a practical *sine qua non* of its existence. So long as there are more persons desiring to broadcast than there are frequencies available to accommodate them, a broadcast frequency is a "scarce" resource.

Despite sharp criticism of the scarcity rationale from some quarters, the Supreme Court has refused to reconsider it without some signal from Congress or the Commission that revision of the long-standing regulatory system is required. See Federal Communications Commission v. League of Women Voters of California (1984).

This, then, is the rationale for government regulation: There is a clear public need that some form of broadcasting exist. Broadcasting must be recognized as a public resource, analogous to an interstate traffic system, or a national park system, or a national environmental policy. Technical considerations make broadcast frequencies allocationally "scarce" and impose an obligation on the government to (a) make choices and (b) set standards to make certain that the "resource" is not wasted or misused. Because the government grants broadcasters a limited monopoly in the sense that it will protect a broadcaster's right exclusively to use a frequency, it is not inappropriate to extract a quid pro quo in the form of requiring that broadcasters operate in the "public interest." The government's traditional "police power" further allows it to impose certain limitations (as, for example, to protect children from "obscene or indecent" material). All governmental regulation of broadcasting can be traced to at least one of these considerations and, although they are not present at all times, together they represent the foundation of broadcast regulation.

To assert, however, that the uniqueness of broadcasting allows some form of government regulation is merely to begin the inquiry. For it is quite clear that the NBC rationale will not support any and every form of governmental action. The First Amendment places limits even upon government regulation of allocationally "scarce" resources. See Columbia Broadcasting System, Inc. v. Democratic National Committee (1973). Congress, for example, cannot forbid a station from editorializing in favor of a particular candidate or issue. Nor (except, perhaps, in the very limited circumstances of appearances by political candidates or the rather unique worlds of "indecency" or pornography) can the Commission regulate the content of broadcasting material. Restrictions on broadcasting can be upheld only when the courts are satisfied that the restriction "is narrowly tailored to further a substantial governmental interest, . . .". League of Women Voters, supra. In addition, although numerical scarcity is not the foundation for the government's control over broadcasting, nevertheless, numerical scarcity can, and does, affect the type of regulation which the Commission has imposed. For example, in the 1950's the Commission created the so-called "Fairness Doctrine," which imposed certain obligations upon licensees to cover controversial issues of public importance and to do so in a fair and "balanced" fashion. Such regulation was justified (and approved by the Supreme Court as constitutional) as necessary to insure that the public have before it a broad diversity of viewpoints. However, as the number of broadcast outlets dramatically increased in the past decade second half of the twentieth century through such technological advances as cablevision and direct satellite cable distribution, the need for such governmentally imposed requirements appeared to the Commission to decrease (the marketplace being viewed as diverse enough to insure broad issue coverage) and the Commission repealed the Doctrine as (a) no longer necessary and (b) constitutionally suspect. See Syracuse Peace Council v. FCC (1989). This is but one example of the fact that the tension between the necessity for governmental regulation and the common recognition of the dangers posed by such regulation forms the matrix in which broadcast law has developed.

B.   STRUCTURAL REGULATION

1.   Allocation of Frequencies

The Commission handles the problem of allocation of frequencies between uses in a rather straightforward manner. Certain frequencies are specifically allocated to commercial "broadcasting uses"; other frequencies are specifically allocated to common carrier uses (i.e., telephone, telegraph and other communications services for hire); other frequencies are dedicated to uses such as industrial communication, marine and ship radio, aviation and medical services. These initial allocations are quite important for a number of reasons: (1) they help establish the relative "scarcity" of frequencies which is the basic justification for governmental action in the broadcasting realm, and (2) they are the warp and woof of the nation's communication's system. As much as any single factor, the FCC's allocations policy determines the shape and content of our communications capabilities.

The Commission has further subdivided the broadcast "band" into distinct portions. One set of frequencies is set aside for standard (or AM) broadcast stations, another group for frequency modulation (FM) stations, and a third for use by television stations. But the manner in which it chooses to assign specific frequencies within these groupings is not the same.

a.   AM Allocation

The Commission immediately confronts a fact of physics: because of electrical interference considerations, the number of individual broadcast stations which can operate in a particular bandwidth varies inversely with their power. The higher the power, the smaller the number of stations which can be accommodated and vice-versa. The Commission could have chosen an allocations policy which would have led to a small number of very powerful stations, each being given the task of covering very large distances. This system was rejected on policy grounds, i.e., that the nation should have a large rather than a small number of individual voices. Conversely, the Commission could have allowed a very large number of stations, giving each low power. The difficulty here was that the coverage area of such stations might be so small as to preclude financial viability. Instead, the Commission opted for a compromise. The present AM allocation policy allows three classes of stations:

(1) The so-called "clear channel" stations, approximately 25 in number, which operate at 50 kilowatts (the highest permissible power for any commercial AM station), cover a radius of approximately 80 to 90 miles during daytime hours and (because of a scientific phenomenon) can be heard during the night at distances which sometimes reach 500 or 600 miles. These few "clear channel" stations are heavily protected from interference by other stations;

(2) Lower power, so-called "regional" stations which operate at a power usually of 5 or 10 kw and which cover a radius of approximately 25 or 30 miles (depending on the terrain); and

(3) So-called "local" stations which operate at a power no greater than 1 kw, cover an area of approximately 8 to 10 miles in radius, and many of which (because of interference considerations) are allowed to operate only during daytime hours.

By far the majority of standard broadcast stations in the United States are local stations which operate on a "local" frequency.

See 47 C.F.R. §§ 73.21–73.29 and Regulations of the Commission for a full exposition of the AM broadcast allocations rules.

The second characteristic of the AM allocation system is that, unlike FM or TV, it operates on a "demand" basis. To illustrate, the Commission could have taken all of the available frequencies in the AM band and allocated specific frequencies to specific communities. New York City could have been allocated 5 clear channel stations, 6 regional stations and 13 local stations. Chicago could have been allocated a different number of specific classes of stations, Des Moines, Iowa yet a third, and so on throughout all communities in the United States. This type of specific allocation by city has the advantage of ensuring that significant cities have a certain number of broadcast stations, and it also has the virtue of reserving frequencies for future use in areas which are now relatively sparse in population, but which later might become more heavily populated.

Instead, in AM the Commission opted for an allocation policy which allowed maximum scope for a "market type" of demand. The Commission first established engineering ground rules stipulating certain power requirements, and also stipulating the amount of allowable interference which a proposed station could cause or accept. Within these ground rules, applicants were entitled to apply for any of the various classes of stations in any community. It was believed (and proved to be the case) that the larger population centers, being able to support the larger number of stations, would attract the largest number of applicants. The Commission put as few restrictions as possible on the number of applicants so that the benefit of radio communication could be realized throughout the country as quickly as applicants could design proposed facilities which would fit within the Commission's overall engineering guidelines.

The "demand" system still governs the allocation of AM stations, although the engineering ground rules are now such that (in light of the number of existing AM stations) it is virtually impossible to design a new AM station which will fit within them. Moreover, as FM stations continue to multiply, their superior technical performance has made them the dominant radio medium, to the economic detriment of AM broadcasting. The number of AM stations has not significantly increased in the past decade, and (absent a radical policy change) is not likely to do so in the future. Indeed, the Commission has suggested (in a rather radical policy change) that there now may be too many operating AM stations, creating technical degradation to their economic detriment. In 1991 the Commission allocated an additional 1000 KHz to the AM band so as to allow some existing stations to migrate to the new band to relieve congestion in the AM service. See, e.g., Report and Order, MM Docket No. 87–

267, released October 25, 1991. Various petitions for reconsideration, as well as engineering errors, delayed final assignment of the channels until 1997.

b.   *FM Allocation*

FM allocation was originally on a "demand" basis. After considerable experience with the "demand" allocation system the Commission had identified shortcomings in it, particularly that it engendered a great deal of complicated, lengthy and difficult engineering litigation. It tended to favor the more populated areas over the less populated, since a station granted to a larger community, by necessity precluded use of that frequency in smaller communities which had not as yet stimulated entrepreneurs to view them as places for radio stations. The demand system was essentially an "unplanned" one in which future growth might not adequately be accommodated.

The Commission therefore discarded the demand system for FM and turned towards a simplified, more specific allocation policy which assigned specific frequencies to specific communities. Certain frequencies were reserved for non-commercial, educational (now termed "public") stations. Specific frequencies are assigned to specific cities according to a table of allocations, which can be changed only through the institution of a formal rule-making proceeding. There are essentially four classes of stations, high-powered ones (which can operate up to 100 kw) and low-powered ones (which are limited to 50 kw, 25 kw or 3 kw). The number of FM stations has been increasing at a rapid rate and the Commission in 1985 allocated hundreds more.

In early 2000 the FCC adopted rules authorizing a new low-power FM service. The NAB, claiming the likelihood that these new stations would cause interference with existing FM stations, opposed the creation of these new stations and lobbied Congress to prohibit the FCC from proceeding with its plans. Congress responded by inserting requirements for increased interference protection in the 2000 appropriations bill. See Creation of a Low Power Radio Service (2001).

Two new classes of stations were authorized, one with a power limit of 10 watts, the other with a power limit of 100 watts. Stations are exclusively noncommercial. For the first two years, licenses were awarded exclusively to local entities. As of 2005, 1175 LPFM construction permits had been issued, including approximately 590 stations that were on the air. Creation of a Low Power Radio Service (2005).

c.   *Television Allocation*

Television has always been allocated through a table of assignments. There are no different *classes* of television stations. All television stations are either on VHF or UHF frequencies. They can all operate day and night, and all have the same maximum power limitations (though, for technical reasons, VHF stations can cover a larger area than UHF stations).

Each city only has available to it those specific frequencies which the Commission has chosen to assign. These allocations are part of the Commission's rules, and any change in them requires a formal request for the Commission to institute a rule-making proceeding in accordance with the Administrative Procedure Act. Certain frequencies are reserved for use only by non-commercial stations, and some of these frequencies, even now, lie fallow, an example of the Commission allowing for future growth. Because there are no interference "ground rules" for television, there is much less engineering litigation in television cases, and there is no need for the Commission to compare in the hearing process (as it does in AM) the relative needs of different communities for a particular frequency. The needs of the various communities have already been evaluated in the rule-making process by which the frequencies were assigned.

The exception to the above TV allocation scheme is the low-power television service (LPTV) inaugurated in 1982. The LPTV service allows low-power stations (maximum power of 100 watts VHF and 1000 watts UHF, encompassing a coverage area of approximately 10–15 miles) to operate on any available channel, on a secondary (i.e., non-interference) basis to regular full service stations. "Secondary basis" means that any low power station creating interference to a full-service station must either eliminate the interference or cease operations. See Final Rule, LPTV General Docket No. 82–107, 47 Fed.Reg. 21468, May 18, 1982.

d.   Digital Television (DTV)

Although a plethora of new systems for delivering television programming (cable, MDS, DBS, and SMATV, all discussed later in this chapter) have been developed, one thing remained constant—the television picture itself. The last major change was the advent of color decades ago.

All this is changing with the introduction of Digital Television. DTV is an outgrowth of the development of High Definition Television (HDTV). The key difference between HDTV and the current U.S. broadcast standard is that HDTV has a much higher number of scan lines (720–1080 as opposed to 525). The result is a sharper, brighter, clearer picture with deeper, more vibrant colors. In addition HDTV uses a 16:9 aspect ratio as opposed to the 4:3 currently in use. Proponents of HDTV claim that its quality approximates that of 35 mm. film. DTV also uses a digital 5.1 (five speakers plus a subwoofer) audio standard.

When the FCC set the technical standard for HDTV, it chose a digital, as opposed to analog, system. Instead of measuring variations in a continuous signal, as is the case with traditional broadcasting, the new system uses discrete codes similar to those used in modern computers. The digital approach has several advantages. First, it is far less susceptible to interference or signal degradation.

The second major advantage is compression. By removing redundant information prior to transmission (e.g. material that doesn't change from one frame to the next) and restoring it at the receiving end, it is possible to transmit more information in less bandwidth. This allows one HDTV signal or five standard definition (SDTV) digital signals to occupy the same bandwidth as an existing standard definition analog television signal.

Finally, it is possible to transmit different formats using the same equipment. Thus, a digital television (DTV) station can not only choose between transmitting one HDTV or 5 SDTV channels, but can switch back and forth between them. It can even utilize part of its signal for high-speed data transmission.

When the FCC began considering HDTV service, in addition to setting a technical standard, it had to answer a number of questions before the new service could become a reality. Should the new service be compatible with the current television standard? How much spectrum should be assigned to this service? Who should be authorized to provide HDTV?

In a series of decisions issued between 1988 and 1999, the Commission answered most of these questions. DTV utilizes the existing television broadcast spectrum. Current television licensees received the initial DTV licenses. DTV is not compatible with existing television service.

In order to provide an orderly transition to DTV, broadcasters were given an additional 6 MHz in which to broadcast DTV. Within as short a time span as possible, licensees will be expected to simulcast 100 percent of their programming on their original channel and their DTV channel. Once DTV becomes the prevalent medium, broadcasters will be required to surrender their original channel. When this spectrum space is recovered, some will be allocated to non-broadcast services while the rest will be auctioned off for additional DTV service.

Broadcasters will be allowed to choose the mix of services they offer, including supplementary or ancillary services. These services can include subscription services. The only restriction is that each licensee must broadcast a minimum of "free digital video programming service that is at least comparable in resolution to today's service and aired during the same time periods as today's analog service."

There is still great disagreement regarding how long it will take to make the transition from analog to digital television. The first DTV stations began broadcasting in 1998. However, there are a number of problems that have hindered the rapid growth of this medium. The first is the high cost of digital sets–thousands of dollars each. The second is disagreement among broadcasters as to how best to utilize DTV. Some want to broadcast HDTV, while others believe it is better to broadcast multiple SDTV channels.

Another problem is the lack of agreement on cable carriage of DTV or even the technical standard for connecting cable boxes to DTV sets. We will discuss cable carriage of DTV further in Chapter XI.

Also hindering a quick transition to DTV has been the need for many stations to erect new towers for DTV transmitters because existing towers can't support the weight. Not only are new towers expensive, but it is difficult to find land for them, and there are a limited number of companies capable of building and erecting these towers.

Initially, the FCC set the end of 2006 as the deadline for returning existing analog spectrum. However, Congress subsequently amended the Communications Act allowing broadcasters to retain analog spectrum as long as any of the following conditions exist.

1. One or more stations in a market affiliated with one of the four major networks are not broadcasting digital signals.

2. Fewer than 85 percent of the TV households in a market subscribe to a multichannel video service carrying at least one digital signal from each local television station.

3. Fewer than 85 percent of the TV households in a market have either a digital television set or an analog set with a digital to analog converter. For a list of DTV stations currently on air: http://www.fcc.gov/mb/video/files/dtvonair.html.

In an attempt to hasten the transition to DTV, the FCC adopted rules requiring all televisions with a screen size of 13 inches or greater, and video recorders to have a digital tuner by 2007. The requirement will be phased in over a three-year period, starting with large screen (36 inches or greater) televisions. Review of the Commission's Rules and Policies Affecting the Conversion To Digital Television (2002).

Another potential barrier to a quick transition to digital television has been the concern of program suppliers that it will lead to widespread illegal copying of their product. The Commission responded to these concerns by adopting regulations requiring all devices capable of receiving DTV signals manufactured after July 2005 to include technology that would recognize the "broadcast flag." "The broadcast flag is a digital code embedded in a DTV broadcasting stream, which prevents digital television reception equipment from redistributing broadcast content." Digital Broadcast Content Protection (2003).

Several organizations including the American Library Association challenged the regulations claiming that the broadcast flag would prevent them from making and distributing lawful copies and that the regulations were beyond the scope of the FCC's jurisdiction. The circuit court agreed. In asserting jurisdiction, the FCC relied on its authority to issue regulations that "are reasonably ancillary to the Commission's specific statutory powers and responsibilities." The court rejected the FCC's argument because its specific authority was limited to regulating the transmission and receipt of communications, not subsequent uses of those communications. "In sum, because the rules promulgated by the *Flag Order* regulate demodulator products after the transmission of a DTV broadcast is complete, these regulations exceed the scope of authority Congress delegated to the FCC.''

In its analysis the court relied heavily on a series of cases involving the FCC's jurisdiction over cable. The court also noted that other regulations governing receiving equipment had been specifically authorized by Congress, e.g. the All Channels Receiver Act. American Library Association v. Federal Communications Commission (2005).

2. Broadcast Licensing

Although there may have been other methods of insuring the existence of a nationwide communications system, as, for example, by lottery or by auctioning off frequencies to the highest bidder and granting the winner a broadcast right in perpetuity subject to defeasance for misconduct, Congress nevertheless chose to institute a licensing procedure by which broadcasters are granted a limited privilege to broadcast over a particular frequency at a particular power for a fixed term. The grant of the privilege gives the licensee no vested property interest in the frequency. 47 U.S.C.A. § 309(h). Section 307(d) of the Communications Act limits the license of a broadcasting station to a maximum of eight years, with a requirement that the broadcaster file for renewal of that license every eight years if it wishes to continue broadcasting. Licenses will be granted only if the ''public convenience, interest, or necessity will be served thereby.'' Section 310(b) of the Act provides that no license may be transferred to any person or entity, directly or indirectly, without the prior approval of the Commission, and Section 310(a) of the Act mandates that station licenses shall be granted only to U.S. citizens and cannot be held by aliens, foreign governments, or corporations of which any officer or director is an alien or of which more than a minority of the stock is voted by aliens or representatives of foreign governments. Interestingly, there is no restriction on foreign individuals or corporations holding ownership interests in cable systems.

Licensees do possess certain constitutional and statutory protections which derive not from any "right" in the license itself, but rather from general constitutional and statutory protections against arbitrary action of government. Although a license can be revoked during its term, the Commission can only do so after giving notice to the licensee and a full opportunity to be heard. 47 U.S.C.A. § 312(c). The Commission carries the burden of proof in such a revocation proceeding. The Commission cannot act arbitrarily or capriciously and must explain its decisions through written findings (Saginaw Broadcasting Co. v. Federal Communications Commission (1938)) on a public record containing full explanation of its rationale and actions. Greater Boston Television Corp. v. Federal Communications Commission (1970). Its actions are subject to the requirements of the Federal Administrative Procedure Act, 5 U.S.C.A. §§ 500–576. The Commission's decisions are appealable to the United States Court of Appeals and the court must be satisfied that the

Commission has exercised its decision-making powers in accordance with constitution and statute.

The Commission's primary statutory function is licensing; indeed, licensing has always been the linchpin on which all Commission broadcasting functions depend. Section 301 of the Communications Act mandates that no person shall use or operate any apparatus for radio transmission except by virtue of a license to operate granted by the Commission. Section 307(a) requires that licenses be granted to applicants only "if public convenience, interest, or necessity will be served thereby." Section 303 gives the Commission the power to classify different types of stations, to prescribe the nature of the service to be rendered by different types of stations, and to assign the bands of frequencies for each individual station. A license from the Commission is, in essence, an exclusive right to operate a station on a particular frequency at a prescribed power.

a. *The Showing an Applicant Must Make—Basic Qualifications*

Having found a frequency which can be used in accordance with the Commission's rules, what type of showing must be made by an applicant in order to convince the Commission that the public interest requires a grant of the license?

The Commission is not always faced with the necessity of choosing between particular applicants; there may be only one applicant. But whether or not a choice is required, there are certain basic qualifications which *all* applicants must meet, some specifically required by the Communications Act and others by the Commission under its policy-making authority.

(1) Citizenship

Section 310 of the Act mandates that a broadcast license may not be held by a non-citizen, a foreign government, a foreign corporation, or any corporation of which any officer or director is an alien or of which more than one fifth of the capital stock is owned by non-citizens. The above restrictions are mandatory. They cannot be waived by the Commission and can be changed only by Congress. If the corporation is a holding company, no more than one-fourth of the capital stock can be owned by non-citizens, unless the Commission finds that the public interest will be served by allowing the increased foreign ownership. Other provisions of Section 310 specifically allow licenses to be held by foreign pilots, ships and radio ham operators under certain circumstances. There are no similar restrictions on foreign ownership of cable systems.

(2) Character

By statute (Section 308(b) of the Act), the Commission must determine whether an applicant possesses the requisite "character" qualifications. But neither the Act nor the Commission's rules spell out the requirements that constitute "good character" or those that will be deemed "bad." The matter is left to the Commission's discretion. Because "bad character" could be as extensive as human experience and considerations of "character" per se could involve the Commission in abstract value judgments which it would rather avoid, the Commission's policy is to concern itself only with the type of bad character traits that would raise questions as to the honesty of the applicant, its potential performance as a broadcaster, or its proclivity towards obeying or violating Commission regulations. See Matter of Policy Regarding Character Qualifications in Broadcast Licensing (1986).

Honesty and candor are essential. The Commission could not function effectively if its licensees were dishonest. It has neither the staff nor the budget to check independently every licensee representation. The information with which it deals is almost always information given to it by its licensees; it relies upon their veracity to do its work. Therefore, a licensee or an applicant who has been found to have knowingly misrepresented a fact to the Commission is in serious danger of having its license application denied, even if the misrepresentation is in an area of little significance. The significance of the misrepresentation is far less important than the fact that the misrepresentation occurred. Federal Communications Commission v. WOKO, Inc. (1946). A review of the cases where the Commission either denied or revoked an application or license shows that by far the greatest percentage of denials occurred where the Commission found knowing misrepresentation to have occurred.

Violations of criminal law also raise character issues, although here the Commission has adopted a more flexible attitude. Felonious violation of criminal law involving moral turpitude (such as murder, robbery, rape, etc.) almost certainly would result in denial, but disqualification is not automatic. There have been instances of felony violations that have not resulted in outright denial. See Las Vegas Television, Inc. (1957). The Commission is likely to be forgiving if the crime occurred years ago and involved a law that had been routinely disregarded, for example, operating a speakeasy during Prohibition at a time and place where such operation was not uncommon. See WGCM Broadcasting Co. (1947). In general, the Commission's policy is that criminal convictions not involving fraudulent conduct are not relevant unless it can be demonstrated that there is a substantial relationship between the criminal conviction and the applicant's proclivity to be truthful or comply with the Commission's rules and policies.

One exception to this position involves drug trafficking. Pursuant to the Anti–Drug Abuse Act of 1988, the Commission announced that absent extenuating circumstances, drug-trafficking convictions are grounds to deny a license application or revoke an existing license. Drug Trafficking Policy (1989).

Criminal violations of the Federal antitrust laws are not necessarily grounds for disqualification. A number of nationwide companies (among them General Electric and Westinghouse) were found to have violated the Sherman Act through price fixing in their non-communications-related businesses. In considering whether to take away their broadcast licenses, the Commission found that the communications sections of these companies were separate from the other areas, were not handled by any of the persons involved in the price fixing, and were characterized by a history of meritorious programming and pioneering broadcast efforts. Weighing these factors led the Commission to renew the licenses. Westinghouse Broadcasting Co., Inc. (1962); General Electric Co. (1964).

However, violations of the Sherman Act by a newspaper which engaged in predatory competitive tactics against a radio station, and with no past broadcasting history against which to weigh them, could be grounds for refusal to grant a license to the offender (see, e.g., Mansfield Journal Co. v. Federal Communication Commission (1950)). Obviously, the outcome of these cases depends upon their individual facts. The Commission will not adjudicate controversies that are the subject of other court proceedings. In such cases the Commission will condition its actions upon the outcome of the adjudication in the courts. See, e.g., RKO General, Inc. (1969). The general rule is that where non-broadcast related antitrust or anticompetitive activity is involved, even adverse adjudications will not be considered relevant unless they suggest a proclivity toward fraud or unreliability. The factors which weigh most heavily in the analysis are the willfulness of the misconduct, the frequency of such behavior and its currency.

At one time, the Commission considered character not only as a *basic* qualifying condition but also as a factor to be weighed on a *comparative* basis. If the alleged misconduct was not sufficient to totally disqualify an applicant, nevertheless, it could be used as a standard to choose one competitor over another. This is no longer the case. The Commission's present policy is that a character defect either disqualifies the applicant or is irrelevant. See Policy Regarding Character Qualifications in Broadcast Licensing (1986).

(3) Financial Qualifications

An applicant must demonstrate its financial capability to construct and operate its proposed facility. The theory is that a "scarce" public resource should not be wasted in the hands of an operator that does not have the financial capability to run it. The Commission has established a minimum standard which applicants must meet. Prior to replacing the comparative licensing process with auctions, discussed later in this chapter, applicants for new stations (AM, FM or television) had to demonstrate financial capability to construct and operate the station for 90 days, even assuming that the station earns no revenue. Financial Qualifications (1978); (1979). The FCC has eliminated this requirement for the new auction process. Competitive Bidding for Commercial Broadcast and Instructional Fixed

Service Licenses (1998). Purchasers of a broadcast station must still have sufficient capital to consummate the transaction and to meet expenses for a three-month period. See Financial Qualifications (1981).

(4) Technical Showing

All applicants must demonstrate that they will meet the applicable technical requirements such as, for example, using equipment that has been appropriately "type approved" by the Commission, proposing to operate within the height and power limitations for the station sought, operating during the hours appropriate for the frequency sought and causing or receiving no more than the allowed amount of interference. This showing of technical qualifications has extremely important procedural ramifications. Although the Commission cannot normally deny a broadcast application without giving the applicant a hearing, the Commission may properly refuse even to consider an application if it fails to meet technical requirements. As a matter of practice, an application is not "filed" with the Commission; it is only "tendered" for filing and must first be "accepted" for filing even before the processing stage is reached. If an application, on its face, patently fails to meet certain technical minimum requirements, it will not even be "accepted" for filing, much less processed. For example, in AM radio the Commission has established a set of engineering "ground rules" which every applicant must meet. In FM and television allocations, the Commission has allocated specific frequencies to specific cities. If an AM application fails to meet the ground rules, or if an FM or TV applicant specifies a frequency other than one already assigned to the particular community involved, the Commission need not (and will not) accept these applications for filing. United States v. Storer Broadcasting Co. (1956); Ranger v. Federal Communications Commission (1961).

There is one caveat to this general rule. The Commission cannot refuse to accept an application failing to meet minimum technical requirements where the applicant makes a strong prima facie showing that because of its particular situation, the requirements should be waived. See Storer Broadcasting Co., supra. Thus, for example, where the Commission's rules did not permit AM applications for nighttime operation of local stations on "clear channels," an applicant which sought such operation argued that its application should be considered because it was a unique "good music" station which would directionalize its antenna to protect the clear channel station. The Commission's refusal even to accept the application for filing was reversed by the court of appeals on the grounds that the applicant had at least made a prima facie showing that the rule should be waived in its case, and the Commission was required to give the application "reflective consideration." WAIT Radio v. Federal Communications Commission (1969). However, such a holding is quite unusual. Absent special circumstances, an application which does not meet fundamental technical standards will not be processed.

(5) Programming

Contrary to a widely held misconception, the Commission never established, even in its pre-deregulatory period, official minimum norms or requirements for any programming category. Although frequently asked to set minimum norms, the Commission has consistently refused to do so, mainly on First Amendment grounds. Section 326 of the Act forbids the Commission to act as a "censor." Setting up required minimums would, in the Commission's view, be tantamount to censorship. See Hubbard Broadcasting, Inc. (1974); Report and Order, 66 FCC 2d 419, 428–29 (1977); National Black Media Coalition v. FCC (1978).

Despite the absence of specific programming minimums, the Commission had evolved a series of unofficial "guidelines" which, prior to 1981, were used as application processing criteria. These "guidelines" became the standard that most applicants for a new or renewed license in fact used. The "guideline" became a de facto quota. As part of its "deregulation" effort, the Commission in 1981 abandoned use of the "programming guidelines" for radio stations (AM or FM) and in 1984 abandoned them for television stations. Programming for radio and television stations is now governed simply by the marketplace, subject to the right of listeners to attack a station's performance at renewal time.

There is one exception. Pursuant to the Children's Television Act of 1990 (Public Law 101–437, 1990), the FCC must review applications for renewal of television licenses to consider the extent to which the licensee has complied with these standards and has served the educational and informational needs of children through its overall programming (47 U.S.C.A. § 303b). The Children's Television Act is discussed in greater detail later in this chapter.

b. *Processing the Application*

Section 307 of the Act provides that the Commission "shall grant to any applicant therefor" a license if the public convenience, interest or necessity will be served. Sections 307(a) and 309(d)(2) of the Act allow the Commission to grant an application making the proper showing without evidentiary hearing, but Section 309(e) states that if (a) a substantial and material question of fact is presented or (b) the Commission "for any reason" is unable to make a finding that the grant would be in the public interest, then the application must be designated for "full hearing" with the "burden of proof" upon the applicant. The key with respect to factual disputes is that they must be material and substantial. Factual ambiguity that would not be significant even if resolved does not require hearing. See Stone v. Federal Communications Commission (1972). The importance of the second condition is that the Commission may be required to hold a hearing even if there are no factual disputes, if there are policy or public interest questions that can only be resolved after public evidentiary hearing. See Citizens Committee to Save WEFM v. Federal Communications Commission (1973); Citizens Committee v. Federal Communications Commission (1970). However, instances of the latter type of hearing (i.e., where there are no substantial or material factual issues) are extremely rare.

c.   *Participation by Non-applicants in the Processing of Applications*

The broadcast application process is not merely a duet between the Commission and the applicant. Others may have a significant role in the process, even if they are not themselves applicants. Generally, non-applicant participants are either (1) other broadcast stations that may be affected by a grant of the application, or (2) representatives of the public who may be affected.

(1) Participation by Other Broadcast Stations

There are essentially two reasons why another broadcast station might be allowed to intervene in the application process:

(a) because a grant would itself act as a "modification" of the intervening station's license, thus requiring a hearing by statute; or

(b) because the intervening station might be a party economically "adversely aggrieved or affected" by a grant, thus being accorded intervenor's status.

An example of the first is the grant of the application to station A causing objectionable electrical interference (as defined in the FCC Rules) to station B. All AM stations have an area in which they are protected from interference. The normally protected contours of station B (as defined in the rules at the time of the grant to B) become part of B's license. Because Section 316(a) of the Act forbids a "modification" of B's license without a "public hearing," B is entitled to protest the grant to A and to be accorded a hearing on its protest. It should be noted, however, that the "modification" would occur only if the grant becomes effective during B's eight-year license term.

(2) Participation by the Public

Until the landmark decision by the United States Court of Appeals for the District of Columbia in Office of Communication of the United Church of Christ v. Federal Communications Commission (1966), the public played virtually no part in the licensing process. Standing to participate in that process was limited to persons who were "parties in interest," a classification limited by Commission practice and interpretation to other stations complaining of electrical interference or to those persons or stations claiming specific adverse economic injury. The interests of the listening public at large were to be represented by the Commission itself, which, by statute, was required to act only in the public interest.

United Church of Christ opened the Commission's forum to broader public participation. Rejecting the notion that only economic injury or electrical interference conferred participatory rights, and recognizing that the Commission may not always be able to reflect public sentiment as effectively as the persons actually affected, the court held that representatives of the public could participate in the licensing process upon a showing that a grant of the application sought would have a particular effect upon them. Any listener to a station, therefore, has potential standing to participate. However, the Commission can protect the orderly character of its proceeding by refusing to allow the public to participate en masse, and by requiring that they do so through representative groups. A citizen cannot gain entry merely by asserting a bare general listenership interest without alleging a specific injury to himself or herself. Unless injury in fact occurs to a person or a member of an organization which claims to speak in his or her name, the courts will refuse to grant standing to sue in court. American Legal Foundation v. FCC (1987).

Since United Church of Christ, citizens' groups have participated with respect to thousands of applications. Public interest law firms have been organized specializing in the representation of minority group interests in application proceedings. Women's groups have been effective in attacking applicants as being unresponsive to women as listeners and employees. Ethnic groups have been allowed to participate on the grounds that particular applicants did not evidence sufficient awareness of their needs.

The form that such participation ordinarily takes is the filing of a "Petition to Deny" the application. If the Petition raises a substantial or material question of fact or a policy issue which the Commission cannot resolve on the basis of the information in the application alone, the application will be designated for hearing. The burden of proceeding with the evidence on the issue or issues raised in the Petition will be placed by the Commission upon the party best suited to do so. The ultimate burden of proof, however, remains with the broadcast applicant as to the grant of its application for license.

d. Comparative Qualifications—The Need for Choice

For many years there were two situations where the Commission had to choose between competing applicants. The first involved applicants for a new frequency. The second involved an existing station seeking renewal of its license and a challenge by one or more competitors desiring to take the license away. In the late 1990's, Congress completely changed the long-standing approach to choosing between these competitors.

(1) The Non-renewal Situation

When faced with more than one applicant for the same license, how did the Commission choose? Until 1965, the criteria used to compare applicants were less than clear, and the relative weight accorded the criteria by the Commission was so inconsistently applied at times as to raise serious charges that the purported criteria were used merely to mask preconceived results. In 1965, to clarify and simplify the comparative process, the Commission set forth a new comparative licensing policy. Policy Statement on Comparative Broadcast Hearings, 1 FCC 2d 393 (1965). Asserting its primary objectives to be (a) the "best practicable service" to the public and (b) a maximum diffusion of control of the media of mass communications, the Commission indicated the material comparative criteria to be:

(i) *Diversification of Control of Mass Communications.* This became, in practice, the most important non-engineering criterion. All other things being equal (and even when all other things were not necessarily equal) the applicant who possessed no other broadcast interests was preferred to the one who had other commercial media interests in the same area. An applicant with significant holdings in other mass media was at a comparative disadvantage.

(ii) *Full–Time Participation in Station Operation by Owners and Local Residence of Applicants.* This factor had been considered to be of "substantial" importance because the Commission believed that an owner who participated in the day-to-day operations of the station, would be more sensitive to the needs of the community. But the importance of this criterion (familiarly known as the "integration" criterion) came to an end when the Court of Appeals (D.C. Cir.) in December 1993 declared the integration policy to be arbitrary and capricious (Bechtel v. FCC (1993)) thereby throwing the entire comparative process into serious disarray.

(iii) *Proposed Program Service.* The Commission did *not* ordinarily use as a comparative criterion the proposed program services of competing applicants. This seems counter-intuitive because programming is, from the public's point of view, the most important aspect of a broadcast applicant's proposal. Why did the Commission fail to consider it at all? The reason was the FCC's experience that applicants generally proposed similar program formats, and even if they differed, the "minor differences among applicants [was] apt to prove to be of no significance." 1 FCC 2d at 397. The Commission was also concerned that forcing it to compare different program formats would cast it in the role of censor, and involve subjective qualitative judgments of the type that it preferred not to make.

(iv) *Past Broadcast Record.* The Commission used an applicant's past broadcast record as a significant comparative factor only if the past record was either "unusually good or unusually poor." A past record that is "within the bounds of average performance [was] disregarded." 1 FCC 2d 398.

(v) *Efficient Use of the Frequency.* Where one or more competing applicants proposed an operation that, for one or more engineering reasons, would be more efficient, this fact was considered of significance in determining the preference.

(vi) *Other Factors.* The above framework did not exhaust the possibilities. Since the comparisons took place on a case-by-case basis, it would be impossible to list all situations which arose. However, it does indicate the nature of the pertinent criteria which the Commission considered. If an applicant desired consideration of another factor not specifically enumerated above, it had to make a special request that the FCC do so.

The entire FCC comparative hearing process came under sharp criticism as cumbersome, unnecessary, a fruitful ground for applicant deceit or dishonesty, unduly time consuming and expensive, and, on balance, indefensible because the process appeared to have little effect on the ultimate programming product in the real world. No matter how the licensee was chosen, most broadcast programming appeared disarmingly similar. What was the point, critics argued, in depending upon such criteria as local ownership and participation in management by owners when, in actuality, most owners (no matter how chosen) hire professional broadcasters to program and operate the station? Worse, the FCC had no effective way of insuring that its comparative criteria had any lasting meaning. Applicants only needed to operate stations one year after receiving their licenses and then they were perfectly free to sell them to the highest bidder. The new owners only had to meet the threshold qualifications. It was the lack of effective Commission follow-up control that led the court of appeals in Bechtel to ultimately declare the Commission's use of the integration policy improper. As a result competing applications that could not be settled were frozen.

The Commission was unable to devise a new comparative licensing process. Finally, Congress, in the 1997 Budget Bill, replaced comparative proceedings with an auction process. 47 U.S.C.A. § 309(j).

(2) The Renewal Situation

Choosing between an existing licensee and a new applicant presented an even more difficult problem. On the one hand, giving preference to the existing licensee would tend to freeze out newcomers. On the other, ignoring past performance would be unfair to a licensee who had spent considerable sums in building up its station, which might not be recovered if its license were to be denied. Moreover, such a policy might introduce an element of instability in the broadcast industry which ultimately would not serve the public interest. However, if credit is to be given for past performance, how much and in what way should it be given?

Essentially, what the Commission did was to apply the same criteria it used in new license cases with one additional criterion. An incumbent that had provided substantial service was given a preference known as renewal expectancy. The exact weight given to renewal expectancy varied, but it could not, by itself, be controlling. See Central Florida Enterprises, Inc. v. FCC (1982).

The tension underlying the comparative renewal problem reflected the conflict between the desire for stability in the broadcast industry, and the view that a broadcasting license is a limited privilege which must be periodically renewed. There is a significant public interest component in stability because unless licensees can be reasonably assured that their heavy investment will not be rendered valueless at the end of the license term; they might not make a long-term investment in public service programming. Rather, they will operate the station solely to maximize short-term profit. Yet, there is also a public interest benefit in insuring licensee responsibility through the veiled threat of loss of license in the event the broadcaster fails to fulfill its public service obligations.

During most of the Commission's regulatory history, the balance was weighed in favor of the latter consideration. Gradually, however, the extraordinarily lengthy and expensive proceedings characterizing license renewal challenges, the extremely limited number of successful challenges and the potential for mischief in challengers filing only for the purpose of being "paid off" made both Congress and the Commission less enamored of the license challenge procedure as a prophylactic device.

In the 1996 Telecommunications Act, Congress eliminated comparative renewals. Now the Commission will grant a renewal application whenever it finds the applicant has served the public interest, convenience and necessity (including providing service to children); has not committed serious violations of the Communications Act or Commission rules and regulations and; has not committed other violations of the Act or the FCC's rules and regulations that would constitute a pattern of abuse. The Commission is expressly prohibited from considering whether another applicant might better serve the public interest, convenience and necessity. If the FCC denies the renewal application, then other applicants will be permitted and the auction process discussed previously will be used to decide who gets the license. 47 U.S.C.A. § 309(k).

3.   Diversity of Media Ownership

Perhaps the major premise upon which the First Amendment is based is the societal necessity of a flourishing marketplace of ideas, with truth emerging not by governmental fiat but, rather, from the clash of many voices. Associated Press v. United States (1945). Where no government regulation is constitutionally permitted, the economic marketplace determines the number of voices to be heard. The government's role is limited to ensuring (through appropriate antitrust involvement and legislation) that the economic model succeeds. Where, as in broadcasting, government regulation is allowed, and where inherently it creates market monopolies, the question arises as to how the Commission should act to ensure hoped-for multiplicity, competition and diversity.

The Commission has historically responded to the problem by enacting rules which restrict persons or entities from acquiring excessive power through ownership of too many radio or television facilities. Congress (or the Commission) might, of course, have limited applicants to only one radio facility, either AM, FM or television, so that no one could own more than one station anywhere in the United States; neither has done so. Yet, the absence of any limitation posed the threat that broadcast economics might well follow the path of newspaper economics where a relatively small number of entities control a large number of daily newspapers throughout the country, and sometimes control all of the daily newspapers in a particular community. The Commission's rules attempt to strike a balance between these extremes, allowing multiple ownership of commercial media by a single entity in certain instances, and forbidding it in others. Over time the Commission and Congress have relaxed the rules allowing individual entities to own more and more stations. Non-commercial stations are exempt from the operation of these rules.

There are basically three types of broadcast media concentration rules: (a) those forbidding ownership of facilities in the same community or area (''duopoly''); (b) those limiting ownership of broadcast facilities by single entities no matter where the facilities are located (''multiple ownership''); and (c) those forbidding newspapers from owning television stations in the same community in which they publish ("cross ownership").

The duopoly rule originally limited licensees to 1 license in each class of service in each community. During the past twenty years, both Congress and the Commission have relaxed the stringency of the media concentration rules so as to allow common control of a larger number of stations than previously was the case. During the past two decades, the number of stations allowed under common control has increased dramatically. The clear reason for the relaxation is the increase in competing media (primarily cable) which has (a) siphoned audiences away from over-the-air traditional broadcasting and has put AM, FM and TV stations under increasing economic pressure, and (b) increased the total available pool of media voices. The Commission's stated purpose in deregulation is to allow the economic marketplace greater sway in ownership decisions and to improve competition by allowing broadcast combinations to become economically stronger and thus be in a better position to compete. Nevertheless, the continued existence of the media concentration rules testifies to the concern that no one group should control broadcasting stations to an unwarranted degree. Diversity still remains a Commission goal.

The current radio rules permit licensees in markets with 45 or more commercial radio stations to "own, operate, or control up to 8 stations, not more than 5 of which are in the same service." In markets with between 30 and 44 stations, the limit is seven stations, "not more than 4 of which are in the same service." In markets with between 15 and 29 stations, the limit is six stations, of which not more than four are in the same service. In markets with 14 or fewer stations, the limit is five stations, with not more than three in the same service, "except that a party may not own, operate, or control more than 50 percent of the stations in such market." Whether stations are considered to be in the same market is determined by the degree to which the stations' signals overlap. 47 C.F.R. § 73.3555.

For television, market is defined by the Neilsen Direct Market Areas ("DMAs"). Ownership of more than one television station in the same DMA is only permitted where there are "eight independently owned, full-power and operational television stations (commercial and noncommercial)" and "one of the stations is not among the top four-ranked stations in the market, based on audience share," or where the two stations, despite being in the same DMA, do not have overlapping Grade B contours (a measure of signal strength).

TV station owners can own: "up to six radio stations (any combination of AM or FM stations, to the extent permitted under our local radio ownership rules) in any market where at least 20 independent voices would remain post-merger; up to four radio stations (any combination of AM or FM stations, to the extent permitted under our local radio ownership rules) in any market where at least 10 independent voices would remain post-merger; and one radio station (AM or FM) notwithstanding the number of independent voices in the market." Parties permitted to own two TV and six radio stations under these rules, may own one TV station and seven stations instead. For the purpose of this rule, voices includes all commercial and noncommercial TV stations in the DMA in question, all commercial and noncommercial radio stations "licensed to, or with a reportable share in, the radio metro market where the TV station involved is located," and all newspapers published in the DMA with at least five percent circulation in the DMA.

The multiple ownership rules originally limited national ownership to seven AM stations, seven FM stations and seven TV stations. The current rules permit ownership of an unlimited number of radio and television stations. The only restriction is that the television stations owned by a single entity have a total audience reach of 35 percent of the country. The audience reach of a VHF station is the total available audience in the DMA in which it is located. For UHF stations the total audience available is divided by 2.

Until 1975, there was no prohibition against ownership of a broadcast station by a newspaper in the same community. Although the Commission acknowledged as early as 1944 that such ownership might lead, at least in certain circumstances, to a monopoly both in the economic and the informational senses, nevertheless, it was not persuaded that the feared results were inevitable nor that the problem could not be handled in ways other than outright prohibition. In 1975, though still finding no specific evidence of monopoly abuse, the Commission nevertheless concluded on policy grounds that the public interest would be best served, and the twin goals of economic competition and competition in the marketplace of ideas furthered, if future newspaper-broadcasting combinations were prohibited by rule. Therefore, it prohibited the ownership of either AM, FM, or TV stations by daily newspapers in communities over which the AM, FM or TV stations place a signal of a particular strength. See Second Report and Order, Docket No. 18110, 50 FCC 2d 1046 (1975). Existing combinations were almost all grandfathered with the proviso that they could not be sold as a unit to a third party. In 16 instances, the Commission actually ordered divestiture by newspaper-broadcaster owners. See FCC v. National Citizens Committee for Broadcasting, et al. (1978).

Pursuant to a provision in the 1996 Act directing the Commission to ''conduct a rulemaking proceeding to determine whether to retain, modify, or eliminate'' its broadcast concentration rules, in 2003 the FCC voted to modify several of these rules. First, the TV Duopoly Rule was changed to allow companies to own two stations in markets with five or more stations, but only one could be among the the top four in the ratings. In markets with 18 or more stations, a company could own three TV stations, but only one could be among the top four in the ratings.

In addition, the reach cap in the National TV Ownership limit was increased from 35 percent to

45 percent. Finally, the broadcast-newspaper and radio-tv cross-ownership rules were replaced by new cross-media limits. Under the new rules, no cross-ownership would be permitted in markets with three or fewer TV stations. In markets with between four and eight TV stations, combinations would be limited to either a daily newspaper, one TV station and up to 50 percent of the radio station limit for that market; or a daily newspaper and up to the radio station limit for that market; or two TV stations and up to the radio station limit for that market. In markets with 9 or more TV stations, there would be no cross-ownership limits.

The new rules proved extremely controversial, both in Congress and with the public. Congress passed a bill setting the national reach cap at 39 percent. Pub. L. No. 108–199, § 629, 118 Stat. 3, 99 (2004). Meanwhile, all of the rules were challenged by various groups, some seeking more limits and others seeking fewer or less restrictive ones. After rejecting the challenge to the national reach cap as moot due to the new law, the court of appeals affirmed some of the FCC actions while remanding others as not justified by reasoned decision making. Specifically, the court remanded the numerical limits chosen for cross-media concentration, the modifications to the local television rules permitting triopolies in some markets and duopolies in others, and its decision to retain existing numerical limits for local radio ownership. The rules were stayed pending the FCC's actions on remand. Judge Scirica, dissented in part, arguing that, given the deference owed a regulatory body's decision-making, the FCC had adequately justified the rules. He asserted that the court "applied a threshold that supplants the well-known principles of deference accorded to agency decision-making. In so doing, the Court has substituted its own policy judgment for that of the Federal Communications Commission and upset the ongoing review of broadcast media regulation mandated by Congress in the Telecommunications Act of 1996." He argued that the stay should have been lifted and the rules allowed to go into effect. Prometheus Radio Project v. Federal Communications Commission (2004).

In applying all these rules, one important determination is what constitutes ownership. The key issue for the Commission is determining what is the minimum level of ownership that carries with it the ability to influence station operation. This minimal level is referred to as a "cognizable interest." The complete ownership attribution rules are too complex to be detailed in this book. However, the basic minimums for a cognizable interest are five percent of voting stock or 20 percent for passive investors such as banks, insurance companies and investment companies. See Review of the Commission's Regulations Governing Attribution of Broadcast and Cable/MDS Interests (1999).

It should be recognized, of course, that joint or common ownership is only one method by which the number of potential broadcast voices can be limited. Diversity can be affected by other types of joint ventures between independently owned stations in

the same community such as, for example, cooperation between separately owned stations in terms of
advertising sales, joint use of technical facilities,
joint program formats and joint sales of commercial
time. The Commission has considered whether
these types of joint arrangements should be brought
under (or made subject to) the multiple ownership
rule caps but in 1992 rejected this approach. See
Revision of Radio Rules and Policies (1992). The
Commission now generally allows such activities, so
long as each licensee retains ultimate control of its
station. The Commission is content, in these circumstances, to allow the question of competition
(and, thus, program diversity) to be left to the
federal antitrust laws enforced by the Department
of Justice. The Commission did, however, place
restrictions on one type of joint venture, local "time
brokerage" arrangements. Time brokerage involves
the sale by a licensee of discreet units of time to a
"broker," who then supplies the programming to
fill that time and sells commercial spot announcements to run within that time unit. The profits
from the sale of these spot announcements go to the
broker so that, in a sense, he becomes a "mini-
licensee" for the time involved. The Commission
recognized that widespread and substantial time
brokerage agreements could adversely affect its
multiple ownership restrictions. Therefore, in order
to prevent the use of such agreements to circumvent its ownership limits, the rules provide that
where an individual owns (or has a cognizable interest) in one or more stations in a market, time

brokerage of more than 15% of the programming of any other station in that market will result in counting the brokered station toward the broker's permissible ownership limits, either with respect to local market totals or to national multiple ownership limits.

A separate diversity issue involves minority ownership of broadcast stations. The Commission developed several policies aimed at increasing minority ownership. The first of these was a licensing preference in the form of an "enhancement" feature in applying the "integration" criterion discussed earlier in this chapter. If two applicants, for example, proposed that all of their owners would actively participate in station operations, but all of the owners of one applicant were black, whereas the owners of its opponent were white, it would be appropriate for the Commission to "enhance" the participation weight of the black applicant because it would be likely that the black applicant might be more sensitive to the needs of the black residents in the area. The Commission applied a similar theory to women applicants to female ownership when comparing applicants who proposed that their owners would all work at the station.

A second policy allowed stations threatened with license revocation to sell their licenses to a minority applicant at a distress sale price. The distress sale policy permitted the challenged licensee to salvage something in return for both increasing minority ownership and saving the FCC the cost of a lengthy hearing.

Eventually, these policies came under sharp constitutional attack as being race- and gender-based distinctions violative of the equal protection and due process clauses of the Constitution. Two District of Columbia Circuit Court of Appeals cases (Shurberg Broadcasting, Inc. v. FCC (1989) and Winter Park Communications, Inc. v. FCC (1989)) considered the constitutionality of preferences based on minority status. Shurberg specifically struck down as unconstitutional the FCC's "minority distress sale" policy. Yet the same court (though a different panel) in Winter Park upheld the minority preference enhancement in FCC comparative cases. It was difficult to reconcile the reasoning of these minority enhancement cases decided the same year by different panels of the same court.

The issue was finally settled by a divided (5–4) Supreme Court in Metro Broadcasting, Inc. v. FCC (1990). Justice Brennan, writing for the majority in his last decision before retirement, stated that neither the minority comparative hearing preferences for minorities nor the minority distress sale policy was unconstitutional. Rather, they were "benign," "race-conscious" measures which served important governmental objectives within the power of Congress and therefore, they passed constitutional muster. The public interest in enhancing program diversity was an important and appropriate governmental objective and there is an empirical connection between program diversity and minority ownership. Race-neutral measures had been found by the FCC to be insufficient to produce adequate program diversity; more expansive methods have been rejected by the FCC. Thus, the FCC had properly chosen the least restrictive alternative.

The victory was, however, short lived. As noted earlier, the integration criterion was thrown out in Bechtel and comparative licensing proceedings have been eliminated. Furthermore, the Supreme Court, in Adarand Constructors, Inc. v. Pena (1995), appears to have undercut the basic holding of Metro. "[A]ll racial classifications . . . must be analyzed by a reviewing court under strict scrutiny. In other words, such classifications are constitutional only if they are narrowly tailored measures that further compelling government interests. To the extent that Metro Broadcasting is inconsistent with that holding, it is overruled."

A third approach to increasing minority ownership was to issue tax certificates, permitting a seller to defer payment of capital gains taxes, to owners selling their stations to minority-controlled groups. However, Congress terminated the tax-certificate program in 1995.

In 1969 the Commission began requiring all applicants to adopt and file affirmative action equal opportunity programs to ensure non-discrimination against minority groups such as Blacks, Native Americans and Spanish surnamed and women. See 47 C.F.R. § 73.2080. This obligated the applicant to take specific and affirmative action in recruiting, advancement, and training to ensure equality of opportunity. Report and Order, 18 FCC 2d 240

(1969). Stringent reporting requirements were imposed upon stations whose employment programs were in less than full compliance with the Rules. Bob Jones University, Inc. v. Connally (1973).

The Commission utilized "guidelines" to determine whether a station's employment profiles merit routine approval of their renewal applications. It continually monitored equal employment opportunity performance by requiring stations with five or more full-time employees to file yearly employment profiles. See FCC Public Notice, EEO Processing Guidelines, 45 Fed.Reg. 16335 (Feb. 13, 1980).

In 1998, the Circuit Court of Appeals for the District of Columbia held that the FCC's equal opportunity regulations were unconstitutional. Lutheran Church–Missouri Synod v. Federal Communications Commission. The court held that the FCC's asserted interest, "fostering diverse programming content," while important, was not a compelling interest. Turning to the question of whether the rules were narrowly tailored, the court found the FCC's justification of the rules was inherently contradictory. The FCC had held that the Lutheran Church's preference for Lutheran secretaries, receptionists, business managers and engineers, was not "connected to the espousal of religious philosophy over the air," while contending that applying affirmative action rules to these positions would enhance broadcast diversity. See 47 C.F.R. § 73.2080.

4. The Network Rules

The Commission, over the years, evolved a series of policies which had specific impact upon the material presented by a network affiliated broadcast station. Networks are, generally speaking, organizations which have been created for the purpose of producing and distributing programming to individual stations and also to act as advertising clearance centers for all network affiliated stations. Although networks can (and do) act as licensees of individual stations, the networks themselves are not licensed by the Commission and the Commission has no power directly to regulate their operations. However, the Commission can and does indirectly regulate the networks through its power over the licenses of individual stations. This regulation is apparent in the so-called "Network Rules" which prohibit any individual station from entering into contracts with networks which contain certain provisions that the Commission finds offensive to the public interest. 47 C.F.R. §§ 73.132 (AM radio), 73.232 (FM radio), and 73.658 (television) (1981). These prohibitions forbid network contract clauses that would prevent the licensee from broadcasting the programs of any other network, or that would prevent another station in the affiliate's area from broadcasting a network program if the affiliate declines to broadcast it. The rules also require that the television affiliate be granted the right to reject network programs that it believes unsatisfactory (§ 73.658(e)).

For many years the most important network rules were the "Prime Time Access Rule" (PTAR) and the financial interest and syndication rules (fin-syn). PTAR provided that television stations owned by or affiliated with a national television network in the 50 largest television markets could devote during the four hours of prime time (7–11 p.m. Eastern Time and Pacific Time and 6–10 p.m. Central Time and Mountain Time) no more than three hours to the presentation of programs from a national network, including programs that formerly had been presented on national networks. There were a few limited exceptions including programs designed for children, public affairs programs or documentary programs, special news programs and political broadcasts, regular network news broadcasts up to one-half hour when immediately adjacent to a full hour of locally produced news programming, and run-overs of sporting events and network broadcasts of national sports events or other programs of a special nature. The FCC, concluding that the three major networks no longer had dominant market power, repealed PTAR effective 1996. Review of Prime Time Access Rule (1995).

The financial interest and syndication rules, issued in 1970, placed significant restrictions on the ability of the then established television networks (ABC, CBS, and NBC) to (a) own television programming produced (or co-produced) by others and (b) engage in the business of "syndication" (the sale of programming exhibition rights to television stations). These restrictions were intended to limit network control of television programming generally and thereby encourage the development of independent program producers. Because of the networks' almost monopolistic power to control access to the nationwide television audience, it was feared that networks could dominate the production and distribution end of television simply by demanding ownership and syndication rights in programs produced by independents, using as a lever the networks' power to act as gatekeeper. Accordingly, the FCC adopted rules which effectively froze the networks out of the prime time entertainment program production business and out of the (even more lucrative) syndication business. This significant restriction of network power was allowed by the Court of Appeals for the Second Circuit as appropriate economic regulation in Mt. Mansfield Television, Inc. v. Federal Communication Commission (1971) and was incorporated into antitrust consent decrees entered into by the networks and the Department of Justice. The ensuing decades saw the growth of program-producing units independent of network control, based primarily in the Hollywood motion picture studios. Program syndication by the independent producers to non-network-owned stations grew. At the same time, however, the growth of non-network programming outlets (primarily cable systems and cable programming networks) and the advent of additional networks such as Fox, WB, UPN and Paxnet loosened the networks' power to act as gatekeeper to the national television audience (from 1970 to 1997 the three original major networks' share of the listening audience decreased from over 90% to less than 50%).

The networks bitterly fought to repeal the financial interest and syndication restrictions and in 1991, the Commission relaxed (although it did not repeal) these Rules. Report and Order, 6 FCC Rcd 3094, as modified at 7 FCC Rcd 345 (1991). The FCC's relaxation order proved unpersuasive to the Court of Appeals for the Seventh Circuit, which remanded the case for a fuller explanation as to why the FCC rejected certain of the networks' arguments and why its limited 1991 relaxation satisfied the Commission's goals of program and outlet diversity. Schurz Communications v. FCC (1992). The Commission thereupon relaxed these rules still further (Second Report and Order, 8 FCC Rcd 3282, reconsidered at 8 FCC Rcd 8270 (1993)), and scheduled them to sunset two years after the equivalent provisions were removed from the consent decrees. As a result the financial interest and syndication rules were eliminated in 1995.

The result of the Commission's relaxed restrictions was to allow the re-entry of the networks into the prime-time television entertainment programming production and syndication business, thus allowing the production and distribution arms of the industry to come into closer common control. Perhaps the best illustration of the effect of these rules and the changes in the media landscape during the period they were in effect was the Viacom purchase of CBS announced in 1999. Viacom was originally a programming library spun out of CBS in the early 1970s as a result of the fin-syn rules and the consent decrees. By 1999 it had become a media conglomerate with holdings that included 19 television stations, several cable networks, Blockbuster Video, Paramount Pictures, Simon & Shuster, and a half-interest in the UPN network.

C. FCC CONTROL OF BROADCAST CONTENT

Although the Commission's primary function is and has been the licensing of broadcast stations, it has been involved from its inception, and increasingly in the past three decades, with the supervision of broadcast content. Section 326 of the Act specifically forbids the Commission to "censor" material broadcast by a radio facility, and an overly broad reading of this restriction might make it appear that the Commission plays no part in the content of program material. Such is not the case; there are some areas in which, Section 326 notwithstanding, the Commission can and does control or influence program content. These areas include: (1) political broadcasting; (2) obscene, "indecent," and lottery programming; (3) "anti-payola" and "anti-plugola" statutes; (4) children's programming and (5) nebulous regulation by "raised eyebrow" in such areas as "family viewing time," drug lyrics and sexually stimulating radio programming.

1. Political Broadcasting

From the inception of broadcast legislation, Congress has recognized the enormous potential of radio as a political tool. A major concern is that a broadcast facility might improperly influence an election by affording only one candidate access to its audience. To prevent this possibility, Congress enacted what is now Section 315 of the Communications Act which provides that "If any licensee shall permit any person who is a legally qualified candidate for any public office to use a broadcasting station, he shall afford equal opportunities to all other such candidates for that office in the use of such broadcasting station," (47 U.S.C.A. § 315) subject to certain specific exceptions. Although clearly a statute which regulates program content, it has survived attacks on its constitutionality. See, e.g., Branch v. Federal Communications Commission (1987). The section, as amended, also provides that the rates charged each candidate must be equal and that during election campaigns candidates must be given the "lowest unit charge" that is offered by the station to commercial advertisers for comparable time. The concept of equality extends not only to rates but also to station business practices. Thus, for example, a station cannot require one candidate to pay by certified check while another is allowed to pay by regular check in the normal course of business. Alpha Broadcasting Corp. (1984). Although rarely invoked, there are civil and criminal penalties for willful and knowing violations of the statute.

The political broadcasting statute (when applicable) is quite precise and leaves virtually no room for broadcaster discretion except in the area of news and news event coverage. It operates with a type of mathematical certainty not usually found in broadcasting regulation. Nevertheless, despite Congress' attempt at clarity, Section 315 law is often misunderstood because of its ad hoc application. Over the years, the statute has accumulated by accretion layers of interpretative rulings to the point where its intricacies have become quite arcane.

a. *"Use"*

Although it is generally thought that the "equal opportunities" provision of Section 315 applies to all election broadcasts, in fact, the provision is limited only to those circumstances where the candidate himself or herself "uses" the program. Section 315 thus does not apply to a broadcast or advertisement on behalf of the candidate where the material is not considered a "use." This is a critical distinction. Unless the broadcast is a "use," Section 315 simply does not apply.

The Commission's interpretation of "use" has changed over the years. Originally, the Commission held that "use" did not encompass, for example, an appearance by a candidate on news programs where the appearance was dictated by the licensee's news judgment. Allen H. Blondy (1957). In 1959, however, the Commission radically departed from that concept, holding that a candidate's appearance (even on a news program) would be considered a "use" whenever his or her identity could reasonably be presumed to be known by the audience and where the appearance was of such magnitude to be considered an integral part of the program. Lar Daly, recon. den. (1959). Thus, a station staff person who was also a candidate could not appear at the station without invoking equal time obligations if his or her voice was distinctive or well known enough to be identifiable. See, e.g., National Urban Coalition (1970); Station WBAX (1969). This was true even where the appearance was not sought by the candidate so that, for example, when Ronald Reagan was a presidential candidate, stations that presented his 20–year-old movies during the political campaign incurred equal time obligations. Adrian Weiss Productions (1976).

In 1991, as part of a general recodification of its political broadcasting rules (Matter of Codification of the Commission's Political Programming Policies, (1991)) the Commission significantly narrowed its "use" interpretation so that a "use" would include only candidate appearances that were controlled, approved, or sponsored by the candidate (or the candidate's authorized committee) after the candidate became legally qualified. The introduction of the concept of candidate approval and/or control as an element in the definition meant, for example, that film actor Reagan's movies would not be considered a "use" after he became a candidate, unless he specifically approved or controlled the presentation of the program. Similarly, the decision by a licensee to include a candidate on its news program would not be considered a use unless the candidate approved or controlled that decision. After experimenting with the narrower definition, however, the Commission (in 1994) elected to return to its more expansive 1959–1991 definition of "use."

The above discussion also illustrates another aspect of the "use" doctrine: a candidate's appearance will be considered a "use" even if the candidate is appearing for a completely unrelated purpose and never mentions his or her candidacy. Letter to United Community Campaigns of America (1964). The classic example would be a station weatherperson, announcer or interview host who is also a candidate for local office. An appearance by any of them in their normal roles, in which they present the news or the weather, would nevertheless (assuming they can be identified) be considered a "use" entitling their opponent to equal time, even if they never mention their candidacy. See Newscaster Candidacy (1965); Station WBAX (1969); RKO General, Inc. (1970).

b. *Legally Qualified Candidates*

"Equal time" obligations come into play only upon "uses" followed by demands by "legally qualified candidates for public office." The determination of whether or not a user (or demander) is a legally qualified candidate for public office is made by reference to the law of the state in which the election is being held. Political Primer (1984). All elections are not for "public office." For example, the position of delegate to a party convention is not a "public office," even though the name of that person may appear on an election ballot. Russell H. Morgan (1976). Conversely, a candidate can be legally qualified even if his or her name is not on the ballot if such a person, under state law, is making a bona fide "write-in" campaign. Political Primer (1984). However, in order to be a legally qualified candidate the person must publicly announce his or her candidacy, even if everyone expects the person to be a candidate. Thus, an incumbent president, for example, cannot be presumed to be a candidate for reelection until such candidacy is announced. Until that time, appearances by the incumbent president would not be considered a "use" triggering equal time requirements. Id. at 1480. If a purported candidate is too young to serve even if elected, he or she could not demand equal time to respond to an opponent. Socialist Workers Party (1972). The question of whether a person is "legally qualified" can be quite complex, and the Commission will follow the laws of the particular state wherever possible. Committee for Mayor Bergin v. Station WATR–TV (1982). In cases of ambiguity, the Commission will be the ultimate arbiter of whether the person is a candidate. CBS, Inc. v. FCC (1981).

c.   *Exemptions From Equal Time Requirement*

The stringency of the "use" doctrine as it then was interpreted by the Commission (i.e., any "appearance" by a candidate was a "use") led Congress in 1959 to create certain specific exemptions to the "equal time" doctrine. Thus, the equal time doctrine is not applicable where the appearance by the candidate takes place on any:

(1) bona fide newscast,

(2) bona fide news interview,

(3) bona fide news documentary (if the appearance of the candidate is incidental to the presentation of the subject or subjects covered by the news documentary), or

(4) on-the-spot coverage of bona fide news events (including but not limited to political conventions and activities incidental thereto). 47 U.S.C.A. § 315(a).

The exemptions were enacted in 1959 to avoid the situation where an appearance by an incumbent at a routine affair such as a ribbon cutting ceremony or a greeting of visiting dignitaries on a newscast could trigger demands for equal time by all of his or her opponents. See Columbia Broadcasting System, Inc. (1959). It was believed that applying the "use" doctrine in all its rigor would, in practice, force stations to ignore such events in their news programming even though, in the exercise of their editorial judgment, they would otherwise have presented such material.

The first three exemptions, i.e., newscasts, news interviews and news documentaries are rather straightforward and have been further defined by extensive legislative history indicating their scope. Underlying them is the notion that such programs are essentially under the control of the station (and not the candidate) so that the candidate cannot misuse his or her appearance to gain an improper advantage. Indeed, the Commission considers such programs to be under the "control" of the station even if the newscasts, news interviews or portions thereof are created by persons other than station personnel; so long as the station retains the ultimate decision to run the program it is still in control. The inclusion of the concept "bona fide" in the exemption represents a restriction on the station. If the appearance on the news program is intended by the station to be aimed at favoring one candidate over another, the appearance would not be "bona fide" under the statute and thus would not be exempt.

The fourth exemption, however, "on-the-spot coverage of a bona fide news event" is less well defined in the legislative history and raises the question whether the definition of "bona fide" news event should be based upon the subjective determination of the broadcaster or upon an objective determination by the Commission. For example, two gubernatorial candidates have been invited by a local professional group to debate important issues. The debate is considered a "bona fide news event" by a local station which desires to carry it live as a matter of interest to its audience. Would the debate be an exempt program so that the station need not offer equal time to other candidates for the same office who are not invited to the debate? Similarly, if a station believed a presidential press conference to be a newsworthy item to be presented in its entirety, would the station's belief in the program's newsworthiness render it an exempt "bona fide news event?" The Commission first held in 1964 that the subjective judgment of the station was not dispositive and that the Commission would ultimately determine exemptions based on objective criteria such as whether the fact of candidacy was an integral part of the appearance or merely incidental thereto. Columbia Broadcasting System, Inc. (1964). The Commission later changed its mind. Now, at least with respect to debates and press conferences by candidates, it is the bona fide subjective judgment of the station which determines the exemption. If the station, in good faith, believes the debate or news conference to be newsworthy, it can cover these items without invoking the equal time rules for opposing candidates. Petitions of the Aspen Institute (1975). It can even sponsor the debate, so long as it does so without intending to benefit a particular candidate. Henry Geller (1983). This interpretation, however, has been limited to debates, press conferences and, on occasion, to speeches by incumbent officials on issues affecting the electorate. The Commission has been wary of extending the exemption much beyond these types of presentation. See King Broadcasting Co. (1991).

The Commission has also expanded its interpretation of "on-the-spot" coverage. Although "on-the-spot" coverage was originally interpreted to mean that the event had to be broadcast within 24 hours, the Commission subsequently relaxed this restriction and now holds that a delayed broadcast of "reasonably recent events" could be considered "on-the-spot" so long as the determination was made by the station in good faith. Henry Geller (1983).

d. *Necessity for Timely Demand*

Equal time rights, though available, can be lost through inactivity or delay. A candidate must make a request of a station for equal time within one week of the day of the first use giving rise to the right to equal opportunity in the use of the broadcast facility. 47 C.F.R. § 73.1940(e) (1981). If the person was not a candidate at the time of the first prior use, he is entitled to equal opportunity only with respect to uses made during the week prior to his announcement of his candidacy. Letter to Joseph H. Clark (1962).

There is no obligation on the part of the station to inform all other candidates, for purposes of equal opportunity, that a particular candidate is appearing on the station. It is assumed, and in essence required, that candidates will be vigilant on their own behalf. The only exception to this rule would be where the candidate—or user—is the licensee of the station involved. Under these circumstances, the Commission has held that the licensee is under an obligation to inform his opponent of the specific days that the licensee would be using the station for his candidacy. Letter to Emerson Stone, Jr. (1964). Absent such special circumstances, however, a licensee is under no obligation to inform candidates of uses by other candidates.

e. *Reasonable Access (Section 312(a)(7))*

Section 315 requires even-handedness, not access. Indeed, Section 315(a) specifically states that "No obligation is imposed under this subsection upon any licensee to allow the use of its station by any such [legally qualified] candidate." Technically, a station could avoid Section 315 entirely simply by refusing to allow any candidate to appear. In so doing it would violate other sections of the Communications Act, however. Thus, with respect to *federal* candidates, Section 312(a)(7) of the Act specifically includes, as a ground for revocation of license, "willful or repeated failure to allow reasonable access to or to permit purchase of reasonable amounts of time for the use of a broadcasting station by a legally qualified candidate for Federal elective office on behalf of his candidacy." Federal candidates, thus, have a clear statutory right of access. CBS, Inc. v. FCC (1981). Although state and local candidates are not specifically mentioned under the access provisions of Section 312(a), the Commission has interpreted the general "public interest" standard of Section 307 of the Act to forbid any station from simply refusing to allow political candidates to use the station's facility in any way simply to avoid equal time obligations. Some access must be given to certain state and local candidates, although the rules in this respect are imprecise.

What represents "reasonable access" for federal and state candidates has not been precisely defined—the concept necessarily varies with the circumstances. The Commission has set forth certain guidelines, however. If, for example, there are dozens of state or local candidates for state or local elective offices, the FCC has never required that every candidate for every office must be given access. A broadcast station is not a common carrier and access cannot be achieved on demand. A station can prune out election campaigns for minor offices and allocate time only for the major offices on the state and local level. This flexibility with respect to state offices arises because there is no specific requirement in the Act that all state or local candidates must be given access and the Commission has refused to create one. See Political Primer (1984); CBS, Inc. v. FCC, supra.

A station's discretion is much more limited with respect to federal offices. All federal candidates, under the strictures of the statute, must be given "reasonable access." Even here, however, the station retains some discretion to determine the manner of access. Even under Section 312, a station is not required to *sell* programming or advertising time to candidates. Stations can, and some do, take the position that they will sell no program time to candidates, but instead will meet their "access" obligations by giving candidates a reasonable amount of free time. Political Primer (1984).

The federal candidate "reasonable access" provisions of Section 312(a)(7) have created complex and vexing questions due to the inherent ambiguity of the concept "reasonable." What seems perfectly reasonable to a station manager trying to maximize profits seems quite unreasonable to a candidate hoping to limit campaign expenses. Although requested to adopt formal rules spelling out "reasonable access," the Commission has consistently refused to do so, instead relying on the "reasonable good faith judgments" of its licensees. The Commission has, however, adopted certain guidelines articulating the essence of "reasonable access." (See Matter of Codification of Commission's Political Programming Policies (1991)):

a) Reasonable access must be provided to legally qualified federal candidates through the gift or sale of time for their "uses" of the station.

b) Reasonable access must be provided at least during the 45 days before a general or special election. The question of whether access should be afforded before these periods or before a convention or non-primary caucus will be determined by the Commission on a case-by-case basis.

c) Both commercial and noncommercial stations must make program time available to legally qualified federal candidates during prime time and other time periods unless unusual circumstances exist that render it reasonable to deny access.

d) Commercial stations must make spot announcements available to federal candidates in prime time. The same rule applies to noncommercial stations that utilize spot time for underwriting announcements. Where a noncommercial station normally broadcasts spot promotional or public or public service announcements only, it generally need not make those spot times available to political candidates.

e) If a commercial station chooses to donate rather than sell time to candidates, it must make available to federal candidates free time of the various lengths, classes and periods that it makes available to commercial advertisers.

f) Noncommercial stations may not reject material submitted by candidates merely on the basis that it was originally prepared for broadcast on a commercial station.

g) A station may not use a denial of reasonable access as a means to censor or otherwise exercise control over the content of political material, e.g., by rejecting it for nonconformance with any of the station's suggested guidelines.

h) Licensees may not adopt a policy that flatly bans federal candidates from access to the types, lengths, and classes of time which they sell to commercial advertisers. Noncommercial educational stations must provide program time which conforms to normal parts of the station's broadcast schedule.

i) In providing reasonable access, stations may take into consideration their broader programming and business commitments, including the multiplicity of candidates in a particular race, the program disruption that will be caused by political advertising, and the amount of time already sold to a candidate in a particular race.

j) Broadcasters may ban the sale of political advertising to federal candidates during news programs; the public interest is served by preserving the journalistic integrity of the licensee in its news programming and does not reasonably hamper access of federal candidates to broadcast time.

k) Licensees may sell a "news-adjacency" class of time to candidates, provided that such a class is sold at rates no higher then the sale of such time to most-favored commercial advertisers.

Acting on a petition for reconsideration, the FCC modified the rules to require broadcasters to give consideration to requests for program lengths other than those sold to commercial advertisers. Broadcasters who deny one of these requests must provide legitimate justification for the denial. Codification of Commission's Political Programming Policies, recon. (1999). See also People for the American Way (1999).

One final note. "Reasonable access" (being included in a portion of the statute pertaining to license revocation) does *not* apply to cable systems since such systems are not primarily licensed by the FCC but rather by state or local governments.

f. *Lowest Unit Charge*

Prior to 1971, Congress required only that stations treat political candidates in ways comparable to commercial advertisers. No station or cable system could charge a political candidate, whether federal or state, a greater amount than was charged for a comparable announcement presented on behalf of a commercial advertiser. The obvious intent was to prevent stations or cable systems from taking advantage of the necessity for political candidates to obtain advertising time during election campaigns.

For most of the year, the comparability criteria still holds true. However, in 1971 Congress amended Section 315 to require that during a specific election period (45 days preceding the date of a primary election and 60 days preceding the date of a federal or special election) a station may charge a political candidate no more than the lowest unit charge for the same class and amount of time for the same period. 47 U.S.C.A. § 315(b) (Cum.Supp. 1976). The station must, during this period, treat the candidate in a manner comparable to its most favored commercial advertiser. The difference between "comparability" and "lowest unit charge" may be illustrated in this way: if a station has an advertiser willing to commit itself to purchasing an advertising schedule which will run an entire year, the station might be willing to give that advertiser a quantity discount so that instead of paying a normal rate of, for example, $10 per announcement, the advertiser need only pay $6 per announcement. Under the comparability standard in effect during most of the year, the station need only give political candidates the $6 rate if the candidate also agreed to purchase a schedule of announcements for the entire year. Because both are being treated in a comparable manner, the equality terms of the Act have been met. However, under the lowest unit charge concept, enforced during the 45– or 60–day period prior to a primary or general election, a station would be required to offer the $6 rate, even if the candidate bought only one announcement, because this would be the "lowest unit charge" being made for the time in question. In other words, lowest unit charge requires a station to give a political candidate a quantity discount even if the candidate does not purchase the same quantity as would be a commercial advertiser receiving the discount.

Even under the lowest unit rate the station still retains some flexibility. It may make distinctions between classes of time so that a candidate seeking, for instance, to purchase prime time advertisements to be run at a fixed time would be required to pay the lowest unit charge for such fixed prime time advertisements. Nevertheless, the lowest unit charge rule has given political candidates a significant price advantage in using broadcast facilities.

It must immediately be noted that the lowest unit rule, easily enough articulated in concept, has become increasingly complicated in actual operation, so much so that in a 1990 surprise FCC audit of major television stations, the Commission found that a majority of them violated the rule at one time or another during political campaigns. This revelation led to a series of suits by candidates in state courts seeking millions of dollars in rebates which, in turn, led the Commission ultimately to federally preempt the question of whether a station has violated the statute. Therefore, any candidate who now believes that a broadcast station has overcharged him or she is limited to seeking redress only at the

FCC, and the FCC has established procedural rules governing such complaints, including limited discovery rights for claimants and the provision of requirements for rebates, if such are necessary. See Exclusive Jurisdiction, etc., Declaratory Ruling, 6 FCC Rcd. 7511 (1991).

During the surprise political audit and the ensuing litigation the Commission recognized that at least some of the violations were due to:

(a) the complexity of the problem coupled with the lack of up-to-date Commission guidance; and

(b) continuing changes in the manner in which stations sell advertising, particularly through creation of myriad "packages" with bonuses, rebates, different time periods, and an increasing tendency to sell advertising time on a virtual auction basis to the highest bidder.

This led the Commission in 1991 to articulate a series of lowest unit charge guidelines: Matter of Codification of Commission's Political Programming Policies:

(i) Stations must disclose to candidates all classes of time, discount rates, and privileges afforded to commercial advertisers. Furthermore, stations are required to sell such time to candidates upon request.

(ii) Stations must continue to apply the "most-favored advertiser" standard to factors which affect the value of an advertisement, including (but not limited to) priorities against preemption.

(iii) Stations are permitted to establish their own reasonable classes of immediately preemptible time so long as some demonstrable benefit besides price or identity of the advertiser (such as preemption protection, scheduling flexibility, or guaranteed time-sensitive make goods) distinguishes each class. The licensee must adequately define each class, disclose it, and make it available to candidates.

(iv) Stations may establish their own reasonable classes of "preemptible spots with notice" time, so long as they adequately define such classes, disclose them, and make them available to candidates.

(v) Stations may treat non-preemptible and fixed position as distinct classes of time, provided that they articulate clearly the differences between such classes, fully disclose them, and make them available to candidates.

(vi) Stations may not create a premium-priced, candidates-only class of time.

(vii) Stations must calculate rebates and provide them to candidates promptly.

(viii) All rates found in all package plans sold to commercial advertisers must be included in the station's calculating of the lowest unit rate.

(ix) Stations need not include in lowest unit charge calculations noncash merchandise incentives (e.g., vacation trips). Bonus spots, however, must still be calculated into lowest unit charge.

(x) Stations may not increase their rates during an election period unless the rate increase is an ordinary business practice.

(xi) Stations must provide make goods prior to the election if the station has provided a time-sensitive make good to any commercial advertiser during the year preceding the 45–or 60–day election period. All make-good spots must be included in the calculation of the lowest unit charge.

(xii) While there is no obligation to sell spots in a particular program to candidates, once a station has decided that it will sell spots in a program, daypart, or time period, it cannot inflate the price of the spot sold to a candidate beyond the minimum necessary to clear by claiming that all "preemptible time" is sold out.

The mere listing of these guidelines suggests the complexities inherent in the lowest unit rate rule.

It must also be emphasized that the lowest unit charge criterion is applicable only to a "use" by a legally qualified candidate. Appearances by spokespersons on behalf of a particular candidate would not fall within the lowest unit charge concept because, as discussed above, it would not involve an appearance by the candidate and thus technically would not be a "use." Political Primer (1984).

The Bipartisan Campaign Reform Act of 2002 (BCRA), Public Law No. 107–155 amended Section 315(b) to deny a federal candidate who makes a direct reference to an opponent in an advertisement entitlement to lowest unit rate unless the advertise-

ment contains a statement identifying the candidate
and a declaration that the candidate approved the
advertisement.

g.   *Censorship*

Section 315(a) specifically provides that no licensee can have any "power of censorship over the
material broadcast under the provisions of this section." A legally qualified candidate for public office
is free to say anything, whether or not it relates to
the candidacy, and whether or not the material is
scandalous or in any other manner unsuitable for
broadcast. The obvious intent behind this subsection is to allow candidates to use radio or television
time free from the fetters of any other person or
entity. As a quid pro quo for such freedom, the
Supreme Court has held that no station can be sued
for libel or slander arising from such use by a
candidate, nor can it be acted against in any manner by a private person or by the government.
Farmers Educational and Cooperative Union v.
WDAY, Inc. (1959). This immunity from suit is, the
Court declared, constitutionally required to insure
free speech by candidates. The "no censorship"
provision is so stringently interpreted that it would
be considered improper for a station to request that
a candidate provide it with a copy of the candidate's
speech or other materials prior to broadcast, the
Commission holding that such a condition might
inhibit the candidate in his or her use of the facility.
Western Connecticut Broadcasting Co. (1973).

There is one caveat to the "no censorship" clause. Although there has been no direct adjudicated case on the point, the Commission's staff has concluded in a memorandum to Congress that the prohibition against censorship would not apply to the broadcast of obscene material forbidden by the criminal code. Legislation to this effect has been introduced into both Houses of Congress, but not yet adopted. Even without legislation, it is likely that the Commission would take this position if an actual case came before it since otherwise it would be requiring a broadcaster to violate the criminal law in order to comply with Section 315. See Political Primer (1984).

If, however, the material in question is not explicitly prohibited by statute, then it must be aired, even if the FCC finds that doing so is against the public interest. For example, in 1994 the Commission concluded that stations should be permitted to limit ads for a Congressional candidate containing graphic representations of aborted fetuses to hours when children were least likely to be in the audience. The FCC held that although the ads were not indecent, they could be psychologically damaging to children and therefore, should be channeled to the same hours as indecent material. (Indecency and channeling are discussed later in this chapter).

The FCC's ruling was struck down on appeal. Becker v. FCC (1996). The court found that the ruling violated sections 312(a)(7) and 315. Channeling the ads to those times when children were least likely to be in the audience would necessarily conflict with the candidate's right under section 312(a)(7) of access to the time periods with the greatest audience potential. It would also prevent a candidate from exercising equal opportunity rights whenever an opponent aired ads during other times of day.

The ruling also conflicted with the "no censorship" provision of section 315. It gave licensees too much discretion to limit ads based on content. In addition, it would cause self censorship as candidates would be loath to include material that would cause ads to be channeled.

In response to the Commission's public interest argument, the court noted there was no evidence Congress intended to subordinate the specific rights granted candidates to the general public interest standard. Rather, the court found that those rights override the programming discretion otherwise allowed by the Act.

It must be stressed that the "no censorship" provision applies only to a use by a candidate. It does not apply to a use by a spokesman on behalf of a candidate, and it did not apply to appearances by non-candidates under the Fairness Doctrine when the Commission was still applying that doctrine.

h.   *The "Zapple Doctrine"*

Although the "equal time" rule applies only to appearances by candidates, the Commission has created what has been termed a "quasi-equal opportunity doctrine," which relates specifically to appearances by spokespersons for candidates. Because appearances by such spokespersons on behalf of candidate A are not "uses," they do not vest any "equal time" rights in A's legally qualified opponents. However, under the "Quasi–Equal Opportunities Doctrine" (known as the "Zapple Doctrine"), when a station sells time to supporters or spokespersons of a candidate who urge the candidate's election, discuss the campaign issues or criticize an opponent, the licensee must afford comparable time to the spokesperson for an opponent. Letter to Nicholas Zapple (1970). If the first group of spokespersons purchases time, then the opposing group can also purchase time if it wishes to respond. If the first group is given free time, then the second group must also be given free time. The Zapple Doctrine is, in essence, a type of hybrid between the "Equal Time Doctrine" and what was known as the "Fairness Doctrine." But although it contains elements of "Equal Time," there are, nevertheless, important distinctions. The Zapple Doctrine does not apply to all parties and all candidates. A station may choose not to provide "fringe candidates or minor parties" with broadcast time under Zapple. First Report, Docket No. 19260, 36 FCC 2d 40 (1972). The Zapple Doctrine does not apply outside of campaign periods. In addition, the Equal Opportunities Doctrine is mutually exclusive with the Zapple Doctrine. If a legally qualified candidate appears in the broadcast with his supporters, then the broadcast is a use under the Equal Time Doctrine and the Zapple Doctrine does not apply.

2. The "Fairness Doctrine"

Perhaps nothing better illustrates the deregulatory thrust of recent Commissions than its repudiation of what was one of the fundamental pillars of broadcast regulation: The Fairness Doctrine.

The Fairness Doctrine arose out of a series of FCC rulings which for over two decades were thought to have been codified by Congress in its 1959 Amendments to Section 315(a) of the Communications Act. P.L. 86–274, 73 Stat. 557. The 1959 amendments refer to the obligation of a broadcaster "to operate in the public interest and to afford reasonable opportunity for the discussion of conflicting views on issues of public importance." For over two decades, this language was construed to be legislative shorthand which enacted into positive law a dual licensee obligation: (a) to devote a reasonable amount of broadcast time to the discussion of controversial issues, and (b) to do so fairly, i.e., to afford reasonable opportunity for the presentation of opposing view-points. That interpretation was upheld by the Supreme Court. Red Lion Broadcasting Co. v. Federal Communications Commission (1969). See also 47 C.F.R. § 73.1910.

The entire "Fairness Doctrine" area was thrown into confusion by a 1986 United States Court of Appeals decision, Telecommunications Research and Action Center (TRAC) v. FCC (1986), in which the court held that the Fairness Doctrine was not, in fact, codified in the 1959 amendments. The court held that, rather than being a statutory obligation, the Fairness Doctrine was the Commission's creation and its enforcement was left by Congress to the Commission, which was free either to apply the doctrine or eliminate it.

The confusion was compounded when, in response to a court mandate, Meredith Corp. v. FCC (1987), that the Commission specifically consider the constitutionality of the Doctrine, the FCC overturned decades of practice to hold that, in its present view, the Fairness Doctrine "contravenes the First Amendment and thereby disserves the public interest." In re Syracuse Peace Council, Memorandum Opinion and Order (1987) at paragraph 98. The Commission reasoned that the Fairness Doctrine both chills speech and is not narrowly tailored to achieve a substantial or compelling government interest. It relied upon the growth of the electronic media which, in its view, removed the "scarcity" rationale of Red Lion. The Commission acknowledged that there still exists "allocational scarcity;" there are still more applicants for stations than spectrum space to accommodate them. However, the Commission concluded that this allocational scarcity could not alone justify controls upon program content, with their "chilling effect" on editorial discretion. In the Commission's view, enforcement of the Doctrine acted to eliminate rather than foster coverage of controversial issues. Because of the increasing multiplicity of media the Commission concluded that the free marketplace would better insure a diversity of opinion than would rules imposed by the federal government. The FCC's decision repealing the Fairness Doctrine was upheld by the courts as an action within the Commission's discretionary authority. See Syracuse Peace Council v. FCC (1989); Arkansas AFL–CIO v. FCC (1993).

The elimination of the Doctrine has led some to argue that the "public interest" standard is now devoid of substantive meaning. The Commission, however, took great pains in its Fairness Doctrine decision, and its Order on Reconsideration (Syracuse Peace Council (1988)) to separate the question of the desirability of the Fairness Doctrine from the issue of licensee responsibility under the "public interest" standard of the Act. The "public interest" standard requires that licensees broadcast programming in response to public issues in the community and failure to do so can raise serious questions at renewal time. The formal Fairness Doctrine may be outdated but the public interest obligations of broadcast licensees (which gave it life) still remains in force.

In this context (i.e., the general "public interest" standard), the charge is often made that a particular news program is "slanted" or "biased." Here, the Commission has held that direct intervention into the thought processes of broadcast newspersons could well have an extremely "chilling effect" in an area explicitly protected by the First Amendment. Absent some direct, extrinsic evidence of deliberate news slanting, the Commission will not entertain complaints concerning the "fairness" of news presentations. Hunger in America (1969); Central Intelligence Agency (1985).

a.   *Political Editorializing*

The Commission's Rules (47 C.F.R. § 73.1930 (1981)) contained special provisions relating to editorializing by licensees. These rules provided that where a licensee in an editorial either endorsed or opposed a legally qualified candidate, the licensee had to transmit to the other candidates within 24 hours notification of the date and time of the editorial, a script or a tape and an offer of reasonable opportunity for the candidate or his spokesperson to respond. Where such editorials were broadcast within 72 hours of the election, the licensee was required to transmit the material sufficiently far in advance of the broadcast to enable candidates to have a reasonable opportunity to present a reply. This obligation only arose with respect to endorsements of candidates. It did not apply to editorials on issues not involving candidates such as, for example, municipal bond issues and referenda.

b.   *Personal Attack Rule*

The Personal Attack Rule (47 C.F.R. § 73.1920) was born as an aspect of the Fairness Doctrine. It related to the right of a person attacked by a broadcast licensee to gain access to the broadcast facility to defend himself or herself. The Personal Attack Rule was quite precise and specific. It held that when, during the presentation of views on a controversial issue of public importance, an attack was made upon the honesty, character, integrity or like personal qualities of an identified person or group, the licensee was required to, within a reasonable time and in no event later than one week after the attack, transmit to the person or group attacked (1) notification of the date, time and identification of the broadcast; (2) a script or tape of the attack; and (3) an offer of a reasonable opportunity to respond over the licensee's facilities. The rule did not apply to:

1. attacks on foreign groups or foreign public figures;

2. personal attacks made by legally qualified candidates, their authorized spokesmen, or persons associated with them; and

3. bona fide newscasts, bona fide news interviews or on-the-spot coverage of bona fide news events.

The rule only applied to a personal attack broadcast during the presentation of views on a controversial issue of public importance. Galloway v. FCC (1985). A person attacked at some other time had no redress from the Commission but had to look to the law of defamation for remedy. Straus Communications, Inc. v. Federal Communications Commission (1976). Moreover, the attack had to be as to the person's honesty, character, integrity or like personal qualities if the rule is to be invoked. An attack, for example, upon a person alleging that a person's ideas are "stupid" would not be considered a personal attack for the purposes of the rule. Mrs. Frank Diesz (1971). The complainant had to show that the person or group attacked was identified with sufficient specificity that the listening or viewing public would have been able to discern the specific person or group. Fairness in Media (M.M.B. 1985). If the Personal Attack Rule applied, the person attacked had an absolute right to appear in his or her own defense. The station had no discretion to require that the defense be made by another person.

Paradoxically, the Commission did not overturn the Personal Attack and Political Editorial Rules in its 1987 repudiation of the Fairness Doctrine. Therefore, RTNDA, which had filed a petition for repeal of the rules in 1980, filed a petition for expedited ruling, contending that because these rules are really only an aspect of the Fairness Doctrine, there would seem to be little logic in continuing the rules. The Commission continued to take no action. Eventually, in 1996 RTNDA filed a petition for writ of mandamus. The court denied the petition, giving the FCC six months to make significant progress toward possible repeal or modification. The Commission then announced a 2–2 split on the issue. After still another petition by RTNDA, the court ordered a formal vote. The court further ordered those Commissioners voting against repeal or substantial modification to supply a statement of their reasons. Again the vote was 2–2 (Chairman Kennard not participating) with all those voting issuing formal statements.

RTNDA appealed. Because the deadlocked vote effectively continued the rules, the court treated the joint statement of the two voting against repeal as the opinion of the agency. The court found the joint statement provided inadequate justification for the rules because it assumed their underlying validity and did not specifically state why the same arguments that mandated repeal of the Fairness Doctrine were not equally persuasive here. However, because it was possible that there were valid reasons and that the statement simply failed to articulate them, the court remanded the case to the FCC with orders to further explain its failure to repeal or substantially modify them. Radio–Television News Directors Association and National Association of Broadcasters v. FCC (1999).

Less than 2 months before the 2000 Presidential Election, the FCC voted, 3–2, to suspend the rules for 60 days for the purpose of compiling a better record on which to review the rules. The Commission directed broadcasters to present evidence of their claim that there would be more editorializing in the absence of the political editorial rule. Broadcasters were also instructed to collect information "regarding complaints concerning personal attacks that are received while the rule is suspended, and to compare the number and nature of the complaints made during those 60 days to a comparable period while the rule was in effect."

One week later, the court of appeals ordered the FCC to repeal the personal attack and political editorial rules, holding that the Commission had failed within a reasonable period of time to provide a justification for retaining them. The court rejected the FCC's argument that because the rules were suspended for 60 days the issue was moot.

The court did note that this was not a decision on whether the public interest was served by the rules. Thus, the Commission was free to institute "a new rule-making proceeding to determine whether, consistent with constitutional constraints, the public interest requires the public attack and political editorial rules." Radio Television News Directors Association v. Federal Communications Commission (2000).

3.   Obscenity, and Indecency

Although not contained in the Communications Act of 1934, the Criminal Code of the United States (18 U.S.C.A. § 1464) contains a specific prohibition against broadcast stations presenting any material which is "obscene," "indecent," or "profane." Rarely invoked, the "obscenity" section of the statute has been held constitutional because obscenity is not protected by the First Amendment. Illinois Citizens Committee for Broadcasting v. Federal Communications Commission (1974).

The standard used by courts with respect to "obscenity" on radio or television is that followed in the normal "obscenity" case, i.e., whether the material taken as a whole is patently offensive and appeals to an average person's prurient interest without serious literary, artistic, political, or scientific value when considered in connection with contemporary community standards. Miller v. California (1973). In practice, the courts have applied a more expansive concept of prurience to broadcasting than that applied to other forms of media. But there are few reported cases and the outlines of such standards for broadcasting have not yet been fully delineated. The courts have approved Commission prohibition of explicitly sexual programming where, during daytime hours, listeners freely discussed their sexual practices in a normal "disc jockey" format readily accessible to children. See Illinois Citizens Committee v. Federal Communications Commission, supra. Beyond this, the line between protected programming and "obscenity" is far from clear. In recent years, the Commission has evidenced a reluctance to become involved in obscenity determinations. While recognizing its concurrent jurisdiction to enforce federal anti-obscenity statutes, it has nevertheless determined to leave to local prosecutors the responsibility of identifying and prosecuting violators of such statutes. Video 44 (1986).

Not so with respect to "indecency." The "indecency" standard as it relates to broadcasting has also been upheld as a constitutionally proper exercise (under certain circumstances) of the state's police power. FCC v. Pacifica Foundation (1978). Significantly, the Supreme Court has allowed the Commission to give the concept of "indecency" a broader definition than that of "obscenity." Material that is "patently offensive," and either "sexual" or "excretory" may, if broadcast during times when children are presumed to be in the audience, be punishable even if not "obscene." The Pacifica Foundation case is instructive because the Court had previously defined the concept of "indecency" to be coextensive with "obscenity" if presented in books and films. Pacifica is an excellent example of the court applying different statutory and constitutional standards to broadcasting, primarily because of broadcasters' ease of access to children and the difficulty of parental supervision.

For almost a decade after Pacifica, the Commission, in practice, limited its definition of "indecency" to the specific "seven dirty words" at issue in that case. Between 1975 and 1987 no broadcasts were found actionable under this narrow interpretation. In 1987, however, the FCC gave notice that in the future it would apply the indecency standard more broadly and take action if such material was broadcast at a time of day when there is "reasonable risk" that children were in the audience. Unfortunately, the Commission gave no guidelines as to what would be considered "reasonable risk" and it warned broadcasters that adult programming after 10 p.m. (which it heretofore had suggested was safe) might not, in fact, be safe. See New Indecency Enforcement Standards To Be Applied to All Broadcast and Amateur Radio Licenses, 2 FCC Rcd. 2726 (1987). Such ambivalence invited a court test, which came immediately and which resulted in a remand by the court to the Commission. Although the appellate court rejected an attack on the Commission's definition of "indecency" on grounds of vagueness and overbreadth, nevertheless, it vacated action against two post–10 p.m. broadcasts on the grounds that the Commission was constitutionally required to create a "reasonable safe harbor" during which programming which might be indecent with respect to children could nevertheless be broadcast to adults. The court mandated the Commission to develop a precisely defined "safe harbor" after compiling an appropriate factual hearing record on which to do so. See Action for Children's Television v. FCC (1988).

Before the Commission could begin these "safe harbor" hearings, Congress intervened and passed a rider to an appropriations bill requiring the Commission to promulgate regulations to enforce the indecency provisions of the Criminal Code on a 24–hour–per–day basis. (Public Law No. 100–459, § 608, 102 Stat. 2228 (1988). Concluding that Congress had left it no discretion, the Commission thereupon promulgated a rule prohibiting all broadcasts of indecent material and enacting no safe harbor.

On appeal, the court rejected the Commission's approach, holding that there had to be some type of safe harbor for adults. Action for Children's Television v. FCC (1991). Congress then included provisions in the Public Telecommunications Act of 1992 requiring the Commission to set the safe harbor as midnight to 6 a.m. Public broadcast stations going off the air by midnight were given a safe harbor of 10 p.m. to midnight. Initially, these rules were also struck down by the court of appeals on the grounds that the Commission had once again failed to provide adequate evidence that the rules were a proper accommodation between the various competing interests. Action for Children's Television v. FCC (1993).

However, a petition for rehearing en banc was granted and the decision reversed. The majority found that the rules served two compelling government interests, protecting children from broadcast indecency and support for parental supervision of children. The court also found that the rules were narrowly tailored to serve that interest, because there are substantially fewer children in the audience late at night, while at the same time there are substantial number of adults up at that time. In addition, adults have other ways to access indecent material.

The court did, however, strike down one part of the rules. There was no reason related to the government's compelling interests that justified different safe harbors for noncommercial stations that ceased broadcasting at midnight. If any station could broadcast indecency starting at 10 p.m., then all stations should be permitted to do so. Thus, the safe harbor for all stations is now 10 p.m. to 6 a.m.

The dissent would have struck down the rules as unconstitutional for two primary reasons. First, the government's two compelling interests are contradictory. By protecting all children against broadcast indecency, the government is not supporting parental supervision by those parents who wish their children exposed to at least some indecent material. Second, because the definition of indecent is not sufficiently specific and decisions are made on a case-by-case analysis, the rules have a significant chilling effect. Action for Children's Television v. Federal Communications Commission (1995).

Throughout these proceedings the FCC continued to fine stations for presenting indecent material during daylight hours when it can be legally presumed that there is a reasonable risk that children will be in the audience. See Evergreen Media Corp. (1991).

By 2004, the Commission was starting to take a much more aggressive approach to enforcing the indecency rules. It issued a warning that it might consider license revocation in an especially egregious case, while changing its policy of counting any program containing indecent material as a single violation to one where separate indecent utterances within a single program could each constitute a separate violation. Infinity Broadcasting Operations, Inc. (WKRK–FM) (2003). When Janet Jackson's breast was briefly exposed during the 2004 Super Bowl Halftime Show, public pressure led both the Commission and Congress to take additional steps in that direction. Legislation was introduced in both the Senate and the House which would increase the maximum fines from $32,500 per violation to as much as $500,000 per violation, permit fines to be levied against the individuals uttering the indecent speech as opposed to just the licensees, allow revocation of licenses for repeated indecency violations and extend the rules to cable and satellite television and radio. However, it was 2006 before the Broadcast Indecency Enforcement Act was finally passed and signed into law. The Act raised the maximum fine to $325,000 (a tenfold increase), but it did not extend the indecency regulations from broadcasting to other media.

Meanwhile, the Commission, in addition to fining CBS $550,000 for the Super Bowl half-time show, Complaints Concerning the February 1, 2004, Broadcast of the Super Bowl XXXVIII Halftime Show (2004), issued a series of record fines against various group owners airing such shows as "The Howard Stern Show," "Bubba the Love Sponge," and "Mancow Morning Madness." Clear Channel Communications, the largest group owner responded by cancelling "Bubba the Love Sponge," dropping "The Howard Stern Show" from the six Clear Channel stations that carried it and reaching a $1.75 million consent decree with the FCC covering all outstanding indecency complaints. Clear Channel also agreed to an extensive compliance plan to prevent future airing of indecent material. Commissioner Copps dissented arguing that the Commission did not have a full record of Clear Channels violations and that until it did, the Commission should not eliminate the possibility of license revocation should the record warrant it. Clear Channel Communications (2004).

Viacom, which produces and syndicates "The Howard Stern Show," filed appeals with the Commission regarding the various findings against its stations, including the Super Bowl fine. The Commission rejected these appeals in 2006. Meanwhile in late 2004, Howard Stern announced that he had signed a five-year, $500 million deal with Sirius Radio, a satellite radio service. He moved to Sirius in 2006, after his Viacom deal expired. Stern stated that his motivation for leaving was to remove himself from the FCC's "censorship."

The Commission also changed its policy regarding isolated and fleeting uses of expletives. At the 2003 Golden Globe Awards, U2 lead singer Bono, upon learning he had won an award, responded "This is really, really, fucking brilliant. Really, really great." Numerous complaints were filed against NBC , which broadcast the awards show. The Enforcement Bureau, relying on earlier Commission decisions held that this was not indecent. The Commission reversed and found the phrase not only inherently indecent, but profane. Responding to NBC's argument that the "F–Word" had not been used as a sexual reference, but rather "as an intensifier," the Commission held that the ' "F–Word" is one of the most vulgar, graphic and explicit descriptions of sexual activity in the English language. Its use invariably invokes a coarse sexual image.' However, NBC was not fined on the grounds that there had been no prior notice of the changed FCC position. Complaints Against Various Broadcast Licensees Regarding Their Airing of the "Golden Globe Awards" Program (2004).

This led to a number of complaints regarding the Veteran's Day 2004 airing of "Saving Private Ryan" on ABC. The FCC held that it was not indecent, establishing an exception to the general rule that the F–Word is inherently indecent and profane. The rule does not apply when "the use is essential to the nature of an artistic or educational work or informing viewers on a matter of public importance." Complaints Against Various Television Licensees Regarding their Broadcast on November 11, 2004 of the ABC Television Network Presentation of the film "Saving Private Ryan" (2005).

In early 2006, the FCC issued another series of indecency rulings. The most significant was the decision to add "shit" to the list of inherently indecent words that can only be used under the exception established in Saving Private Ryan. An airing of the Scorsese documentary "The Blues: Godfathers and Sons" was found indecent because use of the "S–Word" was not essential to the nature of the work. At the same time the FCC rejected adding various other words including dick, ass, bitch and piss to the list of inherently indecent words. Complaints Regarding Various Television Broadcasts between February 2, 2002 and March 8, 2005 (2006). These rulings present a problem for broadcasters who must predict in advance which words are inherently indecent and whether the FCC will find the use of certain words essential to the nature of the work broadcast.

The Commission also changed its policy of fining all stations that aired an indecent program outside the safe-harbor time period to one of only fining those stations that were identified in a viewer or listener complaint. Complaints Against Various Television Licensees Concerning Their December

31, 2004 Broadcast of the Program "Without A Trace" (2006). Note that all these actions took place prior to the passage of the Broadcast Indecency Enforcement Act.

4. Children's Programming

As television became increasingly pervasive in the American home, various public interest groups, most notably Action for Children's Television (ACT), began to voice their concern over its influence on children. These concerns centered around three specific areas: too many commercials in children's programming, too few educational programs for children and violent programming.

For years, despite numerous petitions from public interest groups, with the exception of commercial limits applied to all programs that were eliminated in 1981, the Commission had resisted issuing specific requirements in these areas. Eventually Congress addressed the first two concerns in the Children's Television Act of 1990. The Act imposed strict limits on commercials in children's television programs: 12 minutes per hour on weekdays and 10.5 minutes on weekends.

The Act also requires the FCC to include service to children as a factor in television license renewal decisions. Initially, the Commission chose not to impose any minimal programming requirement, but did require renewal applicants to detail their service to children. When a report to the House Telecommunications Subcommittee indicated that broadcasters were listing programs such as "The Jetsons,' The Flintstones' and 'Yo Yogi!" as programs designed to meet children's educational needs, pressure was brought on the FCC to strengthen its requirements.

The Commission responded by imposing a minimum requirement of three hours per week of regularly scheduled "core" educational programming. This programming must be aired between 7 a.m. and 10 p.m. In addition, the FCC narrowed the definition of core educational programming. To qualify, programming must "be specifically designed to meet the educational and informational needs of children ages 16 and under and have educating and informing children as a significant purpose." Broadcasters must also provide on-air identification at the beginning of these programs. Children's Television Programming (1996).

With the advent of digital television, supra, questions arose as to how to apply the guidelines to broadcasters transmitting multiple SDTV channels. Should the 3–hour minimum apply separately to each SDTV channel? Should it matter whether these channels were free or pay? In early 2005, the FCC addressed these and other related questions. Digital broadcasters will be required "to air at least ½ hour of core educational children's programming for every increment of 1 to 28 hours of free video programming provided in addition to the main program stream." This additional children's core programming does not have to be aired on the same programming stream. Thus, it could be aired on the main programming stream or another secondary stream. No more than 50 percent of the additional core programming can be a repeat of the initial three hours of core programming and pay programming is exempt from the new requirements.

The FCC also changed its definition of commercial matter subject to the time limits of the CTA "to include promotions of television programs or video programming services other than children's educational and informational programming." Children's Television Obligations Of Digital Television Broadcasters (2004).

Some critics had long demanded government control over the depiction of violent events on television, but until 1996 neither the Commission nor Congress had ever enacted such legislation. The Department of Justice had extended waivers of the antitrust laws to allow networks to cooperate in voluntary joint efforts to control violence, but the critics deemed those efforts unsatisfactory.

As part of the Telecommunications Act of 1996, Congress mandated the inclusion of a computer chip (the V-chip) that will allow parents to program televisions to block shows based on content ratings carried in the shows. The Act also directed the FCC to establish an advisory committee to set up guidelines for content ratings unless within one year video programming distributors adopted voluntary rating rules acceptable to the Commission and agreed to transmit these ratings.

Initially, broadcasters and other video programmers threatened to challenge the V-chip requirements on First Amendment grounds. The argument was that the V-chip would have a chilling effect on programmers causing them to avoid content that would cause shows to be blocked in large numbers of homes. In addition, they contended that the chip would not achieve its purpose because of logistical issues, including the impossibility of consistent ratings for hundreds of thousands of hours of programming, the difficulty of devising a ratings system complex enough to be useful for children of different ages and parents with differing ideas of what is suitable content for children, yet simple enough for parents to use, and the problem of designing a device that parents can program but children can't bypass.

After further consideration, program distributors opted to propose an age-based system similar to the MPAA ratings used for movies. The proposal drew widespread criticism for its lack of specific information on violence, nudity and language. In response the system was modified to include some of this information.

The ratings appear on-screen for the first 15 seconds of each show. They are also carried in the television signal in a form that can be read by the V-chip. The ratings, which are used for all television programming except news, sports and unedited MPAA rated movies on premium cable channels, are as follows:

For programs designed solely for children:

TV-Y (All Children—*This program is designed to be appropriate for all children*). Whether animated or live-action, the themes and elements in this program are specifically designed for a very young audience, including children from ages 2–6. This program is not expected to frighten younger children.

TV-Y7 (Directed to Older Children—*This program is designed for children age 7 and above*). It may be more appropriate for children who have acquired the developmental skills needed to distinguish between make-believe and reality. Themes and elements in this program may include mild fantasy or comedic violence, or may frighten children under the age of 7. Therefore, parents may wish to consider the suitability of this program for their very young children. Note: For those programs where fantasy violence may be more intense or more combative than other programs in this category, such programs will be designated **TV-Y7–FV**.

For programs designed for the entire audience, the general categories are:

TV-G (General Audience—*Most parents would find this program suitable for all ages*). Although this rating does not signify a program designed specifically for children, most parents may let younger children watch this program unattended. It contains little or no violence, no strong language and little or no sexual dialogue or situations.

TV-PG (Parental Guidance Suggested—*This program contains material that parents may find unsuitable for younger children*). Many parents may want to watch it with their younger children. The theme itself may call for parental guidance and/or the program contains one or more of the following: moderate violence (V), some sexual situations (S), infrequent coarse language (L), or some suggestive dialogue (D).

TV-14 (Parents Strongly Cautioned—*This program contains some material that many parents would find unsuitable for children under 14 years of age*). Parents are strongly urged to exercise greater care in monitoring this program and are cautioned against letting children under the age of 14 watch unattended. This program contains one or more of the following: intense violence (V), intense sexual situations (S), strong coarse language (L), or intensely suggestive dialogue (D).

TV-MA (Mature Audience Only—*This program is specifically designed to be viewed by adults and therefore may be unsuitable for children under 17*). This program contains one or more of the following: graphic violence (V), explicit sexual activity (S), or crude indecent language (L).

Adoption of the new guidelines was not unanimous. NBC chose to use age-based ratings only and Black Entertainment Television does not use any ratings at all. Nevertheless, the FCC approved the voluntary system, eliminating the need to set up an advisory committee and mandate a specific ratings system. Implementation of Section 551 of the Tele-communications Act of 1996 (1998). In 2005 NBC started using the more detailed rating system.

5.   Lotteries

The federal criminal code generally prohibits any station from broadcasting any information concerning a lottery. 18 U.S.C.A. § 1304. Section 73.1211 of the Commission's rules essentially follows this criminal code section. A lottery is any game or contest which contains the elements of prize, chance and "consideration." These elements are construed in terms of a type of federal common law of lotteries followed by the Federal Communications Commission, the Post Office Department and the Department of Justice. See Federal Communications Commission v. American Broadcasting Co. (1954). This area of the law can become quite complex particularly in determining whether "consideration" is present. The federal common law of "consideration" means a monetary or other detriment to the participant in the contest rather than merely a benefit to the contest operator. For example, the requirement of the listener mailing in a post card to a station would not be considered "consideration," even though the station may thereby "benefit" by obtaining a list of members of its audience or by the contest enlarging the station's audience. Federal Communications Commission v. American Broadcasting Co., supra; cf. Caples Co. v. Federal Communications Commission (1957).

Until recently there were three exceptions to the general lottery ban. The Supreme Court decision in Greater New Orleans Broadcasting Association, Inc. v. United States (1999), infra, has now expanded them. A station is allowed to broadcast any information about a state authorized lottery so long as the station is located in a state which has its own official lottery. It can also broadcast advertisements of lotteries conducted by non-profit organizations or by commercial organizations using lotteries as an ancillary promotional activity. 18 U.S.C.A. § 1307, 47 C.F.R. § 73.1211(c)(1). Additionally, a station may broadcast information concerning a fishing contest if such contest is not conducted for profit. 18 U.S.C.A. § 1305; 47 C.F.R. § 73.1211(c)(2).

The "state-authorized lottery" exception raises an interesting dilemma: A station in a state which does not allow state lotteries cannot broadcast commercials for a legal lottery run by an adjacent state, while a station in the adjacent state can broadcast lottery information into the state that has no legal lottery. This situation was addressed in United States v. Edge Broadcasting Co. (1993), which involved a North Carolina station that wished to carry advertisements for the Virginia state lottery.

Both the district and appellate courts found the statute unconstitutional as applied. The Supreme Court reversed. Applying the Central Hudson test, the Court rejected the lower courts' finding that the regulation did not advance the government's interest in supporting each state's right to implement its own policy with regard to lotteries. The Court's analysis focused on whether the statute in general advanced the government's interest, whereas the lower courts had focused on the statute as applied to Edge. The Court argued that the question of the statute's application to Edge was more properly addressed in assessing whether or not there was a reasonable fit between the regulation and the governmental interest.

Here the Court held that despite the fact that the vast majority of Edge's listeners were in Virginia and that its North Carolina listeners had access to all kinds of Virginia media carrying advertisements for the Virginia lottery, there was a reasonable fit. The ban still reduced the amount of lottery advertising to which the station's North Carolina listeners were exposed.

In dissent, Justice Stevens argued that the lottery advertising restriction was "a ban on speech imposed for the purpose of manipulating public behavior." As such its effect on Edge's First Amendment rights was disproportionate to the federal government's "asserted interest in protecting the antilottery policies of nonlottery States."

However, in Greater New Orleans Broadcasting Association, Inc. v. United States (1999), the Court unanimously struck down the application of § 1304, supra, to advertising for Louisiana casinos on Louisiana broadcast stations. Relying on Rubin and 44 Liquormart, the Court focused on the numerous exemptions to the rule, especially the exemption for casinos owned by Indian tribes. Given the exemptions, there was no reasonable fit between the regulation and the government's asserted interests, "reducing the social costs associated with 'gambling' or 'casino gambling,' and assisting States that 'restrict gambling' or 'prohibit casino gambling' within their own borders."

6. Contests

Both Congress and the Commission have adopted standards of conduct governing broadcast contests. Section 73.1216 of the Rules mandates that a station must fully and accurately disclose the material terms of any contest which the station presents and the contest must be conducted in the manner advertised. The material terms include, inter alia, entry qualifications, eligibility restrictions, deadline dates, prize information, basis for valuation of prizes and tie-breaking procedures.

Section 509 of the Communications Act provides that, in contests of "intellectual knowledge, intellectual skill or chance," it is illegal to supply any contestant with any special or secret assistance, to persuade or intimidate a contestant from refraining from using his knowledge or skill or to engage in any prearrangement or predetermination of the outcome.

7. Sponsorship Identification Rules: "Anti–payola" and "Anti–plugola" Requirements

Congress and the Commission have expressed concern that the airwaves not be used by "hidden persuaders." Although most sponsors purchase time specifically to identify themselves and/or their products, there are occasions when persons wish to use programming time anonymously to further their own purposes. Such use can occur in a number of ways. Record promoters may offer money to disc jockeys to induce them to play their records ("payola") or to advertise certain activities ("plugola") without the public being aware that such material is being broadcast for pay. Other examples include broadcasting paid political matter or material concerning controversial issues without identifying the person or group presenting the material.

Because it is believed important that the audience be aware of the person paying the piper, Section 508 of the Communications Act and Section 73.1212 of the Commission's Rules stipulate that any person who pays or receives money or other valuable consideration for including any material as part of programming to be broadcast over a station must report that transaction to the licensee or licensees over whose facilities the program is aired. In turn, under Section 317 of the Act and Section 73.1212 of the Rules, the licensee is required to identify over the air, clearly and concisely, the person making the payment, and the fact that payment was made.

The sponsorship identification rules have caused some particular anomalies in the public broadcasting field where commercial sponsorship, per se, is prohibited, while identification of "sponsors" is required by Section 317 of the Act. The Commission has resolved this anomaly by holding that a public broadcaster is required to identify the name of a donor, and may even refer to the donor's product or service, but may not "promote" the product or service in the sense of urging viewers to purchase it. See Educational Broadcasting Stations (Promotional Announcements) (1982); Educational Broadcasting Stations (1984). Admittedly, the line between "identifying" and "promoting" becomes rather thin. The Commission has recently become more active in policing the sponsor identification rules with respect to public broadcast stations and has fined a number of them for engaging in what clearly is "commercial" promotional matter rather than merely identification of public broadcast benefactors.

Section 73.1212(d) of the Rules also requires that if any material or service is given to a station as an inducement to use such material or service in the broadcast of political matters or during the discussion of controversial issues of public importance, an announcement must be made indicating the material or service that was received by the station and identifying the person or entity which provided that material or service.

The advent of personal video recorders such as TIVO, that make it much easier to skip or delete commercials has led advertisers to seek other ways to reach viewers, including having their products featured within shows. Although product placement had been common in movies for a long time, its use in broadcast programming had always been limited by the payola rules. The sudden increase in broadcast product placement raised some questions as to whether the rules were always being followed. At the same time a public outcry had arisen over the use of video news releases, especially sponsored prepackaged news stories. Responding to these concerns, the FCC issued a new Payola Fact Sheet that included both the rules on Payola and instructions on how to file a complaint with the F.C.C. Http://www.fcc.gov/cgb/consumerfacts/PayolaRules.html.

Meanwhile, an investigation by New York State Attorney General, Elliot Spitzer resulted in Sony BMG Music Entertainment paying a $10 million fine in 2005 as part of a negotiated agreement. Sony admitted some of its employees had bribed radio stations to increase the play of songs by various Sony artists. In 2006 Spitzer filed a lawsuit against Entercom alleging that various Entercom stations had accepted payments to play certain songs.

8. Public Broadcasting

There is one striking exception to the general rule that American broadcasting follows the marketplace wherever possible. The exception is the growth and development of what has come to be known as "Public Broadcasting," i.e., a wide-ranging coalition of nonprofit (both private and governmental) broadcast stations operated by state governments, private and state colleges, private nonprofit organizations, religious groups, etc. The single unifying factor in this diverse group (other than their non-profit status) is their mission which is, in large part, to broadcast material which would *not* ordinarily be demanded by the commercial marketplace. These stations are, in effect, programmed for specialized audiences. They were created precisely to fill the lacunae inevitably left by mass market tastes.

That such a system exists is due to the foresight of the Congressmen and Commissioners who specifically fought for and ultimately adopted a policy of reserving from the commercial allocation system certain frequencies (both radio and television) specifically to be used by noncommercial entities for "educational" uses. Although at first limited to educational licensees (colleges, high schools, state university systems, etc.) these were later joined by other types of nonprofit licensees. The public broadcasting base evolved beyond televised classrooms and sunrise semesters to a whole range of cultural programming, including operas, literary presentations, concerts, "how to" shows, plays, nature documentaries and ultimately into the diverse public broadcasting network known as PBS.

The basic Public Broadcasting structure is quite simple: stations operating on the frequencies reserved for noncommercial use must be licensed only to nonprofit entities and cannot broadcast "commercials" promoting or advertising goods and services. The stations are to be supported not through the purchase of specific portions of time by commercial entities in return for advertising the goods and services of those entities, but instead, by:

(a) public funding through donations by private individuals and businesses;

(b) public funding through government sources; and

(c) sale of programming and related materials to the public (such as, for example, the sale of the cassettes of the popular "Civil War" series).

Although the line between "identification of donations by commercial businesses" and "the promotion of goods and services by commercial announcements" can become very blurred, nevertheless, the difference between commercial broadcasting stations and public broadcasting stations is usually readily apparent to viewers.

Aside from the reservation of operating frequencies for noncommercial use, the principal federal governmental role in Public Broadcasting is twofold:

a.   Through the Department of Commerce, the Federal Government has established a matching grant program (not subject to judicial review) under which the Federal Government will give matching grants (up to 75%) to noncommercial stations for the purpose of purchasing equipment and for other capital costs; and

b.   Making available, through the Corporation for Public Broadcasting, significant funds to public stations and networks for the production and distribution of programming to be presented on public broadcasting stations.

The Corporation for Public Broadcasting is a private, nonstock corporation chartered by the federal government, all of whose Board of Directors are appointed by the President. The Corporation, however, is not a government agency in the same sense as the FCC or FTC. It receives its funding through government grants and then proceeds to carry out its own grant programs as would any other private foundation or endowment. It operates under the rules established in its enabling statute (47 U.S.C.A. §§ 396–399B) which requires, inter alia, that grants shall be made available "with strict adherence to objectivity and balance in all programs or series of programs of a controversial nature" (47 U.S.C.A. § 396(g)(1)(A). The FCC has no jurisdiction or authority to enforce the statutory rules governing the Corporation, however. Nor does any member of the public have the power to do so; the Public Broadcasting Act creating the Corporation did not confer a private right of action upon any private group or individual. See Network Project v. Corporation for Public Broadcasting (1977). The only governmental body overseeing the Corporation's work is Congress which, of course, has the power to revise or amend the Corporation's enabling statute.

The statutory provision concerning the need for "objectivity and balance" and a corresponding statutory provision (47 U.S.C.A. § 399) that no public broadcasting station may support or oppose any candidate for public office, illustrates the tension between the need for government funding on the one hand and the First Amendment on the other. Ordinarily, he who pays the piper calls the tune. However, the First Amendment's prohibition against government regulation of the media places severe restrictions on the government-payor. Where does illegal government action end and appropriate government oversight of public funding begin? This vexing question comes up in many guises (such as, for example in the National Endowments for the Arts and Humanities) and it arose in the Public Broadcasting field in Section 399 of the Communications Act. As originally drafted, Section 399 prohibited public broadcasting stations from engaging in "editorializing" or in supporting or opposing any candidate for public office. The prohibition against "editorializing" was attacked on First Amendment grounds and struck down as unconstitutional by the Supreme Court in FCC v. League of Women Voters of California (1984). The Court, by a 5–4 margin, held that the broad ban on editorializing by stations merely because they receive Corporation for Public Broadcasting funds was a content-based restriction going beyond anything necessary to protect against the risk of undue governmental interference into public affairs.

Interestingly, however, the prohibition against endorsing (as distinct from editorializing in favor of) candidates for public office still stands; it was not specifically at issue in the League of Women Voters case. Furthermore, a strong dissent by Justice (now Chief Justice) Rehnquist argued that stations which take government funding can legitimately be required to conform to the restrictions placed by Congress upon that funding, even with respect to editorializing, a position which, although not in the majority in 1984, nevertheless ultimately became the law with respect to federal funding for family planning clinics as regards their abortion counseling. See Rust v. Sullivan (1991).

A somewhat different question was presented when a state-owned public broadcaster excluded an independent candidate from a station-sponsored debate. The candidate sued, claiming a constitutional right to be included. The Supreme Court held that the debate was a non-public forum and as such, subject to some constitutional requirements. "To be consistent with the First Amendment, the exclusion of a speaker from a nonpublic forum must not be based on the speaker's viewpoint and must otherwise be reasonable in light of the purpose of the property." In this case, there was extensive evidence that the candidate was not excluded because of his viewpoint but because he was not considered a viable candidate by the station, other media or the public. Arkansas Educational Television Commission v. Forbes (1998).

It must be recognized, of course, that in one sense Congress has the ultimate power of censorship. It can cut off CPB funding completely or at least reduce it significantly. Just such an attack on CPB funding was recently mounted by some who argued that in times of budget deficits there is simply no warrant to fund public broadcast programming rather than other more pressing governmental needs. The attempt was defeated by the full Congress, a significant demonstration that public funding of public broadcasting programming is indeed popular. The visionaries who saw a public need and desire for some nonmarket-driven programming appear to have been vindicated.

CHAPTER XI

CABLE AND NEW TECHNOLOGIES

A. TELEVISION BY CABLE

CATV (cable television) arose because of inherent limitations in commercial television. Television is merely the wireless transmission of visual and aural material over the air. Because of its physical characteristics, the distance that the television signal can travel over the air is limited. This fact, together with the Commission's television allocation policy whereby only a limited number of frequencies were assigned to designated cities throughout the country, posed significant reception problems for many residents of outlying areas, or areas on the fringe of larger cities. The problem was exacerbated by the fact that even some of the larger cities to which frequencies were assigned were only assigned three VHF channels, and some only two; thus there were large areas of the country that could receive no more than two or, at most, three signals. Because television signals only travel a line-of-sight path, there were some communities located in mountainous terrain that could not even obtain adequate reception from the two or three stations that they theoretically should have been able to receive over the air.

The solution to the problem for many of these communities was to erect extremely tall receiving towers at the highest point in the area to pick up the off-the-air signals and then retransmit the signals over wires run from the tower to various homes (subscribers). Typically, the home subscriber would pay a one-time installation fee for the wiring and a monthly fee for the service.

Although the original CATV systems were intended mainly to fill in the blanks within stations' normal coverage areas, it soon became apparent that CATV could also bring in service from distant cities which, under the Commission's allocation plan, were never intended to render service to that particular cable community. Thus, for example, a city such as Kingston, New York, located 90 miles from New York City, was never intended by the Commission to receive off-the-air service from the New York City television stations; the Commission intended Kingston to be served by the closer Albany, New York, facilities. However, cable television could bring in all of the New York stations, an obvious benefit to the residents of Kingston, but also a possible economic detriment to the Albany station, which could have its "natural audience" in Kingston fragmented. Moreover, CATV system operators could offer other communications services, including programming services such as sports events and feature films. This latter capability caused many to begin referring to CATV as "cable television," implying that the new service was much more than merely a community antenna.

Cable television also posed legal problems:

(a) Was cable television subject to FCC jurisdiction? It was not in existence when the Communications Act was passed, and might be considered merely a receiving rather than a transmitting unit, thus not "broadcasting."

(b) If the Commission did have jurisdiction, did the federal government preempt the field of regulation so that state or local governmental bodies were deprived of jurisdiction over such systems? This question was particularly important since cable television systems required local construction of wire lines and thus had a significant effect on the local citizenry;

(c) If jurisdiction was to be shared between a federal and local agency, how should the power to regulate cable be allocated?

(d) How was the Commission to reconcile the new technology of cable and its potential for carrying distant signals over the entire country with the existing Commission policy of station allocation?

(e) How did cable television comport with the copyright laws?

1. Jurisdiction

a. History

At first, the Commission refused to take jurisdiction over cable on the grounds that its power to do so was in question and that it did not feel the impact of cable television at the time was sufficient to invoke discretionary jurisdiction. Frontier Broadcasting Co. v. Collier (1958). In 1966, the Commission changed course and adopted the first general federal regulation of cable systems, asserting that some overall comprehensive federal regulation was necessary to meet the Commission's responsibility to promote, maintain, and supervise an effective television service throughout the country. Second Report and Order, 2 FCC 2d 725 (1966). The Commission's power to assert jurisdiction under its general grant of power from Congress and in the absence of specific legislation concerning cable television was affirmed by the Supreme Court in United States v. Southwestern Cable Co. (1968). The Commission's jurisdiction was limited, however, "to that reasonably ancillary to the effective performance of the Commission's various responsibilities for the regulation of television broadcasting."

Some clarification of what the Court meant by reasonably ancillary came in United States v. Midwest Video Corp. (1972) when, by a 5–4 vote, the Court upheld regulations that required specified cable systems to originate local programming. However, the Chief Justice (who voted with the majority) took pains to point out that in making such a requirement the Commission appeared to be reaching the limits of its authority under the Communications Act. Actually, the Commission had voluntarily stepped back from its position during the course of the Midwest litigation. It suspended the mandatory program origination rule and never reinstated it.

The Chief Justice's remarks were prophetic. The mandatory program origination rules appear to have been the high water mark of Commission cable regulation. Not long thereafter, the court of appeals struck down Commission rules restricting the ability of cablevision systems to present certain feature films and sports programs, holding that such regulation was beyond the power of the Commission because it was not "reasonably ancillary" to the Commission's long-term regulatory goals and responsibilities. Home Box Office, Inc. v. FCC (1977). Then in 1979, the Supreme Court struck down the Commission's rules requiring cablevision systems to offer separate channels for public, educational and government use ("PEG channels"), as well as at least one channel available on a lease basis for commercial use ("leased access channels"), on the grounds that these provisions also went beyond the Commission's regulatory powers. FCC v. Midwest Video Corp. (Midwest Video II) (1979).

In cable, unlike in broadcasting, the Commission accepted a bifurcated jurisdictional scheme that also allowed state and local authorities regulatory authority over cable. Under this scheme state or local authorities issued the franchise or license for the specific cable operator, imposing whatever obligations they thought necessary. For example, access channel requirements, similar to those held beyond the Commission's jurisdiction in Midwest Video II, were common in franchising agreements. The franchise agreements were, however, subject to certain minimal FCC limitations, such as a ceiling of 5% of gross revenues on franchise fees.

By the early 1980s, the jurisdictional scheme was becoming increasingly controversial. Cable operators felt that some franchising authorities were making excessive demands. Of even greater concern was the question of renewal. With no renewal standards or guidelines and no specific requirement of renewal expectancy, cable operators were worried about what would happen when initial franchise agreements expired.

Meanwhile, the FCC was becoming more aggressive in asserting its jurisdiction at the expense of the state and local authorities. For example, the Commission preempted rate regulation of premium cable services (pay services such as HBO). The preemption of franchising requirements for SMATV was seen as a foreshadowing of even more preemption in the cable area. See New York State Commission on Cable Television v. FCC (1984).

Then in 1984, the FCC received strong support for its authority to preempt state and local regulation of cable in Capital Cities Cable, Inc. v. Crisp (1984) (application of Oklahoma ban on alcoholic beverage advertising to out-of-state signals carried on Oklahoma cable systems held preempted by FCC signal carriage regulations). Further limitations on state and municipal franchising authority seemed inevitable.

b. *The Cable Communications Policy Act of 1984*

Cable operators, represented by the National Cable Television Association (NCTA), and state and local authorities, represented by the National League of Cities (NLC), sought legislative relief. Eventually a compromise bill was drafted and, in late 1984, enacted into law as the Cable Communications Policy Act of 1984 (P.L. 98–549, 47 U.S.C.A. § 151 et seq.).

The 1984 Cable Act created Title VI of the Communications Act, 47 U.S.C.A. §§ 521–559, setting explicit rules for cable that clearly delineated the jurisdictional division between the FCC and state and local authorities. Franchising authority still rested with state and local authorities. In addition, they were given explicit authority to require PEG channels. In contrast, leased access channels were mandated by the Act itself, with the number of leased access channels dependent on the overall number of channels provided by the cable system. Franchise authorities could not, however, regulate cable as a common carrier, nor could they require specific video programming services. Specific guidelines for franchise renewal were set out, giving extensive protection to the incumbent franchisee. There were also guidelines for franchise modifications that permitted an operator to appeal the denial of requests for modification.

c. *The Cable Television Consumer Protection and Competition Act of 1992*

Cable flourished under this new regulatory structure. By 1992, cable service was available to 96 percent of the nation's homes. Approximately 60 percent subscribed to cable. However, consumer complaints regarding both rates and service had also increased dramatically. Responding to these complaints, Congress passed the Cable Television Consumer Protection and Competition Act of 1992. P.L.102–385, 47 U.S.C.A. § 151 et seq.

Whereas the 1984 Cable Act could be viewed as cable-friendly, the 1992 Cable Act was anything but. It required rate regulation for the vast majority of cable systems, imposed several measures designed to improve the competitive position of broadcast television stations, and directed the FCC to develop mandatory customer service standards for cable systems. It also gave the FCC greater authority to oversee state and local regulation.

The new scheme proved unsuccessful in reducing consumer complaints, especially with regard to cable rates. Four years later, in the 1996 Telecommunications Act, Congress reversed course and opened cable to competition, by allowing phone companies to obtain cable franchises for the first time, while reducing the scope of rate regulation

2. Cable System Ownership

At the heart of all cable regulation is the government's ability to choose who will be permitted to offer cable television service. As previously noted, this is subject to a bifurcated jurisdictional scheme. State and local authorities award cable franchises subject to federal limitations. These limitations include concentration rules and restrictions on the demands franchising authorities can make on franchisees. For example, franchising authorities are not permitted to establish requirements for video programming or other information services. (47 U.S.C.A. § 544). Both initial franchising proceedings (47 U.S.C.A. § 541) and renewal (47 U.S.C.A. § 546) proceedings must conform to procedures set out in the Communications Act.

Finally, the Communications Act imposes some requirements of its own. For example, § 612 requires each cable system with 36 or more channels to set aside a percentage of its channels for commercial lease. The percentage depends on the total number of channels available on the system (See 47 U.S.C.A. § 541).

a. *Franchising*

Among the more common provisions in cable franchise agreements are requirements that the franchisee make service available to all homes in the franchise area ("universal service") and that they install state-of-the-art technology. Franchising authorities will usually require cable operators to designate a portion of their channel capacity for public, educational and governmental use. Other than the right to prohibit programming that is obscene or otherwise unprotected by the U.S. Constitution, cable operators have no editorial control over these "PEG" channels.

Prior to the 1992 Act, most franchising authorities awarded only one franchise in any given area. Cable companies were forced to bid against each other for what was essentially a de facto monopoly. (The 1992 Act prohibits the award of exclusive franchises.) This allowed the franchising authorities to extract the maximum in terms of service and equipment. For many years cable companies were loath to challenge franchising regulations—probably because of fear that such an action would damage the challenging company's chances of obtaining the franchise. Then in 1984 Preferred Communications Inc. sought to bypass the City of Los Angeles' franchising regulations by asking various utility companies to provide space on their poles for the express purpose of constructing a cable system. The companies refused because Preferred had not obtained a cable franchise from the city.

Preferred then brought an action seeking to have the cable franchising regulations declared unconstitutional under the First and Fourteenth Amendments. Los Angeles' successful motion to dismiss for failure to state a claim upon which relief could be granted was appealed by Preferred. In a strongly worded opinion, the court of appeals reversed the district court's grant of the motion to dismiss. Preferred Communications, Inc. v. City of Los Angeles (1985).

Although the Supreme Court affirmed the appellate court's decision, it did so on very narrow grounds. Justice Rehnquist's majority opinion stated that the activities engaged in by cable television companies clearly implicated First Amendment activities but then noted, consistent with the Court's new hierarchical approach to the Amendment, that "[E]ven protected speech is not equally permissible in all places and at all times." He also noted that the construction and operation of a cable television franchise involved a mixture of speech and conduct, thus presenting special questions regarding the right of the state to regulate the non-speech elements involved. The Court was unwilling to decide the appropriate degree of First Amendment protection to be afforded cable without the more complete factual record that an actual trial could provide. Justice Blackmun concurred to emphasize that the proper First Amendment standard for cable was still undetermined. City of Los Angeles v. Preferred Communications, Inc. (1986).

Without a clear Supreme Court holding on the First Amendment status of cable, lower courts continued to produce inconsistent holdings on this issue. One district court judge rejected a First Amendment attack on the franchise fee and access channel provisions of a franchise agreement, applying the standard for broadcasting set out in Red Lion. "In its effort to preserve an uninhibited marketplace of ideas, government is entrusted with protecting the First Amendment rights of cable television viewers." Erie Telecommunications, Inc. v. City of Erie (1987).

A different approach was taken by the court of appeals in Chicago Cable Communications v. Chicago Cable Commission (1989). In determining the constitutionality of a requirement that the cable system supply 4½ hours per week of local programming, the court applied the O'Brien test. Because localism was a substantial government interest and the 4½ hours-per-week requirement an incidental burden, the court found the requirement constitutional. The court also seemed influenced by the natural monopoly characteristics of cable.

Still other courts used a mix of O'Brien and strict scrutiny analysis. For example, in the Preferred remand the court set up two categories of franchise requirements. The O'Brien test was applied to those requirements imposing an incidental burden on speech. These included awarding a de facto exclusive franchise, prohibiting transfer of the franchise without the city's consent and requiring universal service. Strict scrutiny was applied to restrictions "intended to curtail expression." Among these were mandatory PEG channels and a state-of-the-art technology requirement. The court of appeals upheld the lower court's finding that de facto exclusive franchising violates the First Amendment. Preferred Communications, Inc. v. City of Los Angeles (1994).

b. Concentration Rules

Both the 1984 Cable Act and the 1992 Cable Act imposed restrictions on cable ownership. Earlier

Commission rules prohibiting a television broadcast licensee from owning a cable system within its signal coverage area or a common carrier from owning one within its telephone service area were codified in the 1984 Cable Act. Network ownership of cable systems was also prohibited, although television network ownership of cable networks is not. For example, ABC is a part owner of ESPN. At the same time state ownership restrictions were preempted.

A few years later, the FCC decided to relax both the network-cable and telephone-cable crossownership rules. The new network-cable crossownership rules permit television networks to own cable systems. However, a television network's cable systems could not exceed 10 percent of the homes passed by cable nationwide or 50 percent of the homes passed by cable within any ADI. Television networks were still prohibited from merging with or investing in major MSOs. Common Ownership of Cable Television Systems and National Television Networks (1992).

The 1996 Telecommunications Act required the FCC to eliminate the network-cable crossownership rule and replace it with new rules designed to prevent network-owned cable systems from discriminating against non-affiliated television stations. Because the broadcast-cable crossownership rule is still in effect, there is still minimal network ownership of cable.

The 1992 Cable Act required the FCC to conduct a rulemaking proceeding establishing reasonable limits on the number of subscribers a cable operator would be authorized to reach and on the number of channels that could be occupied by a program supplier in which the cable operator has an attributable interest. An initial facial challenge to the statutory provisions was unsuccessful. Time Warner Entertainment Company v. United States (2000).

The FCC then enacted specific regulations setting the subscriber limit at 30 percent and the affiliated channel capacity limit at 40 percent of all channels up to a 75. Capacity over 75 channels was not subject to the limit, thus capping the unaffiliated channels requirement at 45 (60 percent of 75).

The specific regulations were then challenged in Time Warner Entertainment v. Federal Communications Commission (2001). The circuit court held that, although the statutory provisions were constitutional, the FCC had failed to adequately justify the specific limits set pursuant to the statute and that the rules therefore burdened more speech than was necessary. There was insufficient evidence that lesser restrictions wouldn't adequately serve the FCC's two asserted interests, diversity in competition and fair competition. In addition, the Commission had failed to consider the impact of DBS, see infra, competition.

Telephone companies were authorized to transmit video programming on a common-carrier basis. The new "video-dialtone" rules still prohibited telephone companies from exercising editorial control of video programming carried under these rules.

Transmission capacity must be offered on a non-discriminatory basis. Neither the telephone company carrying programming pursuant to the video-dialtone rules nor the customer supplying the programming was subject to franchising requirements. Telephone–Cable Cross–Ownership (1992). The FCC's decision was affirmed on appeal, NCTA v. FCC (1994).

In 1993 a U.S. District Court held that the crossownership rules were unconstitutional as applied to one of the regional Bell operating companies. Chesapeake and Potomac Telephone Company of Virginia v. United States (1993). Applying an O'Brien analysis, the court addressed two asserted government interests: "promoting competition in the video programming market and preserving diversity in the ownership of communications media." The court quickly rejected the first interest because the crossownership prohibition reduced the number of outlets through which programming could be transmitted and thus, reduced rather than enhanced competition in the video programming market.

With regard to the second asserted interest, the court found that given the FCC's video dial-tone decision, the telephone companies were already in a position to monopolize the video transmission market. Thus, there was not a reasonable fit between the asserted government interest and the means chosen to advance that interest.

In the 1996 Telecommunications Act, telephone companies were given three alternative ways to enter the cable business. The first is to lease their lines to others subject to the common-carrier rules of Title II. The second option is to obtain a cable franchise subject to the requirements of Title VI.

The final option is a hybrid called open video system (OVS). An updated version of video dial-tone, OVS subjects a phone company to some common-carrier-like regulations and some Title VI requirements. For example, OVS operators cannot discriminate between video programming providers and, if demand exceeds capacity, must make two-thirds of their capacity available to companies that are not affiliated with the OVS operator. At the same time, OVS operators are subject to the must-carry and PEG-channel requirements discussed later in this chapter.

The OVS option has not proved popular, with most LECs who provide video programming doing so by obtaining cable franchises. However, there are some problems with this approach. For example, Verizon has started to offer a new combination broadband, telephony and video service (FiOS)delivered through fiber optic cable connected to the home (FTTH). As soon as the fiber is deployed Verizon can offer the broadband and telephony components to consumers. However, before offering video service, Verizom must obtain separate cable franchises from each community. Concern that this process can be used by incumbent cable companies to slow the entry of a viable competitor has led the FCC to announce it was investigating the problem.

There are also proposals to amend the Communications Act to permit regional or national cable franchising.

c. *Rate Regulation*

As noted previously one of the first areas of regulation preempted by the FCC was rate regulation of premium cable channels. The 1984 Cable Act went further and prohibited rate regulation except where there was a lack of effective competition. Even where there was a lack of effective competition only basic cable rates could be regulated.

The FCC initially defined effective competition as the presence in the market of at least three off-the-air television signals. However, the circuit court found the definition arbitrary and capricious. American Civil Liberties Union v. FCC (1987).

On remand, the FCC defined effective competition as the availability of three or more off-air signals in all geographic areas served by the cable system. The three signals did not have to be the same ones throughout the cable system's service area. Cable Communications Policy Act Rules (Signal Availability Standard), 3 FCC Rcd. 2617 (1988). Under this definition less than 4 percent of all cable systems were subject to rate regulation.

Three years later the FCC changed the definition again. Effective competition required meeting one of two alternative conditions. The first was the availability of six off-air signals throughout the entire area served by the cable system. The second was the presence of an independently owned, competing multichannel video service available to a minimum of 50 percent and subscribed to by a minimum of 10 percent of the homes in the cable system's area. Effective Competition, 6 FCC Rcd. 4545 (1991).

Despite the new definition, complaints about unreasonable cable rates continued, prompting Congress to enact a much more stringent system of rate regulation as part of the 1992 Cable Act. As was the case with the 1984 Cable Act, cable systems subject to effective competition are exempt from rate regulation. Effective competition is defined as meeting one of three conditions. The first is "fewer than 30 percent of the households in the franchise area subscribe to the cable service of a cable system." The second is that the franchise area must be "served by at least two unaffiliated multichannel video programming distributors each of which offers comparable video programming to at least 50 percent of the households in the franchise area; and the number of households subscribing to programming services offered by multichannel video programming distributors other than the largest multichannel video programming distributor exceeds 15 percent of the households in the franchise area." The third is that "a multichannel video programming distributor operated by the franchising authority for that franchise area offers video programming to at least 50 percent of the households in that franchise area." 47 U.S.C.A. § 543.

Section 623 of the Act directed the Commission to issue regulations ensuring that rates for basic cable systems not subject to effective competition are reasonable. The actual regulation is to be done by franchising authorities, unless a franchising authority does not do this consistent with the FCC's regulations. In those cases the FCC can claim jurisdiction and regulate rates for systems franchised by that authority. However, the FCC has decided that where a franchising authority opts not to regulate (as opposed to regulating improperly) the FCC will not claim jurisdiction.

In April 1993, the Commission adopted a series of regulations governing cable rates. These regulations established three classes of rates—basic, premium and other. For basic cable the FCC created a table of benchmarks "based on the average September 30, 1992 rates of systems subject to effective competition." Basic rates that were below the applicable benchmark were to be presumed reasonable. Basic rates that exceeded the benchmark had to be reduced by 10 percent or to the benchmark, whichever was higher. Once these initial rates were set, they became subject to a price cap which is adjusted annually. Cable Rate Regulation, 8 FCC Rcd. 5631 (1993).

Premium channels, services offered on a per-channel or per-program basis, are not subject to this provision. Finally, the FCC was required by the 1992 Cable Act to establish a system for resolving complaints about other cable rates, i.e., those that are neither basic or premium. The Commission announced it would use the same table of benchmarks to determine the reasonableness of these rates. However, the FCC had to receive a complaint from a subscriber before it starts this process.

When the Commission's rate regulations took effect, many cable customers found that the expected reduction in their rates did not materialize. In response to public outcry and Congressional pressure, the Commission revised its table of benchmarks. As of May 15, 1994, cable systems not subject to effective competition had to set their rates so that their regulated revenues did not exceed their September 30, 1992 revenues, reduced by 17 percent, as opposed to the 10 percent reduction imposed by the Commission's original rate regulation.

Section 623 also prohibits cable operators from requiring subscription to any tier above the basic tier as a condition of receiving programming offered on a per-channel or per-program basis.

As noted previously, the 1996 Telecommunications Act reversed course. Rate regulation of non-basic channels terminated in 1999. In addition, the definition of effective competition was amended to include comparable video programming services, utilizing the facilities of a local exchange carrier (LEC)(phone company) or its affiliate. The LEC can be operating as a cable franchise, an OVS, or can be distributing the programming through MMDS (discussed infra).

3. Copyright Problems

One of the earliest legal problems to be faced with the advent of cable television was whether a cable system, by the act of receiving a program broadcast over the air and then sending the program by wire to various subscribers, was undertaking a "performance for profit," thereupon subjecting itself to liability either to the television station whose program it was re-transmitting, or to the copyright holders of the work being presented on the station. It was argued by the cable interests that cable systems were not "performing" in the sense contemplated by the copyright laws since they were merely receiving material sent out over the air by stations which had already paid a copyright fee. Imposing liability on the cable system would, the argument ran, result in double payment to the copyright holder. Others argued that whether or not copyright fees should be paid depended upon whether the cable system merely filled in the blanks within a station's normal service contour or whether the cable system extended the range of a station's service beyond the normal service contour.

The Supreme Court dealt with the issue in two landmark cases absolving cable systems of copyright liability for material picked up over the air and then sent through wire, on the ground that this was not a "performance" but merely a mechanical, passive act no different in quality than the erecting by a single person of an extremely tall receiving antenna to improve his or her own reception. Because such an act did not subject the individual to copyright liability, the provision of such a service for profit did not change the quality of the act for copyright purposes under the then existing copyright act.

Fortnightly Corp. v. United Artists Television, Inc. (1968); Teleprompter Corp. v. Columbia Broadcasting System, Inc. (1974).

a.   *The Compulsory License for Retransmission of Broadcast Signals*

The Fortnightly and Teleprompter decisions led Congress to enact significant revisions of the copyright statute. Under the Copyright Act as it now reads, cablevision systems are free to retransmit television signals containing copyrighted materials without obtaining permission of the copyright holder. There is no fee for retransmission of local broadcast signals. However, systems must pay a compulsory license fee for retransmission of distant signals. Originally, the amount of that fee, and the manner in which the fee was to be disbursed, were determined by the Copyright Royalty Tribunal (CRT), a statutory body created by Congress for this purpose. With the 1994 elimination of the CRT, these duties have been delegated to the Library of Congress. See 17 U.S.C.A. § 111.

The compulsory license has proven quite controversial. Not only were broadcasters dismayed at receiving no compensation for local retransmission, but they were also dissatisfied with the CRT's distribution formulas. The Motion Picture Association of America (MPAA), which represents those holding copyrights in televised motion pictures and syndicated programs, has consistently been awarded the lion's share of the license fees. Broadcasters have received very little by comparison.

b.   Retransmission Consent

Broadcasters consistently argued that the compulsory license should be replaced by a system known as retransmission consent. As the name implies, cable operators would be prohibited from retransmitting broadcast signals without first securing the broadcaster's consent. Broadcasters assumed that cable operators would be willing to pay for retransmission rights.

The 1992 Cable Act created a retransmission consent option for broadcasters, but it is applicable only to carriage by local cable systems, carriage for which broadcasters received no compensation under the compulsory license. Each television station can choose between must-carry status, discussed below, and retransmission consent. A broadcaster who opts for retransmission consent must then negotiate for carriage with each local cable system. Any cable system unable to obtain the broadcaster's consent is prohibited from retransmitting that broadcaster's signal. Every three years broadcasters have the option of changing their status.

The underlying assumption was that higher-rated stations would opt for retransmission consent, while the others would retain must-carry status. Retransmission consent was not what broadcasters had hoped it would be. For the most part cable companies refused to pay cash for retransmission consent. As the deadline for obtaining consent approached, several broadcast groups found a compromise that proved acceptable to both sides. If a cable operator agreed to carry a cable channel from the broadcast owner, the broadcaster would agree to allow retransmission of its broadcast signal. For example, Hearst and Cap Cities/ABC reached agreements with a number of MSOs, including Continental Cablevision and Jones Intercable, whereby the cable operator agreed to pay for and carry ESPN2 (co-owned by Hearst and Cap Cities/ABC). In turn, Hearst and Cap Cities/ABC granted those cable companies retransmission consent for their broadcast stations. Other broadcasters, including CBS, gave retransmission consent without receiving anything in return.

When subsequent opportunities to switch status came up at three-year intervals, there was very little change.

4. Signal Carriage Rules

The potential impact of cable television upon the Commission's television allocation scheme has two aspects. First, the importation of distant signals might fragment the audience of the local television station since the local station would now be required to compete with "outside" signals not originally anticipated in the Commission's allocations policy. This is the so-called "distant signal" problem. Second, unless the local cable system is required to carry the signals of the local stations, viewers who choose to subscribe to the system usually would not be able to receive the signal of the local station because they would probably disconnect their regular antennae.

To complicate matters further, the cablevision impact upon independent, non-network and UHF television stations is paradoxical. To the extent cablevision systems carry local, non-network, UHF stations, the cablevision system helps them by eliminating most of the technical advantages which off-the-air VHF reception possesses over UHF reception. On the other hand, to the extent these systems carry distant signals and cable networks, they tend to fragment the audience and therefore harm local non-network UHF facilities.

a. The "Must–Carry" Rules

The Commission in 1972 attempted to resolve these issues and integrate cablevision in the television scheme by enacting a series of rules aimed at protecting local stations. These rules essentially fell into two categories: "Must Carry"—rules requiring cable systems to carry local stations—and "May Carry"—rules limiting the number or type of competing signals cable systems may carry. We will return to the latter later in this chapter.

The must-carry rules were designed to ensure that cable subscribers would still receive the local broadcast stations and that these stations would have the same signal quality as competing signals. They remained in effect until 1985.

The constitutionality of the must-carry rules went unchallenged for years, probably because most cable operators believed them to have been a trade off for the compulsory license. Thus, they feared that if the must-carry rules were eliminated, the compulsory license would be in jeopardy. As a result the must-carry rules were in place for over a decade before a court was asked to decide their constitutionality. In Quincy Cable TV, Inc. v. FCC (1985), the court declared the must-carry rules, as written, unconstitutional under the First Amendment. The case involved two petitions. Quincy Cable, located in Quincy, Washington, was appealing an FCC order requiring it to carry some Spokane, Washington television stations as well as a $5,000 forfeiture for its failure to comply with the Commission's order. Turner Broadcasting System (TBS) was appealing the Commission's denial of TBS's petition to have the must-carry rules eliminated.

The court began by stating that the more limited scope of First Amendment protection enjoyed by the broadcast media as a result of Red Lion is not appropriate for cable. The court rejected any application of the scarcity rationale, noting that cable does not use the airwaves to deliver its programming to its subscribers. The court also rejected an economic scarcity argument based on the idea that cable is a natural monopoly. Not only was the court skeptical of cable's status as a natural monopoly, suggesting that the pattern of one cable system to a market was primarily a result of municipal franchising policies, but the court observed that economic scarcity had been rejected as a ground for infringing First Amendment rights in Miami Herald Pub. Co. v. Tornillo (1974).

The court found it unnecessary to decide whether the rules should be examined under the O'Brien test or some more exacting level of scrutiny, because in the court's analysis the rules failed even the more relaxed O'Brien test. The court held that the Commission had failed to prove that the rules served an important government interest. Although the Commission asserted that the interest served by the rules was preserving free, locally-oriented television, it failed, at least in the court's eyes, to prove it. Even though substantial deference to the Commission's expertise is required, the court concluded that after twenty years of regulation, something more than unsubstantiated assumptions and speculations was needed to support the Commission's conclusions.

The court went on to state that even if it assumed that the rules served the asserted government interest, they would still fail the O'Brien test as overinclusive. In the guise of protecting local broadcasting the rules were protecting local broadcasters regardless of the quality of their service or the number of stations in the market. The rules imposed no requirement that a station offer at least a minimum amount of local programming or demonstrate that its programming was not completely duplicative of another already in the market.

Finally, the court of appeals majority indicated that it had "not found it necessary to decide whether any version of the rules would contravene the First Amendment," leaving the door open for the Commission to draft new rules.

The Commission ceased enforcement of the old rules in September 1985. Then in August 1986, under pressure from Congress, the Commission announced a new set of must-carry rules. The purpose of the new rules, according to the Commission, was to provide time to educate consumers as to the availability of a device, an A–B switch, that would allow them to easily switch between an antenna for broadcast reception and the cable feed. Reinforcing the transition concept, the Commission included a five-year sunset provision in the rules.

These rules were also struck down on appeal. Again the court found it unnecessary to determine the appropriate level of scrutiny because the rules failed even the O'Brien test. In the court's view the FCC neither proved that consumers were ignorant of A–B switches nor that, without must-carry rules, cable systems would drop local broadcast stations. Therefore, there was no proof that the must-carry rules furthered a substantial government interest. In addition, the court found no evidence that it would take five years to learn about A–B switches and thus, the rules were not narrowly tailored. As in Quincy, the court emphasized that it was not declaring must-carry rules per se unconstitutional. Century Communications Corp. v. FCC (1987).

The 1992 Cable Act contained provisions requiring the FCC to promulgate two new must-carry rules, one for commercial stations, the other for non-commercial stations. With regard to commercial stations, cable systems with 12 or fewer channels must carry at least three local broadcast signals. Larger systems must carry all local commercial stations up to a maximum of one third of the system's total number of channels. Where the number of local commercial stations exceeds this maximum, the cable operator may choose which stations to carry. In so doing the operator cannot choose a low-power TV station unless all full-power stations are carried, and if a network affiliate is chosen, it must be the affiliate of that network closest to the system's head end. 47 U.S.C.A. § 534. In addition, each broadcast station carried pursuant to the requirements of § 614 must be carried on either the channel number on which it is broadcast, "the channel on which it was carried on July 19, 1985, or the channel on which it was carried on January 1, 1992, at the election of the station." Carriage on any other channel must be mutually agreed upon. 47 U.S.C.A. § 534(b)(6).

As far as noncommercial stations are concerned, systems with 12 or fewer channels must carry one local noncommercial educational television station. Systems with 13–36 channels must carry all local noncommercial educational television stations up to a maximum of three. Systems with a channel capacity greater than 36 must carry all local noncommercial educational television stations. 47 U.S.C.A. § 535.

As required by § 23 of the 1992 Cable Act, challenges to both must-carry provisions were heard by a special three-judge panel of the United States District Court for the District of Columbia. In Turner Broadcasting System Inc. v. FCC (1993), the district court, 2–1, granted summary judgment holding the rules constitutional.

Judge Jackson found that in enacting the must-carry provisions of the 1992 Cable Act, "Congress employed its regulatory powers over the economy to impose order upon a market in dysfunction, but a market in a commercial commodity nevertheless." In his view the commodity being regulated was the means of delivery of video signals to individual receivers, not the actual signals themselves. Thus, the 1992 Cable Act was nothing more than "industry-specific antitrust and fair trade practice regulatory legislation."

Recognizing however, that First Amendment values were implicated, Judge Jackson held that the O'Brien test was the appropriate standard to be applied. He found that the record compiled by Congress when combined with the deference the court should accord Congress was adequate to sustain a finding that there was a substantial government interest in sustaining local broadcasting. Again noting the deference due Congress, he found the must-carry rules were narrowly tailored to achieve the substantial government interest in sustaining local broadcasting. Finally, the rules did not unduly burden cable operators because they retained editorial control over the majority of their channels.

Judge Sporkin also viewed the case as dealing with economic regulation that only minimally implicated the First Amendment. He dismissed the cable operators' argument that the rules impermissibly interfere with their editorial discretion, finding that their editorial discretion does not rise to the level of detail-oriented, content-based decision making exercised by newspaper editors. Similarly, he rejected the programmers' argument that the rules favored one class of speakers—local broadcasters—over others, holding that it was only necessary that the statutory classification bear a rational relationship to a substantial government interest.

In dissent, Judge Williams took a very different approach. He focused on the leased access channels required under § 612 of the 1992 Act. If, in fact, cable operators were capable of exercising monopoly power over the delivery of video signals, the requirement that they lease a percentage of their channels to unaffiliated programmers provided an adequate remedy. In contrast, the must-carry rules favored a specific class of speakers, one that is required by the FCC to "provide programming responsive to issues of concern to its community." In Judge Williams' view, this meant that the must-carry rules were content-based and, as such, required strict scrutiny.

Applying strict scrutiny to the must-carry rules, he found two interests that the government claimed were furthered by the rules. The first was diversity, which is arguably a compelling interest. However, the rules were not a narrowly tailored means of advancing that interest. Increasing the number of access channels would be a less burdensome method of increasing diversity.

The second interest asserted by the government to be served by the must-carry rules was the preservation of local broadcasting. For the purpose of his analysis, Judge Williams divided this interest into two parts. One was Congress' desire to ensure the availability of local programming. The other was the need to ensure that noncable subscribers had access to video programming. Judge Williams doubted whether the desire for local programming could ever reach the level of a compelling government interest. Even if it could there was a less restrictive means of assuring local content. The government could subsidize the provision of local programming.

Turning to the need to ensure that noncable subscribers have access to video programming, he found that the figures cited by the government did not constitute evidence that, absent must-carry, there would be widespread failure of over-the-air stations. Even if cable systems should drop a lot of broadcast stations (which Williams believed to be highly unlikely) leading to a serious drop in advertising revenues, a less restrictive solution would be to expand the number of leased access channels and, if necessary, subsidize the cost of leasing for local broadcast stations.

The Supreme Court vacated the judgment and remanded the case for further proceedings. Turner Broadcasting System, Inc. v. FCC (1994) (Turner I). A bare majority of the Court, in an opinion written by Justice Kennedy, decided that the rules were subject to the intermediate level of scrutiny set out in O'Brien. The Court rejected the less vigorous Red

Lion—broadcast—level of scrutiny because spectrum scarcity and signal interference do not exist with cable.

The Court also rejected strict scrutiny because in its view the must-carry rules were content neutral. The rules distinguish between speakers based on the method of transmission as opposed to content. Because most cable subscribers either take down their TV antennas or allow them to fall into disrepair, cable operators effectively controlled access to the 60 percent of the television households that subscribed to cable. Breaking this "bottleneck" control (not the favoring of a particular content) was Congress' objective in adopting the rules, and justified the differentiation in treatment between broadcast and cable.

Applying O'Brien, the Court found that the rules furthered three important government interests unrelated to the suppression of free expression. These were "(1) preserving the benefits of free, over-the-air local broadcast stations, (2) promoting the widespread dissemination of information from a multiplicity of sources, and (3) promoting fair competition in the market for television programming."

Turning to the questions of whether the must-carry rules advanced these government interests, and whether they burdened speech no more than necessary to achieve those interests, the majority split 4–1. Justices Kennedy, Souter, Blackmun and Chief Justice Rehnquist held that, even giving Congress' predictive judgments the substantial deference required, the government had not adequately proven either. Therefore, because genuine issues of material fact remained, summary judgment should not have been granted.

Justice Stevens argued that in fact the government had provided adequate evidence that they did not burden more speech than necessary to advance those interests. He would therefore have voted to affirm the lower court's judgment. Because so voting would mean that no disposition of the case would command a majority of the Court, however, he concurred in the judgment vacating and remanding for further proceedings.

Justice O'Connor, joined by Justices Scalia, Thomas and Ginsburg, dissented. She argued that the must-carry rules were clearly not content neutral, and thus should be subject to strict scrutiny. She noted that the findings enumerated in the 1992 Act cited "[p]references for diversity of viewpoints, for localism, for educational programming and for news and public affairs." In her view, these findings proved that the government interests were not compelling, and thus the rules were unconstitutional.

Even assuming arguendo that the rules are content neutral, O'Connor would still have found them unconstitutional because they were overbroad. "They disadvantage cable programmers even if the operator has no anticompetitive motives, and even if the broadcasters that would have to be dropped to make room for the cable programmer would survive without cable access."

Justice Ginsburg wrote a separate dissent, adopting the reasons contained in Judge Williams' dissent from the district court judgment. She characterized the rules as "an unwarranted content-based preference." She also termed the harm the rules are supposed to prevent "imaginary."

Perhaps the most important effect of Turner I was the clear rejection of the broadcast standard of scrutiny as appropriate for cable. Instead, in determining the constitutionality of cable regulation, the O'Brien standard should be used for content-neutral regulations imposing only an incidental burden on speech, and strict scrutiny for content-based regulations. Of course, determining whether a given regulation is content neutral or content based (and teasing out the elements of the O'Brien standard) still proves difficult.

On remand, after holding hearings and collecting evidence, the district court panel again upheld the must-carry rules, 2–1. The three judges essentially reiterated their earlier views.

This time the Supreme Court upheld the rules 5–4. Turner Broadcasting v. FCC (Turner II)(1997). In an opinion by Justice Kennedy, the majority started with the conclusions of the Court in Turner I. They applied intermediate scrutiny and with one exception concluded that the three governmental interests identified in Turner I were important. Justice Breyer, who supplied the key fifth vote to affirm the lower court decision, only recognized two important government interests, "preserving the benefits of free, over-the-air local broadcast television," and "(2) promoting the widespread dissemination of information from a multiplicity of sources." He did not accept the third, "promoting fair competition."

The Court then concluded that there was adequate evidence for Congress to conclude that the rules would serve these interests "in a direct and effective way." This evidence included statistics on broadcast stations that lost carriage during the period between the elimination of the original rules and the passage of the new ones and arguments concerning the financial incentives for cable systems to drop broadcast stations.

Finally, the majority concluded that the rules were narrowly tailored. The reasoning was that the burden–the number of cable programming channels dropped–was equal to the benefit–the number of broadcast channels gaining carriage.

The dissenting Justices, in an opinion by Justice O'Connor, began by reiterating their view that the rules were not content neutral, and thus, should be subject to strict scrutiny. They further argued that the rules should not survive intermediate scrutiny. First, there was not clear evidence that, absent the rules, there would be a serious reduction in the "benefits of free, over-the-air local broadcast television" or the "widespread dissemination of information from a multiplicity of sources." The stations that would be dropped would be those with minimal viewership.

Second, the rules were not narrowly tailored. The majority's assertion that the benefits were equal to the burden is not only simplistic, but a tautology. The benefit to the non-cable subscribers of the minimally-viewed stations that might go out of business if denied carriage was not necessarily equivalent to the harm to cable operators, who could lose advertising and/or subscription revenue, as well as the harm to the cable programmer who would be dropped and the cable subscribers deprived of access to that programming. Further, it was not clear that non-carried broadcast stations would be forced to reduce service or go out of business.

One noteworthy aspect of Turner II is the minimal weight given to the harm to cable programmers displaced by must-carry broadcast stations. Although non-carriage by the cable system can make it harder for a broadcast station to reach its audience, it can make it impossible for the cable programming service.

The advent of DTV has created a new must-carry dilemma. How should the must-carry rules be applied to the additional signals? The issues here are far more complex than with the current rules. On one hand, the government may have a more important interest served by digital must-carry, the rapid growth of DTV, enabling a quick transition to the new system of broadcasting. This in turn would allow the recovery of the analog spectrum, which could then be auctioned.

On the other hand, the burdens are also greater, especially during the transition period. It would increase the number of must-carry stations, in many cases with duplicative programming due to simulcasting on the analog and digital channels. In many cases, it would also require upgrading the cable system to enable carriage of the DTV signals.

Even defining what constitutes a must-carry channel would be difficult. If a station is broadcasting multiple SDTV programs on its channel, which must be carried? If a station switches between SDTV and HDTV, how does that affect the carriage requirement? What if some of the SDTV channels are subscription or pay signals? Given that multiple SDTV channels are the equivalent of a single analog channel, in terms of cable capacity required to transmit them, how do they count towards the one-third of capacity limit on must-carry channels?

In 2001 the FCC issued a series of digital must-carry regulations. First, "usable activated channels" was determined to include not only that portion of the cable spectrum used for regular video programming, but also the portion used for Internet service, pay-per-view, video-on-demand and telephony. To calculate the one-third cap for commercial must carry, that capacity is expressed in megahertz and divided by three. For non-commercial stations, the FCC continues to use the original definition of channels with any system that carries more than 36 channels required to carry all local non-commercial channels. Carriage of Digital Television Broadcast Signals (2001).

With regard to defining picture quality for digital coverage, the requirement is that "a cable operator may not provide a digital broadcast signal in a lesser format or lower resolution than that afforded to any digital programmer (e.g. non-broadcast cable programming, other broadcast digital programming, etc.) carried on the cable system, provided, however, that a broadcast signal delivered in HDTV must be carried in HDTV. The one exception to these requirements is that a digital station that qualifies for must carry can require the cable operator to supply one its HDTV or SDTV programming streams in an analog format. This requirement is designed to aid the transition to digital by allowing subscribers without the necessary home equipment to view a digital signal to properly view the signals.

The Commission also announced two important tentative decisions. The first was not to require carriage of both analog and digital signals for any given station during the transition from analog to digital television. Broadcasters had argued that this was needed to speed the transition and to make DTV viable. The second was to interpret the must-carry requirement that only primary video be carried to mean that when a digital television broadcaster multicasts only one programming stream need be carried. Several years later the Commission affirmed these tentative decisions. Carriage of Digital Television Broadcast Signals (2005).

b.   *The "May–Carry" Rules*

The may-carry rules took several forms. One, no longer in effect, was a limit on the number of signals from distant stations that a cable system could transmit. This limit varied according to market size and the number of available over-the-air signals within the market.

A second restriction on distant signals involves syndicated programming. Generally, syndicated programming is sold on a market-exclusive basis, but the importation of syndicated programming made it impossible to guarantee market exclusivity. The Commission therefore requires cable systems in major markets to black out distant syndicated programs when local commercial stations own the exclusive rights to the broadcast of these programs.

Any station that has obtained local exclusivity can enforce that against local cable systems. Stations are also permitted to obtain and enforce national exclusivity. This provision, which benefits superstations, also exempts such stations from the territorial exclusivity rule discussed at p. 521, supra. Syndicators may also enforce exclusivity contracts for the first year after the initial syndication. See United Video, Inc. v. FCC (1989).

One may-carry rule that remains is the network nonduplication rule. It is aimed at the problem that arises when the same cable systems carry "local" and "distant" stations which may both be broadcasting the same network program. Because such duplication through the use of cable television could have a detrimental economic effect on the local station that had obtained exclusivity for the program under its network agreement, the Commission enacted rules which require that cable systems with more than 1000 subscribers delete the network programs of duplicating distant stations under certain circumstances. When the Commission reinstituted the syndication exclusivity rules, the network non-duplication rules were expanded from simultaneous network programming to all network programs. See 47 C.F.R. §§ 76.92–76.99 (1981). The deletion is made in accordance with certain priorities set forth in the Commission's Rules: a "local" television station has the right to require the deletion of a duplicating network program from the signal of a lower priority station. See 47 C.F.R. § 76.92. In order to invoke such protection the station requesting deletion must formally notify the cable system.

In sum, the only programming restrictions that still remain upon the type of material that can be presented on cablevision systems relate to the syndication exclusivity rules (See 47 C.F.R. § 76.161), the non-duplication protection afforded network programs (47 C.F.R. §§ 76.92–76.99 (1981)), and those portions of the Commission's rules placing a blackout upon the cablecasting of sports events taking place locally (See 47 C.F.R. § 76.67) (1981).

5. Content Regulation

The Commission has imposed upon cable systems certain operating requirements similar to those imposed upon broadcast stations. Thus, despite the fact that cable may not be considered "broadcasting" in the usual sense, nonetheless, to the extent cable systems originate their own programs, the

Commission's Rules require that these systems follow all of the "equal time" and "lowest unit rate" political broadcast regulations promulgated pursuant to Section 315 of the Communications Act, adhere to the rules concerning the Personal Attack and Political Editorial Rules, not transmit obscenity, even on the so-called "access" channels, identify all material that is sponsored, and maintain certain records.

Most of the constitutional challenges to content regulation of cable have involved laws aimed at limiting the carriage of indecent programming. Under Miller v. California (1973), chapter IV, supra, it is clear that obscenity over cable can be proscribed. The question of indecency over cable has led to a series of fact-specific and sometimes seemingly contradictory decisions.

In Cruz v. Ferre (1985), a Miami ordinance banning the distribution of obscene and indecent programming over cable was struck down on overbreadth grounds. The court distinguished Pacifica on the basis of differences between broadcasting and cable. Cable requires the affirmative decision to subscribe and juveniles can be protected through the use of lockboxes that permit parents to lock out channels and put them out of reach of their children.

Even if these differences did not exist, the court would still have found the ordinance unconstitutional because it banned indecent programming outright. In Pacifica the U.S. Supreme Court had indicated that indecent programming might be permissible in appropriate time periods or programming contexts. No such allowances were made in the Miami ordinance.

Similarly, in Jones v. Wilkinson (1986) the court of appeals affirmed a lower court decision striking down the Utah Cable Television Programming Decency Act. However, one member of the court argued in his concurrence that Pacifica was the appropriate standard by which cable indecency regulations should be judged. He then found that the Act could not even meet the more relaxed Pacifica standard. The U.S. Supreme Court affirmed without issuing any opinion. Wilkinson v. Jones (1987).

The 1992 Cable Act contained several provisions aimed at limiting cablecasting of indecent material on either leased access channels or PEG channels. The FCC was required to promulgate regulations requiring cable operators to place on a single channel all indecent programming intended to be carried on leased access channels and to block access to that channel absent a written request for access from the subscriber. Also required by the 1992 Act were regulations permitting cable operators to prohibit obscene or indecent material on leased access or PEG channels.

In compliance with these provisions of the 1992 Cable Act the Commission adopted indecency rules for leased access channels, Cable Access Channels (Indecent Programming) (1993), and PEG channels,

Cable Access Channels (Indecent Programming) (1993). An initially successful challenge on First Amendment grounds, Alliance for Community Media v. FCC (1993), was reversed in a rehearing en banc.

In an extremely fragmented opinion, the Supreme Court found constitutional, 7–2, the section of the 1992 Act that permits cable operators to prohibit indecent programming transmitted over leased access channels (§ 10(a)), but struck down, 6–3, the provision that required cable operators to segregate and block indecent programming if they broadcasted it (§ 10(b)) and, 5–4, the provision that permitted cable operators to prohibit indecent programming on public access channels (§ 10(c)). Denver Area Educational Telecommunications Consortium, Inc. v. Federal Communications Commission (1996).

The 1996 Telecommunications Act contained a provision requiring all multichannel video distributors to scramble both the audio and video portions of any "sexually explicit adult programming or other programming that is indecent on any channel of its service primarily dedicated to sexually-oriented programming" to prevent non-subscribers from receiving such channels. Distributors who could not fully scramble those signals were required to limit them to the FCC's safe-harbor hours for indecency. Playboy Entertainment Group challenged the provision on the grounds that full scrambling without any "signal bleed," an occasional moment of clear audio or video, was prohibitively expensive and thus the law was in effect a daytime ban on the company's programming.

The Supreme Court held, 5–4, that the provision violated the First Amendment. In an opinion authored by Justice Kennedy, the Court found that it was a content-based regulation subject to strict scrutiny. Although the government interest in shielding young children from indecent material was compelling, there was almost no hard evidence that the problem was serious or widespread. In addition, the existence of the voluntary blocking provisions (allowing parents to request blocking of specific channels), which could be coupled with an adequate informational campaign to alert parents of this option, provided a less restrictive alternative. United States v. Playboy Entertainment Group (2000).

The increased controversy over indecent programming that followed the infamous Janet Jackson Super Bowl performance has led to proposals to extend the restrictions on indecency to cable. If Congress were to amend the law in that manner, there is serious question as to whether it would pass constitutional muster. In the past the Supreme Court has been careful to limit Pacifica to broadcasting.

An alternate approach to the problem, requiring or encouraging cable operators to offer a la carte program subscription or theme tiers such as a family tier was originally rejected by the FCC as not economically feasible and against consumer interests. Report on the Packaging and Sale of Video Programming Services to the Public (2004). However, a subsequent mass media bureau report criticized the 2004 report and suggested that these alternatives were economically feasible and would be beneficial to consumers. Report on the Packaging and Sale of Video Programming Services to the Public (2006).

B.   MULTIPOINT DISTRIBUTION SERVICE (MDS)

By the early 1980s, despite the emergence of cable television and pay television, and despite the nationwide saturation of receivers, there were still approximately 1.2 million households that had no access to television service and there were approximately 4 million households that received only one or two channels (see 47 Fed.Reg. at 1967, Jan. 13, 1982). There were additional millions of households that received only three or four channels. In an attempt to alleviate the shortage, alternative technologies have been developed.

Multipoint distribution service (MDS) is one such technological alternative. In its early years, this service typically consisted of a microwave transmitter and antenna at the transmitting site broadcasting over a microwave frequency omnidirectionally covering a line of sight area of approximately 10 to 20 miles. The signal was then received by a receiving antenna at a particular site. The signal was converted from the microwave frequency to a lower frequency compatible with the customer's television set. The signal was passed from the downconverter through a cable to the customer's set on a VHF channel which was vacant in the community (see 45 Fed.Reg. 29350 at ¶ 24 (May 2, 1980)).

Economically, the arrangement was as follows: the transmitting equipment was licensed to an entity which acted as a common carrier. The licensee as a common carrier did not have control over the programming presented on the channel. Persons wishing to present programming over the system (called "subscribers") leased air time on the transmitter and made the programming available for transmission. Time was usually sold to a programmer on a block basis. The subscriber also typically owned the receiving antenna and the downconverter. The subscriber then contracted with the customer for delivery of the program to the customer's set. In essence, the transaction was very close to a point-to-point transmission, using the air waves rather than a wire.

Originally, most markets had only one or two microwave channels available for MDS service. They were allocated via the comparative hearing method with all its attendant delays and expenses. Then in 1983 the Commission reallocated eight of the 28 instructional television fixed service (ITFS) microwave channels to MDS. ITFS (MDS Reallocation), 48 Fed.Reg. 33,873 (July 15, 1983). At the same time, the FCC authorized MDS operators to lease extra channel capacity from ITFS operators and changed its method of allocating MDS channels from the comparative hearing to a lottery system. The expanded service created by the rule changes was called multichannel multipoint distribution service (MMDS). It is often referred to as "wireless cable."

In 1987, noting that MMDS was for the most part being used to deliver broadcast-type services, the Commission decided to allow MMDS operators to choose the regulatory model to be applied to them based on the type of service provided. 47 C.F.R. §§ 21.900–21.908.

Because the service developed as a "common carrier" service neither licensees nor subscribers (i.e., programmers) were subject to the equal time or fairness rules, the access rules for political candidates, or the other doctrines which control broadcast operations. Unlike cable system operators MDS operators do not have to obtain a franchise grant from a state or town because the FCC has preempted state and local regulation of MDS. See New York State Commission on Cable Television v. FCC (1982).

Continuing demand for spectrum and the advent of new services such as 3G led the FCC to make further changes in the rules for MMDS and ITFS, starting with a name change for each. MMDS was renamed "Broadband Radio Service" (BRS) and ITFS was renamed, "Educational Broadband Service" (EBS). Other changes included restructuring "the 2500–2690 MHz band into upper and lower-band segments for low-power operations (UBS and

LBS, respectively), and a mid-band segment (MBS) for high-power operations" and "designating the 2495–2500 MHz band for use in connection with the 2500–2690 MHz band." In addition, the FCC implemented geographic area licensing for the entire band, consolidated licensing and service rules for EBS and BRS, authorized spectrum leasing and set signal strength limits. Amendment of Parts 1, 21, 73, and 74 of the Commission's Rules to Facilitate the Provision of Fixed and Mobile Broadband Access, Educational and Other Advanced Services in the 2150–2162 and 2500–2690 MHz Bands (2004).

As a competitor of cable, BRS has several advantages. Installation is much less expensive, especially in urban areas where cable must be placed underground. Because there are no franchising requirements, BRS does not have to provide expensive community services such as access channels and studios. Long expensive franchising battles are not required and an MMDS operator can offer service to all the surrounding communities.

On the other hand, until recently, even with the new channels made available, BRS was limited to less than thirty-five channels, whereas some urban cable systems have the capacity to provide 100 or more. However, by using recently developed digital compression technology, BRS systems can now offer up to 300 channels. The same techniques permit 500–channel cable systems. Perhaps more important, cable is already established in many communities and it may be difficult for BRS operators to convince existing cable subscribers to switch. As a

result, by mid–2005 the total number of BRS subscribers had fallen to approximately 100,000 and
most companies are focusing on data transmission
as opposed to video services. Annual Assessment of
the Status of Competition in the Market for the
Delivery of Video Programming (2006).

C.   SATELLITE MASTER ANTENNA TELEVISION (SMATV)

One of the earliest alternatives to cable, satellite
master antenna television (SMATV) is really a cable
system that does not cross a public right of way. A
SMATV operator sets up one or more earth stations
on an apartment building or residential complex.
The programming received by these earth stations
is distributed throughout the building or complex
by wire.

In 1983, the FCC preempted state and local entry
regulations for SMATV. The Commission's decision
was affirmed in New York State Commission on
Cable Television v. FCC (1984). As a result SMATV
is an essentially unregulated industry.

Because a SMATV system cannot cross a public
right of way, SMATV is limited to large apartment
buildings, hotels and private residential complexes.
In those areas it has several advantages over other
services. The absence of any franchising requirements allows immediate entry into the market. Like
MMDS, SMATV cannot be required to provide access channels and studios, thus reducing the cost of

operation. However, unlike MMDS, SMATV has no limit on channel capacity.

Increased competition from DBS, infra, has reduced the demand for SMATV. As a result, by mid–2005 there were only 1 million SMATV subscribers in the United States. Annual Assessment of the Status of Competition in the Market for the Delivery of Video Programming (2006).

D.   DIRECT BROADCAST SATELLITES (DBS)

As satellite communications technology improved, both the cost and size of earth stations capable of receiving satellite transmissions decreased. As a result direct transmission to individual homes appeared to be both technologically and economically feasible. In 1980, the Commission began conducting inquiries into how best to initiate such a service. See Notice of Inquiry, 45 Fed.Reg. 72,719 (Nov. 3, 1980).

Among the questions that needed to be addressed were the type of service to be offered (pay or advertiser-supported), the number of satellites and channels to be used, and the frequencies to be allocated to the service. Permanent answers had to await the decisions of an international conference allotting frequencies and orbital slots to the Western Hemisphere nations.

However, in an attempt to hasten the development of this new service the Commission in July, 1982 issued interim guidelines for DBS operators.

Licenses would be granted for five years, and licensees would be required to meet international guidelines. DBS services with broadcast characteristics would be subject to the broadcast sections of the Communications Act, but not subject to non-statutory Commission policies with the exception of the Commission's equal employment opportunity rules. DBS operators offering common carrier-type services were to be subject only to the common carrier sections of the Act. The interim guidelines were challenged in National Association of Broadcasters v. FCC (1984) and were upheld except for the exemption from the broadcasting sections of the Communications Act of programmers leasing DBS channels.

In response to the Court's decision, the FCC changed its method of classifying subscription video programming services from a content-based system to an intent-based system. This meant that these subscription services would not be subject to broadcast regulations despite their offering broadcast-like services because the programmers' intent would be to limit access to their signals. Subscription Video (1987).

The 1983 international conference set aside 12.2 to 12.7 GHz for DBS and awarded orbital slots. Other allocation questions were left for a 1985 conference which in turn left them for another conference scheduled for 1988. At that conference it was decided to resolve allocation disputes through flexible, multilateral planning meetings.

In 1983 United Satellite Communications, Inc. (USCI) became the first company to offer DBS service. Less than two years later, after huge losses, USCI discontinued its service. Meanwhile, a number of the other companies that had originally applied for licenses to offer DBS service abandoned their DBS plans.

The advantages of direct broadcast satellites had appeared obvious. A single satellite could provide programming to a large area of the country. Most importantly, satellites offered a way to serve those areas of the country (primarily rural) where cable cannot be profitable due to high per-subscriber installation costs.

Unfortunately, less immediately apparent were some of the key disadvantages. DBS service turned out to be very expensive because of the costs involved in putting satellites in space. There were not enough potential subscribers to make advertiser-supported service feasible. Instead subscribers had to pay several hundred dollars to buy a receiving dish in addition to a monthly charge of more than $20/month for a limited number of channels. Thus, in those areas where cable was available, DBS could not compete. The uncabled areas were insufficient to support DBS by themselves.

New technology revived DBS. High-powered satellites permit the use of smaller, less expensive receiving equipment. Digital compression techniques also enable DBS operators to offer hundreds of channels. Several companies launched DBS service in the mid–90s. The most successful of these were DirecTV and Echostar, which bought out some of their competitors, allowing them to offer even more channels.

In 2001 Echostar announced it was buying DirecTv. Proponents of the deal argued that combining the two companies was necessary to provide adequate competition for cable. Opponents feared a monopoly in DBS service would lead to higher prices and lower service for customers in rural areas where there were no cable systems to compete with DBS. The FCC agreed with the latter and rejected the deal.

The primary competitive disadvantage for DBS was its inability to deliver local broadcast channels and/or broadcast network programming ("local-into-local"). DBS operators could only deliver network stations to those subscribers unable to receive a viewable signal from a local broadcast station.

The passage of the Satellite Home Viewer Improvement Act of 1999 changed this by authorizing DBS providers to deliver local broadcast channels. This allowed the DBS companies to provide much stronger competition for cable. By mid–2004 DirecTv had 14.67 million subscribers and Echostar had 11.45 million, giving DBS approximately 27.7 percent of the multi-channel video program distribution (MVPD) market. DirectTv and Echostar are now the second and third largest MVPDs in the country. Annual Assessment of the Status of Competition in the Market for the Delivery of Video Programming (2006).

The 1992 Cable Act imposed some content regulation on DBS, including equal opportunity and reasonable access. See discussions of §§ 315 and 312(a)(7), in chapter X, supra. In addition, the Act required DBS to make available non-commercial educational and informational channels at reasonable rates, and provide service to local communities. A district court held this provision violated the First Amendment. Daniels Cablevision v. United States (1993). The circuit court reversed, applying Red Lion. The court concluded that the set-aside provision "represents nothing more than a new application of a well-settled government policy of ensuring public access to noncommercial programming." Time Warner v. Federal Communications Commission (1996).

One concern voiced by each of these alternative delivery systems, MMDS, SMATV and DBS, was access to programming. The question is whether program vendors have been unfairly favoring cable operators, by far their biggest customers. Pursuant to requirements of the 1992 Cable Act the Commission conducted a rulemaking proceeding to "establish regulations governing program carriage agreements and related practices between cable operators or other multichannel video programming distributors and video programming vendors." Exclusive programming arrangements between vertically integrated programming vendors and cable operators in areas not served by cable are illegal *per se.* In areas served by cable they are enforceable only after an FCC determination using criteria set forth in § 628(c)(4) that they serve the public interest. Similar provisions apply to "the activities of cable operators and other multichannel programming distributors when dealing with programming vendors." Video Programming Distribution and Carriage (1993).

CHAPTER XII

INTERNET LAW

A. INTRODUCTION

The advent of interactive computer communications, most importantly the Internet, has had arguably the greatest impact on communication law of any communication technology. The reason is that no previous technology affected as many different communication industries.

Many of the legal issues raised by the development and growth of the Internet involve the application of existing laws to this new technology. Some of the more difficult of these include copyright, defamation and privacy. In addition, there are some new legal issues such as encryption, spamming and cybersquatting that are peculiar to computers and the Internet. Although a body of Internet law has started to develop, there are still far more questions than answers in this area.

In addition to specific substantive legal issues, the Internet presents several unique jurisdictional questions. One is the problem of applying U.S. law to sites located in other countries. How can a law prohibiting a specific type of speech be effective if sites in other countries containing the same speech are readily accessible to U.S. residents? If it can't be effective, how can such a statute survive strict scrutiny? This is one of the questions raised by the district court deciding the constitutionality of COPA (discussed later in this chapter).

A different jurisdictional issue is suggested by United States v. Thomas (1996). A couple who operated an adult bulletin board in California was prosecuted in Tennessee for violating federal obscenity laws, 18 U.S.C.A. §§ 1462 and 1465, based in part, on material downloaded by a United States Postal Inspector in Tennessee. They were convicted based on the obscenity standards in Tennessee and their convictions were upheld on appeal.

The court relied on the fact that access to the bulletin board required applying for membership and paying a fee. Because the inspector's application listed a home address and phone number located in Tennessee, the court reasoned that defendants knew that their materials would be downloaded in Tennessee. It was therefore not unreasonable to extradite them to Tennessee and subject them to the standards of Tennessee.

However, what if instead of running a bulletin board, Mr. and Mrs. Thomas had posted their materials on the Internet and allowed access to anyone paying with a credit card? Would it still be reasonable to subject them to the standards of Tennessee? A similar question is raised by defamatory statements published on Web sites. Does the fact that they can be accessed from any state, not to mention other countries, subject them to potential law suits in all of these jurisdictions?

Still another jurisdictional question involves the line between state and federal regulation of the Internet. Several courts have struck down state attempts to regulate the Internet under the Interstate Commerce Clause. See e.g., ACLU v. Miller (1997); American Library Association v. Pataki (1997); and ACLU v. Johnson (1998); WhenU.com, Inc. v. State (2004).

B.   INDECENCY

Children's access to indecent and obscene materials has probably received more publicity than all the other legal issues involving the Internet combined. Parents, confronted with a technology that in many cases they do not understand as well as their children, have sought ways to restrict what their children can access. In response Congress passed the Communications Decency Act (CDA) as part of the Telecommunications Act of 1996.

Included in the CDA were provisions criminalizing the knowing transmission of indecent messages to children under 18 years of age, as well as the knowing sending or displaying of patently offensive messages in a manner available to a person under 18 years of age. The constitutionality of these provisions was immediately challenged by a coalition of electronic publishers and public interest groups. After a three-judge district court panel enjoined the challenged portions of the statute, the case was heard by the Supreme Court.

The Court affirmed the judgment of the district court, finding the provisions at issue both vague and overbroad. The government had argued that "[b]ecause the CDA's 'patently offensive' standard (and we assume arguendo, its synonymous 'indecent' standard) is part of the three-prong Miller test ... it cannot be unconstitutionally vague." In the Court's opinion, the flaw in this argument was that the Miller definition includes three limitations, not just one. It is the combination of the three that give sufficient specificity to the definition.

Turning to the scope of the CDA, the Court found that even though the government has a compelling interest in protecting children from harmful materials, the CDA suppressed "a large amount of speech that adults have a constitutional right to receive and to address to one another." Among the reasons for this finding were the cost and often fallibility of existing methods of verifying ages on the Internet, the impossibility of enforcing the CDA against sites located outside the country, and the availability of less restrictive means of enabling parents to control their children's access to Internet material, e.g. blocking software. Reno v. American Civil Liberties Union (1997).

In response to the Court's decision, Congress passed a new statute designed to meet the constitutional infirmities of the CDA. The Child Online Protection Act (COPA) prohibits knowingly by means of the World Wide Web making "any communication for commercial purposes that is available to any minor and that includes any material that is harmful to minors." Using a specific definition of harmful to minors was an attempt to address the vagueness problems of the CDA and limiting the application of the Act to commercial uses was designed to meet the Court's overbreadth concerns.

A request for a preliminary injunction against enforcement of the statute quickly followed. A federal district court, applying strict scrutiny, held the Act would likely be found unconstitutional and granted the injunction. Although protecting children was again recognized as a compelling public interest, the court held that the Act was not the least restrictive means of achieving that interest. First, minors would still be able to gain access to the prohibited material through foreign web sites, as well as non-web Internet services, e.g. newsgroups, chat rooms and file transfers (ftp). Second, other less restrictive means of achieving the goal of limiting minors' access to this material might be available. Finally, the inclusion of writing and any communication of any kind in the Act was unnecessary to protect against the pornographic "teasers" that Congress had directed the statute against. According to the court, limiting the prohibited material to pictures, images and graphic image files would accomplish Congress' objective, while restricting far less speech.

The decision was appealed and the Court of Appeals for the Third Circuit upheld the district court's decision, but on a different ground. The court found that the use of "community standards" in the statute rendered it unconstitutionally overbroad. This holding was reversed by the Supreme Court, and remanded to the circuit court for consideration of the district court's findings.

After the circuit court again affirmed the district court, this time on the same grounds as the district court, the Supreme Court again granted certiorari. The Court, relying heavily on its decision in Playboy Entertainment Group, held that where there is a choice between "a blanket speech restriction" and "a more specific technological solution that [is] available to parents who choose to implement it," the government must show that the alternative would be less effective. Here the government had failed to show that a proposed less restrictive alternative, filtering software, would be less effective.

The Court also noted that there were strong practical reasons for sending the case back for a trial on the merits. Most important of these involved a problem that exists in almost all cases involving the Internet. The rate of technological change is such that the trial court's findings of fact do not reflect the factual reality in existence at the time the appellate court considers the case. Here the problem was exacerbated by the court of appeals and Supreme Court each hearing the case twice. Ashcroft v. American Civil Liberties Union (2004).

Filtering software, relied on in Ashcroft, is the most commonly suggested alternative to laws restricting Internet content. This software allows a parent to limit the sites a child can access on the Internet. However, when that software is mandated or is used by public facilities, most commonly libraries, it raises serious First Amendment questions. Some of this is due to the nature of blocking software. Often these programs screen for other categories of speech including violence, profanity and hate speech. In addition, the software is far from 100 percent accurate. For example, these programs have blocked access to such sites as the Heritage Foundation, the M.I.T. free-speech society, the U.S. Central Intelligence Agency, a banned-book archive and the National Organization for Women. One such program even blocked the White House Web Site—it blocked anything containing the word "couples."

When a county library in Virginia installed blocking software on all computers with Internet access, some library patrons filed suit claiming a First Amendment violation. The asserted purpose of installing the software was to "minimize access to illegal pornography and avoidance of creating a sexually hostile environment." Adults could access blocked sites, but only by filing an official, written request with the librarian stating the patron's name, the site and the reason why the patron wanted access to the site. The librarian had unlimited discretion to decide whether or not to unblock the site.

The court, having determined this was content regulation of a limited public forum, applied strict scrutiny. It found that although the government's interests were compelling, there were numerous less restrictive ways to further those interests including privacy screens on computer monitors, casual monitoring by library staff, installation of the software on only some computers and restricting minors to those computers, and permitting adults to turn off the filtering software. Mainstream Loudoun v. Board of Trustees of the Loudoun County Library (1998). The trustees did not appeal.

In contrast, in California a city was sued for failing to install blocking software on library computers. A woman whose 12–year-old son accessed pornography using a library computer sought an injunction requiring installation of filtering software on the library computers. The court denied her request and the decision was affirmed on appeal. Kathleen R. v. City of Livermore (2001).

However, the Minneapolis Public Library was forced to pay $435,000 to settle a civil suit filed by librarians who alleged that unfiltered access to the Internet created a "sexually hostile work environment." The suit was filed after an EEOC ALJ had found for the librarians in a probable cause hearing.

The Supreme Court finally considered the question of mandating filtering software in libraries after Congress passed the Children's Internet Protection Act (CIPA) in 2001. CIPA disqualifies any library or school from receiving discounted Internet access, Internet services, and internal connection services under 47 U.S.C. § 254(h), unless it can certify that measures to block or filter certain visual depictions have been installed. These include visual depictions that are obscene, child pornography, or, with respect to use of computers with Internet access by minors, harmful to minors.

The Act was challenged by a group of libraries, library associations, library patrons and Web site publishers. A district court three-judge panel held the statute was a content-based restriction on access to a public forum, subject to strict scrutiny. The use of software filters was not narrowly tailored to furthering the government's compelling interest "in preventing the dissemination of obscenity, child pornography, or, in the case of minors, material harmful to minors," and thus, it violated the First Amendment. The decision was appealed directly to the Supreme Court.

The Supreme Court reversed. Chief Justice Rehnquist, joined by three other Justices, rejected the lower court's finding that Internet access in public libraries is a public fora. It could not be a traditional public forum because the technology was too new to have a long history of "being used for purposes of assembly, communication of thoughts between citizens, and discussing public questions." It was not a designated public forum, because the purpose of Internet access in libraries is "facilitat[ing] research, learning and recreational pursuits by furnishing materials of requisite and appropriate quality," as opposed to "encourag[ing] a diversity of views from private speakers." Thus, the statute did not require heightened judicial scrutiny.

Turning to concerns regarding overblocking, Rehnquist found that the provision allowing adults to ask a librarian to unblock a site or turn the filter off, adequately addressed the problem. That some patrons might be too embarrassed to request unblocking was not relevant because the "Constitution does not guarantee the right to acquire information at a public library without any risk of embarrassment."

Although concerned that unblocking might not be as readily available as the government had asserted, due to lack of trained personnel, Justice Kennedy concurred in the judgment, reasoning that such issues should addressed through an as-applied challenge as opposed to the facial challenge before the Court.

Justice Breyer, applying intermediate scrutiny found that statute was narrowly tailored to serving the compelling interest in restricting access to obscenity, child pornography and, in the case of minors, material harmful to them. The unblocking provision reduced the burden on First Amendment rights to an acceptable level.

Separate dissents by Justices Stevens and Souter, focused on the problems of underblocking and overblocking. Due to the substantial amount of sexually explicit material that is not blocked, "the statute will provide parents with a false sense of security." As far as overblocking is concerned, not only is there the problem of unblocking not being readily available, but a larger one of people not knowing that something has been blocked. When a filter prevents a site from being included in search results, the library patron will not know to ask for access to that site.

In addition, Justice Souter rejected the plurality's argument that filters were analogous to the traditional freedom that libraries have been given to select which books they will acquire. That freedom is necessitated by the reality that cost and space limitations force libraries to make choices regarding what to acquire. In contrast, there are no such limitations with Internet access. Filters merely restrict access to materials already available. In Justice Souter's view, this would make it unconstitutional for even individual libraries to install filters on computers used by adults.

A somewhat different question was presented when a group of professors from various public colleges and universities in Virginia challenged the constitutionality of a Virginia law restricting state employees from accessing sexually explicit material on computers that are owned or leased by the state. The district court found the statute unconstitutional, but the court of appeals reversed, holding that the speech being restricted was only that of individuals speaking in their capacity as Commonwealth of Virginia employees, not as citizens. As such their speech was not entitled to First Amendment protection. Urofsky v. Gilmore (1999).

C. SAFETY AND VIOLENCE

New technologies always seem to be viewed with fear and apprehension. This is certainly true of the Internet. The same material that is tolerated in print is considered far too dangerous when distributed over the Internet. For example, after the Oklahoma City bombing, numerous Senators and Representatives supported proposals to ban bomb-making information on the Internet, even though the exact same information is readily available in libraries, newsstands and bookstores.

An unusual case involving a University of Michigan student typifies this reaction to new technologies. Jake Baker posted a fictional account of the rape, torture and murder of a young woman to the Internet newsgroup, alt.sex.stories. Newsgroups are a series of electronic bulletin boards organized by subject matter that are publicly available through the Internet. The woman had the same name and physical description as one of Baker's classmates.

Based on this story, as well as e-mail messages Baker sent to a Canadian individual named Arthur Gonda, Baker was charged with threatening to kidnap or injure (18 U.S.C.A. § 875(c)). Gonda was also charged, but he was never located or even identified beyond the name, which was almost certainly a pseudonym.

After Baker was held without bail for a month and expelled from the university, the original charge was dropped and five new counts, based solely on the e-mail messages were filed, but quickly dismissed. The judge was extremely critical of the government's actions in the case. He noted that the original charge was based on "a savage and tasteless piece of fiction." The fact that it was transmitted over the Internet as opposed to printed in a newspaper did not eliminate its First Amendment protection. The subsequent charges were merely an attempt to salvage the case, which failed because the e-mails did not contain the "unequivocal, unconditional and specific expressions of intention immediately to inflict injury" that would remove them from the protection of the First Amendment. The dismissal of the charges was upheld on appeal. United States v. Alkhabaz (1997).

In 1997 Planned Parenthood, some doctors and a clinic sued the creators of The Nuremberg Files, an anti-abortion Internet site, claiming the site violated the 1994 Clinic Entrance Act. The site listed detailed personal information about doctors who performed abortions and their families. Doctors who were murdered appeared on the list crossed out. It also contained "wanted posters" naming specific physicians. The plaintiffs argued that the site incited people to murder the doctors listed. After the trial judge instructed the jurors that a finding of intent to cause violence was unnecessary as long as a " 'reasonable person' would consider the harsh words and graphics to be threats," the jury awarded the plaintiffs $107 million.

The court of appeals reversed, holding that the defendants' speech was protected and that it did not fall within the "true threats" exception. A rehearing en banc was then granted and a closely divided court affirmed the district court's holding. The key issue was whether or not the web-site material constituted a true threat.

The majority defined true threat as follows: "whether a reasonable person would foresee that the statement would be interpreted by those to whom the maker communicates the statement as a serious expression of intent to harm or assault." Under this definition, there is no requirement that the speaker intend to, or be able to carry out the threat. Rather, as long as the speaker could reasonably foresee that the speech, given its entire context, would be interpreted by the recipients of the speech as a serious threat of physical harm.

Relying on the fact that three earlier "wanted posters" (not posted on this site) had been followed by the murder of the physicians named, the majority found that reasonable people would view the posters and the list of physicians as a serious threat of physical harm. The fact that this case involved public political speech was seen as irrelevant to the inquiry.

The dissents relied heavily on NAACP v. Claiborne Hardware (1982). In that case, Medgar Evers, while calling for a boycott of white merchants gave several public speeches in which he stated that people who broke the boycott would have their necks broken and warned that the Sheriff couldn't sleep with them at night. In addition, names of boycott violators were published in a local newspaper. A number of violent acts, including shots fired at individual's homes, were committed against the boycott violators. The Supreme Court applied Branzburg and held that the speech was protected.

The majority distinguished Claiborne Hardware on the ground that there had been no evidence in that case that the people who heard Evers' speeches took his statements as a serious threat. In contrast, the dissents found the two cases remarkably similar. They also argued that a distinction needed to be made between statements made directly to the "threatened" parties and statements made as part of a public protest.

The ultimate problem is determining which test is appropriate, incitement or true threat. The primary disagreement between the judges here involved two key distinctions. The first was whether the speaker would be the one inflicting the threatened harm, rather than inciting others to do so. The majority rejected that as a requirement for a true threat. The second was whether statements made as part of public, political speech should be treated differently than targeted statements made to individuals. The majority held no. Planned Parenthood of the Columbia/Willamette, Inc. v. American Coalition of Life Activists (2002).

D.   DEFAMATION

The development of computer bulletin board sites (BBSs) and the Internet raised some very difficult liability questions in defamation. They revolve around the role of the providers of the services and the degree of control they have over material accessed through them. Initially, in trying to resolve these questions, courts sought analogies to traditional media. For example, in Cubby, Inc. v. CompuServe (1991), a federal district court held that CompuServe was not liable for the contents of an electronic newsletter because CompuServe was, in the court's view, an electronic for-profit library with "little or no editorial control."

In contrast, a New York trial court held Prodigy liable for a message posted on one of Prodigy's electronic bulletin boards. Because Prodigy used human monitors and automated systems to remove objectionable material, it exercised sufficient editorial to be considered a publisher. Stratton Oakmont, Inc. v. Prodigy Services, Co. (1995). After Prodigy eliminated these monitoring systems, a New York appellate court took a completely different view of the company's services, holding that because it exercised no editorial control, it was the equivalent of a telephone company. As such it was not liable for e-mails or bulletin board postings that used its service. Lunney v. Prodigy Services (1998).

The passage of the Communications Decency Act, discussed earlier in this chapter, brought a consistent approach to this confusing issue. Section 230 provides that "no provider or user of an interactive computer service shall be treated as the publisher or speaker of any information provided by another information content provider." Early cases applying § 230 to defamation cases indicate it provides extensive protection to online and Internet service providers.

In Zeran v. America Online, Inc. (1997), an unknown individual posted a message on an AOL bulletin board advertising T-shirts with offensive slogans related to the 1995 Oklahoma City bombing. The message said to call Ken at a phone number that was the home number of Kenneth Zeran. After receiving numerous abusive phone calls, Zeran complained to AOL and eventually the message was removed. However, several similar messages were posted over the next few days and the number of abusive and threatening calls reached a level of one approximately every two minutes. The situation was exacerbated when an announcer for an Oklahoma City radio station read one of the messages over the air and urged listeners to call.

Zeran sued AOL arguing that AOL should, at a minimum, have removed the messages as soon as it was notified of the problem. However, a federal court of appeals held that AOL was explicitly protected by § 230, regardless of its knowledge of the defamatory messages.

What if AOL had instead hired someone to post material on its service and some of this material turned out to be defamatory? This question was addressed in the context of a defamation suit against Matt Drudge, author of the online publication, "The Drudge Report." AOL had hired Drudge to publish his report, and then publicized the report's availability on AOL. When the report charged

White House aide Sydney Blumenthal with a history of spousal abuse, Blumenthal sued both Drudge and AOL. A federal district court held that § 230 required dismissal of the case against AOL, but allowed the case against Drudge to proceed. No appeal was taken. Blumenthal v. Drudge (1998).

Courts have continued to take an expansive view of the protection afforded by § 230. In Carafano v. Metrosplash.com (2002), an unknown person posted a trial profile on a computer dating service for Christianne Carafano without her knowledge and consent. The profile which described her as "looking for a 'hard and dominant' man with a 'strong sexual appetite, included an e-mail address that generated an automatic response with Carafano's home address and telephone number. Carafano received a number of sexually explicit voicemails and a fax that threatened her son. She sued for defamation, invasion of privacy and misappropriation of the right of publicity.

The circuit court reversed a district court holding that § 230 did not apply to the computer dating service because it was an information content provider. The appellate court found that the questionnaire used to generate the computer profile only provided a structure as opposed to actual content.

E. PRIVACY

Internet pornography has drawn the most public attention, but many would argue that the ability of both companies and the government to gather, correlate and distribute detailed information concerning individuals should be the primary concern. There are many ways this information can be gathered. Some are open and voluntary such as filling out questionnaires. Others are trade-offs for convenience or financial incentives. For example, an online grocer stores previous orders to allow a consumer to duplicate common purchases, or a bookstore keeps a record of purchases in order to notify customers of new books by their favorite authors.

More surreptitious methods include the use of cookies, small data files stored on people's hard drives which can be used to keep track of the sites visited during browsing. Although it is possible to block cookies, a large percentage of Internet users are unaware of the existence of cookies or how they can be used.

Finally, although difficult, it is possible to intercept material sent over the Internet. In addition, anything sent over the Internet also resides on various computers. Many people and companies have learned this the hard way when copies of E-mails have been used as evidence against them.

These privacy issues have led to proposals for laws restricting data collection and distribution. Although efforts to do so have been largely unsuccessful in this country, other countries have extensive privacy regulation. With the developing emphasis on international E-commerce, the gap between the U.S. position and that of other countries led to the threat of a major trade conflict.

In 1998 the European Union Data Protection Directive took effect. Under the directive, member states must take a number of specific measures to protect individuals' privacy. The most important measure from a U.S. perspective is one prohibiting businesses in E.U. countries from transferring data to countries that don't have adequate privacy protection. The problem is that the U.S. approach relies almost exclusively on self-regulation. Initially, the U.S. and the E.U. were unable to resolve the conflict.

Hindering the U.S. position were a series of revelations concerning companies gathering information contrary to their publicly declared policies. The most highly publicized of these involved Double Click, the leading provider of banner ads to Web sites. Using cookies, Double Click tracks Internet users across the approximately 1500 sites where the company has placed ads. When Double Click merged with Abacus Direct, the country's largest catalog database firm, its SEC registration statement referred to plans to combine Double Click's tracking information with detailed personal information contained in the Abacus database. Highlighting the potential privacy problems was the revelation that a number of medical and health information sites that guaranteed user privacy carried ads placed by Double Click.

When the statement was publicized and complaints were filed with the FTC against Double Click, the company issued a revised privacy policy allowing people to opt out of the data-gathering process. Critics of the policy argue that the opt-out approach is ineffective because many people are unaware of the privacy problem and others find the opt-out procedure too burdensome. Privacy advocates prefer an opt-in policy that requires an individual to affirmatively agree to participate in the data collection.

After more than a year of negotiation the U.S. and the EU agreed on a compromise that allows U.S. firms to comply with the EU requirements without a major change in U.S. law. Under the compromise U.S. organizations that participate in a U.S. Safe Harbor Program are considered to be in compliance with the European Commission Directive on Data Protection. The voluntary program, administered by the Department of Commerce, requires participating organizations on an annual basis to self-certify in writing that they agree to adhere to the safe harbor's requirements. These requirements cover seven basic areas: notice, choice, onward transfer, access, security, data integrity, and enforcement.

One type of data collection that has provoked U.S. legislative action involves children. The Children's Online Privacy Protection Act required the FTC to establish regulations governing data collection from children. The regulations which took effect in 2000 impose extensive notice and parental consent requirements on commercial Web sites or online services that are primarily directed at children under 13. The Act applies to individually identifiable personal information obtained directly or through the use of cookies or other tracking mechanisms.

Parental consent must be verifiable. Acceptable methods of verification include "getting a signed form from the parent via postal mail or facsimile; accepting and verifying a credit card number; taking calls from parents, through a toll-free telephone number staffed by trained personnel; e-mail accompanied by digital signature; e-mail accompanied by a PIN or password obtained through one of the verification methods above."

F.   ACCESS AND SPAM

Although akin to more traditional marketing methods such as direct mail and phone solicitation, the practice of spamming—indiscriminately sending e-mail to large numbers of people—raises some unique legal issues. Whereas the cost of direct mail or phone solicitation is proportional to the number of people contacted, there is almost no incremental cost in increasing the number of people to whom a specific e-mail message is sent. In addition, large quantities of Spam actually impose costs on and affect the quality of service of the Internet Service Providers (ISPs) involved. As a result, many of these providers try to limit the amount of spam entering their system.

America Online (AOL) took a series of actions designed to discourage the ISPs used by Cyber Promotions, a company that was sending millions of e-mails to AOL subscribers, from continuing to give the company access to the Internet. When some ISPs then refused to do business with Cyber Promotions, the company filed a series of complaints against AOL alleging antitrust and First Amendment violations. Cyber Promotions argued that by providing e-mail boxes to which it was the sole conduit, AOL was performing a public function and thus was a state actor similar to the company town in Marsh v. Alabama (1946).

The court rejected this argument. AOL was not performing any municipal functions. In addition, there were numerous alternative avenues of access to AOL subscribers. For example, Cyber Promotions could set up a Web site which interested AOL subscribers could visit. Cyber Promotions, Inc. v. America Online (1996). AOL subsequently took further steps to prevent Cyber Promotions from continuing to send e-mail to its subscribers.

Government attempts to limit spam raise different questions. Several states passed anti-spamming statutes and others were considering doing so. These statutes varied in their approach to the problem. For example, the California statute granted ISPs the right to develop and enforce their own anti-spamming policies. In contrast, the Nevada statute established civil liability for commercial e-mail messages that do not meet specific guidelines. The Washington statute took still another approach. It prohibited commercial e-mail messages, originated in Washington or sent to a Washington resident, that misrepresented any identifying information or contain false and misleading information in the subject line.

These statutes were preempted in 2003 when Congress passed the CAN–SPAM ACT of 2003 (Controlling the Assault of Non–Solicited Pornography Act). The most significant features of the Act are bans on false or misleading header information and deceptive subject lines, and requirements that the e-mail provide the recipient with an opt-out method and that commercial e-mails be identified as advertisements and contain the sender's valid physical postal address. Violations can result in fines or, in some cases, imprisonment.

The Act also directed the FTC to establish additional regulations governing sexually explicit commercial e-mail. Pursuant to this mandate the FTC adopted a regulation requiring all such e-mail to contain the label "SEXUALLY EXPLICIT" in the subject line, as well as in the initial screen of the body of the message. 16 C.F.R. § 316.

Despite several successful prosecutions under the CAN–SPAM ACT, many people believe that it will have little effect on the overall volume of spam. Reasons for this include the difficulty in tracing the senders and the fact that much of the spam originates in other countries.

G. COPYRIGHT & TRADEMARK

Another area of law dramatically affected by the development of the Internet is copyright law. There are numerous definitional and enforcement problems with applying copyright law in cyberspace. Although copyright is beyond the scope of this book, there are certain specific Internet copyright issues that should briefly be noted.

One problem area that gained widespread publicity, especially on college campuses, has been digital audio. A widespread digital format, MP3, allows songs to be compressed to approximately one tenth their normal size with minimal loss of quality. This aids storage on computers and transmission over the Internet. With the advent of MP3 players, Web sites with large catalogs of songs, many of which were illegal copies, proliferated. The Recording Industry Association of America (RIAA) and its members have tried numerous different legal strategies to restrict the traffic in MP3 copies. Early approaches included an attempt to enjoin production of an MP3 player, the Diamond Rio. This failed because the device had substantial non-infringing uses. RIAA also put pressure on universities to restrict access to MP3 sites, an action that some universities took, not for legal reasons, but to reduce the excessive demand on university systems. Some universities estimated at one point that more than half of all traffic on their systems is MP3 related.

RIAA next filed, on behalf of major record labels, a copyright infringement suit against Napster.com, a site that provided peer-to-peer (P2P) software that allowed users to exchange MP3 libraries. Napster also stored on its own servers indexes and lists of the songs available for copying. A district court, finding it likely that Napster would be held to be both a contributory and vicarious infringer, issued a preliminary injunction prohibiting Napster "from engaging in, or facilitating others in copying, downloading, uploading, transmitting, or distributing plaintiffs' copyrighted musical compositions and sound recordings, protected by either federal or state law, without express permission of the rights owner." Although the Ninth Circuit required some narrowing of the scope of the injunction, it affirmed the district court's central findings on Napster's liability. A & M Records, Inc. v. Napster, Inc. (2001).

Although the circuit court's order regarding the scope of the injunction had the effect of staying the injunction, Napster never resumed service until it was sold to Roxio, which converted it to a legal download service. Meanwhile, other companies distributing P2P service tried to structure their service in a way that would not subject them to copyright liability. The primary difference was that they avoided keeping lists or indexes on their own servers. Lower court results were inconsistent. The Seventh Circuit upheld a preliminary injunction issued against Aimster, finding that by providing the file-sharing software and indexes allowing users to locate music files belonging to other users, Aimster was likely to be found a contributory infringer. In Re: Aimster Copyright Litigation (2003). However, the Ninth Circuit affirmed a district court finding that there were substantial non-infringing uses of the software provided by Grokster and Kazaa, thus preventing a finding that they were contributor infringers. Metro–Goldwyn–Mayer v. Grokster, Ltd. (2004).

A petition for certiorari was granted in the Grokster case and the decision became one of the most widely anticipated in Internet law, drawing a number of amicus briefs on both sides. Record companies and movie studios argued that they stood to lose control of their business if nothing could be done to stop wide-spread distribution of illegal copies of their product. Meanwhile, software companies and public interest groups expressed concern that the chilling effect of having software developers liable for illegal uses of their product by others would chill innovation and new product development.

Prior to the Court's decision, most people expected the Court's holding in Sony Corp. v. Universal City Studios, Inc. (1984) to be the key. In that case the Court found that Sony could not be held a contributory infringer based on the manufacture and sale of the Betamax VCR because the machine was capable of substantial non-infringing uses. Grokster could have been decided by a clear definition of what constitutes substantial non-infringing uses, or by new rules for when equipment or software manufacturers are liable as contributory infringers.

The Court, however, avoided the need to revisit Sony, by holding there was sufficient evidence to withstand the motion for summary judgment that the defendants had induced copyright infringement.

In contrast to the Sony focus on the uses of the product, here the focus was on the conduct and expression of the software distributors. By marketing their product to former Napster users and failing to take any steps to develop filtering tools or other methods of limiting the infringing use of the product, the companies sent a clear inducing message to potential customers.

The Court's decision did have an immediate effect on various P2P distributors with some shutting down their business and others changing their marketing and even technical support approaches to avoid any evidence of inducement. However, the decision left the exact meaning of the Sony decision unclear. Although the majority opinion, written by Justice Souter, did not address whether contributory infringement could have been found based on Sony, three Justices in a concurrence by Justice Ginsburg argued that it should have been found. In contrast Justice Breyer, joined by two Justices argued that it should not.

Congress has also addressed the issues raised by digital copying by passing the Digital Millenium Copyright Act (DMCA) of 1998, implementing provisions of the World Intellectual Property Organization Copyright Treaty and the WIPO Performances and Phonograms Treaty. The DMCA makes it illegal to manufacture, import or in any way traffic in devices that circumvent technologies that protect copyrights. When someone created a software program, DeCSS, that allowed people to make and distribute digital copies of DVDs, and posted it on the Internet, movie studios tried various legal actions to stop the widespread distribution of DeCSS. Among these was asking a federal district court judge to enjoin certain individuals from posting DeCSS on their Web sites. A preliminary injunction was granted. Universal City Studios, Inc. v. Reimerdes (2000).

One key aspect of the DMCA is its safe-harbor provision for ISPs. The DMCA safe-harbor protection differs in one key respect from that afforded by § 230. The DMCA's protection is subject to a "notice-and-takedown" limitation. If notified of copyrighted material on its system, an ISP must expeditiously remove the material or disable access to it. There are specific requirements for notification and authorization to act on behalf of the complaining party, so the rights of the party who posted the material and the rights of the complaining party are both taken into consideration. However, critics say that the process can be used to persuade ISPs to remove material that is not actually infringing, e.g., material that is a fair use.

Other Internet-related copyright issues include deep-linking (one site providing a link to another company's site that bypasses the second company's home page); and framing (linking in such a way that one company's site appears in a window on another company's site). Each of these practices has led to law suits, but so far they have either settled or are still at trial.

H.　DOMAIN NAMES

One key to the success of the World Wide Web is the Domain Name System, which translates the numeric addresses for each Web site to alphanumeric combinations that can be used to create easily remembered addresses. The root address is limited to certain specific suffixes including .com, .org, .net, .gov, .edu, .pro, .info, .biz, .name in addition to country suffixes, e.g., .us for United States. These suffixes are referred to as top-level domain names (TLDs). The segment of the name immediately preceding the TLD is the second-level domain name. The problem arises from the desirability of addresses (second-level domain names) that are both easily remembered and related to the individual or business running the site.

Traditional trademark law was not well-suited to resolving these conflicts because more than one trademark holder could have an equally valid claim to a particular address. For example, who should have the best claim to www.ford.com: Ford Motor Company or Ford Modeling Agency? Abbreviations such as MS (Microsoft or Morgan Stanley) or MLB (Morgan, Lewis & Bockius or Major League Baseball) are equally difficult to analyze. The lack of geographic boundaries only exacerbates the problem. There may be a Blue Note Cafe in both New York City and Kansas City, but there is only one www.bluenotecafe.com.

There are other conflicts besides those between two claimants with legitimate interests in the domain name. In some cases people have registered domain names incorporating the names of companies or famous people and then offered to sell the names to those companies or people. This practice became known as cybersquatting.

Other practices leading to conflicts between domain name holders and companies included registering a name close to that of a company selling similar products in hopes of syphoning off a percentage of that company's business (e.g., if a razor company were to register www.shick.com or www. schik.com), or critics of a company registering a site with the company name followed by a disparaging term, (e.g., www.acmesucks.com).

Some companies chose to file trademark suits over disputed domain names with mixed results. See, e.g. (Panavision International v. Toeppen (1998); Planned Parenthood Federation of America, Inc. v. Bucci (1997); Hasbro, Inc. v. Clue Computing, Inc. (1999); Data Concepts Inc. v. Digital Consulting, Inc. (1998). Others, due to the difficulties outlined above, sought relief from Network Solutions, Inc. (NSI), which from 1993–1999 had sole control over the root addresses, .com, .net and .org. NSI changed its policy on domain name disputes several times during that period without ever achieving a satisfactory solution to the problem.

Domain name assignment has now been transferred to the Internet Corporation for Assigned Names and Numbers (ICANN), which in turn licenses a number of companies including NSI to assign domain names. ICANN has adopted a new Dispute Resolution Policy. The policy requires registration applicants to warrant that the registration will not "infringe upon or otherwise violate the rights of any third party," is not being done for an unlawful purpose, and will not knowingly be used "in violation of any applicable laws or regulations."

If a third party brings a complaint alleging that a domain name is identical or confusingly similar to the complainant's trademark or service mark, the registrant has no legitimate interest in the name and that the registrant has acted in bad faith, a mandatory administrative proceeding ensues. If each of these elements are proven to the administrative panel's satisfaction, ICANN will cancel the name. ICANN will also do so upon receipt of an order from a court or arbitral panel.

Meanwhile, Congress has attempted to address the problem with the Anti–Cybersquatting Consumer Protection Act, passed in late 1999. The Act creates a civil cause of action against someone who, in bad faith with intent to profit, registers, traffics or uses a domain name that is identical or confusingly similar to a distinctive or famous mark (including a personal name) or a registered trademark. A cause of action is also available, with certain limited exceptions, against anyone who "registers a domain name that consists of the name of another living person, or a name substantially and confusingly similar thereto, without that person's consent, with the specific intent to profit from such name by selling the domain name for financial gain to that person or any third party.''

The most controversial aspect of the Act is its provision for in rem jurisdiction over the domain name if in personam jurisdiction over the registrant of the disputed name is unavailable or the registrant cannot be found through due diligence. In the case of in rem actions, the only remedy is a court order requiring the domain name registry to cancel the name or transfer it to the prevailing party. Critics argue that applying a U.S. statute to an international medium will place an undue burden on registrants residing in other countries. They also raise the question of conflict with the laws of other countries.

I.   CONVERGENCE AND THE FUTURE

In just a few short years the rapid growth of the Internet has raised numerous legal issues. However, far more difficult issues remain to be addressed. The central problem is that communication law has always been based on different rules for different media—different regulations, different jurisdictions, even (as discussed in Chapter 1) different levels of First Amendment protection. Unfortunately, this ''silo approach'' to regulation no longer reflects technological reality.

For example, telephone and cable service are no longer separate services offered by separate companies. The change is the result of both technological advances and regulatory changes. However, even though both services may now be offered by the same company using a single wire into the home, they are subject to different regulations, often administered by different agencies on the state and local level. The cable service will usually be franchised on the municipal level, subject to additional state and federal regulation. The phone service will usually be subject only to state and federal regulation and the state agency regulating the phone service may not be the same one regulating cable service. Meanwhile, other video distributors competing with the cable company may be delivering their product through other technologies, each subject to different regulatory schemes. Recall our discussion of MMDS and DBS in the previous chapter. Now television programs are being delivered directly to cell phones.

In addition, the jurisdictional problems discussed earlier in this chapter may require a shift in the balance between state and federal regulation. Early examples of this include the Can–Spam Act and proposals to allow regional or national cable franchises.

As the Internet continues to develop, these anomalies will proliferate. Voice over the Internet Protocol (VOIP) is now a competitor for phone companies. Soon there will be sufficient bandwidth to allow high-quality streaming video. How should this be classified, given the existing regulatory structure? However, the Telecommunications Act of 1996 was passed at a time when broadband access was in its infancy. At some point a new regulatory scheme based on the reality of current communication technology needs to be developed.

As this new regulatory structure is being developed, one key issue is becoming a central focus. Net neutrality is the idea that all broadband networks should be legally required to keep their networks open to all content, services and equipment. Although, much of the debate centers on telecommunication services and equipment, and is thus beyond the scope of this book, the potential for favoring some content providers over others does have serious implications for mass communication. For example, one telephone company has proposed establishing a separate, higher-priced tier for the exclusive use of content providers selected by the telephone company.

Unfortunately, communication technology changes far more rapidly than the law. It will be interesting to see how Congress and the FCC, as well as state legislative bodies and regulatory agencies, will meet the challenges presented by the Internet during the next few years.

INDEX

References are to pages

SUNSHINE LAWS
See Freedom of Information Act

TELECOMMUNICATIONS ACT OF 1996, 642–643

UNFAIR COMPETITION
See Commercial Speech

USA PATRIOT ACT, 249–253

†